*Colonial Rule and
Political Development
in Tanzania:*

## THE CASE OF THE MAKONDE

J. GUS LIEBENOW

*Colonial Rule and
Political Development
in Tanzania:*

THE CASE OF THE MAKONDE

NORTHWESTERN UNIVERSITY PRESS

EVANSTON 1971

Copyright © 1971 by J. Gus Liebenow
All rights reserved
Library of Congress Catalog Card Number: 72–126898
ISBN 0–8101–0332–X
Printed in the United States of America

J. Gus Liebenow is Professor of Political Science and Direc-
tor of the African Studies Program at Indiana University.
He is the author of *Liberia: The Evolution of Privilege.*

# Contents:

*Figures and Tables*     *vi*

*Acknowledgments*     *vii*

*Preface: The Significance of Micropolitical Studies*
   *in Africa*     *ix*

1:   Introduction     3
2:   Origins of the Makonde of Tanzania     20
3:   Fragmentation and Cohesion
      in Traditional Makonde Society     40
4:   The Beginnings of Alien Rule     72
5:   Indirect Rule     93
6:   The Forces of Innovation     126
7:   Return to Direct Rule: The Liwali System     163
8:   Encouragement to Tribalism     190
9:   The Experiment in Multiracialism     200
10:  The Grouping of Forces, 1956–1958     227
11:  The Triumph of TANU     257
12:  The New Political Order in Tanzania     275
13:  Post-Independence Social Change
      in Umakonde     285
14:  Political and Economic Institution-Building     305
15:  Perspective     332

*Bibliography*     342

*Index*     353

# Figures and Tables:

## FIGURES

1: Makonde Districts of Tanzania    14
2: Makonde Migration Routes    22
3: Ethnic Groups of Southern Tanzania    32
4: Succession to the Office of Mkulungwa    53
5: *Wazimu wa Mzungu* (White Man's Madness):
   Enforcement of Native Authority Rules
   and Orders, Mikindani District,
   1938–1950    *following* 146
6: Tenure of District Commissioners,
   Newala, 1919–1962    148
7: Tenure of District Commissioners,
   Mikindani, 1917–1950    149
8: Makonde Native Authorities, 1956    171

## TABLES

1: Asian Population in Makonde Districts, 1957    151
2: Newala District Revenue Receipts, 1955    212
3: Newala District Expenditures, 1955    213
4: School Enrollment in Mtwara Region, 1966    303
5: TANU Membership in Newala District,
   1955–1965    307

# Acknowledgments:

In writing this volume, I owe an enormous debt of gratitude to the kind assistance of many Tanzanians, Europeans, and Asians. Their numbers are legion, and I wish to avoid associating any single individual with the conclusions drawn by me in this study. I nevertheless want to express my special thanks to Thekla and Frederick Mchauru, Leopold Pallahani, Rashidi Mtalika, Justino Mponda, Saidi Nantanje, Dr. Marion Robinson, Douglas Healey, J. Hornstead, and to George Saidi, who served as my research assistant. A very personal thanks is due to Jean and Clem Wills (and their wonderful children), who managed the Mkunya Leprosarium, which served as my research base in 1955–56.

I also wish to acknowledge the generous support of the Ford Foundation (1954–56) through an inaugural grant of the Foreign Area Fellowship Program as well as the support provided by Indiana University and the University College of Dar es Salaam, which made the second phase of this study possible. I am indebted as well to the staff of the Tanzanian National Archives for their very helpful cooperation.

Above all, I want to thank my wife, Beverly, and our children—Diane, Debra, Jay, and John—who shared part of this experience with me and who endured the extended gestation of this volume. Without Beverly's patience, encouragement, and constructive comments, this work would never have been completed.

J. G. L.

# Preface:
# The Significance of
#    Micropolitical Studies
#    in Africa

The people of Tanzania, their diverse history, the country's magnificent landscape, and, above all, the quality of its contemporary leadership have an irresistible and euphoric fascination for those who have had only a passing exposure to this East African state. It is not charm alone, however, which has attracted those of us who have scholarly interests in Tanzania. Rather, we have found this to be one of the most interesting regions on the continent for fruitful research in the social sciences. There is probably no other African state which contains within its boundaries such a wide range of social, religious, economic, and political situations for the comparative study of human behavior. The complexity of indigenous political organization among its 120 or more ethnic groups, for example, ranges from the highly bureaucratized and centrally organized kingdoms of the Hehe, Haya, and Chagga to the rather unsophisticated political systems of the Gogo and Barabaig. Among the latter the kinship unit has served multiple purposes, and there is very little signaling as a family head moves from his social to a political, religious, or economic role. Tanzania, too, has been a significant arena for the analysis of interracial conflict and accomodation as the African majority has come to terms with the Arabs, Indians, and Europeans who have pursued their special interests in East Africa during the past centuries. For students of colonial rule and its impact upon development, Tanzania presents an unusual experience. It has undergone three distinct types of subordination to alien rule—to the Arabs, the Germans, and the British—in the century preceding independence.

In recent years, the country's leadership has continued to provide models for economic and political development which contrast sharply with patterns emerging elsewhere on the African continent. Julius Nyerere, for example, has provided some social-science credibility to the useful but much-abused term "charisma." His party, the Tanganyika African National Union (TANU), constitutes one of the few examples of a nationalist movement which has sincerely attempted to organize itself on a country-wide basis with genuine mass participation in decision-making. Nyerere's experimentation with diverse means of economic development constitutes one of the more heroic attempts to recognize that Africa is a rural rather than an urban continent and that "instant industrialization" may not be the panacea for African poverty. Finally, Tanzania's sometimes quixotic ventures in foreign affairs have provided models worthy of emulation by developing countries seeking to break the chain linking foreign economic aid with foreign political control.

In addition to a long-standing interest in Tanzania, the present study of the Makonde reflects a firm conviction that students of African politics should pay greater attention to developments at the micro level. We should not ignore the very fruitful and provocative ideas which have been generated in the analyses of nationalist movements, state formation, and the operation of parliaments and other structures at the macro level. Often this has been "where the action was" in the period immediately preceding and following the dramatic achievement of independence by more than 30 African states. Nevertheless, in searching for enduring, rather than journalistic, contributions to a science of politics, we find ourselves returning to the more painstaking studies done in recent years on politics at the village or urban-ward level, to the detailed analyses of bureaucratic and other less political roles, and to in-depth studies of trade unions, cooperatives, and structures other than the dominant political parties. Micro-studies have more readily gone beyond the rhetoric of prescription and aspiration to an examination of actual political relationships. They have focused more sharply upon changes in the basic dispositions and attitudes of individuals and upon the capacity of social structures to accomplish stated goals. Gross data on increases in national production, on elections, and on other activity at the macro level may provide very deceptive indices regarding nonelite participation in the economic and political structures left behind by the colonial administrators. Statistical "progress" may merely reflect increased alien participation in the system or the increased ability of the national elite to manipulate the communications media and regiment the masses without actually changing fundamental popular attitudes. The ideologies, five-year plans, and other facets of political life evolved at the center fall on sterile soil if the resistance or apathy of the people at the grass-roots level is ignored. The leadership cadre is still in the formative stage in most African states and is desperately competing for mass support against a rural-based traditional leadership that has all the advantages of face-to-face contact, "old shoe" familiarity, and kinship support. Unless there is interaction between the central and peripheral elites, the task of nation-building in Africa is a difficult one indeed.

In conducting micropolitical studies, the political scientist in Africa must be fully cognizant of the concepts, methodologies, and field methods of sociologists, anthropologists, economists, and historians. One has to probe deeply into the nature of kinship relations, religious beliefs, the organization of technology and economic distribution, and even aesthetic values of a people to discover that which is still central to the political processes of .most African societies. Unlike the student of American or Western European politics, one does not find the most relevant political structures and norms in African societies clearly labeled *political*. Documentation and statistical data on the political process, moreover, are fragmentary and in many instances nonexistent. Imaginative use of safari notes of district officials, tax registers, records of court proceedings, diaries of missionaries, and other written forms of evidence was able to tell me much about the political system of the Makonde. Such documentation, however, was sparse, incomplete, and literally scattered around the countryside in remote divisional and village headquarters. Far greater reliance had to be placed upon data which could only be secured through observation of the political system at work and through interviews with local government officials, missionaries, peasant farmers, teachers, traders, witch-finders, and other relevant actors. Hundreds of hours were spent during 18 months in 1955–56 and briefer periods in 1967 and 1968 traveling through the three Makonde districts, attending meetings of local government councils, observing court proceedings, accompanying African and European officials on safari through their districts, administering questionnaires to students, and conducting semi-directed interviews with liwalis, jumbes, teachers, and others. One could not engage in this kind of research comfortably ensconced in the university library or the national archives in Dar es Salaam, although some of the documentation had been moved to the national capital by the time of the second phase of research in 1967 and 1968. During 1955–56 I operated out of my base at Mkunya Leprosarium, in Newala, where a vacant house had been offered to me by the district commissioner (in a gesture which I am convinced was calculated to frighten me away from the district). Being ten miles from the district commissioner's doorstep, I was relatively free to move about the district without official impediment. In fact, the very generous cooperation afforded me by African officials upon my return to the area in 1967 was almost matched by the assistance and candor of most of the European officials with whom I earlier worked in the colonial period.

Political scientists accustomed to analyzing the contemporary political processes of Western societies may find the chronological framework of this study disturbing. They tend to ignore the very heavy burden they normally place upon the reader to sort out the complicated historical threads that make up the warp of contemporary American or European politics. Political analysts in Africa cannot leave the historical foundation implicit. Indeed, it is readily apparent that the contemporary political system of most African states is a fast-moving and constantly changing kaleidoscope whose separate parts can only be comprehended through in-depth political analysis within discrete historical contexts. In the absence of such historical perspective, the contemporary political system appears to be an utterly chaotic and irrational melange. Without the historical perspective, we are unable to differentiate the ephemeral from that which is enduring or recurrent, and we are unable to fathom the complexity of the relationships among current values, institutions, and social groupings. Ignorance of, or indifference toward, the historic context of traditional institutions was one of the major sources of instability during the European colonial period, and it continues to pose serious problems for nationalist leaders as they introduce new schemes for political, economic, and social development. The historical framework permits the political analyst to make visible the patterns, issues, and relationships at the local level and to relate them to the broader context of Tanzanian politics and to the formulation of more general theoretical statements about the developmental process.

Since I rely upon oral traditions and historic reconstructions, some comments are also in order on this point. First of all, while I am aware of the arguments which have raged back and forth among social scientists for decades regarding the positing of historical "zero points" and the use of the "ethnographic present," the establishment of a reasonable historic base line is useful in evaluating subsequent political changes. Second, in response to those who place greater credence in the written than in the spoken word, it has not been established that nonliterate people have a monopoly when it comes to falsifying the record or being afflicted with convenient lapses of memory. Added to the human frailties of both the scribe and the teller of tales is the fact that the peculiar location of the historian gives him a parochial version of what may be a more generalized phenomenon. No historian is fully aware of all the variables which might have influenced the outcome of an event, and the telling and retelling of a tale leads to a constant restructuring and even "deselection" of personalities, values, and events which may be regarded as unfavorable by current standards or which threaten important groups within the society. Thus all history, whether written or oral, tends to be a subjective rather than a completely objective statement of forces and factors. Distortion, however, should not be decried, for in itself it is a social fact which must be analyzed by the scholar.

Finally, I would suggest that procedures of social science should also be historical in the sense that the systematic study of human behavior would profit through replication by contemporary scholars of previously conducted research or by longitudinal studies—that is, studies of a single community conducted by the same scholar over a period of years. The opportunity of achieving the latter, however, does not come easily, and it is frequently more a matter of fortunate coincidence than design. Indeed, I acknowledge that it was the distraction of other research projects in Tanzania and West Africa as well as the press of teaching and administrative duties that interrupted my research on the Makonde. I did the initial investigation on political development in the Ruvuma River Valley during an eighteen-month period in 1955–56 when Tanganyika was still under colonial rule. It was not until 1967 that a combination of circumstances made it possible for me to return to the Makonde region for a second view of the pace of political development. The eleven-year interval gave me a new perspective, based upon experience in other parts of Africa, by which to judge my previous findings. Moreover, the enlightened policy of the Tanzanian government with respect to declassifying documentation on the pre-independence period provided access to vital materials which had remained closed to scholars under the colonial regime. I was delighted to find through an examination of the official records in the National Archives of Tanzania that many of my "educated guesses" with regard to explaining British administrative behavior had proved to be correct. I also found that in the eleven-year interval many of the Tanzanians as well as those expatriates who were still resident in Tanzania were now receptive to discussing openly and in some detail situations which could only be referred to obliquely during my previous field research.

Thus, if I am charged with having written a volume on the Makonde that is as much anthropology or history as it is political science, I willingly plead guilty.

*Colonial Rule and
Political Development
in Tanzania:*

THE CASE OF THE MAKONDE

# 1:
# Introduction

The passion for modernization on the part of African leaders has become one of the dominant themes in the politics of that continent. Without modernization of the political, economic, and social systems of the new states, the achievement of independence in the 1960s will seem like a hollow victory indeed. Modernization spells the difference for Africa's millions between the ability to control their own destinies and subjugation to the same external forces which overwhelmed their grandfathers in the nineteenth century. Without modernization, the promises made by the nationalist elite of a better life in which poverty, illness, and human degradation will have disappeared become more and more illusory. The revolution of rising expectations soon becomes a revolution of rising frustrations in which coups and countercoups, rather than orderly growth, characterize the political scene.

When does a society which seeks modernization actually become modern? Each discipline has its unique way of approaching this question, and the indices are, to a great extent, quantifiable. To an engineer, for example, modernity is measured in terms of physical changes: the building of steel mills and hospitals, expansion of the network of roads and telephone

lines, or the replacement of hoes and digging sticks by auto-
mated cultivators and harvesters. An economist might add that
modernity consists of more than changes in the environment,
that a modern society is one with a high and steadily rising
gross national product based upon industrialization, where the
cash sector predominates over subsistence activities. A sociologist, on the other hand, might be more concerned with
equating modernity to a high degree of urbanism, on the assumption that only through concentrated residence and collective action can man acquire the organizational capacity and
technological skills necessary to create and distribute the material and psychological benefits of modernization. To the
educator, the key variable in the transition from a traditional
to a modern society is literacy, together with the acceptance
of a rational, scientific explanation of natural phenomena. The
political scientist also has his quantifiable indices of modernization: the expansion in scale of the political community; the
increasing effectiveness of the political center over its periph-
ery; the establishment of institutions which self-consciously
deal with the problems of defense, material security, and other
problems of the community; and the increasing network of
relationships among the citizenry and between the citizen and
the political elite. Finally, the political leader himself might
measure political modernization in terms of the degree of popular involvement in national elections and referenda and the
reduction of primordial ties based upon kinship and religious
and ethnic differences.

While each of these indices of modernization is significant, it
may be that any or even many of these conditions exist in societies that are neither modern nor even undergoing a noticeable
advancement toward modernization. For modernity and modernization relate not simply to changes in the environment and
in activities which can be measured in gross terms by the social
scientist; they relate primarily to changes in human attitudes.
A modern or modernizing man (as opposed to one oriented to
tradition) is a person who accepts the notion of change in his
environment and in his social, economic, and political relationships as being *at least potentially* desirable. This does not
mean that modern man considers all existing conditions bad or
that all reform is for the better; it means that modern man is at

least willing to entertain the idea that his present condition can be improved. In addition to a positive posture toward change, the modernized man assumes that improvements in his condition must come about largely through the application of the canons of science rather than by resorting to witchcraft, prayer, or star-gazing. In making judgments, moreover, about whether a change is beneficial or detrimental, modern man will tend to employ pragmatic and secular criteria rather than rely on spiritual or aesthetic considerations.

To achieve the goal of creative and scientific responses to crises a modernizing society creates institutions which are intended to initiate, articulate the need for, and sustain innovation. Modernizing institutions are expected to engage in a constant questioning of society's values and its procedures for realizing its goals. Parties, parliaments, bureaucracies, and village development committees are some examples of political institutions which are created to sustain innovation. A modernizing society, however, also mounts a frontal assault on the range of economic, social, and religious challenges that confront it. In doing so it establishes cooperative societies, trade unions, universities, family-planning agencies, credit associations, religious lay organizations, and literary societies.

The prerequisites of successful institution-building in a modernizing society are several. Foremost, perhaps, is the requirement that the innovating institution be perceived as beneficial by the individuals whose lives are directly affected by the day-to-day functioning of the institution. It is not sufficient that the agents of innovation themselves regard the institution as good, for their value system and cultural experience may be completely alien to the individuals whose cooperation is expected. Nor is it sufficient that the institution has the *appearance* of support, for the threat of force, bribery, and other inducements may bring about mechanical compliance without a psychological commitment on the part of the masses. The application of force suggests the absence of legitimacy, and it may actually undermine the establishment of legitimacy. Consequently, in the face of a challenge to the institution or a relaxation of coercive acts, the masses may withhold their energies and the institution can only be kept functioning through an extraordinary expenditure of scarce resources.

Successful institution-building requires not only commitment but also the meaningful involvement—or at least potential involvement—of an ever-expanding segment of the affected population. Indeed, it is one of the tenets of modernization that the ability to comprehend and apply rationality should be spread throughout society and not limited by accident of birth or historic circumstances. Hence, the political, economic, and social institutions of a modern society are fashioned to take advantage of this widespread pool of talent. The citizenry generally is provided with avenues of access to the training and experience needed to make rational decisions about the functioning of innovative institutions.

Complementing the need for mass commitment is the requirement of institutional leadership. Modern society is complex, and, though one assumes potential is everywhere, actual demonstration of the leadership needed to man the range of differentiated and interrelated institutions is scarce. Despite the dream of a fully participatory society, the overwhelming mass of society seems destined to be engaged in subsistence and other nonleadership activities. This poses problems with respect to the establishment of legitimacy on the part of the leadership cadre. Successful innovating leadership does not merely do things *for* or *to* a people; it manages to convince the people that innovation is performed *by* or *with* the people's energies or talents—or at least with their explicit or tacit consent. Consent freely given, moreover, should be complemented by the power to withdraw consent when the leadership fails to deliver.

Finally, successful modernization entails the maturation of innovating institutions and their successful adaptation to a potentially hostile environment. Leadership of an innovating institution needs time to convince the masses of the beneficial qualities of the institution. It also needs time to develop internal strategies of operation and to evolve doctrines that will permit it to function without daily confrontations and challenges to its legitimacy. The establishment of a novel institution generates the creation of new groups that inevitably challenge the power and privilege of other groups in that society. Therefore, cautious prior planning of resources and programs is essential to get the institution through its infancy. This also means that drastic shifts in program objectives or premature public discussion of abandonment of an institution not only undermine that particular institution but may also discredit the very notion of induced change. The affected masses will soon come to regard institution-building as the sport of the agents of change, with little relevance to their perceived interests.

## Alternative Paths to Modernity

The means by which political leadership in the recent past has attempted to hurry the transformation of men's attitudes toward change have varied considerably. Mustafa Kemal (Atatürk), in Turkey, assumed that all aspects of life in the Islamic Ottoman sultanate, from the alphabet to articles of dress, had to be altered—by coercive means if necessary—if the society was to enter successfully upon a course of modernization, Westernization, industrialization, and secularization. It was further assumed that the political elite had a special responsibility to carry the masses and the nonpolitical elites through an extended period of tutelage prior to the full involvement of society in the decision-making process. Eventually, however, the political system was to become participatory to the extent that an opposition party was permitted to use the ballot to displace the dominant revolutionary party.[1]

The modernization of Soviet society under Lenin and Stalin represents a more extreme version of the Turkish model, with a highly articulated and universally oriented ideological program that went far beyond the parochial nationalism of the Turkish revolution. The deeper entrenchment of traditional political, economic, and religious forces, moreover, seemed to compel Soviet leadership to place a greater reliance upon terror and other coercive sanctions in transforming Czarist institutions and altering the values of the peasant majority. The continued elitist character of the Communist Party indicates an intention to prolong the period of tutelage rather than to permit significant mass participation in societal planning even after dramatic

1. Richard H. Pfaff, "Disengagement from Traditionalism in Turkey and Iran." *Western Political Quarterly*, XVI (March, 1963), 79–98.

transformations have taken place in the political, economic, and social sectors.

Iran under Reza Shah Pahlevi represents a further model for modernization in which the ideological content of the revolution has remained largely unstated and reform has been undertaken on an *ad hoc* basis. The entrenchment of traditionalist forces, such as the landlord class, has been great in contrast to the power of the reforming elites. Thus, the traditionalists have been permitted to retain the form and some of the substance of political power while the modernizing Shah whittled away at land privileges and attempted to generate new forces in society through the development of areas and resources which fell outside the traditional domain. Instead of openly displacing the existing elite, the Shah has attempted to cultivate the peasantry as a partner in the modernizing process.[2]

Still a fourth model of development is presented by Liberia and Ethiopia, in which the traditional aristocracy that dominates a heterogeneous polity employs the rhetoric of modernization for the purposes of retaining political power. The outward trappings of modernization in the form of new roads, splendid skyscrapers, port facilities, and other physical changes substitute for basic alterations in the political, social, and economic order. The exploitation of resources is achieved through the skillful manipulation of foreign capital and personnel by the traditional aristocracy. Expansion of the economy further entrenches the ruling class, who use their new wealth to perfect the techniques of surveillance and control over the masses. Involvement of the latter in the economic growth of the society is limited with respect both to skills which may be acquired and to distribution of benefits from the new enterprises.[3]

## The Tanzanian Blueprint for Development

TANU (the Tanganyika African National Union) under the leadership of Julius Nyerere has attempted to provide the people of Tanzania with yet another model for political

2. *Ibid.*
3. Cf. my volume, *Liberia: The Evolution of Privilege* (Ithaca: Cornell University Press, 1969).

and economic development. TANU established its legitimacy as an innovating institution by having successfully pressed the British administrators during the 1950s to grant independence to Tanganyika—as the trust territory was then called. The achievement of this goal on December 9, 1961, and the subsequent union of Tanganyika with Zanzibar led many citizens of the united republic to assume that the millennium was at hand. Many had not taken literally Nyerere's dual slogan of *Uhuru na kazi*—"Freedom and *Work*." The reality of Nyerere's statement became apparent to some only as the tax collector once again made his familiar rounds, as local officials continued to enforce compulsory cultivation rules, and as the prices of coffee, cotton, and other crops remained the same or even suffered a decline.

Generally, however, there is a great deal of optimism apparent in Tanzania regarding its future despite several severe crises in the political order and difficulties in meeting economic targets. There is almost universal acceptance of the fact that the government of Tanzania is not only one of the most fiscally honest governments in Africa but also that its leadership displays a moral honesty which is rare anywhere. Julius Nyerere has always insisted that his people must have the "bad news" regarding the sacrifices they are required to make if they are to overcome poverty, disease, illiteracy, and the other ills afflicting a developing society. Nyerere has thus hoped to avoid creating unrealistic hopes.

Tanzania's version of development, which Nyerere presented as TANU policy on socialism and self-reliance in the Arusha Declaration of 1967, represents a radical departure from previous models. It strives to be participatory. Development is not seen as leading simply to a change in the status of the educated elite; rather, there is to be a significant involvement of the time, talents, and energy of the masses both in the decision-making process and in the implementation and evaluation of plans. Furthermore, since more than 90 per cent of Tanzania's citizens reside outside Dar es Salaam and the other urban centers, development—Nyerere insists—should mean *rural* development. Those who contribute most to the earnings of a poor society—the peasants—should not be exploited for the benefit of the urban elite and the unemployed. Rather than following the will-o-the-wisp of instant industrialization, Nyerere would concentrate instead on improving the agricultural sector. Tanzania thus might escape the dualism of other African states in which an ever-widening gap develops between the traditionally oriented cultivators and the more modernized urban minority. The gap has been more than psychological, for it has also led to a disproportionate share of income and government services going to the towns at the expense of the countryside.

The prerequisites for development set forth in the Arusha Declaration are simple: people, land, good policies, and good leadership. It is clear, however, that the conversion of good intentions into hard economic and political realities is a difficult task. Nyerere faces, for example, the problem of equalizing participation and benefits not merely between the urban and the rural population but between various rural sectors as well. Physical geography, historical accident, natural economic advantage, and other factors have already placed a considerable distance between the wealthy and well-educated coffee-producing Chagga of Kilimanjaro and the illiterate Gogo of the central Tanzanian steppe, who still eke out a meager existence with their crude hoes and digging sticks in the midst of the tsetse-infested bush. Unfortunately for Nyerere and TANU, probably more of Tanzania's 120 tribal groups fall closer on the scale to the Gogo than to the Chagga. Indigenous technology and traditional attitudes toward local political leadership and social organization persist in spite of the rigorous efforts by the nationalist leadership to transform Tanzanian society.

Traditionalism, however, is not the only major barrier to rapid modernization. A legacy which is of equal significance is the impact of colonial rule. Much has been written and said, even by African political leaders, regarding the material benefits which have come from the Western colonial experience in Africa. There were even claims made in the early 1960s regarding the democratic heritage of colonialism—in terms of the British, French, and others leaving behind parliamentary institutions, political parties, and stable bureaucracies. Time has demonstrated the absurdity of the latter claim. Colonial rule was far from being an ideal environment for inculcating the notion of self-reliance, which is essential not only for democracy but also for the self-sustaining institutions needed for development. Colonial rule, even within a single territory, moreover, vacillated between the extremes of rigidly maintaining the traditional status quo and of assuming that any aspect of the indigenous culture could be subjected to manipulation at the whim of the colonial administrators. Thus, whether the indigenous society stagnated or underwent dramatic changes in its physical setting, it was clear that the choice was made by others. The subject of colonial rule had things done *to* him and *for* him, but seldom *with* and *by* him. He was made to feel like a marginal participant in programs that were nominally for his benefit. He was not encouraged to think on his own, to formulate plans, and to organize pressure group activity in pursuit of rational interests. It was the colonial administrator who reserved the right both to propose and to dispose, and what might be proposed one day could be rejected the next. *Indeed, it was the caprice (almost a whimsical attitude) of colonial administrators with respect to economic, social, and political change that probably more than any other factor undermined the confidence of colonial people in the idea of modernization.* In terms of contemporary European standards of morality during the nineteenth and early twentieth century, the innovative colonial administrator may have been regarded as a humanitarian, who had responded to Kipling's challenge to take up the "white man's burden." To the subjects of colonial rule, the administrator was—at best—a benign meddler, as this study of the Makonde of Tanzania will demonstrate. It is to the consequences of this benign meddling that Julius Nyerere and other leaders must address themselves if they are to successfully encourage the modernization of the new African states.

## The Case for Analysis

The Makonde area of southeastern Tanzania was often referred to as the "Cinderella region of a Cinderella territory" by the British colonial administrators who governed Tanganyika until 1961. By 1969, no one had as yet managed to rescue the one-third-million Makonde from their plight of poverty, illiteracy, and disease.[4] Although they constitute the third-largest of the 120 ethnic groups of Tanzania, size bears little relationship to their economic, social, and political development. On various scales of modernization the Makonde rank far behind the Chagga, Nyakyusa, Haya, Sukuma, and Nyamwezi, and not much higher than the Gogo and Ha, who are often cited as the stereotypes of underdevelopment in a society which is undergoing rapid change. The enrollment of Makonde children in school, for example, is well below the national average. It has only been within memory of the adult population of the Makonde region, moreover, that the residents have made the difficult and painful transition from a substantially subsistence economy to one in which a sizable proportion of the population is engaged in migratory labor, production of salable crops, or other phases of a cash economy. Except for a few small enterprises around the deep-water port of Mtwara, there has been no substantial industrial development in the region. Cooperative societies, which have been a stimulus to modernization in other parts of Tanzania, were only recently introduced, and they still lack dynamism since participation by Makonde is mandatory rather than voluntary. The region, furthermore, is well below the national average in terms of hospitals, clinics, and other medical institutions.

One of the most striking indices of underdevelopment in Umakonde — as the inhabitants refer to their homeland — is the relatively small contribution made by the area to the pool of human talent needed for nation-building. It is true that some of the leading members of President Julius Nyerere's administration in 1969 were Makonde; nevertheless, the group as a whole has lagged numerically behind many of the smaller tribes in contributing its share to national leadership.[5] At the local level as well, participation by the Makonde in the modern political system is marked either by lethargy or by resistance to innovation.

4. The Makonde population in 1957 was placed at 333,897 for Tanganyika as a whole. The majority of the Makonde live in the three districts of Newala (165,631), Mtwara (82,390), and Lindi (49,064). They are the dominant tribal group in Newala (90 per cent) and Mtwara (86 per cent), but constitute only 30 per cent of Lindi District (Tanganyika, *African Population Census, 1957*).

5. An analysis by Gordon Wilson, based upon the responses to the questionnaires used for the 1963–64 *Who's Who in East Africa* (Nairobi: Marco Surveys,

Various reasons have been presented to explain the lack of development in Umakonde. Most frequently cited is the geographic isolation of the three districts. (See Figure 1.) Even today, torrential rains and the absence of all-weather roads to the north leave the Makonde largely isolated from the rest of the nation and its capital for six or seven months of the year. In recent decades, East African Airways has provided one means of contact, but the limited schedule and the cost of travel restricts its use to Tanzanian officials, Asian traders, and European missionaries, businessmen, and technicians. Ships calling at the port of Mtwara do provide links with the outside world. The small coastal steamer that operates between Tanga and Mtwara, however, has an irregular schedule even in the best of weather and invariably puts in for repairs at the height of the rainy season. Mail service is unreliable during the months from December to July, and even the telephone lines are frequently down one week in three during the wet months.

Geographic and climatic conditions, however, do not present insuperable obstacles to change if government policy, revenues, and human technology can be consistently, and in a massive fashion, directed toward road and rail construction, the development of resources, and the establishment of markets, schools, and other facilities that will permit sustained internal growth. Unfortunately for the contemporary Makonde, the low level of technology in traditional society as well as the fragmented character of the political and social system did not permit their ancestors to do more than barely cope with the shortage of water, the presence of tsetse fly, and other problems of the physical environment. Often the most creative response of traditional Makonde to a natural or a human challenge to survival was to move on to a more hospitable location.

When societies possessing better material resources or more

---

1964), indicated that the Makonde, with 6 per cent of the population of Tanzania, contributed only a fraction of 1 per cent to the leadership sample. The Chagga and Haya, who also constitute 6 per cent of the population, contributed 12 per cent and 7 per cent, respectively, to the elite sample. The Makonde ranked proportionately with the Gogo and Ha—two of the least-developed communities in Tanzania. See Gordon M. Wilson, "The African Elite," in *The Transformation of East Africa*, ed. Stanley Diamond and Fred G. Burke (New York: Basic Books, 1966), p. 443.

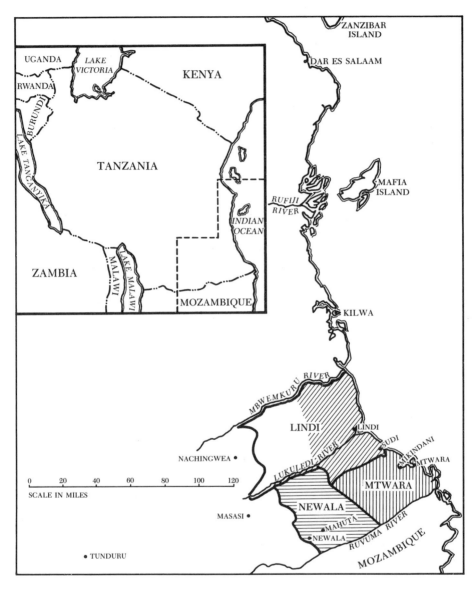

FIGURE 1:
MAKONDE DISTRICTS OF TANZANIA

sophisticated systems of political, military, and economic organization came into contact with the Makonde, moreover,
there was no guarantee that development would take place. The
decades of Ngoni and Arab contact that preceded the impo-

sition of European rule in 1885, as well as the nearly eight decades of German and British colonial administration, did relatively little to set the Makonde on the road to development. Alien domination of, or even contact with, Makonde society took one of three forms. First, contact was frequently counter-productive with respect to development, since it resulted in the harassment or exportation of its human resources. Second, those who tended to monopolize the mechanisms of change regarded the Makonde homeland as being of marginal interest in the pursuit of economic, religious, or other interests, and hence they concentrated their administrative and material resources elsewhere. And third, when innovation was at-tempted, it was frequently done in an arbitrary and capricious fashion without any effort being made to involve the Makonde in developmental institutions in a sustained and significant fashion.

The first and second forms of contact were present in the earliest relationship that the Makonde had with people from outside the continent of Africa. During the eighteenth and nine-teenth centuries, Umakonde was crucial to the East African slave trade, with the area itself being a source of slaves as well as lying astride the various Arab caravan routes connecting Lake Nyasa (now Lake Malawi) with the slave entrepôts at the coast. Mikindani, which was the terminus of the Ruvuma Valley caravans, saw many Makonde and their neighbors shipped to the French plantations on Mauritius, Réunion, and the Mas-cerene Islands.[6] An even more significant route was the north-erly one, which skirted to the north of the Makonde plateau of Newala and terminated at Kilwa Kivinje. The Reverend J. Lewis Krapf, who visited the coast in 1850, estimated that be-tween 10,000 and 12,000 slaves passed through the markets at Kilwa each year on the way to other coastal towns, the islands of Zanzibar and Pemba, or Arabia.[7]

The Makonde region underwent the second form of contact — marginal concern — when the European missionaries appeared on the scene in the middle of the nineteenth century. Africa's

6. Sir John Gray, "Mikindani Bay before 1887," *Tanganyika Notes and Records* (hereafter cited as *TNR*), no. 28 (January, 1950), pp. 29–37.

7. *Travels, Researches, and Missionary Labours, during Eighteen Years' Residence in Eastern Africa* (London: Trübner, 1860), p. 423.

most famous missionary-explorer, David Livingstone, appeared
at Mikindani in 1866. His interest was not conversion of the
Makonde; rather, he had been spurred on by the suggestion of
Reverend Krapf that the "Lufuma or Rufuma is said to have its
source in the Niassa, which must mean in the eastern shore of
the lake."[8] If the latter had been true, Livingstone would have
found a water route to the more fertile missionary fields of
Central Africa, where Islamic influence was still spotty. Convinced that Christianity would provide a strong bulwark against
the spread of Islam and put an end to the intertribal raiding that
kept the Arab caravans supplied with the bulk of their human
cargo, Livingstone started out from Mikindani in 1866 on what
was to become his last journey into the interior of Africa. The
hardships of the almost pathetic march of men and camels
through the Ruvuma Valley was capped by the disappointment
in finding that the Ruvuma did not, after all, originate in Lake
Nyasa, nor was it even navigable during most of its course to
the sea.[9] Had the Ruvuma River fulfilled European expectations, the ports of Lindi, Mikindani, and Mtwara would undoubtedly have been intense rivals of the ports to the north,
which ultimately became the focal points for European activity
in East and Central Africa. Instead, the European commercial
interests sought markets farther north in Tanganyika. The
missionaries largely bypassed the Makonde coastal and plateau
areas where the Muslim influence was strong and moved instead to the edge of the Makonde Plateau and the Masasi area,
where Africans were more receptive to proselytizing activities.

During the German period of occupation (ca. 1885–1917),
European interest in Umakonde both waxed and waned. In the
end, the area presented nothing like the promise of economic
reward which the Kilimanjaro, Tanga, and Lake Victoria areas
provided. A few sisal and coconut plantations were established
at the coast, but this was almost the extent of German invest-

8. *Ibid.*, pp. 419–29.

9. *Last Journals of David Livingstone in Central Africa from 1865 to
His Death* (London: John Murray, 1874), Vol. I; and George Shepperson, ed.,
*David Livingstone and the Rovuma* (Edinburgh: Edinburgh University Press,
1965). A plaque on a building in Mikindani indicates, with typical British
caution, that it was the "Reputed Dwelling Place of Dr David Livingstone,
24th March to 7th April 1866, From Here He Began His Last Journey."

ment. The area was not considered to require close administration in order to control native rebellion; there was some sporadic resistance, but in the major African uprising against the Germans—the Maji Maji Rebellion of 1905—the Makonde remained aloof. Indeed, the area took on importance only during the closing days of German rule in East Africa. In 1917 the German forces made a last stand near the Newala *boma*, or headquarters, before fleeing across the Ruvuma into Mozambique, with the British forces in hot pursuit.

During the four and a half decades of British rule in Tanganyika the Makonde region experienced in turn—and even simultaneously—the three forms of alien domination noted above. During the first three decades of British administration of Tanganyika as a League of Nations Mandate Territory, the Makonde region was relatively neglected in terms of positive economic development. The understaffed and underfinanced administration in Tanganyika devoted its attention to the same productive areas the Germans had singled out for concern. To the Makonde, consequently, European rule continued to mean law enforcement, compulsory labor for road construction, and tax collection. Indeed, the Makonde peasant, in order to pay his taxes, was frequently forced to leave his home district to find wage employment, since very few cash crops had been introduced and since industrial, missionary, and government employment within the Makonde area was minimal. The same exportation of human resources occurred with respect to the few Makonde who had managed to receive an education at the mission schools in Newala, Lindi, or the neighboring Masasi District. When educated, they could find no outlet for their talents in the Makonde districts.

The most significant feature of British rule, however, was administrative caprice. Geographic isolation of the region from the territorial capital, compounded within the region by isolation of the districts from the provincial headquarters at Lindi (later Mtwara), afforded the administrator on the spot a dangerous amount of leeway in terms of innovation. While innovation was, of course, necessary for modernization, the constant manipulation of the economic, political, and social structures without regard to previous actions and without guarantees of continuity of programs tended to undermine Makonde trust in modern government. British district officers would come and go with great frequency and with an even greater store of new ideas. It was the Makonde peasant who had to remain on the scene and experience the frustration of seldom seeing fruition of the grandiose schemes to which he had been required to devote his time, talent, and money.

In rather bold relief, the mischief of adminstrative caprice in carrying out a program of modernization is revealed in the postwar fiasco, the Groundnut Scheme. In 1947 the slumber of the Southern Province of Tanganyika was rudely shattered as the windmill fury of the Overseas Food Corporation burst forth upon the region. This was the brainchild of John Strachey, minister for food in the British Labour government. He was convinced that the food-oil shortage in postwar Britain could be solved by a massive scheme of mechanized cultivation of groundnuts (peanuts) in various parts of Tanganyika and other British African territories. Although the vast estates of the Overseas Food Corporation were located in Nachingwea District, immediately to the north of the Makonde districts, the scheme had a direct impact, both negative and positive, on the Makonde economy as well as on its social order. Labor recruitment not only took Makonde from their villages but also resulted in a flow of Europeans, Asians, and other Africans through the Makonde districts and a further concentration of non-Makonde in the coastal towns of Lindi, Mikindani, and Mtwara. Makonde migrant workers acquired new skills and new forms of wealth, but the area also experienced a mild epidemic of theft, prostitution, and other social problems.

One of the most dramatic developments occurred at the small fishing village of Mtwara, which had been selected as the port for the activities of the Overseas Food Corporation. The visions of the developers were almost without bound, since Mtwara's blue lagoon provided Tanganyika with its first deep-water harbor. In a fever-pitch of activity, port facilities were installed and a railway line was laid from Mtwara to Nachingwea. Broad avenues were carved through several hundred acres of a sisal estate near Mtwara connecting what was hopefully to become, in a decade or so, the commercial and government centers, a sports arena, the public library, and even an opera house. All the sterile imagination of a British postwar city planner was

brought to bear upon the problems of creating the future me-
tropolis of a hundred thousand inhabitants.

Alas for the Makonde, poor planning, unpredictable weather,
a lack of African artisans, defective war-surplus equipment,
and even the obstinate baobab tree combined to doom the
Groundnut Scheme to failure. Just as abruptly as it had begun,
the bubble of the Groundnut Scheme burst a brief four years
after the dreams had started.[10] The bright prospects of Makonde
prosperity vanished. The rails began to rust and were eventually
removed. Sisal, weeds, and brush reclaimed many of the roads.
And British officials whom I encountered in Mtwara in 1955
were cursing the thirty-mile "safari" one had to take each day in
Mtwara town as he made his rounds from home to the office, to
the shops, to the cinema or bar, and home again. To the Makonde
peasant, the plans for Mtwara—and indeed the whole Groundnut Scheme—were but another example of the "white man's
madness."

It was precisely at this stage of depression and frustration
among the Makonde that TANU, under the leadership of Julius
Nyerere, began its successful drive for the independence of
Tanganyika from British colonial rule.

10. For a journalistic account of the fiasco, see Alan Wood, *The Groundnut
Affair* (London: Bodley Head, 1950).

# 2:
# Origins of
## the Makonde
## of Tanzania

## The Migrations from Mozambique

The Makonde of Tanzania do not possess a well-inte-
grated myth of origin beyond the almost universal agreement
among the various *litawa,* or kin groups, that the cradle area of
the Makonde people was the *Ndonde.* The latter, however, is
merely a vague geographical expression which refers not only
to the undulating grassy plain which stretches south of the
Ruvuma River into Mozambique but also to the area of Masasi
District north of the Ruvuma. Various informants in 1955 identified the birthplace of the Makonde as Lichelo Hill, the top of
which was called Mkundi. From there the "founders" moved to
Msumbiji, which was at the base of the hill. It was not until they
had gathered at Ngomano (the Portuguese call it Negomano)
that the various litawa had developed the sense of group con-
sciousness which set them apart from the neighboring Makua,
Matambwe, and Yao. Other informants, however, insisted that
the birthplace was a place called Mkula, the exact location of
which is not known today.

In any case, there was no single recognized founder of the
Makonde tribal group as a whole. The fragmented character of
the origin myth stems from the fact that the migration from the

Ndonde to the present Makonde homeland in Tanzania did not occur as one great heroic march. Rather, movement was an affair of isolated individuals, families, or groups migrating at staggered points in time. Each family or group tended to emphasize those events of its migration which were most important to its own struggle for survival. Since many of the myths stress that the founders were in flight from their enemies — both human and environmental — the fugitives were compelled to travel with only light baggage. The light baggage apparently applied as much to the remembered repertoire of legends, folktales, and proverbs as it did to hoes, pieces of cloth, and cooking pots.

Despite the uncoordinated character of Makonde migration from Mozambique, one can reconstruct a series of vague patterns indicating that there were several waves of migration, with the itinerants in various periods taking one of at least four fairly distinct routes. (See Figure 2.) Dating these waves, however, is another matter, for the Makonde are anything but precise about time spans, and the genealogies of the litawa elders I interviewed during my first visit to Newala in 1955–56 seldom went back beyond five or six generations. The best we could obtain was an educated guess, based partly upon oral tradition, the sparse historical record, and the recorded investigations of early British administrators. These suggest that the bulk of the migration from Mozambique took place between the second and third quarters of the nineteenth century, bringing the Makonde — either directly or by a series of stages — to the Newala Plateau, where the majority of the Tanzanian Makonde reside today.

### The Ruvuma River Migratory Route

The major exception to this relatively recent history of migration is the insistence by the coastal inhabitants near Lindi that their ancestors came much earlier — perhaps in the middle of the eighteenth century. They insisted, too, that their ancestors were hunters who had moved eastward along the Ruvuma River to its mouth and then followed the coast northward as far as the Mbwemkuru River, with a few even traveling as far as Kilwa Kivinje. The bulk of these early coastal immigrants, however, clustered in the vicinity of Lindi near the hill

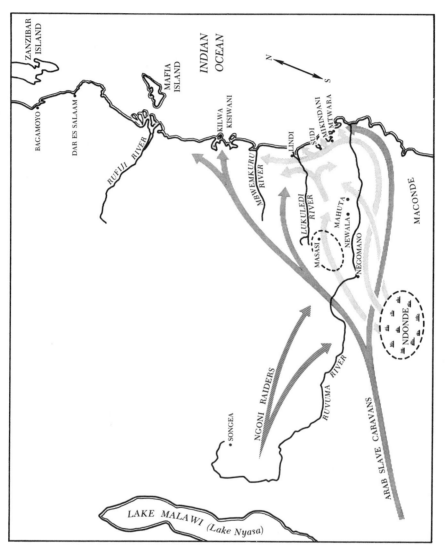

FIGURE 2:  MAKONDE MIGRATION ROUTES

called Maraba and, until the present century, were called Maraba rather than Makonde.[1] Early Swahili texts confirm the existence of this older migration by attributing the establishment of the port of Lindi to Makonde rather than Arab efforts and by chronicles which refer to the affairs of the Makonde "sultans" of the coastal towns of Sudi and Mikindani.[2] The European record also supports the contention that the Ruvuma Valley served as a fairly-well-established route to the interior of Africa by the middle of the nineteenth century. The Reverend J. Lewis Krapf, who reached Mikindani in 1850, stated that "those of Mikindani often journey to the Lake Niassa, and declared themselves ready to accompany us to it if we would give them brandy."[3] Travel of Makonde along the Ruvuma route, however, was not always by choice, for they were frequently the merchandise in which the Arabs, the Yaos, and their fellow Makonde residents of Mikindani trafficked. As early as the end of the eighteenth century, Mikindani had become significant as a slave entrepôt for the shipment of Makonde and other captives to the French plantations of Mauritius and Réunion.[4] Makonde, however, did

1. The two liwalis who related this story insisted that they had not been aware of the similar legend recorded in the Lindi District Book by W. Fryer, an administrative officer, in 1928. Fryer's informants were more conservative, dating the migration at about 1775 to 1825. They also insisted that the group presently called Machinga in Lindi District were Makonde rather than Yao. The Machinga have been treated as a distinct ethnic group by the British administrators and by the present nationalists. See also Lindi Province, Annual Report, 1925 (Tanzanian National Archives, Dar es Salaam [hereafter cited as TNA], Vol. 21, 1733/10:75).

2. "The Ancient History of Lindi," "The History of Sudi," and "The History of Mikindani" first appeared in *Prosa und Poësie der Suaheli*, by C. Velten (Berlin, 1907), pp. 265–84. English versions of the first two appear in G. S. P. Freeman-Grenville, ed., *The East African Coast: Select Documents from the First to the Earlier Nineteenth Century* (Oxford: Clarendon Press, 1962), pages 227–32. There has been no precise dating of the founding of Lindi, and even Freeman-Grenville states that the Makonde are "confessedly descendants of nineteenth century arrivals pressed thither from beyond the Rovuma" ("The Coast, 1489–1840," in *History of East Africa*, Vol. I, ed. Roland Oliver and Gervase Mathew [Oxford: Clarendon Press, 1963], pp. 131, 148–49).

3. *Travels, Researches, and Missionary Labours, during Eighteen Years' Residence in Eastern Africa* (London: Trübner, 1860), p. 429.

4. Sir John Gray, "Mikindani Bay before 1887," *TNR*, no. 28 (January, 1950), p. 29. Edward Alpers notes the primary importance, too, of the port of Mongalo at the entrance of Sudi Bay. See "The Role of the Yao in the Development of Trade in East-Central Africa, 1698–c. 1850" (Ph.D. diss., University of London, 1966), p. 156.

travel voluntarily along the Ruvuma in search of game and trade, and it is even recorded that, in times of famine, Makonde would come to Mikindani and sell themselves into slavery.[5]

The hypothesis that the Ruvuma route to the coast is the oldest of the four migration trails is also supported by conjecture. Following the river, for example, presented an easier approach to the coast than did the more direct northward route, which entailed the difficult scaling of the Newala escarpment. After reaching the plateau, moreover, one still had a journey of many days' duration across a relatively waterless expanse, where one's axe or knife would be constantly in use cutting through the dense thicket of lianas, bamboo, wild rubber, and scrub trees. A more northerly "end-around run" of the Makonde plateau was, of course, a possibility in the early days, just as it was to become the more favored route in the middle of the nineteenth century at the height of the Zanzibari slave trade. The small Makonde family, however, was probably not as well organized as the commercially minded Arabs and Yaos in dealing with the problems of survival in crossing a relatively uninhabited tract of wilderness. The fact that much of the area north of the Ruvuma was a wilderness in the seventeenth century is at least suggested by the reconstruction of the remarkable journal of the Portuguese traveler Gaspar Bocarro, who traversed the hinterland area from Lake Nyasa to Kilwa in 1616.[6]

## The Mahuta Legend

Chronologically, the second migratory route was probably the one which brought the Makonde across the Ruvuma below the Makonde plateau, with the ascent being made at Nambunga. Residents of Mahuta and Namahonga in 1955

5. Freeman-Grenville, "The Coast, 1489–1840," p. 154.

6. Although the reconstruction of his journey by Rangeley and Hamilton has Bocarro skirting the present Makonde homeland, his remarks have application to a wider area. See W. H. J. Rangeley, "Bocarro's Journey," *Nyasaland Journal*, VII (July, 1954), 15–23; R. A. Hamilton, "The Route of Gaspar Bocarro from Tete to Kilwa in 1616," *ibid.*, pp. 7–14; and Sir John Gray, "A Journey by Land from Tete to Kilwa in 1616," *TNR*, no. 25 (June, 1948), pp. 37–47. Bocarro's chronicles appeared in *Extractos da decada 13 da história da India* (Lisbon, 1876).

insisted that their ancestors came up the escarpment via this very difficult climb prior to the settlement by means of the more northerly approach. Since many of the origin myths refer to a man from Mahuta who carved a female figure that became his wife, there is perhaps some substance for the belief in the earlier use of the Nambunga approach. It is largely in this area of the plateau, incidentally, that one finds a supernatural rather than a rational explanation for why the Makonde decided to live on an almost waterless plateau. Although the tale has been modified by a number of Europeans who have resided in the area, the earliest English translation is as follows:

> The place where the tribe originated is Mahuta, on the southern side of the plateau towards the Rovuma, where of old time there was nothing but thick bush. Out of this bush came a man who never washed himself or shaved his head, and who ate and drank but little. He went out and made a human figure from the wood of a tree growing in the open country, which he took home to his abode in the bush and there set it upright. In the night this image came to life and was a woman. The man and the woman went down together to the Rovuma to wash themselves. Here the woman gave birth to a still-born child. They left that place and passed over high land into the valley of the Mbwemkuru, where the woman had another child, which was also born dead. Then they returned to the high bush country of Mahuta, where the third child was born, which lived and grew up. In course of time, the couple had many more children, and called themselves Wamatanda. These were the ancestral stock of the Makonde, also called Wamakonde, i.e. aborigines. Their forefather, the man from the bush, gave his children the command to bury their dead upright, in memory of the mother of their race who was cut out of wood and awoke to life when standing upright. He also warned them against settling in the valleys and near large streams, for sickness and death dwelt there. They were to make it a rule to have their huts at least an hour's walk from the nearest watering-place; then their children would thrive and escape illness.[7]

7. The original appeared in Pater Adam, *Lindi und sein Hinterland* (Berlin: Dietrich Reimer, 1902); the English translation appeared in K. Weule, *Native Life in East Africa*, trans. Alice Werner (London: Pitman, 1909), p. 259.

In the past there may have been a more rational explanation for the reluctance of the Makonde to live near water. The disastrous recurrent flooding of the Ruvuma Valley may account for the Makonde proverb: "We Makonde prefer to have food in plenty and go far for our water rather than to sit near the water and starve."[8] The cooler climate of the plateau, moreover, as well as the absence of mosquitos and crocodiles, must have made the higher land just as attractive to the Makonde as it was later to the European missionaries and administrators. Whatever the rationalization for the residence of the Makonde on the plateau, the fact is that the majority of the residents of Newala District lived away from sources of water until the opening of the Makonde Water Scheme in 1957. The consequence of this was that Makonde women for generations were required, several days each week during the dry season, to spend ten to twelve hours journeying down to the rivers and springs to fetch water for their family needs. Even in 1967, women in those parts of the plateau not serviced by the water corporation faced this prospect.

## Famine and the Ngoni Raiders

The third migratory route entered the Newala Plateau at Mnima via the gradual rise at Luchemo near Majembe. This was apparently the most frequently used approach, and present residents have a different explanation for their ancestors' behavior than that provided by the Mahuta legend. The migrants who used this approach were part of a two-stage movement from Mozambique which was occasioned by a series of crises. People in Mnolela village in 1955 related that roughly before the middle of the nineteenth century a great famine struck the Ndonde area of Mozambique.[9] This sent the Makonde across the Ruvuma in search of game and edible grains. It was said that the dead bodies outnumbered the living and that there were few persons left to bury the dead. The desperate struggle for food found the surviving Makonde fighting one another, and the additional slaughter brought about another exodus across the

8. M. Gillman, Newala District Book.
9. This version differs from the rather confusing legends recorded in the District Books of Newala, Mtwara, and Lindi districts.

Ruvuma into the Ndonde area of Masasi District. Both the famine and the fratricidal warfare were referred to as *Mapende*, which means "that which has no reason." In the Masasi grasslands, the Makonde took up residence at Lumesule, Malumba, Matihu, and other places between the Mbangala and Lukwika rivers.

The residence of the Makonde in Masasi District was but an extended pause in the migration which took them eventually to the Newala Plateau. Tradition indicates that this was a pause of approximately two decades' duration. This explains the apparent discrepancy between Livingstone's assumption in 1866 that the Makonde plateau was relatively underpopulated (due to its "having been thinned by the slave trade") and Bishop Smythies' observations in 1884 that the plateau had a fairly large population.[10]

The major cause of the flight from Masasi to the plateau was the eastward press of slave-raiding neighbors. Fulleborn suggested that the Makonde had been more directly harried by the Yao.[11] Others, perhaps basing their evidence on the fact that the Makua occupied the land vacated by the Makonde when they fled Masasi, attributed the harassment to the Makua. The ultimate source of discord in the entire Ruvuma Valley, however, was the Ngoni raiders, variously called *Mafiti, Maviti,* and *Mafita.* The Makonde in the 1870s and 1880s were being pressed by the outermost shock wave of a military explosion which had actually commenced half a century earlier and several thousand miles to the south. The Ngoni who terrorized more than twenty tribal groups in Tanzania were part of the Zulu-Ngoni diaspora from South Africa that began during the time of Chaka in the second decade of the nineteenth century. Although I encountered one pocket of Ngoni as far north as Kahama District, near Lake Victoria, the main bastion of strength in Tanzania was in Songea District, from which the Ngoni terrorized much of southern Tanzania from 1840 till almost the end of the century. Although the raiders were in some instances "true" Ngoni, the

10. *Last Journals of David Livingstone in Central Africa from 1865 to His Death* (London: John Murray, 1874), I, 19; see also *Journals and Papers of Chauncy Maples* (London: Longmans, Green, 1899), pp. 14 ff, 61.

11. Friedrich Fülleborn, "Das Deutsche Njassa und Rovuma-Gebiet," in *Deutsch Ost-Afrika* (n.p., 1906), pp. 47–48.

preponderance of those who veered eastward to plunder the Masasi and Newala inhabitants were the *Magwangwara*, or "new" Ngoni. That is, they were people who had been conquered by the Ngoni and had identified with their conquerors by adopting their language, customs, and their love of military exploit. Although the "new" Ngoni could operate as freebooters in search of slaves, ivory, and other loot, they could not enjoy the full privileges of military leadership and high political office. Indeed, their lack of discipline and their own status insecurity appears to have made the Magwangwara even more bloodthirsty plunderers than the true Ngoni.[12]

The Makonde quest for security from the Ngoni raiders took them to the Newala Plateau via the Mnima route. Realizing that the raiders would most likely follow the river valleys, the Makonde were ready to sacrifice convenience in obtaining water for the safety that the waterless plateau provided. The plateau was in many respects a natural refuge. The difficulties of scaling the steep escarpment, for example, gave all the advantages of cover and position to those who held the summit. Legends of various kin groups relate how boulders the size of men were rolled over the escarpment to thwart raiding parties. Even if the Ngoni reached the top, the thicket provided such an excellent cover that a Makonde had only to push deeper into the thicket to escape his pursuers. Two cultural traits of the Makonde, moreover, enhanced the security value of the thicket. First of all, the Makonde use a system of stump cultivation, whereby tree stumps are left in a cleared field, and this results in a very rapid regeneration of the original vegetation. Within a period of roughly three years, the maze of new growth and the loss of soil fertility require that the land be left fallow. The regenerated field becomes even more difficult to penetrate than was the natural thicket. Second, the Makonde have traditionally preferred to scatter their homesteads instead of clustering in large villages. Like Daniel Boone on the American frontier, when a Makonde could begin to see the smoke from his neighbor's hut, it was time to move on. From the standpoint of defense, the scattering of homesteads meant that it was difficult

12. Among other references on the Ngoni, see Philip H. Gulliver, "A History of the Songea Ngoni," *TNR*, no. 41 (December, 1955), pp. 16–30.

for Ngoni raiders to do more than pick off one family at a time, for the sounding of the alarm would give other families time to withdraw further into the thicket or to organize some sort of defense.

By the time the Anglican missionaries of the Universities Mission to Central Africa (UMCA) had established stations in Masasi in the 1870s, most of the Makonde had already withdrawn to the plateau for safety. It was only the military adroitness of the Yao chief Matola I and the collective diplomacy of the Arabs and the Anglican missionaries that saved the Makonde from being further pursued in the great Ngoni raids of 1876 and 1882. The last serious raid by the Ngoni took place in 1888, and once again a Yao chief—Machemba—inflicted a decisive defeat upon the Ngoni, which compelled the Songea Ngoni to call a halt to further harassment of the Makonde.[13] Despite many decades of European-imposed peace and the half decade of independence, the Makonde still prefer to live on the waterless plateau. The animosity between the Makonde and Ngoni, moreover, persists. Several of the elders I interviewed in Kitangari referred to the Ngoni as "evil ones."[14]

## The Continuing Migration

The fourth and final migration was much more diffuse in character and took place over a longer period of time; indeed, it continued into the present century. This was the migration of Makonde from the Newala Plateau itself, eastward to Lindi and Mikindani, where the migrants settled behind those Makonde who had arrived at the coast at a much

13. *Journals and Papers of Chauncy Maples*, p. 3; George H. Wilson, *The History of the Universities Mission to Central Africa* (London: UMCA, 1936), pp. 56–58, 79–81; and Joseph Thomson, "Notes on the Basin of the River Rovuma, East Africa," *Proceedings of the Royal Geographical Society*, n.s. IV (1882), 73–79.

14. The animosity is reciprocated. When I visited Songea in 1955, the Southern Province—which included the Makonde districts as well as Songea—was represented in the Legislative Council by a Makonde, Liwali Justino Mponda. One very important Ngoni official volunteered the statement that "the next time Mponda dares show his head in Songea, he will be laughed out of the district. The Makonde tell lies, and they still act like slave people. They try to act like big men. It is fortunate for them that the Europeans are here to protect them."

earlier period via the Ruvuma Valley route. Although there were specific crises, such as an incidence of famine or intra-tribal raiding, that brought about spurts of migration beyond the plateau, on the whole the process was steady and relatively undramatic, caused largely by increased pressures on the land.[15]

## THE PROBLEMS OF ETHNIC IDENTITY

As will be noted in Chapter 3, it is difficult to ascertain the precise point in time that the Makonde began to consider themselves a separate people, distinct from their neighbors. The neighboring tribes were for the most part also Bantu and therefore possessed many linguistic, cultural, and other traits in common with the Makonde, as well as occupying the same general area along the Ruvuma. The problem of analysis becomes particularly acute when it is realized that there are actually two groups of Bantu Africans who are designated as Makonde, and on occasion both historic and contemporary observers have failed to differentiate between the two. The first group of Makonde are the principal residents of Mtwara, Newala, and Lindi districts in the Mtwara Region of Tanzania. The second group carrying the same name regard Mozambique as their homeland, although during the past several decades many have migrated northward across the Ruvuma and have become temporary, or even long-term, residents of Tanzania. Although the migrants from Mozambique insist that they, too, are Makonde, they are frequently called by their neighbors—and have often referred to themselves as—*Mawia*.[16] The latter name, however, is a pejorative term which means "fierce" or "terrible" in Kima-konde, and its use today is often regarded as an insult by most of the refugees from Portuguese oppression.[17] To refrain from

15. R. S. B. M. Hickson-Mahony recorded in the Mikindani District Book in 1928 that one great famine on the plateau, called the *lumaja*, drove many Makonde eastward from Mnima to Lindi and Mikindani in search of food.

16. Various other spellings include *Mabi, Mahiba, Maviha, Mavia, Mawiha, Wawia,* and *Wamawia.*

17. A. Jorge Dias states that the term implies aggressive reactions, because the Mozambique Maconde have a reputation for being violent and for using

the fruitless controversy over which group is the "true" Makonde, and also to avoid confusing two distinct ethnic groups, the Portuguese spelling *Maconde* will be employed here to indicate the tribal group in and from Mozambique.

Although ethnically distinct, the Makonde of Tanzania and the Maconde of Mozambique have much in common. They are the same group only insofar as all Bantu are assumed to have traits in common. The oral tradition of each, for example, confirms that they had similar origins in the Ndonde area of Mozambique west of the present homeland of the Maconde.[18] What members of either group called themselves prior to their eastward migrations is not known. Indeed, since "Makonde" actually means "thicket-covered plateau" in the language of each, it is reasonable to assume that they only utilized the place name in referring to themselves after each had settled on the two high plateaus on their respective sides of the Ruvuma River valley. (See Figure 3.)

Apart from the common place of origin, the patterns of social, economic, and political organization manifest in each society during the traditional period had some striking similarities. Each tribal group, for example, followed a matrilineal system of inheritance of property and succession to office rather than reckoning descent through the father. The political organization of society, moreover, into a series of loosely linked small-scale communities was characteristic of peoples on both sides of the river. Furthermore, the agricultural techniques developed by the Tanzanian Makonde in dealing with the lack of water on the Newala Plateau resemble those employed by the

---

the *panga*, or cutlass, on the slightest provocation. See *Os Macondes de Moçambique* (Lisbon: Centro de Estudos de Antropología Cultural, 1964), I, 65. Dias insists that the reputation is undeserved, and he cites as proof one of the earliest European visitors to the area, H. E. O'Neill, "Journey in the District West of Cape Delgado Bay," *Proceedings of the Royal Geographical Society*, Vol. 5 (1883), p. 402.

18. The common origin of the two is confirmed in the oral data I gathered in Newala in 1955–56 as well as in the data secured by Jorge Dias in Mozambique. See his "The Makonde People: History, Environment and Economy," in *Portuguese Contributions to Cultural Anthropology* (Johannesburg: Witwatersrand University Press, 1961), p. 30.

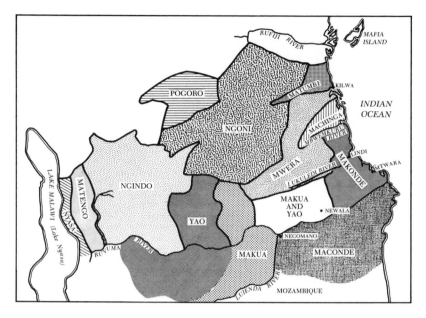

FIGURE 3:
ETHNIC GROUPS OF SOUTHERN TANZANIA

Maconde in Mozambique. Even with respect to the very important initiation rites for young men and women, the rituals and practices parallel each other in the two societies.[19]

Although similar in certain respects, the economic, social, and political systems of the two groups are nevertheless sufficiently distinct to justify our treating them—as they in fact treat themselves—as two distinct ethnic groups. Even more marked, however, are the linguistic differences. Despite the existence of mutual intelligibility between members of the two groups, Lyndon Harries, the British linguist, insists that the language of the Portuguese-controlled group is not simply a dialect of Kimakonde. Indeed, Harries asserted that the Maconde not only possess a distinct language but that Kimaconde

19. The definitive works on the Maconde of Mozambique are the studies by Jorge Dias cited above. The second volume of *Os Macondes de Moçambique* (1964) was written by A. Jorge Dias and his wife, Margot Dias. These are the first two of five contemplated volumes and deal with the history, economics, and culture of the Maconde.

(or Maviha, as he called it) has at least five distinct dialects of its own.[20] In addition to citing differences in vocabulary and tone, Bishop Chauncy Maples, who traveled through the Newala area and northern Mozambique in the nineteenth century, noted that the language of the people to the south was not unlike that of the Makonde but that it had a "great preponderance of dentals."[21]

It is doubtful whether the vague boundary which the Ruvuma River presents can account for the differences in language and other aspects of culture between the two groups. Even today, as the struggle for Mozambique liberation makes the Ruvuma River valley a combat area, the river is only a barrier to contact during the months of high flood. For many decades now the Maconde have moved rather freely back and forth across the international boundary. Both groups, moreover, probably shared the "Ndonde" region of Mozambique as recently as the first quarter of the nineteenth century. Despite the constant and sometimes intimate contact, nevertheless, the differences in language and culture were already noticeable to European visitors in the 1870s. This suggests that many of the linguistic and cultural distinctions had emerged prior to the period of migration. It would also exclude our attributing the ethnic differences to variations in policies and practices of two different sets of European colonial administrators. For the Portuguese — despite a legal "claim" of several centuries' standing — only began to occupy the Maconde plateau on the southern side of the Ruvuma during the fighting which took place between German and Portuguese troops at the close of the First World War.[22]

20. Lyndon Harries, "Linguistic Notes from the Southern Province," *TNR*, no. 19 (June, 1945), pp. 45–48; and *idem*, "Outline of Maviha Grammar," *Bantu Studies*, XIV (1940), 91–146.

21. *Journals and Papers*, pp. 9–10. Very little work has been done on Kimakonde, and one of the works often cited ignores the problems of tone; see Frederick Johnson, "Notes on Kimakonde," *Bulletin of the School of Oriental Studies, London Institution*, II (1922), 417–66. Harries, in "Linguistic Notes," observes that the language of the Makonde, "Mawia," Makua, Matambwe, Mwera, and Ndonde all belong to the Yao cluster of languages. Yao is the standard of linguistic comparison inasmuch as most of the other speakers can converse in Yao even if a Yao cannot converse in the others.

22. Dias states that the Portuguese only effectively occupied the Maconde plateau of Mozambique in 1922; see *Portuguese Contributions*, p. 23.

Undoubtedly, differences in colonial policies and practices with respect to local government, labor recruitment, and attitudes toward the spread of Islam and Christianity have reinforced pre-existing ethnic difference; they did not, I suggest, create them.

It is my hypothesis that the Makonde of Tanzania and the immigrants from Mozambique coexisted in a castelike relationship. The pejorative term *Mawia* employed by the Makonde — and long accepted without protest by the Maconde — is one index of a superordinate-subordinate relationship. Invariably, moreover, in my interviews with Makonde elders as well as in conversations with Makonde schoolboys, the immigrants from Mozambique were undeservedly characterized as being "unclean," "untrustworthy," and otherwise antisocial. The former mkulungwa mkuu (roughly, paramount chief) of Newala supported the notion of a castelike relationship. He indicated that intermarriage of Makonde could take place with Mwera, Makua, Yao, and other groups — including those with whom the Makonde did not enjoy the special friendship relationship called *utani* — but that "Makonde men do not prefer to marry a Mawia woman."

The disdainful attitude of the Makonde toward the Maconde was also evident in the beliefs which were firmly held by my informants regarding the dietary predilections of the Maconde. The visitors from Mozambique were regarded as almost a class of subhumans who were credited with eating snakes, rats, wild pigs, and even monkeys — animals which are generally regarded as unclean or obnoxious by most of their Bantu neighbors. Several Makonde informants, moreover, were convinced that Maconde would — in times of severe famine — eat the flesh of a person who had died of starvation. None of my informants, however, went so far as to indicate that the Maconde were cannibals by preference or that they were unusually addicted to ritualistic murder.[23]

23. The fastidiousness of the Makonde with respect to diet was commented upon by David Livingstone, who noted that the Makonde — unlike their neighbors — did not eat the flesh of the leopard, because the "leopard devours men." He took this as contributing evidence to his notion that the Makonde were not cannibals. See *Last Journals*, I, 25. More recent evidence of the Makonde belief in the cannibalistic tendencies of the Maconde of Mozambique is contained

Furthermore, as is true of many of the caste rel/
Africa, there are marked craft and labor distinctior
subsequently) which set the immigrants from
apart from the Makonde of Tanzania. Although tʰⁱᵉ.
Tanzania, for example, have been regarded as the originatoᵣᵢ
the ebony sculpture being exported from Dar es Salaam in
recent years, in fact this sculpture is almost without exception
the product of artists and craftsmen who are immigrants from
Mozambique.[24] The Makonde do, however, use the wooden
bowls, snuffholders, and even dolls carved by the Maconde. The
only exception to the generalization about the absence of a
carving tradition on the part of the Tanzania Makonde is the
balsawood masks which have been used in the initiation rites

---

in Robert Dick-Read, *Sanamu—Adventure in Search of African Art* (London: Rupert Hart-Davis, 1964), p. 65, which describes a journey in 1956 by a European art dealer.

24. Unfortunately, the recent commercial exploitation of "Makonde" art, as well as several studies which purport to be scholarly, have confused the issue. My own investigations over the past fifteen years in Tanzania have consistently revealed that the sculptors and craftsmen were all immigrants—many very recent—from Mozambique and that the Makonde of Tanzania are not responsible for the ebony carvings which are being exported. In 1955, for example, during my residence at Mkunya Leprosarium I found that all of the patients who carved as a form of physical therapy or to pay their fees were Maconde from across the river. Again, in inquiries at Bagamoyo, Konduchi, Lindi, and Newala in 1967, the "factory" employees who were engaged in carving were without exception from Mozambique.

My own findings aside, there is the previous scholarly record which either explicitly or implicitly supports this position. Such meticulous chroniclers of detail as Livingstone, Thomson, and Weule, for example, make no reference to ebony sculpture being done on the northern side of the Ruvuma, but they do attribute a rich artistic tradition to the Mawia (Maconde), who carved powder horns, medicine and tobacco boxes, and portrait dance masks. Indeed, the wooden carvings of tribal ancestresses which Weule referred to in 1908 were not executed in ebony, and they were attributed somewhat vaguely to "the Mavia, Makonde, and Matambwe tribes"; see *Native Life in East Africa*, p. 260. H. D. Collings, two decades after Weule, in "Notes on the Makonde (Wamakonde) Tribe of Portuguese East Africa," *Man*, XXIX (February, 1929), 25–28, clearly attributes the carving tradition to the people from Mozambique. Lyndon Harries, who worked as a missionary in Newala District of Tanganyika for many years, commented categorically in "Notes on the Mythology of the Bantu in the Ruvuma District," *TNR*, no. 12 (December, 1941), p. 41, that the "Makonde people do not carve from wood." I suspect that he meant that they did not carve in ebony. Still later, the commercial-minded Robert Dick-Read, whom I encountered in 1955, had to venture south of the Ruvuma in search of the sculpture he was merchandising as Makonde art; see *Sanamu*, pp. 62 ff.

of the young Makonde. Unlike the helmet masks of the Maconde, which are worn on the forehead, the masks of the Tanzanian Makonde are face masks.[25] Hence the craft differentiation which is characteristic of many caste relationships, is largely maintained.

A further artistic and cultural difference which has status significance today but which may be the consequence of the differential European impact is the varied attitude of the two ethnic groups with respect to the alteration of the human body. Although the *pelele*, or lip plug (sometimes called an *Ndonya*), is still fairly common among the females on both sides of the Ruvuma, it was only among the Maconde of Mozambique that males were encountered wearing stone disks in their upper lips during the journeys of Livingstone and Bishop Maples in the nineteenth century.[26] Similarly, many of the male immigrants from Mozambique whom I encountered in Newala in 1967 exhibited filed teeth, but this practice was long ago dropped by the male Makonde of Tanzania. One of the most interesting points of differentiation with regard to body art, however, is the continued use of cicatrice (or cicatrix) by both the male and female Maconde of Mozambique. Among the Makonde—at least the males—this practice of scarifying the face and torso with elaborate geometric and naturalistic designs was already dying out at the turn of the century.[27] It was not at all apparent among Makonde males during my investigations in 1955–56 and 1967.

25. One of the earliest references to this distinction is contained in E. C. Chubb, "East African Masks and an Ovambo Sheathed Knife," *Man*, XXIV (October, 1924), 145–46. Two later articles provide further evidence: M. S. Bennett-Clark, "A Mask from the Makonde Tribe in the British Museum," *Man*, LVII (July, 1957), 97–98; and Werner Lang, "Makonde Masks in the Ethnological Collection of the Göttingen University," *Ethnology*, LXXXV (1960), 28–35. The last-named work is interesting because of its curious conjecture about the origin of Makonde stilt dancing.

26. Livingstone, *Last Journals*, I, 24; and *Journals and Papers of Chauncy Maples*, p. 7. Maples noted that in the 1880s the custom was "no longer universal amongst the Maviha with the males." Joseph Thomson, who later achieved fame in Masailand, noted that the pelele had ritual as well as artistic significance; see "Notes on the Rovuma," p. 74. A more extended and illustrated discourse on the lip plug is contained in D. F. Bowie, "The Lip Plug, or 'Ndonya,' among the Tribes of the Southern Province," *TNR*, no. 27 (June, 1949), pp. 75–77.

27. Weule, *Native Life in East Africa*, p. 361.

As has been indicated above, the disparate European colonial traditions of the two peoples could not create these deeply rooted variations in culture and status rankings; nevertheless, European actions and policies undoubtedly reinforced the castelike attitudes of superordination and subordination. There is, for example, the restrictive legislation which the British administrator in Newala had enacted with respect to Maconde refugees. The latter, during the depression of the 1930s, had crossed the Ruvuma in increasing numbers in order to escape the more ruthless Portuguese tax collectors and to search for food. The Newala ordinance strongly implied that the migrants from Mozambique were a disruptive social element by making it an offense for immigrant Maconde to carry weapons and by requiring any Tanzanian Makonde who gave lodging to a refugee from Mozambique to report this event to his headman immediately and to assume all responsibility for any wrongful acts committed by his guest.[28] Commenting on conditions in the southern region as a whole, the senior commissioner of Lindi Province in 1931 stated that the Maconde refugees

> wander from place to place, accompanied by their womenfolk and dogs, doing a few weeks' work at one plantation, and then passing further afield, submitting themselves to no control and paying no dues. Numerous thefts and burglaries have been traced to these wandering natives and numbers of them are in gaol or awaiting trial. The Native Authorities are sorely exercised over these peripatetic strangers and find it difficult to deal effectively with them, owing to their numbers and nomadic propensities. They accept low rates of wages and Planters find them a useful means of cheaper production, though I have repeatedly pointed out the bad economic results of paying thousands of pounds in wages to alien Natives, who spend little or nothing in this Territory and contribute nothing to its revenue. . . . Local Natives found it hard to obtain work and I have strong reason for believing they were generally refused [by estate owners], in favour of alien Natives.[29]

Not all Europeans shared the viewpoint of the administrators regarding the relative merits of the two groups of "Makonde."

28. Newala, *Annual Report*, 1931.
29. Lindi Province, *Annual Report of Senior Commissioner*, 1931 (TNA 11679).

Many Europeans, in fact, regarded the immigrants from Mozambique as the superior of the two peoples. Ironically, however, the very qualities which the European sisal grower, garage
owner, or missionary admired in the Maconde inadvertently
reinforced the superordinate-subordinate status rankings of
the Makonde and the Maconde. The ability of the trans-Ruvuma
immigrants to adapt quickly to complex mechanical tasks as
well as their early and eager appreciation of the values of a
money economy were underrated by the mission-educated and
by the semiliterate Makonde of Tanzania during the postwar
period. The new elite among the Makonde aspired to white-
collar positions in government or with the missions.[30]

The modern buttressing of the castelike relationship by occupational stratification is revealed in a number of ways. One
piece of evidence, for example, was almost obscured by the lack
of perception on the part of a scholar who mistakenly regarded
the two people as a single group. J. A. K. Leslie, in his very interesting study of immigrant communities in Dar es Salaam, appeared almost upset by the "statistical misbehavior" of the
"Makonde" (he made no reference to Maconde or Mawia in his
study), as is revealed in his comments:

> A tribal breakdown shows which tribes are mainly com-
> posed of career men: the Pogoro and the Makonde (many of
> whom, however, are target men, working on construction
> or in the one sisal estate inside the municipality). . . .
> . . . The Makonde are of two groups, the career men like
> those of the Pogoro and Ngoni, Christian and educated, and
> the contract labourers, who are also seldom unemployed,
> but for the different reason that when their services are no
> longer required it is the obligation of the employer to re-
> patriate them.[31]

A most striking example of this occupational stratification was
revealed during my return visit to Newala in 1967. I was im-

30. The European manager of a large sisal estate in Tanga interviewed by
me in 1955 stated that he felt that Mawia (i.e., Maconde) were among his best
employees. "They work hard during the day," he said, "keep out of trouble at
night, and always rely upon each other for assistance." On the other hand, he
complained of the fact that the Makonde were difficult to train and that they
"became homesick" after only a few months on the estate.

31. *A Survey of Dar es Salaam* (London: Oxford University Press, 1963), pp.
258, 122.

pressed by the fact that Makonde cultivators in recent years had taken so readily to the production and marketing of cashew nuts. Several of the more enterprising growers had acquired cashew estates ranging up to 150 or even 200 acres in size. Curious as to how such extensive control of land could be reconciled with the traditional tenure rules (which are based upon usufructory right of occupancy), I probed more deeply. The information was readily volunteered that Maconde refugees from Mozambique were employed to do the weeding and gathering of crops since it was exceedingly difficult to find local residents who were interested in working on other persons' farms for wages. So, the Makonde have become a "landlord class" with the trans-Ruvuma Maconde serving as the "bracero" or transient tenants.[32]

Thus, the recurrent contact and even residence of the low-status Maconde in the homeland of the Makonde both during the formative period in Mozambique and later in Tanzania was probably a factor in the development of Makonde ethnicity. The strangers in the Makonde midst served, through constant contrast, to preserve a feeling of Makonde commonality among the people of a society which was highly fragmented in political, economic, and social terms.

---

32. Even before the liberation crisis the Portuguese attempted, without success, to curb the northward migration of Maconde. They lost not only manpower and revenue but also the produce which the Maconde carried across to Tanganyika, where the prices for cashews and other crops were invariably higher. Rather than "volunteering" for labor in South Africa (an arrangement which in the past brought the Portuguese government a considerable number of shillings for every African "recruited" in this fashion), the Maconde would wander as far north as Tanga to seek employment on the sisal estates.

# 3:
# Fragmentation
## and Cohesion
## in Traditional
## Makonde Society

The study of traditional African societies has greatly contributed to the reformulation by political scientists of the nature of their discipline. No longer adequate — unless one assumes that there were some societies which lacked political systems — are definitions of political science as the study of "the state," of "legal government," of "the monopoly over the use of force," or of specific institutions such as parliaments, courts, bureaucracies, and parties. The study of politics in Africa has revealed many situations in which formal structures of government analogous to those of Western societies were absent; in which force was not regularly monopolized by a specifically identified group of individuals but rather its use was diffused throughout society; or in which the exercise of territorial jurisdiction of authority was vague and poorly defined. It thus became necessary to formulate a definition of politics which would have a more nearly universal application.

David Easton's definition of the political process as "the authoritative allocation of values for society" has permitted us to analyze an essential activity without being restricted to specific "governmental" structures, to the typical activities associated with government in Western societies, or with territorial limits upon the influence of societal authority. Thus, in examining the traditional political system of the Makonde we address ourselves to more relevant questions, such as the limits to the notion of political community, the express and implied goals which the political community seeks in common as well as the means selected for arriving at those goals, the kinds of decisions made with respect to goals and means which are regarded as morally binding upon the members of the political community, and the kind of leadership it is prepared to accept as legitimate in the making of these critical decisions on behalf of the community.

The significance of our concern with a more satisfactory definition of politics becomes apparent when we attempt to delineate the traditional Makonde political system. In common with many of the Bantu groups of East and Central Africa, the Makonde lacked a centralized political authority having jurisdiction over all persons who called themselves Makonde. Indeed, it was only the overriding bonds of kinship, language, belief system, and myths of common origin that permitted a Makonde fisherman of Lindi to identify with a Makonde cultivator of the Newala Plateau for the purpose of economic exchange or social interaction. The fisherman and the cultivator regarded themselves as having political allegiances to different membership groups.

Polycentrism was even more extreme among the Makonde than it was among their neighbors. Unlike the Ngoni and Yao, among whom the institution of chieftainship was at least crudely developed, and unlike the Makua, who regarded kinship as the fundamental basis for political, economic, and social action, the Makonde recognized the pull of two competing basic units of membership. A Makonde was, first of all, a member of one of the several hundred matrilineal kin groupings, or *litawa*,[1] into which the tribal grouping was divided, and this unit of

1. The term *litawa* has been translated as clan, but since the size and conditions of development differed radically—depending upon the proximity of its members and upon the value which members attached to remembering all those who were remotely related to them—we prefer to translate litawa as simply "kin grouping." Rashidi Mfaume Mtalika reported to me in 1956 that litawa names indicated good reputations as farmers (e.g., *wanamnimi, wanampunga*), as keepers of animals (*wanang'uku, wanyuchi*), or as hunters (*walukanga*). Other names indicated the place of origin of the litawa (*wachitama, wantandi, wanyahi, wananonji*), a food taboo (*wananyuwele*), or some other item of significance to the members of the kin group.

membership gave him a series of kinfolk upon whom he could depend for the performance of certain vital services. Overlapping these family units, however, were political groupings – numbering perhaps a hundred at the time of the European arrival – which were at least vaguely territorial in jurisdiction. The latter unit was called a *chirambo* (plural: *virambo*). The leader of the chirambo, the *mkulungwa* (plural: *wakulungwa*), achieved office by virtue of being the first settler in the area or his matrilineal descendant. As such, he possessed spiritual duties with respect to the safety and wellbeing of the entire chirambo and was involved in all major decisions affecting the peace and good order of his village. Depending upon the strength of his litawa, of which he was normally the head, he could require new immigrants to the area to come to him to receive an assignment of land. The requests were usually granted, since the addition of new members to the chirambo enhanced the prestige of the mkulungwa, but the prospective tenant could be denied land entirely or provided a plot of land on a probationary basis.

The polycentric character of the Makonde political system was reinforced by the constant fragmentation of existing virambo, with immigrants hiving off to form new communities. In the "cradle area" south of the Ruvuma, the original hiving-off may have come as famine forced the Makonde to seek out new sources of game and edible grains. When they reached the Newala Plateau, the very reasons which brought some of the Makonde northward – that is, flight from Ngoni and Yao slave raiders – called for a repetition of the fragmentation process. For, as the thicket was cleared on the plateau and the population became more dense, the raiders found their chances of success enhanced. Hence, further flight of the Makonde into the thicket was indicated. Flight and resettlement kept the chirambo typically a unit of small scale. The refuge that the thicket provided, moreover, made it unnecessary for the Makonde to develop large-scale military organizations to defend themselves. There were certainly no formalized military age-grades among the Makonde comparable to the organizations which appeared among more northerly tribal groups in Tanzania. As far as I could determine, almost no attention was paid to the problems of village defense during the young men's initiation rites. Indeed, Makonde informants in 1956 admitted almost with pride that neither they nor their ancestors relished armed combat—a factor which further distinguished the Makonde from the Maconde of Mozambique, who enjoy a reputation as fierce fighters. The Makonde, it should be noted, played a relatively minor role in the Maji Maji Rebellion against the Germans in 1905 and had a very low enlistment record during World War II.

Another factor contributing to the constant fragmentation of Makonde traditional society was the system of cultivation employed by the Makonde when they reached the plateau. The particular system of agriculture is called "stump cultivation" or "bush fallowing." There appears to be no oral tradition regarding the rationale for this particular variation of shifting cultivation, but it has proved to be a fairly effective system for dealing with the problems of water erosion, rapid water run-off, and the maintenance of fertility in the sandy soils of the plateau.[2] With bush-fallowing techniques, tree stumps are left in the cleared fields and the seeds are planted around them. Although this means that the soil is retained during heavy rains, it also means that the regeneration to thicket condition takes place at a more rapid rate—in roughly three years. Almost immediately after clearing his first plot, the cultivator must start clearing the second and third plots for what will eventually be a four- or five-unit cycle of rotation, with each plot being at some stage of clearance, cultivation, or regeneration. Since the mkulungwa, in assigning land to a newcomer, had to take into account the full rotation cycle, there was a technological barrier to high-density settlement. Apparently, however, even in the lower areas of Newala, Mtwara, and Lindi districts, where the need for such frequent rotation was not apparent, social preference still dictated a dispersed pattern of farm settlement. Modern documentation of this is found in the lament of the British district officer in Mikindani in 1925, who noted that "the tendency of the Makonde is to live in small separated settlements of 3 or 4 houses, and this no doubt makes it difficult for a Jumbe to keep in close touch with his people."[3] This statement was

2. See Harold Gillman, "Bush Fallowing on the Makonde Plateau," *TNR*, no. 19 (June, 1945), pp. 34–44.
3. Lindi Province, *Annual Report of the District Officer of Mikindani District*, 1925 (TNA 1733/10:75).

echoed in the remarks of the executive officer of the Mtwara Local Council in 1967. The officer, who was not himself a Makonde, expressed distress over the reluctance of the Makonde to settle in village clusters near the roads, thereby making it more difficult to provide them with the services of local government.

Dispersal to escape raiders or the search for new land effectively put the migrating Makonde out of day-to-day contact with his original village. Distance made it more and more inconvenient for the individual to honor his chirambo responsibilities or to enjoy the benefits which his territorial community could provide. Eventually the hived-off group would be reconstituted as a separate chirambo, with perhaps a representative of the family of the original mkulungwa assuming the leadership and performing the religious rites in behalf of the new polity. If the distance was not too great many of the original ties and obligations would remain theoretically in force, unless of course it was dissension within the original chirambo which was the principal cause of the migration. Essentially, the limits of the political community was a problem of feasible social communication and meaningful social interaction.

The last point brings us back to the original statement that each Makonde recognized a social as well as a political jurisdiction. This meant that the concept of membership was a complex one, even though a Makonde, because of his upbringing, was able to accept his overlapping and even conflicting loyalties with ease. While recognizing the cluster of economic, social, and religious ties which bound him to his mkulungwa, he also acknowledged his loyalties to his *mwenyekaya* (the head of his litawa) and to the fellow members of his litawa. Indeed, with respect to inheritance, the performance of more personal religious rites, the observance of taboos, and assistance in times of old age or dire need, a Makonde would place less stress on his chirambo ties than upon his membership in a litawa. Since his kinsmen were invariably under the jurisdiction of another mkulungwa, this meant that there was a potential conflict or at least overlap between a Makonde's social and territorial obligations. This situation arose largely because of three basic principles of marriage which were manifest in Makonde society. The first of these was the rule of exogamy, which required a man to find a marriage partner from outside his own kin group. "To do otherwise," said one informant, "would bring idiocy to the village." The second principle was the requirement of matrilocality, which compelled a male to reside in the village of his wife's parents, at least until the first child was born and frequently longer. This meant that the search for a spouse would frequently take a male Makonde away from his original chirambo and place him under the family jurisdiction of a non-kinsman. Although this might create some personal conflicts for the individuals directly involved, when viewed from the society as a whole it created inter-virambo linkages that might be instrumental in the mitigation of conflict when disputes arose over virambo boundaries or other problems. The third marriage principle which added to the complexity of social and territorial loyalties was the recognition of polygamy as an ideal form of marriage. Although a man could (and occasionally did) take the sisters of his first wife as junior wives, polygamy often compounded the situation of cross-polity allegiances, with a man having his wives in several virambo, which he visited in turn for a few days or weeks at a time.

## INTER-VIRAMBO BONDS

In addition to the inter-virambo ties which kinship and marriage established, reference has also been made to the links between a parent chirambo and its hived-off colonies. There were, moreover, linkages of historic character which related litawa to each other on the basis of the route they followed in arriving at their present locations in Tanzania. *Maraba,* for example, refers to the Makonde who took the Ruvuma-coastal route to Lindi, and *Mnima* refers to people whose ancestors entered the plateau via Mnima in the west. Aside from the question of whether such groupings of Makonde are historically valid, there do not appear to be political, social, or economic bonds of any consequence which were created by this co-journeying. My informants indicated that the relationships today are largely sentimental.

Of a more significant character were those inter-virambo ties which arose as a consequence of co-residence in a region.

Thus, there were informal alliances, for example, which were established for the purposes of dealing jointly with threats posed by lions, pigs, baboons, and other animals in a given area. Such intervillage cooperation is still a vital factor today in the hinterland areas of all three districts. The institutionalization of this collaborative effort, however, depended entirely upon the qualities of imaginative leadership that one of the wakulungwa was able to manifest. There were instances in the past when the authority of such a gifted mkulungwa could be generalized to cover other situations beyond the original agreement. Such a supra-virambo leader (discussed later) was called *mfaume* or *sultani*, employing the Arab term but certainly not the full content of that role.[4] It appears that the title was accorded primarily to Yaos and in any event was not transmitted to the mfaume's heir.

In addition to kin, historic, and residential bonds, there were instances in which ties of a more mystical character united the members of two or more villages. The term *utani*, which is loosely translated in the anthropological literature as a "joking relationship," indicates ties which transcend membership-group limits – whether the groupings in question are villages, kinship units, or even whole tribal groups. In the case of the Makonde there were a number of utani ties among litawa. Lyndon Harries, who was for many years a missionary in Newala, recorded that the Nanyambe and Nantengo litawa established utani after the Nantengo had purchased the freedom of their former neighbors, the Nanyambe. The latter had been captured by Yao raiders and were being transported to the coast as slaves when they were intercepted and freed by the Nantengo.[5] The significance of an utani relationship lies not merely in the fact that it creates positive linkages which require the parties to provide hospitality to each other, to assist in the burial of each other's dead, and to help in the installation of new litawa or chirambo heads. Of equal importance is the fact that utani establishes a measure of verbal tolerance that permits the full and frank discussion of any situation which may cause conflict. In the absence of utani, the discussion of the

4. J. W. Large, Newala District Book, 1928.
5. Notes in the Newala District Book.

fundamental elements of a situation may in itself constitute an offense which is far more serious than the original act itself. The verbal license of an utani relationship permits insignificant offenses to be treated as annoyances rather than as occasions for armed combat.[6]

Where the various foregoing intercommunity ties were not sufficiently strong or numerous, great reliance had to be placed upon the negotiating skills of the wakulungwa in resolving disputes affecting two or more virambo. The disparities in Makonde tribal law were great (as the British administrators in the period of Indirect Rule were to realize with some dismay), and the exercise of rights and privileges tended to depend upon the forces present in a given situation rather than upon the existence of a universally accepted code of moral behavior. There were no superior or neutral arbitrators for the tribe as a whole to whom aggrieved parties could take their disputes, even though one of the mfaume or sultani noted previously might briefly enjoy such a role. There was, however, the accepted procedure whereby the wakulungwa directly concerned might — if the dispute had not gone too far — meet on neutral ground and negotiate a settlement. The former liwali, Justino Mponda, explained to me in 1954 that in minor disputes

> the aggrieved man went to his clan head and put his case. The elder went with the aggrieved to the village of the offender and said to the clan head: "This man says that he has been wronged. For long now our villages have lived in peace. Must we cause hardship because of the foolish actions of one of your men?" Then the two elders bring the men together and put questions to them and talk the matter out. Finally, the clan head of the second village says [to his kinsman]: "Why have you brought bad feeling between our two villages? Do you not know that when we are threatened by a lion or other ills that the members of this man's village come to help us? Do you want this to end?" The accused usually consents to make some offering; both are required to shake hands; and a white chicken is killed [the symbol of reconciliation].

6. For a discussion of utani among the neighboring Makua which roughly parallels that of the Makonde, see T. V. Scrivenor, "Some Notes on *Utani,* or the Vituperative Alliances Existing between Clans in the Masasi District," *TNR,* no. 4 (October, 1937), pp. 72–74.

In the case of a more serious offense—such as accidental death—in which the village of the accused did not wish to risk war, the people depended upon the mkulungwa's success in negotiation. He went back and forth between the villages, making the legal settlement. Finally, he brought some token— usually a bolt of cloth—from the offending village indicating that it was ready to accept a judgment involving compensation to the offended village. The advocate took part of the cloth as his fee.

Where the talents of the wakulungwa were limited or the dispute had progressed to the crisis stage, armed conflict between two or more virambo became a possibility. Often the fighting was limited to arrows, but later homemade or Arab guns were employed. Considering the general reluctance of the Makonde to engage in sustained conflict, the battle usually lasted only until a sufficient number of the members of the weaker community had been killed or captured as slaves. A truce was then called and further compensation, if such was still required, was agreed upon.[7]

Finally, it should be noted that during the pre-European period a number of Makonde virambo had unity imposed upon them from the outside. There were several instances in which Yao leaders exacted fealty from Makonde wakulungwa as the price for defending the Makonde against Ngoni raiders. The Yaos were in many instances themselves fugitives from the Ngoni but the Newala Plateau gave them certain strategic advantages, and there they were able to regroup their forces in opposing and pressing back the Ngoni raiders. Matola I, who reached Newala in the mid-nineteenth century and who cooperated with the UMCA missionaries, was one such Yao leader. Machemba was another Yao who managed, as a result of defending the Makonde and Makua of the plateau against the slave raiders, to extend his influence and authority throughout the northern portion of the plateau and down to Sudi, on the coast. Machemba also organized resistance to the Germans at the end of the century. The influence of these Yao leaders,

---

7. I am indebted here to the elders of Mnolela and the former mkulungwa mkuu of Newala for this information, which corroborates, corrects, and expands upon some of the notes in the Lindi, Mtwara, and Newala District Books.

however, did not give them the authority to radically alter the basic political structures of Makonde society.

## POLITICAL SOCIALIZATION

Polycentrism in the Makonde traditional political system was reinforced by the structures of political socialization. These structures, which were formal as well as informal, oriented Makonde youth with respect to local personalities, local myths of origin, local norms of behavior, and local precedents, even though they were somewhat exposed to the more universal values of Makonde society. The most significant of the formal structures of socialization was the initiation rites performed for the young. These were usually called *jando,* but occasionally the term *unyago* referred to the collective rites for both boys and girls.[8] There were no tribe-wide initiation rites. Occasionally as many as seven virambo might combine their efforts for convenience, but in most cases the leader of each chirambo would decide that the time was ready for a new group of youngsters in his village to undergo training for adulthood. Following three days of drum beating at the various centers of the chirambo, the young would be presented to the elders for initiation. The girls' initiation — called *malango* or *chiputu* — was a less formalized affair than boys' rites. Girls were considered ready for instruction in the obligations of marriage and

8. Aside from my own interviews with ten youngsters in Newala who had recently gone through the jando, I relied heavily upon the numerous notes found in the District Books in Mtwara, Newala, and Lindi, Although these provided useful clues, there were many discrepancies, which might have indicated some local variation in procedures.

Although he apparently relied on some of the official sources as well as on K. Weule, *Native Life in East Africa,* trans. Alice Werner (London: Pitman, 1909), pp. 295 ff, Lyndon Harries gives a very helpful overview of the Makonde jando as observed in Newala; see "The Initiation Rites of the Makonde Tribe," *Rhodes-Livingstone Institute Communications,* no. 3 (1944).

For an essay dealing with the initiation rites for the neighboring tribes, which influenced Makonde practices in the peripheral zones, see A. M. Hokororo, "The Influence of the Church on Tribal Customs at Lukuledi," *TNR,* no. 54 (March, 1960), pp. 1–13. Finally, there is the description contained in the section on the Makonde in Mary Tew [Douglas], "Peoples of the Lake Nyasa Region," *Ethnographic Survey of Africa,* Part I, *East Central Africa* (London: Oxford University Press, 1950), pp. 28–29.

motherhood at the time of puberty, and after a few weeks of instruction they were considered eligible for marriage.[9]

The boys' initiation ceremonies brought together all uncircumcised youths between the ages of nine and sixteen; they were circumcised and then secluded from women for three to four months. During this period, while waiting for their surgery to heal, they were instructed in hunting, cultivating, proper sexual behavior, respect for the property of others, and similar matters. Among the items most frequently emphasized by my informants was that the *likumbi* (the leader of the jando) taught the young "good conduct, honesty, and respect for the elders." As a schoolboy wrote: "If we are not polite to our elders today, then no one will honor us when we are old. When we die, we will be nothing." The induction of the young boy into manhood was symbolized at the end of the ceremonies by presents of new clothing and the acquisition of a new name. His ties with his own mother, moreover, were broken and he might even go to live with his senior maternal uncle.

There were specialists, called *wakukomela*, who performed the circumcision operations throughout Makonde country. The wakukomela were members of special litawa which claimed to monopolize the required mystical powers (*chihero*) and the ritual paraphernalia (*mchira*). One achieved the role by bearing the expenses of the village for three initiation rites. Thereafter, one not only enjoyed high status as a mkukomela but also shared in the profits of future initiation rites.[10] The wakukomela, it should be added, did give a tribal character to the local initiation rites. This was partially offset, however, by the fact that the instruction which followed the surgery was not in the hands of specialists. Any adult male member of a

9. Weule, at the turn of the century, insisted that no clitoredectomy was performed; see *Native Life in East Africa*, p. 304. A more recent scholar, referring to practices prevalent among both the Makonde and the Maconde, describes the clay representation of the phallus used in the defloration of the young girls at the end of the chiputu; see Margot Dias, "Makonde-Topferei," *Baessler-Archiv*, n.s. IX (August, 1961), 105.

10. Harries indicates that at times the role of Father of the Rites—i.e., the person who sponsors the initiation ceremonies and who enjoys the profit— is separate from the role of mkukomela, in which case the latter is merely the medicine man who performs the operation; see "The Initiation Rites of the Makonde," pp. 2–3.

chirambo could participate in the educational process. Hence, local experience and history tended to be emphasized.

Where bonds of social solidarity were created by virtue of the initiation ceremonies, moreover, these bonds were parochial and local rather than tribal in character. All the youths who went through the initiation together were considered to be members of a common village group, having special friendship obligations to one another. Although Weule in 1908 referred to the initiation group as an "age class," this was not comparable to the highly formalized age-sets of the pastoralist peoples of northern Tanzania in which generational linkages cut widely across kinship, neighborhood, and all other kinds of loyalties.[11] The jando only united the youth of a given age within a single chirambo or at best a few virambo which had cooperated. Although some of the older informants insisted that the jando ties were limited to mutual hospitality, some of the youth in Newala in 1956 stated that it obliged them to "arrange" meetings for a jando-mate with a potential marriage partner; to provide him with money, food, or clothing if he were in need; to provide burial expenses; to help his mate with work in the fields; and to "repair his bicycle free of charge."

In addition to the political socialization provided by the jando, there were less formalized agencies of socialization operative in Makonde society. The liwali of Namikupa, for example, told me in 1955 that it was a fairly common practice in the olden days for the mkulungwa and the elders (*wazee wa vijiji*) to partake of evening meals in common. These meals were served near the *baraza*, or court building, next to the mkulungwa's hut. The building was used during the day for instruction of the women in pottery-making, basketry, and other crafts. It had a thatched roof but no walls, thereby leaving its activities public to all. The communal ritual of breaking bread emphasized in symbolic terms the proper order of things in a Makonde village. First of all, the meal was limited to men. Hence, although women were to be respected because one inherited through his

---

11. Weule, *Native Life in East Africa*, p. 304. For examples of more sharply defined age-grade systems, see M. J. Ruel, "Kuria Generation Classes," *Africa*, XXXII (January, 1962), 14–36; and Robert LeVine and Walter Sangree, "The Diffusion of Age-Group Organization in East Africa: A Controlled Comparison," *Africa*, XXXII (April, 1962), 97–109.

mother, who also gave him birth, women were not normally involved in the public affairs of the community. Second, no one would eat until the mkulungwa did, and this emphasized that it was his ancestors who first gave the people of this village their food. Following this, the breaking of bread by each of the elders in turn reestablished his respective seniority regarding the order of arrival of members of his litawa in the chirambo. In addition to establishing rankings, it showed, as the liwali stated, "that the mkulungwa without his wazee wa vijiji would be nothing. Who would respect an mkulungwa who had no followers?" Beyond its symbolic value, the talk after the meals had a more direct heuristic significance. At that time the mkulungwa and the elders would discuss the events of the day in terms of experience of the past. In the presence of the women and children, the mkulungwa would begin with a long recitation about how things were "in the days gone by, when people did not steal and they respected their elders. . . ."

A similar latent educational agency was the proceedings of the mkulungwa's court, where the mkulungwa and the elders resolved controversies within the political community and arrived at other decisions regarding its safety and well-being. The court was never an enclosed building; frequently it was a circle of stools set up under a tree or in the shade of a house. There the children could take in every word of wisdom and be exposed at an early age to the legends, customary laws, and the claims to rights and privileges that governed relations of the chirambo with its neighbors and among its members.

## Recruitment of Political Leadership

Manifestly political roles in traditional Makonde society were few in number, and, in fact, the performance of activities associated with these roles was frequently done on an intermittent basis. Except in a very large chirambo with several hundred families, the mkulungwa was generally a cultivator whose style of living and day-to-day activities did not noticeably distinguish him from his neighbors. In the small chirambo, his social role as head of a litawa predominated over his political role as head of a chirambo. Nevertheless, the mkulungwa in even the smallest chirambo was more than simply the equal of his neighbors. By virtue of his biological relationship to the first settler in the community, he became a central figure in every recitation of the history of that chirambo. As the direct descendant, moreover, he had special responsibilities with regard to every decision affecting the expansion of the chirambo, its defense against outsiders, and its preservation against internal dissension.

Succession to the key political office was in theory narrowly ascriptive. Biological relationship through the female line was the primary consideration. The order of succession would be roughly as follows: younger brothers, sons of the sisters of the mkulungwa, half-brothers having the same mother as the mkulungwa, and sons of half-sisters with the same mother. Other qualifications enter into the choice of a successor, however, permitting some flexibility. For example, age was a factor and minor nephews would be passed over for those who were lineally junior but chronologically older. Moreover, in a number

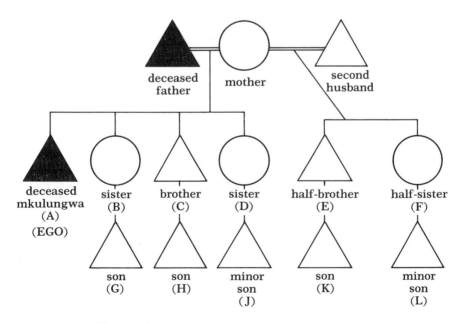

FIGURE 4:
SUCCESSION TO OFFICE OF MKULUNGWA

of instances women have succeeded to the office of mkulungwa when no suitable male heir was available. Hence for the family group shown in Figure 4, at the death of A the probable order of succession would have been: C, G, E, J, L, and B.

Although the above might constitute an ideal model of succession, it was apparent that there was sufficient flexibility in the system that other choices could be made. A strong mkulungwa, for example, might indicate a favorite nephew before his death and bestow the religious powers of office upon him. There were other instances cited in which the elders themselves interposed and dictated the choice of a successor. The elders looked for various qualities in a potential mkulungwa: he must be a good speaker—one who could make his decisions appear wise and thereby terminate dissension; he must know well the traditions of his chirambo; and he must evidence fairness in his dealings with all members of the chirambo, without respect to their litawa. It was indicated by my informants that the members of the late mkulungwa's litawa normally went along with such interposition even though it meant that they had to accept the new mkulungwa as mwenyekaya of their litawa as well; the only alternative would have been the withdrawal of the dissatisfied litawa from the jurisdiction of the governing group. In any event, the selection of a new mkulungwa was not a hurried affair. The chirambo as a whole was vitally concerned that the right man should be chosen for the task.

## SANCTIONS FOR POLITICAL AUTHORITY

Perhaps the most fundamental sanction for the political authority of the mkulungwa was religious in nature. It was he alone who controlled the performance of rites in behalf of the entire community. His spiritual power was called *Inghopedi* in the Makonde language, but sometimes the Yao phrase, *mbepesi,* was used to describe the power which the mkulungwa received through sprinkling ritual flour on the graves of the founder of chirambo. Invocations to the ancestors during the ritual were undertaken to protect the community against drought, famine, and other impending disasters; to scourge the people of a present evil, such as an epidemic of marauding lions; to guarantee the success of the chirambo in the opening of new lands or other uncertain ventures; or to ensure the good behavior of a prospective settler.[12]

As was true of certain other Tanzanian groups where political authority was supported by religious sanctions, the mkulungwa was protected against the possibility that performance of mbepesi rites did not achieve the desired end. This was accomplished by having someone other than the mkulungwa perform the actual ceremony. This could be an old man or a boy. The success of the performance was presumed to be self-evident. The assumed failure of the performance reflected not upon the mkulungwa who employed the artisan but upon the artisan himself. It was the latter who was forced to resign in favor of an understudy in the case of repeated failure.

The primary economic sanction for political authority was the mkulungwa's control over the assignment of land to strangers. Normally the petitioner would be vouched for by a relative, friend, or acquaintance in the chirambo who could give testimony regarding his reputation. The mkulungwa would usually welcome the new settler, who would share in the communal enterprises and add to the prestige of the mkulungwa. Good reasons, however, existed for denying the applicant's bid if he were unknown, if there were doubts raised regarding his character, if land was in short supply, or if the mkulungwa suspected that the factional balance among litawas would be upset by the newcomer. If the petition was successful, the allocation of land and the designation of areas for future expansion did not become binding until the mbepesi rites were performed in behalf of the newcomer. Should a stranger attempt to cultivate without complying with these procedures, he would be evicted and not permitted to harvest his crops. Even the successful applicant, however, had to go through a two-year probationary

---

12. Although some Makonde insisted that the ancestors were acting as intercessors to a High God, a German scholar indicated that the god who was the creator of the universe withdrew from the affairs of man after the creation and only appeared to men in storms, drought, and earthquakes. God left direct contact with men to the ancestors; to mischievous spirits, called *mahoka*, who live anywhere and have to be appeased; and to special representatives of the High God. See Chlodwig Hornung, "Die Religion der Bantu im Süden Tanganyikas," *Zeitschrift für Missionswissenschaft und Religionswissenschaft*, XLII (1958), 313–25.

period. If he failed to meet the chirambo's standards of good behavior, his trees would become the property of the chirambo and he would be permitted to take only that which he brought with him and any cassava that he could harvest quickly. In extreme cases of antisocial conduct, the house of the probationer would be ceremoniously burned to the ground, and he and his family might be forced to flee for their lives.

As a sanction for political authority, however, the allocation of land was a limited kind of control. Beyond the probationary period, the new resident enjoyed the same usufructory rights as the established resident. He could, for example, sell or exchange the fruits of his labors. Trees and other more permanent additions remained his property even in the case of extended absence from the chirambo. He could, moreover, leave other members of his family to maintain his claim if his absence would be for more than two growing seasons. It was only in the event of an extended absence of a cultivator and his family, the bidding of a formal farewell, or the flight of a cultivator to avoid punishment that the mkulungwa could reclaim land for the community.

Beyond control of land, the economic sanctions of the traditional Makonde political system were few. There were no cattle or other preservable commodities whose ownership could be monopolized by the ruling elite. Since famine was a recurrent possibility, wakulungwa who made elaborate demands in the form of tribute payments would soon find themselves without followers. Gifts given by passing strangers, by those who had been successful in the hunt, or by those who were grateful for the good harvest or other good fortune attributable to the success of the mkulungwa's mbepesi were invariably of a token character. A white chicken, the liver of an animal caught in the hunt, some of the beer brewed at harvest time, and other small gifts were normally the extent of tribute. It was also expected that the young men in the chirambo had an obligation to build and repair the mkulungwa's house without any expectation of reciprocity. It was only as the intensity of the slave-trading increased in the third quarter of the nineteenth century that the basic economic relationship between an mkulungwa and other members of his chirambo began to alter. This will be discussed later.

The third authority sanction of the mkulungwa was derived

from his role in the control of disruptive behavior. All cases of murder, assault, robbery, and other actions which threatened harmony within the chirambo as a whole were to be brought to the mkulungwa for a judicial settlement. A suspect would be seized by agents of the mkulungwa amid much shouting and beating of the accused. If the suspect wanted to be escorted to the court without being bound and beaten on the way, he had to pay a bribe—called *kingombwa*—half of which went to the mkulungwa. The bribe was normally paid, since the man who appeared in court with bound hands was presumed to be guilty!

Many cases that would today be labeled criminal actions were treated as civil matters under traditional Makonde law. That is, the offended litawa sought not merely punishment of the deviant but compensation for its injury. There were, however, the beginnings of a civil-criminal law distinction in that people who threatened the community as a whole were punished. Among the forms of punishment mentioned by my informants were the following:[13]

1. In the case of minor assault or destruction of property, the guilty party would pay a fine, half of which went to the mkulungwa, the other half to the offended party.
2. In the case of theft, the convicted person could have his hands tied in a fire; he could be beaten; he might be deprived of food for several days; or he might be placed on public display in a pillory, consisting of a forked tree or pole.
3. In the case of murder or adultery, the man might be required to provide service to the offended litawa; he might be sold into slavery; or he might even be put to death if he were a chronic offender.

## Counterbalancing Forces in the Chirambo

It would be a mistake to assume, as the British advocates of Indirect Rule did in 1927, that the mkulungwa was the sum and substance of the political system. In fact, the

13. In addition to the assistance provided by the jumbe and elders of Mnolela village in 1955 in securing this information, I relied on some notes made

mkulungwa seldom exercised authority without consulting others in the chirambo who represented corporate interests. Moreover, many of the social, economic, political, and judicial decisions affecting the members of a chirambo were made without reference to the opinion of the mkulungwa.

The most obvious counterweight to the authority of the mkulungwa was the residence within his village of men who were members of other kin groups. The elders, as representatives of the stranger litawas, jealously guarded the prerogatives and interests of their respective groups. Indeed, if an action such as inheritance of property involved only members of a single kin group, the elder would insist upon resolving the conflict on his own, inasmuch as the fines and punishments meted out by the mkulungwa would only further deplete the resources of the litawa. Even in the case of murder or theft involving only members of one litawa, the senior males of that group would inflict the beating or agree to place the offender under the close supervision of his maternal uncle. In the extreme case of repeated antisocial behavior the offender could even be put to death by his elder brother or maternal uncle on the grounds that his actions threatened the litawa both directly and indirectly, since it was the corporate group as a whole that would be liable for payments of compensation to other offended litawa.

Where two or more litawas were involved in a situation, the wazee were obliged to refer the action to the mkulungwa. Even there, however, the head of the chirambo was required to act in concert with the elders of the community, including the representatives of the litawas involved in the case. The decision on guilt or innocence as well as the determination of the type of punishment, moreover, was actually a collective decision. Similarly, many informants insisted that the mkulungwa's authority in the allocation of land was limited because he had to get at least the tacit approval of the wazee in general and the explicit approval of the prospective neighbors of the new tenant.

---

by A. C. Donne, an administrative officer in Lindi Province in 1927, entitled "Native Government before the Arab Domination" (TNA 7794/5).

In judicial actions, furthermore, he had to rely upon the active support of the wazee in seeing that accused parties were brought to court, that undesirable probationers were evicted from their land, and that decisions of the court were carried out. The mkulungwa who attempted to govern without being ever mindful of the interests of the other litawas would soon find himself without followers. The possibility that the members of a litawa could withdraw farther into the thicket was a constant safety valve against autocratic behavior.

In addition to intra-litawa restraints upon autocracy, there were institutions beyond the jurisdiction of the mkulungwa which permitted the Makonde to receive social, economic, and political satisfaction without involving the head of the chirambo. Jando-mates, for example, had special obligations toward one another that made the individual less reliant upon the generosity of the mkulungwa. A very special relationship, moreover, was created in the jando between the young initiate and the older boy, or *mnobo,* who was assigned to help him at every stage in the rites. The mnobo had great influence upon the later behavior of the younger boy and even had the privilege of sexual access to his wife. He also, however, had substantial obligations with respect to meeting the material needs of the younger man.[14]

A further sub-chirambo grouping was the neighborhood. Although the arrangements seem not to have had the degree of formalization that Abrahams noted among the Nyamwezi, it was understood in Makonde society that neighbors had special mutual obligations to assist in clearing new fields, building houses, and meeting threats to life, limb, or property.[15] At the beating of drums or the blowing of whistles signaling distress, everyone within hearing distance was obliged to drop his own work and come to the assistance of his neighbor. The only payment the assisting neighbors expected was the ritual beer, or *pombe ya Mkumi,* which came almost as a matter of right.

14. Notes of R. S. B. M. Hickson-Mahony, Mikindani (Mtwara) District Book, 1921; and Mary Tew [Douglas], *Ethnographic Survey,* p. 29.

15. R. G. Abrahams, "Neighbourhood Organisation: A Major Sub-System among the Northern Nyamwezi," *Africa,* XXXV (April, 1965), 168–86.

Neighbors, moreover, were expected to assist a new settler through at least the first growing season by providing food for him and his family. Negatively as well, neighbors played a role — that was often more effective than the sanctions meted out by the mkulungwa — in maintaining good social behavior. A troublesome neighbor would soon be the object of ridicule, which could be carried to great extremes in the case of a persistent fool. Several informants stated that the women of the neighborhood would bring pressure on the wife of a trouble-maker to give her husband his rice and meat uncooked and tell him to eat it raw with the children rather than with the rest of the men. In cases of persistent foolishness a man would be taken to the jando on the last day and ridiculed before the initiates, who would be permitted to vent their pent-up hostilities upon him.

Two other forces which affected social cohesion within the chirambo and which were not always under the control of the mkulungwa were the use of masks as agents of social control and the occasional appearance of "witch-finders" within the community. Although the carved masks mentioned previously were employed largely in the *mdimu,* or spirit dance, which took place at the conclusion of the jando to frighten the initiates, the masks were also used on other occasions. Nominally, the masks worn by stilt dancers at various festivities were for recreational purposes. Actually, they were also effective devices in the conveying of social messages. The masks, for example, were often caricatures of local personalities and emphasized some unfortunate trait of the person being chided. Since the identity of the wearer of the mask was kept secret, the dancer could engage in ridicule, abuse, and songs of derision without the offended party having any recourse. He could not "sue the mask," since the mask itself was not a member of any litawa, even though it was assumed to have a personality of its own. The mask dances were also instrumental in dealing with those who had become too prosperous and were lacking in generosity. The mask — actually the masked dancer — would be paraded around the village to the huts of the more wealthy citizens, and, following the dancing and singing, the benefactor was expected to give grain or beer (and later money). If the wealthy man failed to give generously he was in danger of losing the very influence which wealth could have given him within the chirambo.[16]

The final balancing force I identified within traditional society has been the act of witch-finding. Normally, the phenomenon of witchcraft is viewed as a disruptive force within a society. Its incidence cannot be predicted, and its use—both by entrepreneurs and by those making accusations—is capricious. In effect it establishes a relatively autonomous locus of power within society. This power is not subject to the ordinary restraints which a community imposes upon those who legitimately exercise influence over the minds and bodies of its members. Its sanctions are the laws of chance, and, moreover, the vagueness of predictions and the latitude permitted in interpreting success or failure mean that the practitioner of witchcraft has covered many, if not all, of his bets. If we limit our consideration of witchcraft to the above factors, it is obvious that Makonde traditional society was frequently disrupted. Early in the period of British rule in southern Tanzania, British officers remarked about the high incidence of witchcraft among the Makonde of the plateau, and one commented that only a strong witchcraft ordinance seemed to be capable of making it difficult for the wizards "to practice their wiles with any degree of profit."[17] The early optimism regarding the eradication of witchcraft was simply not justified. Indeed, on the very eve of the liquidation of British rule in Tanzania, an administrative officer in Newala recorded that at Mnyambe there was an old man who claimed that he could turn sticks, specially treated with medicine, into lions. The lions, it was claimed, would then do the bidding of the old man and bring terror to the countryside. The wizard not only made a considerable profit in selling charms against his own powers but also enjoyed a great reputation because of the firmness of Makonde belief in his abilities.[18]

Concurrent with the practice of witchcraft there emerged a professional group of witch-finders, who frequented the

16. See Weule, *Native Life in East Africa*, pp. 235–36; and E. C. Chubb, "East African Masks and an Ovambo Sheathed Knife," *Man*, XXIV (October, 1924), 145–46. Much of this information was secured in Mnolela village.

17. Lindi District, *Annual Report*, 1923.

18. L. Dyke, Newala District Book, 1961.

southern region of Tanzania. For a modest fee the witch-finder would perform purification ceremonies which were supposed to cleanse villages of present and impending misfortunes and also to identify the practitioners of witchcraft. Although an mkulungwa might have been reluctant to welcome the witch-finder, he usually had no alternative. Refusal to permit the witch-finder to practice his craft raised questions regarding the possibility that the mkulungwa himself was a witch.

The integrative aspect of witch-finding is that it frequently did reveal the identity of individuals who were secretly practicing the art. Since the witch-finder was an outsider—usually a Pogoro or Ngindo, but occasionally a Mwera or a Maconde from Mozambique—he was regarded by the community as an impartial agent. For this reason, witches frequently confessed before having to be identified. A second integrative aspect was that the cleansing ceremonies reestablished and redefined kin and other kinds of relationships within Makonde society. If one felt he was the victim of a witch, then all those who were related to him were required to take the oath because their influence was assumed to be greater than that of strangers or even neighbors. Hence, during a witch-finding ceremony, individuals had to decide the strength of their relationship to the victim and act accordingly. In the process, the extended family was once more publicly defined.

In later periods the witch-finder cults were called by various names—indicating either a very important witch-finder or the place of origin of the finder. Among the most prominent cults were Ngoja, Malinda, Pemba, and Lipanga. Although the British administration initially attempted to suppress the activities of the witch-finders, toward the end of the colonial period the witch-finders were utilized by the administration to go through various districts collecting witchcraft paraphernalia and were actually paid for their services. I encountered a witch-finder, Nguvu Mali, in Lindi and Kilwa districts in 1955, and I even assisted the district commissioner of Kilwa in burning artifacts that Nguvu Mali had collected and stored at the boma.[19]

19. For a broader treatment of this subject, see Terence O. Ranger, "Witchcraft Eradication Movements in Central and Southern Tanzania and Their

## EGALITARIANISM IN MAKONDE SOCIETY

Overlapping group affiliations throughout Makonde society, the balancing of forces between the mkulungwa and the wazee, and the constant possibility of further flight into the thicket to escape autocratic leadership contributed to the maintenance of a society with fairly democratic norms. The open character of Makonde society was further emphasized by the level of egalitarianism which was manifest in the social, economic, and religious spheres. In the social realm, for example, there were really no royal litawas. Although the members of the litawa of an mkulungwa might claim certain privileges while actually residing in that chirambo, this was only a temporary advantage. The rules of exogamy and matrilocality eventually required the males to submit to the authority of another litawa head and perhaps even to move to another chirambo in order to secure a spouse. So numerous, in any case, were the virambo that the members of any given litawa could claim that their kinsmen were the dominant litawa in at least one chirambo on the plateau or at the coast. Moreover, while an occasional litawa acquired regional prominence because its leader had distinguished himself as an arbitrator, as a hunter, or because of some other leadership quality, the respect that was accorded such a gifted leader was not passed on automatically to his descendants.

Even though women were treated somewhat more liberally in Makonde society than elsewhere in East Africa, equality of the sexes was not a dominant characteristic of Makonde traditional society. Women were largely excluded from the public discussion of community affairs; they worked long hours in the fields; and during the long dry season they hauled water up the escarpment from the valley.[20] Moreover, one should not mistake a matrilineal society for a matriarchal one. A person

---

Connection with the Maji Maji Rising," seminar paper delivered at University College, Dar es Salaam, November 30, 1966.

20. For a discussion of one aspect of craft specialization by sex, see the discussion of how Makonde women make clay pots (which they use in their twelve-hour treks up and down from the plateau in quest of water) in Margot Dias, "Makonde-Topferei."

counted his kinsmen through his mother and respected her, but women did not normally dominate affairs in Makonde society. Still, women were not slaves. Girls, for example, were permitted some voice in the selection of marriage partners, and matrilocality ensured that at least in the early stages of marriage a wife's interests would be protected by the presence of her own male kinsmen nearby.[21] Dias goes so far as to suggest that the defloration of Maconde women in Mozambique that takes place at the end of the initiation rites placed a low value on virginity and hence encouraged the sexual freedom of women.[22] In economic matters, men and women cooperated in agricultural production and did not necessarily occupy a super-ordinate-subordinate relationship to each other. Finally, although women did not normally participate in barazas, where public affairs of the community were discussed, they did exercise considerable political, social, and economic influence over their husbands. In a few instances, at least, they actually held the office of mkulungwa.

Egalitarianism among the members of a chirambo was even more apparent in the economic realm. The Makonde did not own cattle, and there were few other commodities which could be hoarded to give one man higher economic status than his neighbor. Agricultural production was largely in terms of perishable crops such as sorghum, maize, cassava, gum copal, millet, rice, honey, and simsim.[23] These items, as well as ivory and the latex which was gathered from the forest, could be transported to the coast and exchanged for muskets, iron hoes, and cloth.[24] Cloth, indeed, acquired such high prestige value

21. Weule, *Native Life in East Africa*, p. 306.

22. A. Jorge Dias, "The Makonde People: History, Environment and Economy," in *Portuguese Contributions to Cultural Anthropology* (Johannesburg: Witwatersrand University Press, 1961), pp. 45–46.

23. *Last Journals of David Livingstone in Central Africa from 1865 to his Death* (London: John Murray, 1874), I, 18, 29; Sir John Gray, "Mikindani Bay before 1887," *TNR*, no. 28 (January, 1950), p. 33; and George Shepperson, ed., *David Livingstone and the Rovuma* (Edinburgh: Edinburgh University Press, 1965), pp. 81 ff.

24. The people of Mnolela in 1955 insisted that their ancestors had smelted iron just as the people of the village were doing during my visit there. Weule, however, stated that the skill of iron-making was not known among the Makonde at the turn of the last century; see *Native Life in East Africa*, p. 266. I tend to believe the former, for they have developed the art of smelting to the

during the last half of the nineteenth century that it came almost to be regarded as sacred, and it brought a very high price in the interior. Nevertheless, disparities in wealth were rare.

Aside from the matter of domestic slaves and pawns, which will be discussed below, the material wealth of Makonde society was shared widely. The tribute payments to wakulungwa were largely token in character and did not create disparities in wealth. Any windfall, such as the discovery of ivory in the forest, was a fortune to be shared with the head of the finder's litawa and his other relatives. Marriage negotiations did not require that a young man amass a considerable bridewealth, which would enrich the maternal uncle, nor were the women monopolized by the older, more wealthy men. Before the coming of the Europeans, all that was expected of the suitor was that he or his relatives give a chicken, a goat, or a plug of tobacco to the maternal uncle and possibly also to the parents of the bride. By the time the Germans arrived, the marriage payments had increased, and a yard of calico was demanded by the girl's kinfolks. By the end of the Second World War, money and property of considerable value was expected, thereby establishing a definite bridewealth system. This, however, was certainly not the case in traditional society, and fortunes did not pass from family to family as a consequence of marriage and divorce.[25]

Finally, the egalitarian character of Makonde society revealed itself in the area of religion. Although the mkulungwa monopolized the performance of religious rites (mbepesi) in behalf of the entire community, each litawa and indeed each individual could appeal to his own special ancestors in seeking assistance for a more purely private venture. When hungry, sick, or about to begin a long safari to the coast, the individual

---

stage where a Makonde-made hoe lasts three or even four seasons whereas a hoe purchased in the Indian shops seldom gets through two seasons. For examples of iron-making in other parts of southern Tanzania, see R. C. H. Grieg, "Iron Smelting in Fipa," *TNR*, no. 4 (October, 1937), pp. 77–81; and R. Wise, "Iron Smelting in Ufipa," *TNR*, no. 50 (June, 1958), pp. 106–11.

25. Lindi, Newala, and Mikindani (Mtwara) District Books; Weule, *Native Life in East Africa*, p. 306; and A. C. Donne, "Native Government" (TNA 7794/5).

Makonde would offer snuff or flour as a gift to the spirit of a powerful ancestor. One did not require a special offertory, for it was assumed that wherever two roads met the spirits would be found; nevertheless, the chances of success were enhanced if one made his offerings in the *mholo* tree, which was regarded as the abode of spirits, or at the grave of the litawa founder.[26]

There is also the religious ceremony of reconciliation between two quarreling members of a litawa, which does not require the intermediation of the mkulungwa. In this ceremony, the junior party in the relationship approaches the senior and begs forgiveness for some act of omission or commission. If the senior person feels that the confession of guilt is sincere, he takes a little water into his mouth and spits it upon the chest of the junior petitioner. This signifies the spiritual reconciliation of the two parties.[27]

## SOCIAL STRATIFICATION IN UMAKONDE

Although the foregoing suggests the basic egalitarian quality of traditional Makonde society, there were three serious exceptions to the generalization. The first, discussed in the introductory chapter, was the castelike relationship which existed between the Makonde and the immigrant Maconde who moved northward from Mozambique. Although the social stratification was more sharply defined with respect to the presence of the Maconde, it existed in a less virulent form in the relationships established between Makonde vis-à-vis the Makua, Yao, Matambwe, and other tribal groups whose settlements were intermixed with those of the Makonde. Traditional practices did permit a Makua, for example, to seek and receive land from a Makonde mkulungwa. Although the tribal stranger was frequently accepted as a co-resident, who enjoyed the same land rights as his Makonde neighbors, there were invariably limits placed upon his participation in the religious ceremonies, circumcision rites, sharing of economic windfalls, and other

26. Weule, *Native Life in East Africa*, p. 326. In asking the aid of the ancestors, one faced the grave, called the ancestor by name, and spit in the direction of the impending danger.
27. Masasi District Book.

aspects of social life in the chirambo. His role in the selection of a new mkulungwa was also restricted. Whether by preference or because of limited social acceptance, Makua males in Newala in the 1950s would journey to Masasi to acquire marriage partners.

The institution of pawning was the second major exception to the egalitarian character of Makonde society. Under this system a man might offer one of his matrilineal kin—most frequently a female—as security in the case of defalcation of a debt or as a substitute for himself where his services were expected as part of the compensation settlement. The pawn was not a slave and did not surrender his or her rights as a member of the litawa. This was, nevertheless, a case of involuntary servitude, and if the debt was not liquidated for a long period of time there was little to distinguish the condition of the pawn from that of a slave, with the exception that children born to a female pawn—but not to a female slave—would be members of their mother's litawa.

Although it did not make the lot of the pawn any easier, pawning did establish bonds within a community and across community lines which helped maintain harmony. The relationship between the debtor and the creditor in the pawn context was significant, for the safety and good treatment of the pawn or the prospect of an early termination of the debt depended upon friendly relations being maintained. The pawn, moreover, being a member of another litawa or chirambo, would do his best to serve as a broker of interests in the case of conflict lest his own redemption be threatened. Finally, it might be noted that the accumulator of pawns could increase his prestige within the community by lending the pawns to other individuals, thereby establishing a series of patron-client relationships.[28]

The most significant exception to the egalitarian principle, however, was the existence of domestic slavery, or involuntary servitude. Slavery was both an aspect of intertribal relations and a cause of intratribal conflict. Thus, on the one hand, the Makonde were the direct victims of Yao, Ngoni, and other

28. For a discussion of pawnship among other matrilineal tribal communities in East and Central Africa, see Mary Tew Douglas, "Matriliny and Pawnship in Central Africa," Africa, XXXIV (October, 1964), 301–13.

raiders who either retained their captives as domestic servants or sold them to the Arab traders. On the other hand, the Makonde treated their fellow tribesmen in a similar fashion. In disputes between litawa or between virambo that could not be amicably resolved, it was apparently common practice for the members of one community to seize as slaves any members of the offending group upon whom they could lay their hands.

Whether the institution of slavery was an indigenous one of long standing that was magnified as a result of the Arab and European demands for slave labor or whether it emerged entirely as a response to the latter situation is a matter of some controversy. David Livingstone's ethnocentric comments, made at the commencement of his last journey, suggest the latter to be the case.

> Since the slave-trade was introduced this tribe [the Makonde] has diminished in numbers and one village makes war upon another and kidnaps, but no religious teaching has been attempted. The Arabs come down to the native ways, and make no efforts to raise the natives to theirs; it is better that it is so, for the coast Arab's manners and morals would be no improvement on the pagan African.[29]

On the other hand, many of my elderly informants indicated that their ancestors had had slaves in Mozambique but did not take them along when they crossed the Ruvuma, either because the owners feared that the slaves would escape or because the owners were themselves in flight from their enemies or in search of food. The antiquity of the institution is perhaps supported by the elaborate character of the rules regulating the treatment of slaves. There were apparently many gradations within the slave category which bore some relationship to the manner in which one became a slave: by capture in war, as a result of unredeemed pawning, by sale of oneself during time of famine, by purchase from Arab or Yao slavers, or by birth. Most of the regulations had the effect of making the institution more humane than was the case in Zanzibar or Mauritius. Slaves and their offspring, for example, were often adopted into the litawa of their owner, especially if the child were a product of the union of a free female and a male

29. *Last Journals*, I, 24.

slave. Slaves were permitted to marry other slaves as well as free persons. They could, moreover, purchase their freedom as a result of accumulating wealth on their own fields, which they could work after having finished their expected labor on the owner's fields. In the latter case, half of the crops or goats went to the slave, the rest to the master. Information from my assistants in 1955 coincided with the notes of the British vice consul on Zanzibar, Frederick Holmwood: "The Makonde rarely attempt to exert further authority than is necessary for regulating the cultivations of their lands." [30]

The penchant of the Makonde for slaves and the fact that it was the Makonde rather than just the Arabs who supported the institution is further evidenced by Holmwood's report that slaves were distributed along the entire coast between Lindi and Mikindani, and that

> in the plantations towards the Rovuma I saw several raw slaves, evidently but a few weeks or days from the slave chain. Some of them belonged to Arabs and half-castes, but the majority to Makonde proprietors who spoke little Swahili.[31]

An even earlier reference noted that the people of Sudi, after they had harvested,

> sow again and so they have food for the year. They sell part of their food, and buy trade goods or silver. When this silver has accumulated they buy slaves with it. They use these slaves in their plantations and cultivate with them. Another of their occupations is hunting elephant. If they get ivory, they sell it for silver or trade goods, and with this silver, they buy slaves.[32]

The Makonde also apparently became involved in the collection of latex from the large stands of wild rubber which abound in Makonde country, and they exchanged the latex at the coast

---

30. Gray, "Mikindani Bay before 1887," p. 35.
31. *Ibid.*, pp. 33–34.
32. "The History of Sudi," first published in *Prosa und Poësie der Suaheli*, by C. Velten; translated in G. S. P. Freeman-Grenville, ed., *The East African Coast: Select Documents from the First to the Earlier Nineteenth Century* (Oxford: Clarendon Press, 1962), pp. 230–32. See also Freeman-Grenville, "The Coast, 1489–1840," in *History of East Africa*, Vol. I, ed. Roland Oliver and Gervase Mathew (Oxford: Clarendon Press, 1963), p. 154.

for slaves. Curiously, the suppression of the seaborne slave trade by the British in the 1870s had the unintended consequence of making it easier and cheaper for the Makonde to acquire the slaves which had been brought to the coast from the Lake Nyasa area for the purposes of transshipment to Zanzibar.[33]

The incidence of slavery on the plateau was apparently not as great as it was at the coast, since slaves had the same opportunities to find refuge in the thicket that were available to the free Makonde. Moreover, there were fewer disparities in wealth created by the ownership of slaves, for the manner in which slaves were purchased within a chirambo often symbolically and materially reinforced the existing social rankings within the community. The elders of Mnolela village in Newala District, for example, indicated that in purchasing captives from Yao traders the mkulungwa always had the first choice. He was followed in turn by the elders in the pre-established system of seniority. The mkulungwa could not make a second purchase until each elder had had his first choice. Thus, the essential balance among litawa was maintained.

## SUMMARY

Traditional Makonde society was an extreme example of polycentrism among the Bantu people of eastern Africa. It was a society in which the limits of political community for the individual were never rigidly defined. Indeed, at any moment he was subject to at least two types of community authorities: that of his litawa, based upon kinship, and that of his chirambo, based upon residence. During his lifetime, moreover, a Makonde could not only alter his commitment to a particular chirambo, but he could actually magnify through migration, marriage, and other actions the number of commitments he might have to include several litawa and several virambo. The overlapping and often conflicting obligations of community as well as the random spread of kinship ties

33. Gray, "Mikindani Bay before 1887," p. 35; and Freeman-Grenville, "The Coast, 1489–1840," p. 154.

throughout the Makonde hinterland made it difficult for any group of Makonde leaders to assert and sustain jurisdiction over a sizable region in matters of defense or in the pursuit of more positive goals. This situation made it equally difficult for alien administrators to effectively exercise control over the Makonde.

The identification of authoritative leadership within the relatively autonomous chirambo was also a difficult proposition. Although the mkulungwa emerged as the most significant political leader, it was clear that there were many matters affecting the defense of the community, the maintenance of peace and good order, and the provision of a minimum level of security from which he was either excluded or at least not directly involved. Even with regard to those matters in which he had an established and presumptive right, his actions were frequently circumscribed by the interests of competing forces operating within society. The tendency toward autocracy was placed under severe restraints by the essentially egalitarian character of Makonde society as well as by the ever-present possibility of further flight into the thicket to escape tyranny.

Makonde society found itself constantly reasserting its basic principles of political organization instead of moving on to higher and more sophisticated levels of organization which could sustain a greater development of its resources and an improvement in its technology. The constant struggle against the physical environment meant that the innovative capacity of the Makonde was sacrificed in the interest of pursuing means of survival that had already been demonstrated to be, at the very least, adequate.

# 4:
# The Beginnings
## of Alien Rule

The nineteenth century was the age of imperialism in Africa, and the Makonde found themselves being subjected to the various kinds of alien pressures that were victimizing Africans throughout the continent. Not all of the imperial pressures, however, originated outside Africa. As was noted previously, the greatest alien threats to the Makonde during the second and third quarters of the century were posed by Ngoni and Yao raiders who attempted to exploit the Makonde and their neighbors for political, economic, and social gains. The most significant competitors of the Ngoni in the exploitation of southeastern Tanzania, moreover, also had a long history of residence in East Africa. I refer to the Arabs, who are reputed to have found settlements along the East African coast even prior to the rise of Islam in Arabia during the seventh century. Despite the earlier history of indigenous or semi-indigenous forms of domination and harassment, it was not until the advent of the Europeans—and in particular the launching of Indirect Rule by the British in 1927—that the traditional values and structures of Makonde society were substantially altered by alien rule. The preceding period of British rule (1917–27) was not much more systematic in its control of Makonde society than that of the antecedent German (ca. 1885–1917). During these earlier periods the agent of alien rule was a sporadic presence who appeared on the scene from time to time, made limited demands, and yet permitted Makonde society to continue functioning without major modifications in its goals or procedures. The Europeans, however, were not the first non-Africans who attempted to dominate the lives of the Makonde. They were preceded by the Arabs, whose influence ranged from a relatively radical transformation of Makonde society at the coast to a very ineffective and almost imperceptible attempt to establish Arab suzerainty over the Makonde of the interior.

## Arab Rule at the Coast

It is impossible to date precisely the first contacts between the Makonde and the Arab settlers at the coast. Undoubtedly the ancestors of the Makonde people had at least indirect contact with Arab civilization while the idea of Makonde ethnicity was still in the formative stages in Mozambique. As early as the thirteenth and fourteenth centuries, the various trade routes westward to Lake Nyasa from Kilwa Kisiwani and the mouth of the Ruvuma were being developed. It was not until the middle of the eighteenth century, however, that a substantial number of Arabs became directly engaged in the quest for ivory, gold, wax, honey, and slaves instead of leaving the trade exclusively in the hands of Bisa, Yao, and other African middlemen. It was undoubtedly the traffic in slaves, which began in earnest at the end of the seventeenth century, that was the primary factor in altering the relationship between the Arab coastal settlements and the peoples of the interior. Kilwa, which had been founded in A.D. 957 (reputedly by Persians), gradually became the leading slave export area in East Africa. Many of the Makonde and other tribal people captured inland passed through Mikindani, Lindi, and other southern Arab towns en route to Kilwa for transshipment to Zanzibar.[1]

Although the beginnings of sustained contact are attributed

1. See Gervase Mathew, "The East African Coast until the Coming of the Portuguese," in *History of East Africa*, Vol. I, ed. Roland Oliver and Gervase Mathew (Oxford: Clarendon Press, 1963), pp. 94–127; and Norman R. Bennett, "The Arab Power of Tanganyika in the Nineteenth Century" (Ph.D. diss., Boston University, 1961), pp. 55–56.

to the Arab slave trade with the interior, some of the movements of Makonde to the coast were undertaken voluntarily. It was asserted, for example, that during times of famine inland, Makonde came to Mikindani and sold themselves into slavery. Others, stimulated by the printed cloth, silver, and other commodities of trade brought by Arab caravans, traveled to Lindi and other ports to exchange wild rubber, gum copal, or their labor for the treasured commodities. Many apparently felt that sustained contact with Arab culture and life at the coast was highly attractive, and they took up permanent residence. Lindi, as was noted previously, is reputed to have had Makonde rather than Arab origins, and the same may be true for Sudi, Mikindani, and other points along the southern coast. Gradually, these Makonde migrants came under Arab jurisdiction; many accepted Islam; and some—especially the women—acquired Arab spouses.[2]

The period of intensified contact between Arabs and Makonde in the nineteenth century coincided with the struggle for Omani control over the fragmented Arab settlements along the entire east coast of Africa. It was not until 1840—when Imam Sayyid Said, the sultan of Oman, moved the headquarters of his empire from Muscat in the Arabian peninsula to Zanzibar—that the various warring factions and families were brought under strong centralized control. Prior to 1840 the sultan of Kilwa, for example, enjoyed relative autonomy with respect to the governing of Arab settlements between the mouth of the Rufiji River southward to Cape Delgado in Mozambique. Indeed, even as late as 1850 the Reverend J. Lewis Krapf noted that the residents near Lindi had demonstrated their independence of Kilwa and Zanzibar by engaging in direct trade with Portuguese slave ships. It was only after a punitive force from Kilwa had set the torch to Muitinge—a town opposite Lindi—that the inhabitants were brought to heel.[3]

Although Sayyid Said attempted to placate local Arab sentiment by employing a form of indirect rule, it was understood

2. G. S. P. Freeman-Grenville, "The Coast, 1489–1840," in *History of East Africa*, Vol. I, ed. Oliver and Mathew, pp. 148–49, 154.

3. Rev. J. Lewis Krapf, *Travels, Researches, and Missionary Labours, during Eighteen Years' Residence in Eastern Africa* (London: Trübner, 1860), p. 427.

that the hereditary rulers of Lindi, Sudi, and Mikindani were subservient to the Omani Arabs of Zanzibar. To ensure, moreover, that Zanzibar rather than the coastal settlements would reap the full benefits of the inland trade, Sayyid Said posted Indians – called *Banyans* – as his customs officials. In return for a fixed sum, the Banyan customs official guaranteed the honesty of the service against local connivance. Banyan traders, moreover, were encouraged to settle under the protection of the Arab governor and his troops. They not only facilitated local exchange and the monetization of the inland trade, but they helped finance through credit the various expeditions into the interior. Thus, although each coastal settlement had its own established routes to the interior and its own pattern of trade with the outside world, the Omani sultan of Zanzibar and his agents managed to bring the trade under centralized control.

The political control which Zanzibar exercised over its mainland possessions was intensified under Sayyid Barghash, who succeeded Sayyid Said in 1856. Omani governors replaced the local Arab politicians in the major towns, and garrisons of Baluchi from India were enlarged at Lindi and Mikindani to strengthen the position of the new governors. It apparently did not take much force to accomplish this objective, however, for David Livingstone reported in 1866 that the Arab governor, or *jemidar,* had only fifteen armed soldiers under his command and that he held court in his house, which was also the quarters for his troops.[4] Under the governor of each town was a series of *walis* (or *liwalis*), who held court in the towns, and *akidas,* who administered justice and kept order in the hinterland immediately beyond the towns. The walis and akidas were, in most instances, natives of Oman. They had under their jurisdiction local Arabs, Makondes, and persons of mixed Makonde and Arab blood who served as *jumbes,* or village headmen. The latter received tribute in produce or labor from their "subjects."

Inasmuch as the dominant Muslim influence was from the Hadhramaut, the Shafi'i school of law tended to dominate in

---

4. *Last Journals of David Livingstone in Central Africa from 1865 to His Death* (London: John Murray, 1874), I, 15; and Sir John Gray, "Zanzibar and the Coastal Belt, 1840–1884," in *History of East Africa,* Vol. I, ed. Oliver and Mathew, pp. 212–23.

the administration of justice.[5] In an attempt to ensure the purity of Islamic law, moreover, many of the more important cases heard at Mikindani or Lindi had to be referred to Zanzibar for an ultimate decision. Nevertheless, the displacement of indigenous law and custom by the *Shari'a*, or Koranic law, was never complete even with respect to such matters as the principles of marriage, divorce, and inheritance. Indeed, the International Delimitation Commission of 1886, which investigated conflicting German and Arab claims in the southern area, found that the wali of Mikindani and Pemba administered a form of justice which took jurisdiction over cases involving matrilineal succession, witchcraft accusations, and other non-Islamic customs.[6] Blendings of traditions, moreover, took place, in which paternal control over children was recognized while Makonde laws of matrilineal inheritance of property continued to prevail. The rites of passage as well as certain other rituals also tended to be a mixture of Islamic and Makonde principles and customs. Rather than either Arabic or Kimakonde, moreover, Swahili — the original language of the coastal people opposite Zanzibar — became the primary medium of communication at Lindi and Mikindani, just as it was later to become the principal language of trade and administration elsewhere in East Africa. Although the Makonde who settled on the coast had been converted to Islam, fasted during the month of Ramadhan, prayed five times daily, and attended Koranic school, they frequently maintained their credentials in good standing with their Makonde relatives in the hinterland. Their ambivalent position was demonstrated in many ways. They realized, for example, that, despite the democratic ideals of Islam, social stratification along the coast tended to follow racial lines, with the Arabs on top, the persons of mixed blood in the middle, and the Makonde peasants at the bottom. The urbanized Makonde, nevertheless, tended in turn to regard his rural kinsmen as *shenzi*, or uncouth bush people, while he himself was possessed of the genteel customs and manners of

5. Shafi'i is one of the orthodox Sunnite schools of law. Sunnites generally seek to interpret Muslim law by the use of critical reason, but they speculate only upon what has already been revealed in the Koran and tradition.

6. J. N. D. Anderson, *Islamic Law in Africa*, Colonial Research Publication no. 16 (London: H.M.S.O., 1954), p. 123.

Arab civilization. The fez and the long white gown, or *kanzu*, became outward symbols of his membership in a world religion as well as his acceptance of a commercial economy and a male-dominated society.

While Zanzibari control over the Makonde who clustered in coastal settlements was strengthened during the reigns of Sayyid Said and Sayyid Barghash, the Makonde of the hinterland remained largely independent even to the eve of the transfer of territorial claims from Arab to German hands. The Anglican bishop Edward Steere in 1876, the Delimitation Commission in 1886, and other European observers had all noted that Arab control did not extend more than two days' march (roughly ten to twenty miles) beyond the coastal towns. The walis at Lindi or Mikindani only arbitrated those disputes which the hinterland Makonde felt like referring to the coast for settlement. Arab trade caravans and soldiers both within the nominal sphere of control and beyond this region were dependent upon Makonde guides and upon the friendly disposition of the local population in securing food and refuge. The lack of Arab urban complexes along the trade routes, the difficulties of the terrain, and the constant fear of attack from Ngoni, Yao, and other Africans left the Arab trader in many respects a "wealthy fugitive." Indeed, even the coastal settlements and their immediate environs were not secure bastions, for the Ngoni offshoots—the Maviti and Magwangwara—raided Lindi and other coastal towns with impunity in 1866 and even later. [7]

This is not to imply that the Arabs were completely without influence among the Makonde of the hinterland. The Arab slave trade, for example, drew many Makonde into its vortex and further fragmented Makonde social cohesion as members of Makonde villages sold their neighbors into slavery. As the slave trade diminished following the ban by Sultan Barghash under British prodding, the Arabs made a more purely economic impact upon the Makonde of the interior. The sultan's agents encouraged Makonde to collect rubber, ivory, and other commodities of legitimate trade as well as to plant mango and

7. Sir John Gray, "Mikindani Bay before 1887," *TNR*, no. 28 (January, 1950), pp. 30–36; E. Steere, *A Walk to the Nyassa Country* (Zanzibar, 1876), p. 3; and Reginald Coupland, *The Exploitation of East Africa, 1856–1890* (1939; reprint ed., Evanston, Ill.: Northwestern University Press, 1967), p. 247.

coconut trees for exchange. Indeed, both the legitimate and illegitimate trade became so active that, by the time of the European arrival, the printed cloth, which was one of the most favored items of commerce, acquired ritual significance. Makonde sacrificed cloth before undertaking a journey or raid and in times of domestic crisis.

The Zanzibari Arabs were much less successful in the areas of politics and religion. The dream of Sayyid Barghash to build a road inland from the coast to Newala remained stillborn at the time of the German takeover. The arbitrator's role, moreover, which the sultan attempted to play in maintaining order in southeastern Tanganyika was also more shadow than substance. The religious impact of the Arabs upon the majority of the Makonde was also negligible, largely due to the fact that the religious and commercial interests of the Arabs were antithetical. That is, the converted African was not a likely candidate for slavery since the *Shari'a* forbids the enslavement of the faithful. The agreement of Sultan Barghash in 1873 to close the Zanzibar slave market and to cooperate with the British fleet in suppressing the slave trade gradually altered Arab attitudes toward the conversion of Makonde and other Africans to Islam. The immediate beneficiaries of the new policy—ironically—were the Christian missionaries, whom Barghash permitted and even encouraged to take up residence along the Ruvuma to minister to the needs of the slaves who had escaped or had been liberated from Arab caravans. The double irony was that the real expansion of Islam into the southern interior took place two to three decades later, when the Christian Germans were utilizing Arab and Yao Muslims as local agents of government in southern Tanganyika![8]

## THE GERMAN PERIOD, CA. 1885–1917

As was true of most Africans during the nineteenth-century carve-up of Africa by European powers, the Makonde were conquered not on the battlefield but at the conference

8. Trimingham notes that in Northern Nigeria the spread of Islam among the masses was intensified under British Indirect Rule in that the tenuous power of Muslim rulers over their non-Muslim subjects was buttressed; see J. Spencer

tables in far-off European capitals. The Makonde came under the imperial sway of Germany as a result of the International Agreement of London in 1886. This treaty gave the approval of the European community to the claims of Karl Peters and his German East African Company regarding the coastal area between the Rufiji and Ruvuma rivers, which had been staked out by Peters in November, 1885. These claims were further consolidated by the Imperial German government, which had in 1889 assumed all obligations and rights of the private company. The most significant of these rights was contained in the agreement of July 1, 1890, in which the German government paid the sultan of Zanzibar four million marks in return for his relinquishing all territorial claims to the Tanganyika mainland opposite Zanzibar.[9]

German colonial policy in Africa has usually been characterized as having favored the direct administration of occupied peoples by German officials and by natives or third-party nationals who had been trained by the Germans and had accepted the ultimate goals of European rule. Actually, during the thirty years of German control in East Africa, there were relatively few areas in which the system of direct administration had displaced completely the traditional political systems of the indigenous African groups. The degree of destruction of traditional authorities and value systems was related to the existence of one or more of the following conditions: (1) the attractiveness of the area to European settlement, which might have

---

Trimingham, *Islam in West Africa* (London: Oxford University Press, 1959), pp. 229–30.

9. For various works on the German period in East Africa, consult Jon Bridgman and David E. Clarke, eds., *German Africa: A Select Annotated Bibliography*, Hoover Institution Bibliographical Series 19 (Stanford: Hoover Institution, 1965), pp. 67–81. Several works of note include Karl Peters, *Die Grundung von Deutsch-Ostafrika* (Berlin: C. A. Schwetschke, 1906); Fritz F. Muller, *Deutschland-Zanzibar-Ostafrika: Geschichte einer deutschen Kolonialeroberung, 1884–1890* (Berlin: Rutten and Loening, 1959); and H. William Rodemann, "Tanganyika, 1890–1914: Selected Aspects of German Administration" (Ph.D. diss., University of Chicago, 1961). For the best summaries of German rule in East Africa, see W. O. Henderson, "German East Africa, 1884–1918," and O. F. Raum, "German East Africa: Changes in African Tribal Life under German Administration, 1892–1914" both in *History of East Africa*, Vol. II, ed. Vincent Harlow, E. M. Chilver, and Alison Smith (London: Oxford University Press, 1965), pp. 123–208.

involved either the removal of the indigenous population from European-coveted land or the recruitment of local natives into a labor pool for work on European estates; (2) resistance on the part of the indigenous leadership to the imposition of German rule; (3) the absence of a traditional system of government which could be utilized to accomplish even the very minimal objectives of German administrators.

With respect to the first condition, the Makonde area in general was not considered a prime target for German exploitation. A few sisal estates were established at Lindi and Mikindani, but this was largely the extent of land alienation for European agricultural purposes. There were a handful of European traders who appeared at the coast to merchandise the crude rubber, beeswax, gum copal, and other commodities collected by the Makonde for the payment of taxes. For the most part, however, even the merchandising of commodities was left in the hands of Arabs and Indians, although the Germans did regulate the coastal trade, which the Arabs had previously monopolized. Beyond encouraging the production of cash crops (needed to pay the three-rupee annual tax), the Germans did exhort the Makonde to continue their planting of rice, millet, simsim, and other subsistence crops to meet the threat of recurrent famine in the Makonde and adjacent areas. Although these demands were viewed by the Germans as being minimal intrusions upon traditional economic patterns of the Makonde, it was obvious that the payment of taxes or tribute was not a traditional political obligation on the part of the Makonde. Nor were the Makonde accustomed to the notion of a cash economy, inasmuch as most of their previous transactions with Arab traders had been largely on a barter basis. Finally, it took a measure of direct administration to "encourage" Makonde participation in the general territorial labor pool required for European enterprises.

The second condition for direct administration—namely, resistance of the indigenous population to German rule—was relatively negligible so far as the Makonde themselves were concerned, although the southeastern coastal region did witness opposition to European domination. In 1888, for example, the Germans found their tenuous hold in East Africa challenged all along the coast by the Arab uprising led by Bushiri. This coincided in the Ruvuma area with the appearance at Mikindani of Yao raiders under the leadership of Machemba, who had established supremacy over the Makonde around Luagala. Encouraged by the local Arab residents of Mikindani, Machemba attacked the small cadres of *askaris,* or native troops, under the command of Baron von Bülow and forced the two German officers and their men to flee in an Arab dhow. Machemba next attacked Lindi and compelled the Germans to evacuate their administrative headquarters and withdraw to Zanzibar.[10] Although the Germans returned the following year and encountered little resistance, Machemba continued to provide sporadic challenges to German rule from 1895 to 1899, largely in opposition to the collection of the hut tax. Gradually, the Germans strengthened the garrison at Lindi, which in 1896 had consisted only of 7 German officers and 121 African troops. By 1899 the German command felt sufficiently strong to attack the Yao troops under Machemba and force him and his followers to seek refuge across the Ruvuma River in Mozambique.[11]

The only direct opposition of the Makonde themselves to German rule came in 1902 when Mkoto, the mkulungwa from Kitangari, organized a tax revolt. Mkoto told his followers that anyone who paid taxes would fall victim to smallpox. The quick dispatch of troops from Lindi and the subsequent hanging of Mkoto and several of his leading elders terminated the rebellion. The relative passivity of the Makonde was again demonstrated in the Maji Maji Rebellion of 1905, which found almost the whole of southeastern Tanganyika in revolt against German rule. Several of my informants insisted that the Makonde around Kitangari and the northern tier of virambo sided with the Pogoro, Mwera, and other tribesmen who were in revolt against the system of forced labor and taxes. There is, however, little concrete evidence of significant voluntary participation by the Makonde in what Julius Nyerere has termed the

10. Sir Charles Dundas, *History of German East Africa* (Dar es Salaam: Government Printer, 1923), pp. 6–7.

11. G. S. P. Freeman-Grenville, "The German Sphere, 1884–1898," in *History of East Africa,* Vol. I, ed. Oliver and Mathew, pp. 447–48.

first step in the struggle for Tanganyikan unity and independence.[12] On the contrary, the elders in one Makonde village told me that some of their people had been conscripted to fight on the side of the Germans in "Mwera-land"—i.e., Lindi District.

The relative passivity of the Makonde thus did not require that the German administrative and military presence in the region be overwhelming. Indeed, it was not until the Mkoto tax resistance of 1902 that the Germans felt obliged to take a more direct hand in the management of affairs either on the plateau or at the coast, and it was only after the Maji Maji Rebellion had been supressed that a resident official was appointed to Newala. Prior to that time, the interior of the Makonde region had been administered from Lindi, where the senior *Bezirksamtmann* resided. Although the European resident at Newala had 30 askaris, recruited widely from East Africa, he had no other European support until 1913, when a police officer was posted to the station. Given only a limited European presence, the resident official could not concern himself with the day-to-day problems of administration or even present himself as a military commander. His role was largely that of diplomat, mediating and arbitrating disputes which might have disrupted general order.

In part because of the third condition, the ultimate form of local administration employed by the Germans in the Makonde area was neither indirect nor direct rule but a combination of both approaches. It was a system of indirect rule in that the Germans lacked the personnel and force required to substantially alter the indigenous polity and they placed great reliance upon the continued operation of the traditional system in the maintenance of peace and good order. It was direct rule in terms of the new demands placed upon the Makonde people and the lack of German administrative knowledge regarding the intricate workings of the pre-European political system. It was only late in the period of German rule that the anthropological writings of Pater Adams, Karl Weule, and others became available to German officers. Prior to this, the German

---

12. See John Iliffe, "Reflections on the Maji Maji Rebellion," *Spearhead*, no. 1 (November, 1962), p. 21.

administrators tended to rely upon their Arab, Yao, and other subofficials for an understanding of Makonde society.

Once order had been established, the Germans extended the Arab system of local rule to cover the entire Makonde region. Walis continued to function in the coastal towns, and akidas were given territorial jurisdiction under German resident officers in the rural areas. In theory the Germans could select for the post of akida any local resident who possessed the necessary literacy and leadership qualifications and who had accepted the notion of European supremacy. In practice, however, the Germans preferred to appoint individuals who had no local conflicts of interest that might impede their efficiency in serving as the vital communication links between the Germans and the local population. Thus, in several instances, members of the Yao tribe, who had made themselves allies of the Germans in subduing southern Tanganyika, were selected as akidas. Matola II, for example, was given the area between Newala and the Mbangala River to administer in return for his having been among the first to accept the German flag. At one point a Songea Ngoni served as akida in the Makonde area, as did an educated Mnyanja from Malawi. It was not uncommon, moreover, for even an Arab to serve as an official of local government. Karl Weule in 1906 noted that Arabs were serving as akidas and walis at both Newala and Mahuta.[13] Arabs were generally regarded as much more abusive of the people than African akidas and more dishonest in collecting taxes. It was only at Namikupa that a Makonde regularly served as akida. By the end of German rule in the area, however, two other Makonde – who were not residents of the areas they administered – were appointed as akidas on the plateau. Thus, three of the five akidates in Newala District were at one time or another in the hands of Makonde akidas. Although in certain cases the Germans sent young Africans to Germany to prepare them for future roles in the administration of German East Africa, there is no record that young Makonde were included in this program.[14]

13. K. Weule, *Native Life in East Africa,* trans. Alice Werner (London: Pitman, 1909), pp. 230, 352, 353.

14. The British in 1932 appointed as liwali of Lindi an African who in his

The akida under the German system bore ultimate responsibility for the maintenance of order, the collection of taxes, and the use of conscript labor in the construction of roads and paths. He exercised both executive and judicial power, although his authority was considerably curtailed in court cases by the German officers who reviewed his work. For the most part the Germans continued to permit Islamic law to flourish at the coast, but inland the akidas administered an eclectic kind of law which drew heavily from Islamic, Makonde, and European traditions. Although the akida drew a stipend for his services, he also pocketed a good portion of the fees and fines collected.

Assisting the akida in his tasks were 15 to 20 jumbes, or head men, as well as several court clerks and messengers. The jumbes helped organize road construction, the introduction of new cash crops, the control over predatory animals, and the regulation of forest areas. It was at the jumbe stage that the weakness of the German overlordship and the strength of the indigenous political system became apparent. Although an akida could appoint his relatives and fellow tribesmen to the posts of clerk or messenger, in many instances the jumbes were in fact the traditional wakulungwa. In Kitangari, for example, the akidas found the wakulungwa so firmly entrenched that they had no alternative but to govern through them. If the wakulungwa in that area did not collect taxes, the most that the akida could do was to cut off their wages. Even in those areas where it was necessary to dismiss the wakulungwa and govern through appointed jumbes, the indigenous system had remarkable survival qualities. The elders and traditional advisers continued to resolve disputes, settle claims, and carry on the other functions of government without reference to the alien jumbes. Thus, a *sub rosa* system of local government, unregulated by the German administration, continued to operate alongside the formal structures of direct rule.

The thinness of the veneer that constituted the German presence in the Makonde region became glaringly apparent at

youth had visited Germany prior to his being appointed as an agent at the coast; see letter of Frierson to Chief Secretary, April 26, 1932 (TNA 21456).

the time of the First World War. Shortly after Germany had declared war on Portugal in 1916, the Portuguese forded the Ruvuma and for a time occupied the wells, the boma, and other locations near Newala. The wakulungwa and appointed jumbes alike appeared to welcome the Portuguese. In any case, few Makonde came to the aid of the beleaguered Germans, who fled north. The latter part of 1916 and the first half of 1917 found Newala in a state of chaos. In the absence of firm European control, bands of young Makonde, Maconde, and others went about killing anyone who had been associated with either the Germans or the Portuguese! The turmoil in the area permitted the Germans to reenter Newala, forcing the Portuguese back across the border. Although a number of the jumbes and wakulungwa fled across the Ruvuma, many who had cooperated with the Portuguese were captured and hanged by the Germans. By November, 1917, the Germans themselves had to flee across the Ruvuma into Mozambique in order to escape the British and allied forces who were pressing down from the north. When they departed from the Makonde area the German troops took many of the goats and movable foodstuffs with them. The chaos, as well as the flight of Makonde males escaping the military recruiters, left the farms untended. Hence, when order was finally restored, one of the most serious problems facing the new military administration was famine.[15]

Despite the bitter events surrounding the last days of German rule and the recollections of harshness and cruelty on the part of both German administrators and their akidas, there was a curious romanticizing of the Germans by the elder Makonde I interviewed in the 1950s. Comments were made as follows: "Although the Germans were strict, we knew what they wanted of us; under the British, they keep telling us new things every day." "Look at that boma [in Newala]. The Germans built it years ago, and it is still standing. The new bridge the British put over that river is the third one in five years." It was not unusual, moreover, to find Makonde youths with names like

15. For accounts of the fighting in East Africa during the First World War, see Ludwig Boell, *Die Operationen in Ostafrika: Weltkrieg 1914–1918* (Hamburg: W. Dachert, 1951); and Brian Gardner, *German East: The Story of the First World War in East Africa* (London: Cassell, 1963).

Kaisa, Bismarck, and Dachi. In many respects, this could have been a device for ridiculing the incumbent colonial administrators.

## THE RECONSTRUCTION PERIOD, 1917–1925

The success of the Allied forces in their East African campaign took the British by surprise in many respects. They were unprepared to deal with the long-range administrative problems of the territory while the war continued in Europe. Even after the Paris Peace Conference had placed Tanganyika under the League of Nations Mandate System, the uncertainties regarding the actual obligations of the Mandatory Power and the future development of the relationship made the British reluctant to engage in long-term planning. There was, moreover, a very serious shortage of the administrative talent needed both for the normal governing of a territory as large as Tanganyika and for the relocation of refugees and the restoring of economic activities that had been disturbed during the military campaign. In view of the financial retrenchment taking place within Britain itself and the general disenchantment of the British public with regard to further colonial adventures, it appeared at one point that the military government of Tanganyika might be prolonged indefintiely.

It was not until January, 1919, that Governor Sir Horace Byatt ultimately relieved the military staff with civilian personnel borrowed largely from the Indian and Kenyan civil services. Like its military predecessor, the civilian administration of Byatt was essentially a holding operation. Its limited staff compelled the new administration to ignore long-range development in favor of more pressing problems, such as recurrent famine, the reestablishment of a communications and transportation network, and the maintenance of order. Administration at the local level did not differ radically in character from that of the Germans. The local officials—whether hereditary chiefs or appointed akidas—were largely retained, with the exception of those who had given direct assistance to the retreating German forces or who had made themselves immensely unpopular during their rule.

The Byatt administration moved with extreme caution in altering the basic character of traditional society. They were simply too understaffed to cope with any problems that might arise from further dislocation of existing economic, social, and political patterns. The government, for example, rejected the scheme suggested by a district officer in Lindi to concentrate the Makonde of that district in villages in the more fertile valleys. Admitting that the problems of increased production and population control might be managed more easily, the governor agreed that this was a project that had "to be most tactfully and carefully handled, as natives as a rule have a great objection to leaving their old haunts." [16]

The governor also exercised extreme caution in dealing with the question of slavery, which was not actually brought to an end in Tanganyika until 1928, when Britain adhered to the League of Nations Convention on Slavery. In theory it had been assumed implicitly that slavery ceased to be legal in East Africa when British forces occupied German East Africa, and this was given explicit expression in the proclamation of Ordinance No. 13 of 1922, which abolished involuntary servitude in Tanganyika. The fact is, however, that, although the slave trade had been terminated by Sultan Barghash of Zanzibar in 1876, the institution of domestic slavery was firmly entrenched in the territory and had been only slightly disturbed by the Germans. It was estimated that, in 1914, Arabs and African notables continued to hold 145,000 persons in involuntary servitude. A number of slaves had been freed when their masters fled with the Germans. British caution in conducting a frontal assault on slavery was due perhaps to recollections of the unmanageable chaos they created in the hinterland of Sierra Leone at the turn of the century when they attempted to peremptorily abolish domestic slavery in West Africa. The financial status of Tanganyika made it unrealistic to think in terms of paying compensation to slave owners. It was recognized, too, that an early frontal assault on the institution would meet with considerable resistance from the very local officials upon whom they were depending to maintain order. Acting Governor John Scott in 1924 acknowledged as much when he stated that the Ordinance

16. Lindi District, *Monthly Report,* August, 1923.

of 1922 was not intended to bring an immediate end to slavery. The ordinance was intended to deal largely with flagrant abuses of the system![17] When slavery was ultimately abolished the British were at that time better prepared to deal with the ill-will they encountered from those demanding compensation. Abolition was a continuing irritant, however, and during the next decade or more after 1928 the local court dockets were sprinkled with unsuccessful suits for compensation on the part of slave owners.

The relative complacency in the matters of witchcraft, abusive compulsory labor practices, and exorbitant tribute payments to chiefs and akidas further confirms the cautious conservatism of the Byatt administration in undermining traditional or semitraditional practices. The government was equally hesitant, as well as financially unprepared, to undertake dramatic programs of social, economic, and political reform. A few areas, such as those around Kilimanjaro, were regarded as economically rewarding to the British government. The Southern Province, however, was viewed as being unpromising and also physically remote. It became the Cinderella province of a Cinderella colony, and its major tribal grouping—the Makonde—found even the meager economic advances of the interwar period passing them by.

During the first decade of British rule the pattern of regional and local administration adhered fairly closely to the German pattern. Lindi, which had served as the headquarters of the German *Bezirksamtmann,* continued as the provincial headquarters of the southern area. The Southern Province was the largest regional unit in Tanganyika; at its peak it extended from Kilwa in the northeast to the mouth of the Ruvuma River in the southeast and included most of the region westward to Lake Nyasa, now called Lake Malawi. The Makonde were the largest tribal group within the province, but they were rivaled for administrative attention by the Makua, Yao, Ngoni, Mwera, Pogoro, and a score of smaller tribal groupings. Although the idea of uniting the Makonde within a single administrative district had come up from time to time, during most of the

---

17. See League of Nations Doc. A.25(a)1924.VI; and letter of A. E. Kitching to Chief Secretary, August 3, 1934 (TNA 11193/8).

fifty years of British rule the Makonde were distributed among three administrative districts: Lindi, Newala, and Mikindani, which was renamed Mtwara in the 1950s. There was a brief period—1926 to 1930—when the Makonde of Newala and Mikindani districts were amalgamated under a single administrator.

The British civilian administrators who were posted to the Makonde area took as their first order of the day the restoration of order. The German system of appointing liwalis for the coastal towns and akidas for the rural jurisdictions was continued as the most efficient means for achieving this goal. The judicial roles of these officials, however, were altered. They were stripped of jurisdiction over all but the most minor criminal cases, and they were barred from the use of caning and other unusually harsh forms of punishment. The payment of tribute, moreover, was eliminated as more and more of the akidas became salaried officials, who were paid 80 rupees a month.[18] In addition to maintaining order, hearing cases involving dowry and debts, and performing Muslim marriages, the akidas relayed the instructions of the British administrators to the Makonde under their jurisdictions.

Although a number of the akidas and liwalis had fled or had been dismissed because of pro-German tendencies, a surprising number of the original officeholders were retained. Akida Sefu of Newala, for example, had been appointed by the Germans in 1904 and was highly respected by the British. Indeed, he was regarded as so industrious and trustworthy that during a six-month period in 1924 Akida Sefu administered the Newala subdistrict in the absence of any European officer.[19] Efforts were made, however, to provide a more popular base for the akida system. In Mikindani, at the retirement in 1920 of Liwali Mohammed Ahmed, who was actually a native of Khartoum in the Sudan, the administration permitted the local populace to choose between two candidates presented to them by the administration. They selected an elderly Makonde who had a knowledge of Islamic law. Apparently the people were satisfied with their choice, for he served for many years, with

18. E. A. Leakey, 1938, in Mikindani District Book.
19. Lindi Province, *Annual Report,* 1924 (TNA 1733/15/94).

few complaints being lodged against him. Gradually the "alien" akidas in the rural areas were replaced by Makonde as posts became vacant. The first areas to experience this reform were the Madimba and Nanyamba akidates in Mikindani District. In the Makonde area of Lindi District an Arab continued to serve as akida during the entire reconstruction period.[20]

The value of the akida system in carrying out British objectives in Tanganyika was the subject of some dispute within the administration. Captain George St. J. Orde-Brown, who served in the military government that preceded civilian rule, stated that he was

> convinced that many of the evils which brought about the perpetual punitive expeditions of German days arose solely because the white official was shut off from direct dealings with the natives. . . . Akidas save trouble. A lazy district officer will appreciate an efficient akida and therefore tends to be biased in his favor. If an akida is efficient, he is dangerous, if he is inefficient, he is redundant.[21]

On the other hand, a decade after the abandonment of the akida system in the Makonde area, a district officer who had been reposted to Lindi District wrote with nostalgia of his own experiences twenty years earlier during the military occupation of 1918:

> Gone are the days when the Administrative Officer, touring his district would be met by the Akida, who, bursting with pride in his area, would ask if there was any advance on Rs. 150/- per frasila for wild rubber; he would have notes on how much gum copal had been collected. . . . Tax collection was not the nightmare described by my predecessor. The akida controlled the village headmen. . . . [22]

His views were supported by a fellow officer who felt that, despite the alien character of the akidas and the akida system,

> the Akida was a person elected for his intelligence, ability, and force of personality. These qualities were essential

20. Lindi District, *Annual Report,* 1925 (TNA 1733/10/75).
21. Quoted in Judith Listowel, *The Making of Tanganyika* (London: Chatto and Windus, 1965), p. 69.
22. E. A. Leakey, quoted in letter of A. E. Kitching to Chief Secretary, February 17, 1937.

to the services which he had to perform. . . . The akida
system was an efficient administrative machine under
which the natives were contented and received a fair
measure of justice.[23]

From the standpoint of British administrators, the weakest
element in the akida system was the cadre of jumbes who were
appointed as administrative assistants to the akidas. In return
for a stipend amounting to 3 per cent of the hut and poll tax
collected in his jumbeate, the jumbe was to assist the akida
in maintaining order, collecting taxes, and serving as the eyes
and ears of the British district commissioner and the akida at
the village level. What authority the jumbe had under the German akida system was derived from two sources—the fact that
many of the jumbes were in fact traditional wakulungwa in
their respective areas, and the judicial authority that they
exercised with respect to local problems. Under the British
akida system many of the traditional wakulungwa-jumbes had
been dismissed as either pro-German or inefficient. Their places
had been taken by the easygoing and relatively weak candidates
who had been proposed as substitutes by the people in order to
preserve the office of mkulungwa for the rightful incumbent.
A weak jumbe would constitute no threat to the traditional
order, which was permitted to function under the very noses of
the district commissioner and the akidas. Although the customary courts had no official standing, in fact the wakulungwa
and their wazee arbitrated disputes and settled minor civil
and criminal cases without reference to the British-imposed
court system. The extent to which this *sub rosa* system of
administration persisted is revealed in the remarks of a district
officer in Lindi, who noted:

> Considering its area and its population crime is conspicu-
> ous by its absence, but I am inclined to think that a certain
> amount of undetected crime (assault, adultery, etc.) is
> going on. These cases, I assume are settled out of court by
> compensation being paid. If my assumption is incorrect
> then all I can say is that Lindi District contains the most
> law-abiding lot of natives I have ever known in any dis-
> trict.[24]

23. Confidential letter of E. K. Lumley, District Office, Lindi, October 31, 1937.
24. Lindi District, *Annual Report*, 1924 (TNA 1733/15/94).

British administrators' lack of confidence in the jumbes was not concealed. A sample of the attitudes held by the British regarding the jumbes is contained in the remarks of the district officer in Lindi in 1924 regarding several jumbes:

> *Mitema.* Mfalme Abdallah. Quite useless as a jumbe. He has no authority whatsoever over his people. People have no respect for him and he is quite unable to enforce respect.
>
> *Mbwemkuru.* Issa Malili. Suffers from Elephantiasis and is unable to get about amongst his people. His work during the past year has been most unsatisfactory. No authority over his people.
>
> *Jangwani.* Nangomwa Asmani. Very old man. Past work. Has in consequence no authority over his people. Tax collection in his area has caused a great deal of trouble during last year.
>
> *Lihangani.* Ali Machenje. Suffers from chronic opthalmia. No authority. Useless.
>
> *Mandwanga.* Hamisi Kiuli. Not to be trusted. Has been previously warned about his behavior but makes no attempt to improve.
>
> *Uloda.* Mkanalinga Hamisi. A very sick man. Has been ill for the whole year. No control over his people and in consequence a considerable amount of trouble has been caused with natives in the Newala sub-district which adjoins his. Has been previously warned but apparently can do nothing with people under him.[25]

Relations between the British administration and the jumbes reached their lowest ebb in the last years of the akida system — 1926 and 1927. Recognizing that the abolition of the akida system would return many of the jumbes to the ranks of ordinary citizens, the jumbes simply failed to collect taxes or enforce any of the unpopular orders of the British government. Life might otherwise have been made intolerable for them. Consequently, the last days of the akida system found local government in a state of near chaos.

25. Lindi District, Comments of Senior Commissioner, 1924 (TNA 2716).

# 5:
# Indirect Rule

Most writers on Tanganyika attribute the introduction of the policy of Indirect Rule in the mandate territory to the arrival of Sir Donald Cameron as governor in 1925. Actually, the seeds of the policy of Indirect Rule – or Indirect Administration, as Sir Donald insisted upon calling it – had already been planted in Tanganyika several months before Cameron's arrival on the scene. The conference of senior commissioners, which Acting Governor John Scott had convened at the end of October, 1924, had unanimously resolved

> that the development of the system of Native Administration should be in the direction of creating an autonomous local native Government having its own legislation, treasury, and authorities, and that gradually the Administrative Officers should assume more and more the functions of Resident Advisers rather than executive officials; and that one of the means whereby this system can be developed is by the establishment of local native councils, and eventually composed of the recognized native authorities over larger native areas.[1]

1. Tanganyika, *Administrative Conference, 27 Oct. to 7 Nov. 1924* (Dar es Salaam: Government Printer, 1924), p. 12.

It was the genius of Cameron, however, which was to provide the driving force and imagination needed to put the policy of Indirect Rule into effect. Cameron, after all, had been one of Lord Lugard's trusted lieutenants in Northern Nigeria, where the modernized version of the ancient practice of governing conquered territories through the use of indigenous political authorities had become a philosophy — indeed, almost a religion — that guided British colonial administrators everywhere.[2] Renouncing the ethnocentricity of British colonial practices of the past, Cameron justified Indirect Administration on the grounds that it would "develop the native politically on lines suitable to the state of society in which he lives." Reminiscent of Lord Lugard's own comments, however, the policy was also justified as being highly pragmatic and one which would please the tax-weary British citizens, who had grown tired of colonial adventures. Cameron commented:

> It must be remembered that it is quite impossible for us to administer the country directly through British officers, even if we quadrupled the number we now employ and that the ultimate end of direct rule is complete political repression, or concession to political agitators.[3]

Ironically, the greatest threat to the success of the policy of Indirect Rule was posed by the zealous British administrators themselves, who became doctrinaire devotees of the new philosophy.[4] Colonial governments in actuality seldom have a simple choice between the introduction of a policy of direct or indirect rule, for there are many considerations that limit the options available to an alien regime. Among the leading factors to be considered are the ultimate as well as the short-term goals of the superordinate power with respect to the dependent population. If the relationship is complex and destined to be of

2. See Donald Cameron, *My Tanganyika Experience and Some Nigeria* (London: Allen & Unwin, 1939).

3. *Principles of Native Administration and their Application*, Native Administration Memorandum no. 1, rev. (Dar es Salaam: Government Printer, 1930), pp. 4–5.

4. I have discussed this at greater length in my article on "Legitimacy of Alien Relationship: The Nyaturu of Tanganyika," *Western Political Quarterly*, XIV (March, 1961), 64–86.

long duration, then a radical departure from existing institutions and norms may be either necessary or more efficient; but it would be unnecessarily expensive to pursue a policy of direct administration if the superordinate power had a limited objective—such as suppression of piracy or the slave trade—which could be accomplished in a short period of time. A further variable limiting the choice of alternative policies is the manner in which the superordinate-subordinate relationship was established. The option of utilizing traditional leaders as agents of the colonial power is eliminated if the dependency relationship is established only after a bloody conquest in which those leaders are either destroyed or humiliated to the point where their legitimacy vis-à-vis the dependent masses has been undermined.

Another significant consideration restricting the choice of the superordinate power is the adaptability or inadaptability of the indigenous authority system to the objectives and techniques of the alien administrators. One should not expect to introduce a modern sanitation and inoculation program or a complex scheme for economic development through traditional political leaders whose functions were largely religious in character or who had the authority to arbitrate but not to command. Underscoring the question of adaptability is the more fundamental problem of cultural barriers to understanding. Colonial administrators, lacking training as anthropologists, often fail to comprehend the nature of the political (and other) relationships that they are attempting to preserve (under Indirect Rule) or destroy (under Direct Rule) within the subordinate society. Conversely, the demands of the superordinate agents may be beyond the range of comprehension or credibility to the members of the subordinate society.

Finally, the range of policy alternatives open to a colonial power is limited by the availability of personnel and other resources; by the political and economic struggles taking place within the superordinate society itself among economic, religious, and political groups having diverse interests vis-à-vis the dependent society; by the attitudes and actions of third societies; and by unplanned and unanticipated responses on the part of the subordinate population.

Sir Donald Cameron was very much aware of the pitfalls of the doctrinaire approach to indirect rule—especially as it applied to the southeastern districts of Tanganyika. He noted with distinct annoyance in 1927 that the administrative officers in the Lindi area

> write as if a system of direct administration could no longer be endured; as if indirect administration must be introduced at all costs. This is, of course, not the case. If the foundations for a Native Administration are not present then we must continue to administer directly, but substituting men of the tribe or unit for the aliens we have previously employed to do our administrative work for us. The headmen of the tribe or unit that we so appoint would be merely mouthpieces of the Government through whom the orders *of the Government* (not a Native Administration) would be conveyed to the People.[5]

The "missionary zeal" which Cameron had inspired in his officers, however, was difficult to repress. It was a case of the disciples being greater zealots than the master, and the disciples in the south were not to be denied their place at the "love feast" for Indirect Rule. They bided well their time. When Sir Donald went on home leave in 1927, the provincial commissioner of Lindi Province, A. M. Turnbull, and his officers set in motion plans which Cameron found difficult to reverse despite his very serious misgivings regarding the whole idea. The physical remoteness of the region gave local administrators in this instance—as it was to do time and again in the future—the ability to manipulate the course of events without interference from the territorial capital.[6]

It was apparent that the administrators in the Makonde area assumed that dedication to an ideal was an adequate substitute for real knowledge. The armchair anthropology of

5. Marginal notes in his own hand, at the end of the Lindi District *Annual Report,* 1926; written on February 4, 1927 (TNA 1733/6/59).

6. Notes of Cameron on Lindi and Coastal Native Authorities, August 13, 1929 (TNA 12800). See also confidential letter of E. K. Lumley to Provincial Commissioner of Lindi, October 31, 1937, Newala District Book. In the revised edition of *Principles of Native Administration,* page 7, Cameron later attempted to provide official sanction to the actions of Turnbull, arguing that the indigenous courts of justice had survived in the Makonde area in a striking fashion. I suggest that he was merely "keeping up the side."

one district officer was patently manifest when he remarked that "ultimately it became evident that the so-called Makonde, Matambwe, Machinga, Maraba, and Mawia could be classified as sections of the Makonde tribe."[7] Lack of knowledge, moreover, did not preclude haste. In Lindi District the system of Indirect Rule was adopted after only a two-month survey of the traditional system, conducted by a district officer who was at the time suffering from blackwater fever. In Newala the investigations were totally initiated by a young cadet who was not an anthropologist and who had no more than a year's administrative service to his credit.[8] Only in Mikindani District did the British officer humbly acknowledge that the task was "enormous and occupied many months of careful and patient investigation."[9]

## ENTHRONING THE WAKULUNGWA

In many areas of Tanganyika, the implementation of the policy of Indirect Administration was complicated by the fact that political systems were highly fragmented and often the largest unit was based essentially upon the extended family. Although the litawa, or kinship unit, did play an important role in traditional Makonde politics, British administrators were able to recognize the several score virambo as political units which were sufficiently large and had at least vague geographic jurisdictions. Having identified a workable unit of administration, however, the British administrators mistakenly assumed that the most visible official within the chirambo— that is, the mkulungwa—was the sum and substance of the traditional political system. As was noted previously, the successful mkulungwa in the past was actually one who knew very well that he was merely one of the significant political actors within his chirambo and that his role was narrowly circumscribed by the authority of the elders who represented their

7. Lindi Province, *Annual Report*, 1928 (TNA 11679).
8. The cadet, F. H. Page-Jones, ultimately became Member for Local Government in pre-independence Tanganyika.
9. Mikindani (Mtwara) District Book; and letter of E. K. Lumley to Provincial Commissioner of Lindi, October 31, 1937, Newala District Book.

respective litawas; by the operation of the vituperative alliances, or utani relationships; by the informal bonds created during the puberty rites; and by other forces within his society. Subsequent administrators who attempted to make Indirect Rule work in the Makonde area of Newala, Lindi, and Mikindani districts realized that no mkulungwa was

> acknowledged by his fellows as having greater authority than themselves; the duty of the ordinary man to his family and [litawa] is well defined and scrupulously fulfilled, but beyond these the Makonde has recognized no obligation to any one.[10]

Nevertheless, sheer administrative convenience drove the British administration to concentrate upon the wakulungwa—however numerous they were—in preference to comprehending the complex network of political forces operating within the chirambo. Indeed, the span of administrative control was already stretched beyond the capacity of most officers to cope with such a delicate situation.

Ironically, the attempt to preserve and resuscitate the traditional political system probably accelerated the rate of change in indigenous values and institutions to a greater extent than had occurred under the previous policies of the British and Germans, which had ignored the traditional political system. Under the Native Authority system of Indirect Rule, the status of the mkulungwa acquired a precision which it had not previously enjoyed. The mkulungwa became the sole point of official contact for the dissemination of orders from European officers and for the gathering of data regarding all phases of local government. His official duties made him a meddler in affairs that were traditionally beyond his jurisdiction, thereby incurring the animosity of the elders. Faced with the possible displeasure of both the European administrator and his own people, the mkulungwa tended increasingly to rely upon members of his own litawa in seeking advice and assistance in the conduct of his office. As a consequence the members of his litawa shared in the few privileges and perquisites of office, and they were favored with exemptions from compulsory road

10. J. W. Large, Newala District, *Annual Report,* 1933.

work and payment of taxes.[11] Gradually there began to emerge
a series of "royal," or at least privileged, litawas in a society
where distinctions of this sort had traditionally been relatively absent.

Identification of the office through which the British administrators would funnel commands was one thing; identification
of the appropriate officeholder was quite another matter. The
claimants to the office and its meager salary were legion in the
three Makonde districts. The candidates included former
akidas, wakulungwa who had long since lost their following,
heads of nuclear families which had only recently hived off
from their parent virambo, as well as legitimate wakulungwa.
The search for legitimate claimants frequently upset the
delicate balance binding Makonde to their respective wakulungwa, for the institutional arrangements had not been very
explicitly defined in traditional society. The search undermined
the very stability the British were hoping to preserve and
restore. The tendency, indeed, to keep open the question of who
was or who was not a legitimate claimant complicated the problems of administration during the entire period of Indirect
Rule. Each new district commissioner was "fair game" for a
disappointed claimant seeking a reversal of a previous decision. Each mkulungwa who was aware that his claim was in
question, moreover, could hardly be expected to be a vigorous
enforcer of Native Authority rules or collector of taxes. Some
appreciation of the magnitude of the problem facing administrators and the insecurity which many wakulungwa must have
experienced is revealed in figures from Newala District. During
the period from 1928 to 1935, forty-seven claims to office
were heard. Although all but five of the claims were rejected,
it is difficult to measure the damage it did to the stability of the
system.[12] In the process, too, an alien administrator, who probably knew very little about the nature of Makonde traditional

11. See Newala District Book; and Newala District, *Annual Report,* 1931.
12. Newala District Book. One of the five successful cases proved to be an
unusual instance of administrative caprice. The Provincial Commissioner
himself intervened in the case and decided to recognize a somewhat dubious
claim presented by the son of Machemba I, who had opposed the Germans and
had been compelled to seek refuge in Mozambique.

society, had become the arbiter of who was and who was not a
"legitimate" claimant to office.

The British administrators found themselves further undermining the authority of the wakulungwa by their efforts to
make the system more manageable for the solitary district
officer. In combining a number of small virambo having few
taxpayers into larger units, the British apparently were ready
to sacrifice legitimacy and traditionalism in favor of greater
administrative efficiency. Thus, at the time of the launching of
Indirect Rule there were in the Makonde area 66 wakulungwa
in Mikindani District, 88 in the Makonde section of Newala,
and 41 in the Makonde area of Lindi District. By 1929 the
number of Native Authorities in the Makonde Council of
Newala had been reduced to 73, and similar reductions took
place in the other two districts. Although the reductions were
nominally carried out by the councils of wakulungwa in each
of the three districts, the guiding hands of the district commissioners were becoming increasingly apparent when the councils seemed to be incapable of reaching the "right" decisions.

The "intervention syndrome" was certainly apparent as the
British officers attempted to improve the caliber of the wakulungwa class. In recommending the recognition of a new
mkulungwa, the district commissioner under Indirect Rule
was to be guided by such considerations as the ethnic origins
of the candidates, the principle of matrilineal succession, the
popularity of the candidates among the wazee, and other traditional factors. It was obvious, however, that these factors
were merely to be taken into account; they were not binding
in making a recommendation for recognition or for withdrawal
of recognition. There were other criteria which were considered of equal or even greater importance. Among these were
youth, ability to read and write, experience, and appreciation of
the goals of the British administration. An indication that the
traditional claims and popularity alone were not sufficient
criteria for remaining in office is revealed in the comments
of one district commissioner:

> Headmen are gradually learning to exercise their powers
> and it is chiefly a question of continual instruction and
> patient education for some years before headmen realize

that they must be prepared to face a certain amount of dislike on the part of "slackers" in ruling their virambo properly.[13]

## STABILIZATION OF TERRITORY AND POPULATION

A further step which altered the character of the traditional Makonde political system was the regularizing of virambo boundaries so that each Makonde tribesman was placed into a distinct territorial unit. The objective was to make each Native Authority responsible within a specific area for tax collection or enforcement of Native Authority orders. It was felt that only in this way could rational planning of programs take place in the fields of health, agriculture, and natural-resource development. The administration required that "all boundaries must be singular and continuous," and the system must be all-encompassing, leaving no "islands of anarchy" where Makonde were not subject to the jurisdiction of a recognized Native Authority.

The boundaries of the Makonde virambo in the traditional period were certainly not precise. The territorial jurisdiction of the wakulungwa were constantly shifting as new immigrants arrived, as land fertility changed, and as the family obligations of the members waxed and waned. The very vagueness of the territorial limits made it possible for dissident Makonde to strike out further into the thicket in search of new lands and political leadership. There were many areas, indeed, where no mkulungwa exercised jurisdiction. There were also areas where the exercise of authority was overlapping with no apparent objection from the citizens of the conflict area, or where authority was exercised in a leap-frog fashion as the expansion of other virambo separated a single chirambo into a series of detached islands of loyalty. If anything, the vagueness of the virambo boundaries had intensified under the periods of German and British direct administration as the Ngoni threat had vanished and as both Islam and Christianity contributed to an alteration in marriage and family ties.

13. J. W. Large, Newala District, *Annual Report,* 1928.

In view of the British penchant for territorial neatness, almost as much time was spent in Newala, Mikindani, and Lindi districts sorting out boundary claims as was spent in examining conflicting claims to the post of mkulungwa. Even after committees of the Makonde councils in each of the districts had laboriously gone through the evidence on boundary settlements, the decisions were not considered binding upon the people in the villages. In Newala a few headmen secretly agreed to fix nominal boundaries to satisfy the district commissioner, with the understanding that each would have authority over his people who were outside the boundaries.[14] Moreover, as the number of virambo was reduced through amalgamations, the boundary question would be opened all over again as a means of circumventing the decision on amalgamation.

Once the limits of the virambo had been fixed, the British administrators attempted to stabilize the population within the respective virambo. The administrators were interested not only in the taking of a census for planning purposes and the identification of taxpayers, but were also interested in preventing a sort of human Gresham's law from operating in the Makonde district. By the latter, I refer to the tendency of Makonde cultivators to gravitate from the chirambo of the mkulungwa who vigorously collected taxes and enforced the various Native Authority rules to the chirambo of another mkulungwa, one who had a reputation for being a lax administrator. The Makonde Councils at the commencement of Indirect Rule were required to pass ordinances preventing the movement of persons without the express consent of the headmen. This may have increased efficiency of tax collection, but it undermined one of the significant checks upon autocratic leadership, namely, the possibility of withdrawing allegiance from a tyrant. Moreover, the registration of people within each chirambo was clearly resented by the mwenyekaya, or family elders, who attempted to maintain their social control over the members of their litawa without regard to residence. It also was regarded as a nuisance by the man who had wives in several villages.

14. Newala District Book.

One of the unintended consequences of the British desire to have compact administrative units was that the delineation of political boundaries compelled "alien" Africans in the southeastern districts to recognize the jurisdiction of Makonde wakulungwa. Previously, the vagueness of the virambo boundaries had permitted Makua, Yao, Matambwe, Ndendeule, and other tribesmen to live in the areas between virambo without having to acknowledge the leadership of a Makonde headman. In certain cases the cluster of non-Makonde residents was sufficiently strong that they could claim an mkulungwa of their own. As a group, however, they were obliged to associate with Makonde for administrative purposes rather than with their fellow tribesmen and kinsmen in neighboring districts or across the Ruvuma in Mozambique.[15] In the process there was a tendency for non-Makonde to "pass" and identify with the Makonde in the hopes of being permitted to participate more fully in the affairs of the chirambo and the district.[16]

## System of Rewards

A further distortion of the traditional relationship between Makonde cultivators and their political leadership came through the establishment of a system of material and psychic rewards which elevated the mkulungwa and even the wazee to positions of higher status within the community. Thus the system of Indirect Rule, which was supposed to support traditional structures, threatened a relationship which had been based upon the notion of service bringing its own reward in terms of respect for the just leader. The mkulungwa in the past did not expect anything beyond token gifts for his services,

15. Thus the twelve Matambwe headmen were considered to be so close to the Makonde that it was felt that no great injustice was done. Regarding the Ndendeule (remnants of the Ngoni), they were so far from Songea that it was impractical to do anything other than include them within the Makonde Council. The Makua headman at Mcholi felt his people had lived so long among the Makonde that they readily consented to joining the Makonde Council.

16. Sometimes a tribal group was eliminated by administrative action! In the 1926 *Annual Report* for Lindi, the Machinga, the Maraba, and the Mawia were lumped together as "branches of the Makonde." In the 1948 census, the Maraba were eliminated entirely as a separate tribal classification.

and even the provision of labor was limited to assistance by the young men of the chirambo in the construction of a new house.

The salaries for Native Authorities introduced under Indirect Rule were small when viewed from the perspective of Tanganyika as a whole (12 shillings per month in Mikindani, for example). In a more localized situation in which few people were involved in the cash economy, however, the paltry sum made a significant difference. The salary was further supplemented by whatever court and other fees the mkulungwa could legitimately or otherwise exact from the citizens of his chirambo. There were, moreover, the tax funds which the wakulungwa and their assistants pocketed, and in view of the number of cases of dismissal for peculation this must have been a considerable sum. The new monetary rewards accounted in great measure for the constant stream of claimants to office, which left the legitimacy of the mkulungwa system constantly under challenge. It encouraged as well the establishment of a hierarchically structured leadership class dependent ultimately upon the new wealth of the wakulungwa. As one very disenchanted district commissioner in Lindi wrote:

> Each mkulungwa kept a good percentage of "wakilis," who in turn kept "mtarishis," who kept "boys." This contingent of ruffianly friends and relatives harried the countryside, collected sums of money from various people under the guise of tax, punishment, fees, which the mkulungwa always put in his pocket.[17]

Finally, since the payment of a salary to an mkulungwa was made dependent upon his successful collection of taxes, the harassment by the mkulungwa of his people differed little from that of the akida under the previous German and British systems of administration. Far from encouraging respect for the mkulungwa, the situation challenged the Makonde cultivators to engage in the game of keeping one step ahead of the hut and wife counters and the tax collectors.

There were also differences of a psychic nature which eroded the essentially egalitarian character of the Makonde political

17. F. W. Bampfylde, "Report on the Wamakonde and Wamwera Tribal Administration," July 12, 1929 (TNA 12800).

and social system. In Lindi, Newala, and Mikindani, for example, it was decided that on all official occasions the wakulungwa should wear uniforms consisting of white *kanzus* (the long cotton gowns worn by Arabs) and embroidered waistcoats (*vizabu*), with different colors signifying the various divisions within the districts.[18] It was felt, too, that proper respect for Native Courts required that the elders should have special mats (*jamvi la wazee*) set out for them in the court buildings. It was considered a gross breach of etiquette, punishable by a fine, for common people to step or sit on these mats. Apparently the young bloods found the temptation too great to resist, for eight of the thirty-five infractions of Native Authority Rules and Orders in Lindi District in 1930 involved "challenges to this new status distinction." [19]

## THE EXECUTIVE ROLE OF THE MKULUNGWA

Many of the activities associated with the executive duties of the wakulungwa were not unknown to Makonde society. Certainly the Makonde had recognized before the Europeans arrived that it was necessary to organize communal drives against marauding pigs and other animals, that keeping the villages clean kept down the rodent population, that cutting the weeds on paths between settlements was necessary for the maintenance of social and political ties, and, above all, that peace and order were necessary for the survival of any kind of community. One of the things that was altered under the system of Indirect Rule was the role that the mkulungwa played in the accomplishment of these tasks. Many of these items had in the past been left to the responsibility of the individual, the nuclear family, or the litawa. Under the Native Authority system these activities became a matter of community-wide concern, and it was the mkulungwa who was held responsible by the British officials for the proper performance of these tasks. He was armed, moreover, with punitive

18. Lindi Province, *Annual Report*, 1929 (TNA 11679).
19. Report of P. E. Mitchell on tour of inspection, to Governor Cameron, September 8, 1930 (TNA 13538); and Lindi District, *Annual Report*, 1930.

weapons he had not possessed in the traditional period to secure adequate cooperation from his people. These weapons included the authority to fine and to put able-bodied males to work on community projects.

The mkulungwa's new authority with respect to matters which were traditionally the concern of others was most noticeable, however, in the matter of morals and interpersonal obligations. In Newala District, for example, rules and orders to be enforced by the Native Authorities included the following:

> ***The brewing of "Pombe" without permission of the Native Authority is forbidden when there is a dangerous decrease of reserve foodstuffs (and during the period of tax collection).
>
> ***Gambling in the forms known as "kamali," with cards and "kupikisa" simping coins is prohibited.
>
> ***The dancing of the "ngoma" known as "maluwela" is prohibited.
>
> ***A sick or wounded person unable to walk to hospital for treatment must be carried by relatives or whoever is concerned when called upon to do so, (by a Native Authority).
>
> ***It is forbidden to wed or allow marriage of girls who have not reached maturity.
>
> ***Food is to be provided for sale at current rates to bona fide travellers provided the notice is adequate and food plentiful.
>
> ***Lazy youths are to cultivate sufficient land for support of their dependents.[20]

Although the British administrators might content themselves with the fact that these ordinances might have been in the best interests of the Makonde people (even though that is a matter for debate), they could hardly have argued that they were attempting to preserve the traditional role of the mkulungwa when they vested him with the authority to enforce these rules. In effect, they made him a "meddler" in affairs which had been none of his business.

The new executive authority of the mkulungwa, moreover, gave him responsibility with regard to matters that were—to

20. Newala District, Orders and Rules passed under Secs. 8, 9, 16, 17 of the Native Authorities Ordinance.

the average Makonde, at least—beyond the range of common sense or decency. For example, several rules and regulations dealt with problems of health, agriculture, natural-resource conservation, and economic development. In this area the Native Authority was expected to require, either by persuasion or by threat of court action, that his fellow tribesmen take action against "threats" to the peace and security of the chirambo which were largely problematical. Native Authority rules and orders covered such matters as the following:

> ***The clearing of trees or grass, cultivating or building within 100 yards below or above a water spring on a level ground, without permission of the Native Authority, is prohibited.

> ***Bathing or the washing of clothes within 30 yards of a water supply on a level ground, or 15 yards on a sloping ground, is prohibited.

> ***The cutting down of large trees without permission of the Native Authority is prohibited.

> ***Any case of smallpox, cerebrospinal meningitis or other serious abnormal disease must be reported by those in contact with the sick person, that is friends or relatives, to the Native Authority.

> ***Infected goats must be quarantined.

> ***Every owner of a homestead must plant cassava to the extent of not less than one acre.

> ***Ample seed must be reserved by every cultivator for the next planting season.

> ***No leper may reside within 400 yards of any non-leper; nor may he or she approach within 50 yards of any communal water supply.[21]

Makonde in the pre-European period were certainly capable of concerning themselves with problematical threats to their safety. Indeed, no society could survive very long if it did not give thought to the future. The difference between traditional Makonde society and the society that the European administrators were attempting to create was the designation of appropriate means for dealing with potential crises. The Makonde of the past was much more concerned with "clear and present"

21. *Ibid.*

dangers, such as the presence of marauding lions or Ngoni raiders. He was less concerned with the problematical threat to future generations which, for example, might result from his indiscriminate cutting-down of trees, especially since there had never been any shortage of trees in his lifetime. The range of affairs with which the Makonde cultivator was concerned was sharply circumscribed, and in the absence of scientific training he failed to see the cause-and-effect relationship between, say, polluted water and illness. He was somewhat humble, moreover, in assuming that mortal man could manipulate his environment in order to secure economic prosperity, freedom from famine, or good health. Changes in technology had only brought limited improvements in the material lot of the Makonde cultivator; the rest depended upon one's good relations with his ancestors. Hence, the Makonde cultivator tended to regard the British administrator as an idle dreamer, a nuisance, or, in some cases, a threat equal to the problematical one with which the Makonde cultivator was supposed to be concerned. The Makonde farmer was frequently asked to sacrifice methods which had proved to be moderately successful in favor of gambling on a technique which was as yet untried.

The responses of the district commissioners to the performance of the wakulungwa in these novel areas of executive action were varied indeed. Some complained bitterly about the failure of the wakulungwa to assume an educational role regarding the necessity of sounder practices in the fields of health and agriculture. Instead, the mkulungwa would too often apologize to his people that he was only carrying out the *amri ya Serkali* (orders of government), which in fact he was.[22] Other officers were somewhat philosophical about the impossible burden that had been placed on the shoulders of the wakulungwa. One district officer, for example, commented that the headmen

> generally reply "Iko" (there is) to any query concerning administration or procedure; but give the same old man a complicated inheritance case to decide, involving barter, gift, and levy in items varying from drums to dried fish, he will ascend the family tree and descend by nine branches

22. J. W. Large, "Tribal Government," Newala District Book, 1928.

and thirteen collaterals and a bend sinister to deliver a perfectly equitable judgment in terms of beeswax, without looking up from his matutinal porridge; ask him how many court receipts have been issued and he will probably say "Iko!" [23]

Another sympathetic district commissioner of Newala in 1938 wondered: "What would a Welsh miner or Clydeside riveter say if he was told one day that his allotment was to be planted with trees 'to avoid soil erosion'?" [24] Oddly enough, up to the very eve of independence, British administration in the Makonde region continued to place a primary emphasis upon coercion as a means of effectuating technological change. The district commissioner of Newala in 1956, for example, wrote:

> We cannot altogether ignore the presence of the dissident and recalcitrant farmer who will not easily see to reason and we must consider the question of protecting the good farmer and the land against the results of the bad actions of the bad farmer. We must therefore frame a few rules for the observance of all cultivators. Such rules may be designed to enforce such measures as the uprooting and burning of striga as a control measure against this sorghum weed, the closing to cultivation of eroded land, the protection of water courses and the forbidding of all cultivation on the slopes of big valleys like the ones in the Kitangari depression as a soil conservation measure. Another useful piece of legislation that will be required in the very near future is a set of Land Settlement Rules. [25]

## JUDICIAL ROLE OF THE MKULUNGWA

The judicial authority of the mkulungwa in traditional Makonde society was either restricted or expansive depending upon a number of circumstances. Foremost among these was the mkulungwa's own position within his kin-group and the strength of his group compared to the other litawa that made up his chirambo. Beyond this the extent of his authority

---

23. Lindi Province, *Annual Report*, 1930 (TNA 11679).
24. I. R. G. Sullivan, Newala District, *Annual Report*, 1938.
25. E. H. Craig, Newala District, "Draft Agricultural Policy Framework" (typed MS.), p. 17.

was determined by the peculiar tradition of the chirambo, the demonstrated leadership qualities of the mkulungwa, and the complex array of factors operative in the particular situation which gave rise to a dispute. Both the territorial and the substantive and procedural jurisdiction of the mkulungwa were determined on an almost *ad hoc* basis. Certainly, the mkulungwa enjoyed no monopoly over the settlement of controversy within his chirambo.

The judicial authority of the mkulungwa under the Native Authority system could hardly be described as an effort to restore the traditional patterns of justice. Instead of the diffuseness which characterized the pre-European system, an attempt was made to regularize matters so that the mkulungwa, rather than other actors within the chirambo, was directly and immediately involved in the adjudication of controversy. Substantively, as well, the jurisdiction of the mkulungwa was broadened to include not only matters which might in the past have come to his attention — minor theft, assault, divorce, and inheritance disputes — but also rules regarding soil conservation, health, and other matters which were unknown to traditional Makonde society.

The Native Authority courts, moreover, were supposed to recognize a clear distinction between criminal and civil matters. As was noted previously, the concern in the past was not necessarily that a guilty party should be punished, although this was a consideration, especially in the case of inveterate violators of the peace and property of the community; what mattered was that the corporate interests of the litawa be kept in balance. Restitution and compensation were regarded as the logical ends of litigation. The distinction between civil and criminal jurisdictions was not accepted readily, and, as late as 1941, one district commissioner complained in his annual report that "in civil matters it is almost impossible to induce the courts to believe that not judgment but justice brings the case to an end."

Perhaps the most radical departure from the traditional approach to justice was the relative inaccessibility of the Native Authority court system. In the traditional period, controversy was an intimate affair, with the community not only being fully aware of most of the facts of the case but also participating in the resolution of the controversy, thereby ensuring that substantial justice was rendered. For the administrative convenience of the supervising British officials, this intimacy was sacrificed. Instead of constituting each mkulungwa and his wazee as a Native Court, the wakulungwa within each district were grouped into a series of Second Class Courts having primary jurisdiction with respect to minor criminal and civil matters, as well as infractions of the Native Authority Ordinance. There were eight such courts in Mikindani and Newala districts and four in the Makonde area of Lindi. The average membership was seven, but they ranged in size from five wakulungwa in the court at Ngunja to ten at Kitangari. The courts would meet monthly at the regional court headquarters, and there would be a token representation of the wazee from the area.

The reluctance of the wakulungwa to act in a corporate fashion in violation of traditional procedure was indicated in many ways. The most obvious evidence was their reaction to the election of court presidents. The British officers constantly stressed that the presidency was a temporary one, which was to be rotated, and did not accord superior status to the incumbent. Suspicions, nevertheless, were always great. In the opinion of British officers, the wakulungwa invariably resolved their doubts by "electing that person who [had] the least intelligence, and [was] the least likely to assert himself, and [had], therefore, the minimum of authority." [26] Taking the British administrator at his word that the court president had no superior authority, the orders of the president were systematically ignored by witnesses, other wakulungwa, and those against whom fines were levied.[27] Consequently, neither the presidents nor the wakulungwa acting in their corporate capacities as area courts took firm stands or meted out harsh penalties. They preferred rather to refer all matters of delicacy to the district commissioner or to the entire district Tribal Council of Wakulungwa, which served as a court of review and appeal. The people themselves, moreover, sensing the weakness of the area courts,

26. Confidential letter of E. K. Lumley to Provincial Commissioner of Lindi, October 31, 1937, Newala District Book.
27. Notes of E. A. Leakey, Mikindani District Book, 1938.

tended to take important matters directly to the district commissioner for resolution. If it was possible to evade the jurisdiction of the Native Court system entirely, many civil matters continued to be resolved by the wazee in a traditional fashion without bringing the matter to the attention of the wakulungwa. The latter was especially true in the areas where the minority tribal people, such as the Matambwe or Ndendeule, felt that they could not secure adequate justice from a council consisting of Makonde wakulungwa.[28]

The British administrators recognized that in many respects they had failed in their efforts both to modernize the Makonde system of justice and to preserve the traditional authority base of the wakulungwa. Without traditional restraints upon the judicial actions of the wakulungwa, the punishments meted out by the courts were often quite innocuous for major offenses and unduly severe when only minor infractions of the law were involved. Many administrators commented on the frequent resort to the lash, imprisonment, and heavy fining in correcting petty situations. Indicative of the general lack of respect for the judicial role of the wakulungwa is evidenced in the diary notes of one inspecting officer who commented that there was

> too much "contempt of court"; people are fined for walking out before the case is finished, speaking out of turn, abusing the headman. . . . Fines for petty contempts are both too frequent and often too high. It is quite common for a man to be fined Shs. 5/- for disobeying a summons to attend, which is equivalent to fining a European in Dar es Salaam £20.[29]

## THE LEGISLATIVE FUNCTIONS OF THE WAKULUNGWA

British administrators also encountered frustrations in their efforts to provide the wakulungwa with legislative authority. If the mkulungwa in traditional society had a legislative role, it was almost imperceptible. True, he could, by

28. Newala District, *Annual Report*, 1941.
29. P. E. Mitchell to Governor Cameron, August 23, 1929 (TNA 13538).

stressing one element of tradition at the expense of others, actually make law when he was resolving a controversy. In theory, however, he merely applied the wisdom of the ancestors to novel conditions as they arose. The collective gatherings of the mkulungwa and his wazee, moreover, were expected to preserve tradition and guard against the possibility of innovation on the part of the mkulungwa. Furthermore, it was a considerable stretching of the spirit of the traditional practices to assume that the various *ad hoc* gatherings of wakulungwa from various virambo to resolve a dispute or engage in concerted action justified the creation of tribal councils.[30] These gatherings organized the wakulungwa of each district into separate district councils, which met four times a year. Although the number of wakulungwa in Lindi remained at 41, the reduction in the number of wakulungwa from 88 to 73 in Newala and from 66 to 63 in Mikindani made the institution slightly more manageable for British officials. Each Makonde tribal council was constituted as a Native Treasury, funded by rebates from the central government hut and poll tax and from fines and fees collected locally. The council had legal responsibility for framing the estimates for road work, health, and programs in natural-resource development. The major expenditures were allocated directly to salaries for Native Authority staff. It was apparent that the various rules and ordinances regulating agriculture, sanitation, and other matters legislated by the councils were in fact the inspiration of the European district officers, with the wakulungwa politely applauding in the background. It could not have been otherwise, given the low educational level of the wakulungwa, their general lack of appreciation of the problems involved, and their reluctance to incur unpopularity. As a consequence, many of the council sessions had to be devoted to the scolding and educating of the wakulungwa with respect to why they should be vigorous enforcers of the rules that they themselves had, in theory, adopted!

As was true of the area courts, the question of electing council presidents found the wakulungwa striving to find the lowest possible denominator in order to avoid a rigorous taskmaster. Only in Newala District was the district commissioner able to

30. Mikindani District Book.

convince the council that it should appoint one of its more energetic members for a five-year term and vest him with genuine responsibility in arranging and supervising meetings, sorting out boundary and other disputes before they were reviewed by the whole council, and carrying out the council's disciplinary actions against inefficient wakulungwa. The significance of this development with respect to the fate of Indirect Rule in Newala will be indicated shortly.

## THE ABANDONMENT OF INDIRECT RULE ALONG THE COAST

At the time of the introduction of the mkulungwa system in the Makonde districts, the provincial commissioner at Lindi stated quite confidently, "While much remains to be done, Indirect Rule is now established on a sound and permanent basis."[31] This enthusiasm was far from justified, as is indicated by the preceding analysis of the operation of the mkulungwa system in Lindi, Newala, and Mikindani districts. Indeed, about the only aspect of the system which appeared to be traditional was the title "mkulungwa" and the concentration upon virambo as units of local administration. The demands placed upon the traditional polities in terms of meeting the obligations of modern administration were perhaps a classic case of new wine in old bottles. Far from having established the system on a "sound and permanent basis," within a decade the experiment was being written off as an exceedingly bad investment. In October, 1937, the Makonde Councils of Wakulungwa in Lindi and Mikindani districts, where the failures of the system were much more glaringly apparent, were dissolved. In their place a new form of local government, based on appointed liwalis and jumbes, was introduced. The wakulungwa in Newala continued to serve as Native Authorities for five years longer; then they too were removed from office and replaced by liwalis.

The failure of the system should not have come as a surprise,

31. Notes on "Inspections of District," Mikindani (Mtwara) District Book, 1928.

for as far back as 1929 an investigation of the wakulungwa
in Lindi District had exposed such fundamental weaknesses
that the survival of the system was bound to be some sort of
miracle – especially given Sir Donald Cameron's initial trepida-
tions regarding the whole experiment. A special investigator
in 1929 found the majority of the people looking back with
nostalgia upon the days of the akidas and jumbes, so abusive
were the wakulungwa in extorting money, suppressing open
discussion in council meetings, exempting their kinsmen and
friends from communal labor, and rendering decisions which
were regarded as unjust. He concluded his indictment by
noting that

> Some of the wakulungwa are so old or ill (one could not
> even walk, two of them at least were lepers) that they have
> never left their homes since being appointed, but sit in
> their houses, like great obese spiders in the centre of a
> web . . . and robbed their people in no mean fashion. I have
> been informed . . . that no person was allowed to bring
> a complaint to the Boma under threats of severest pen-
> alties.[32]

Further evidence of failure came in 1931, when the resistance to tax payment became so acute that the administration
was compelled to forego collection of the tax in Mikindani in
order to avoid a direct challenge to the authority of the wakulungwa as agents of the British administration. Certainly the
integrity and the ability of the wakulungwa to accept responsibility for unpopular tasks were questioned by the British
when a second European had to be brought to the district for
the express purpose of collecting the taxes and ensuring that
the wakulungwa would keep honest accounts. The Makonde
Councils in the three districts, moreover, were reluctant in
the extreme to punish those of their number who had been lax
in this affair. Although several wakulungwa had their salaries
cut or withheld, this did not prove to be an effective weapon in
securing greater efficiency for it undercut the very delicate
clientship relations that permitted the wakulungwa to get anything done at all in their virambo! Action apparently went
beyond salary cuts, however, for a later provincial commissioner

---

32. Bampfylde, "Report on the Wamakonde" (TNA 12800).

made reference to the "strenuous and distasteful measures which it had been necessary to take to restore equilibrium." [33]

Whether or not the situation actually demanded drastic action, it seemed to be the conviction of the administrative officers at the provincial and district levels that the system at the coast had utterly failed. The marshaling of evidence in Lindi District in 1937 was overwhelming. Of the original 69 wakulungwa, 20 had been dismissed and imprisoned for peculation, 7 had been discharged for serious neglect of duty, 5 for habitual drunkenness, and 9 as usurpers of the title of mkulungwa. Still others of the original group had been encouraged to resign when it was found that they were incapable of shouldering the new duties placed upon them. For such a system to have been effective, an investigator in 1937 insisted,

> Every mkulungwa would in practice require individual supervision by an administrative officer if he were to be moved to any kind of useful action. This supervision could never be efficient, and would be an intolerable strain on officers." [34]

In Mikindani District the British officers seemed to be equally convinced that the efforts to establish Indirect Rule on these lines was a sham and that the British government "had no alternative but to reject the effort to disinter ancient history." [35] The record of failure in the various virambo paralleled that of Lindi. There was adverse criticism of 39 of the original 61 wakulungwa in Mikindani District. A sample of the commentary by the district officer is illustrative of the low esteem in which the wakulungwa were held by British officers:

> *Nanyamba:* Still alive; deposed for laziness and inefficiency in 1929. Successor was accused of theft of tax money in 1931 with many other headmen. . . .
>
> *Namkuku:* Leper. Deposed in 1936 on account of sickness and holding witchcraft ceremonies.
>
> *Kiromba:* Old useless idiot, who declines to retire and puts in useless and lazy relatives to do his work, one of whom

33. A. E. Kitching to Chief Secretary, September 6, 1937, "Reorganization of Native Administration in Mikindani District" (TNA 26752).

34. E. K. Lumley, "Report on Indirect Rule in Lindi District," October 31, 1937.

35. Mikindani (Mtwara) District Book.

stole money in 1935. The village is virtually unadministered by the Native Authorities.

*Kianga:* Her village is inefficiently administered for her by relatives. She authorized witchcraft ceremonies resulting in conviction in 1931. She stole tax money in 1932 and ran away to Portuguese East Africa for a year.

*Mirumba:* Head of Islam in Mikindani. All work is done by a relative who was obviously a partner in theft of large sums of tax money in 1934.

*Kitere:* Cheated [government hut tax collectors] for years by hiding his three plural wives, revealed only after his death.

*Nambu:* A lazy fool and out of sympathy to government almost to the point of revolutionary.[36]

The condemnation of the mkulungwa system by the provincial commissioner, A. E. Kitching, was forceful in the extreme. Referring especially to Mikindani and Lindi districts, Mr. Kitching stated the following:

> As executive authorities responsible for the maintenance of peace, order, and good government and the collection of revenue, they have been a complete failure throughout the whole of the period during which they have been in office. It is a complete mystery to me how the system has managed to survive so long. Frankly I regard the whole edifice as a "damnosa hereditas" which has impeded the proper administration of the districts ever since it was erected and which should now be renounced.
>
> The decision to appoint the heads of certain families as native authorities necessarily entailed the appointment of many persons – very old men, imbeciles, women, lepers, and others – who were entirely unfitted for the posts they were expected to fill.[37]

In many respects the administration in Dar es Salaam felt that the provincial commissioner and others in the Makonde area did protest too much, and they feared that once again geographic isolation might encourage the opponents of Indirect Rule to act as impetuously in 1936 as the advocates of

36. Notes on Mikindani headmen compiled by District Officer, 1936 (TNA 12800).
37. "Indirect Rule in the Lindi and Mikindani Districts," July 15, 1936 (TNA 12800/II).

the system had acted a decade previously. What disturbed the
governor and chief secretary was the sudden hostility toward
a system which had been regarded as relatively tolerable (with
the exception of the tax strikes in 1931) during most of the
decade. Even Provincial Commissioner Kitching, in his Annual
Report of 1934, wrote that "the Makonde Native administra-
tions are not autocracies and their development as units of
local self-government is not noticeably rapid but they perform
their simple duties with reasonable efficiency and to the satisfaction of the people they represent and of the officers." The
reports for preceding years as well as for 1935 were equally
calm in their assessment of the wakulungwa.

There were two other aspects of the plan to alter the form of
local government that disturbed officials in Dar es Salaam. The
first was the constant reference to the possible restoration of
the akida system. Kitching went so far as to invite back to Lindi
an officer who had served in the area during the military period,
who wrote:

> It is twenty years since I safari-ed on foot, in the Makonde
> country, and since my arrival here, I have been able to do
> so again. . . . I consider 60% [of the wakulungwa] are up
> to the old Jumbe standard of 1918. The balance would not
> have been tolerated in any circumstances.[38]

For those who had been steeped in the mystique of Indirect
Rule, the return to the akida system would have constituted a
psychological defeat. Moreover, it was regarded as retrogressive
politically since it would exclude the people from participating
in the selection of their own leaders and would also create a
new cadre of disgruntled former officeholders.

Equally obnoxious to the governor were the frequent references to Islam and the assumption that the new system of local
rule should be based upon Islamic principles. Taking into account that the coast people were overwhelmingly Muslim,
Kitching and his staff were insisting that Islam had made the
Makonde appreciate a hierarchical structure of authority and
therefore what the people and the wakulungwa needed was a
"superior Native Authority to whom they can look up, rather

38. E. A. Leakey, quoted in *ibid.*

than a Council of themselves." [39] The new officials were to be selected for their competence in Islamic law and custom. These arguments in favor of Islam did not register at all well with the new governor, Sir Harold MacMichael. It was, after all, Sir Harold who, as civil secretary of the Sudan government, had been responsible for carrying out the systematic policy of insulating the non-Christian Negro population of the southern Sudan from the "corrupting" influence of Arabs and Islam.[40]

The insistence on the part of the officers in the south that the situation had become intolerable, plus the reluctance of the chief secretary and governor to act hastily created an embarrassing impasse which lasted until March 3, 1937, when the provincial commissioner met the governor and the chief secretary, Mr. G. F. Sayre, in Dar es Salaam. After prolonged discussion it was agreed that the wakulungwa system should remain in force for the time being. Gradually, however, a cadre of appointed officials — designated liwalis rather than akidas — would be selected from among local men of talent to replace the wakulungwa. Throughout the conference it was stressed that the experiment should proceed slowly, with changes taking place in successive stages. The changeover, furthermore, was to be tried in Mikindani District before being attempted in the remaining areas. It was felt that a more gradual approach would ensure that the liwali system would have a greater measure of permanence. It would, moreover, as Sir Harold MacMichael explained,

> meet with less opposition and apathy if it is done after explanation and consultation with the elders who carry some weight in local councils and in such a way as to meet their wishes so far as they can be lured into elucidation and are not repugnant to governmental policy.[41]

Once more the administrative flexibility which geographic isolation provided officials in the south became apparent.

39. Mikindani District Book.

40. See Robert O. Collins, "The Sudan: Link to the North," in *The Transformation of East Africa*, ed. Stanley Diamond and Fred G. Burke (New York: Basic Books, 1966), pp. 377–85.

41. "Minutes of Conference on Native Administration in the Coastal Areas, March 3, 1937" (TNA 12800/II).

Shortly after his return to the Southern Province, the provincial commissioner convened a baraza of headmen, elders, and notables at Mikindani. There, on March 31, 1937, he explained to the assembled that the Native Authority system had failed. So impressed was Kitching with the enthusiastic response of the gathering that he decided not to delay the next stage until this lesson had had a chance to sink in. Instead, he moved immediately to an explanation of the proposed liwali system and asked for nominations of good men for the posts![42] Events, moreover, "forced" the administrators in Lindi District to move with equal haste in abandoning the mkulungwa system without waiting to secure the results of the experiment in Mikindani District. It was claimed that the news of change in Mikindani had led the people to assume that the wakulungwa were being deposed everywhere, and the people decided to withhold their tax payments until the new liwalis were appointed. In two areas of Lindi, moreover, the elders decided on their own to depose two wakulungwa and appoint a liwali in their stead.[43] By early 1938 the provincial commissioner had nominated liwalis for Lindi District to forestall a complete breakdown of administration. The officials in Dar es Salaam, however, were apparently annoyed by the rapid turn of events, and they withheld the formal order establishing the liwali system in Lindi until February 17, 1941. By that time, however, the system was an accomplished fact.

## Reprieve in Newala

Indirect Rule in Newala was given a reprieve at the time of its abandonment in the two other Makonde districts. That it was spared there was perhaps attributable to personalities as much as to any other single factor. The first of these personalities was the district commissioner, J. W. Large, who

42. A. E. Kitching to Chief Secretary, September 6, 1937, regarding "Reorganization of Native Administration in Mikindani District" (TNA, vol. 21, 26752).
43. E. K. Lumley to Provincial Commissioner of Lindi, October 31, 1937 (TNA 12800/II).

had been in charge of the district (with the exception of home leaves) from December, 1927, to July, 1936. This long tenure stood in sharp contrast to Mikindani District for the same period, where there were no less than six changes of administrative officers, and Lindi District, where the record was comparable. Mr. Large was a man of varied and intense interests, and Sir Donald Cameron had commented that the District Book in Newala was one of the most remarkable collections of information about native law and custom, agriculture, ornithology, linguistics, and other subjects available anywhere in colonial Tanganyika. Although weaker men found that the lack of developed communications and recreational outlets managed to bring out their worst talents, Mr. Large seemed to find this a challenge. He turned his entire attention to the district, over which he could preside like a benevolent potentate. If he was an autocrat, he appeared to be a beloved one. In my standard questions on African attitudes toward non-Makonde in the district, the older men invariably singled out Mr. Large as a European whom the Makonde respected. "He knew our customs and respected them"; "he knew when to speak and when to listen." If the inability of district officers to supervise each and every mkulungwa in Lindi and Mikindani was one of the causes for the failure of Indirect Rule there, J. W. Large certainly did all within his capacity to avoid that situation in Newala. He was an inveterate cutter of trails, and many of the present roads in the district were personally traced by Large in an effort to bring every chirambo into contact with the boma, or district headquarters.

At the time that district officers in Lindi and Mikindani were writing scathing denunciations of the wakulungwa and the artificial traditions they represented, the impact of J. W. Large's close administration was recognized by his successor in Newala:

> To summarize the results of ten years of indirect rule—
> On the whole the system is working well. Where it fails the failure is due principally to an attempt to force upon the people laws which they do not understand and for which they are not yet ready. Where the authority of an Mkulunga appears to be weak it is almost invariably due to the

fact that the people . . . no longer accept him or to the fact
that he has been placed in authority by virtue of his family
right to succeed . . . and not by virtue of his ability to
lead.[44]

The second personality factor which set Newala apart from
the two coastal districts related to the office of *mkulungwa
mkuu,* or council president. There was obviously no traditional
basis for the office of "paramount" chief other than the fact
that the Yao chiefs Matola I and Matola II had exercised a
generalized jurisdiction over a number of Makonde virambo in
the pre-German period. The functions of the office of mku-
lunga mkuu, moreover, were much broader than those of the
Yao overlords. The position, nevertheless, was apparently
widely accepted both by the people and by the wakulungwa of
Newala District. Unlike the experience elsewhere, the wakulungwa of Newala took the advice of the European district
commissioner and accepted one of the more forceful wakulungwa as their council president. Nangololo Chepepwa, the
first mkulungwa mkuu, had had considerable experience in
government under both the Germans and the British. In the
German period he had served as an *mziri,* or adviser, who
had the responsibility of keeping the akidas and the German
administrators informed regarding the wishes and sentiments
of the Makonde people. Although he had gone into official retirement during the early phases of British rule, he continued
to exercise considerable influence in his chirambo. When the
British dismissed the Yao akidas, Nangololo was named mkulungwa of Mtopwa chirambo near Kitangari. In 1928 he was
elected mkulungwa mkuu for Newala District.

To emphasize the point that the mkulungwa mkuu was not
simply *primus inter pares,* a successor was chosen in his chirambo as mkulungwa when Nangololo assumed his new office.
Furthermore, his duties were continuous with respect to the
entire district, whereas the individual wakulungwa only concerned themselves with the district as a whole during the quarterly meetings of the Makonde Council of Newala. Nangololo
Chepepwa took his work seriously and had the full support of
J. W. Large in chastising wakulungwa who were derelict in

44. Newala District, *Annual Report, 1938.*

collecting taxes as well as in his supervision of the work of the area courts. One of his major successes—and one which relieved the European officer of a great burden—was his skillful handling of boundary disputes. The mkulungwa mkuu also proved to be a much more effective salesman of European ideas of government than any European officer could possibly have been. To underscore the genuine delegation of responsibility to the mkulungwa mkuu, the headquarters of the Native Authority was at Mahuta, some twelve miles distant from the district headquarters at Newala. Although this did not mean that the district commissioner isolated himself from direct contact with the people or the other wakulungwa, it did indicate a desire on the part of the British officer to have all contentious matters channeled through the mkulungwa mkuu first.

The very significant role which personalities played in the success of the Native Authority system in Newala became increasingly obvious after J. W. Large left the district in 1936, followed a year later by the death of Nangololo Chepepwa. The succeeding mkulungwa mkuu, Rashidi Mtalika, was regarded as a strong personality and one whose prior experience rivaled that of Nangololo. He had received rudimentary education under the German administration and had served as an efficient and popular jumbe. Indeed, it was his education and popularity that convinced the British officer in charge of the district to retain his services. At the introduction of the Native Authority system, Rashidi's credentials as an mkulungwa were impressive. Indeed, his maternal grandfather had been one of the earliest family heads to cross over from Mozambique and settle on the southern edge of the Makonde plateau near Makote. His father, moreover, had been one of the early *mwenye* of Mkunya, a short distance from Makote. Although the latter fact should not have influenced his claims to office under a matrilineal system of succession, he was nevertheless first appointed mkulungwa of Mkunya, where he served several years before "inheriting" the more legitimate title of mkulungwa of Makote. That Rashidi Mtalika was a man of considerable talent was beyond dispute as far as I am concerned. When I interviewed him at Mkunya in 1956, he was over sixty years of age and yet was more alert and quick-witted than most men ten or twenty years his junior.

Rashidi Mtalika's misfortune was to follow Nangololo in office. The other wakulungwa, having grown restive under the strong hand of the first mkulungwa mkuu and recognizing that the same close bonds of mutual trust did not exist between Rashidi and the new district commissioner, began to engage in intrigue. Soon complaints began to drift into the district headquarters that Rashidi Mtalika was favoring the people from his own area in making appointments to clerkships and other offices. He was plagued, moreover, by the reopening of many of the boundary disputes which had been settled by Nangololo. Intrigue was the order of the day. Privately, the word was spread that Rashidi Mtalika was not even a Makonde but was in fact a Matambwe. The undermining of popular confidence was matched by an apparent indication of loss of confidence on the part of the British administration symbolized by the removal of the Native Authority headquarters from Mahuta to Newala. It was obvious that J. W. Large's successors wanted to be more closely involved in the operation of local government. From a career standpoint, this might have been understandable; from the point of view of encouraging local initiative and responsibility, it was a disaster. The breakdown in confidence was obvious, five years after Large's departure, in the comments of one of his successors, J. W. T. Allen:

> It has been a bad year of poor harvests and poor tax collection and it has been made increasingly clear that this is an area of inadequately staffed direct rule disguised as indirect rule by a meaningless congeries of futile old men called native authorities. There is little hope of progress until they are removed and a workable form of local government replaces them.[45]

In 1967, J. W. T. Allen commented to me that he had been criticized by the provincial commissioner for his flippancy in describing the dilemma he faced in working with the wakulungwa. He had suggested that the idea of introducing modern ideas of local government through an archaic system of hereditary rulers was analogous to wondering "how the city planner of a Tudor town would have designed his petrol station!"

By 1942 Dar es Salaam was no longer able to resist the com-

45. Newala District, *Annual Report,* 1941.

plaints of officers in the Southern Province regarding the last vestiges of the Native Authority system in the Makonde area. Accordingly, the liwali system was introduced in Newala along the lines previously established in Lindi and Mikindani. Despite the contempt which European officials displayed toward the wakulungwa at that time, it was apparent that the system of Indirect Rule had a more profound impact upon the development of local politics in Newala than it had had in other districts. Of particular importance was the establishment of the office of mkulungwa mkuu, which contributed greatly to a sense of supertribalism on the part of the Newala Makonde. For the modernists and traditionalists alike, Nangololo—and, to a lesser extent, Rashidi Mtalika—stood as a proud symbol. For the modernists, he was a symbol of unified action, which suggested that the Makonde might achieve the same sort of lofty status as the Chagga, Nyakyusa, Hehe, and others who had acquired paramount chiefs. In the minds of the modernists, political unity was a major factor in the educational, economic, and social success of the latter tribes. To the traditionalists, the period of the mkulungwa mkuu was regarded as a sort of golden age, when leaders were selected on the basis of hereditary qualifications rather than on the basis of education and experience alone.

Thus, the experiment in the misapplication of the principles of Indirect Rule to the Makonde political system was ended a decade and a half after its introduction. Given the conditions of the traditional Makonde polity, its failure was perhaps inevitable. The only area in which at least the spirit of Indirect Rule was observed was Newala District during the long administration of J. W. Large. Eventually, even there, however, as in the coastal areas during the entire experiment with the Native Authority system, the "intervention syndrome" was one of the significant factors in the ultimate demise of the rule by wakulungwa. Given the demands of a colonial civil service which recognized those officers who accomplished things, it was difficult for young officers to exercise self-restraint. One was not rewarded for simply standing back and letting the Africans govern or misgovern themselves.

# 6:
# The Forces
# of Innovation

The emphasis thus far has been upon the overt manipulation of the Makonde political system by a series of British and—to a lesser extent—Arab and German administrators. In many respects, however, the changes in the political system which were to be of long-range significance were initiated by external agents of innovation who were only tangentially concerned with the alteration of the political values and structures of traditional Makonde society. Even those who were concerned with a frontal assault on the political system, moreover, often failed to perceive that the unintended (and frequently undesired) consequences of their actions were more significant than the actions themselves in altering the character of the political system. Hence, the performance of the district commissioners and other colonial officers, as well as their attitudes and aspirations, have to be examined from a broader standpoint than their immediate relevance in the carrying-out of official policies.

The focus of this chapter is upon the contribution which various external agents and externally relevant events were making in the alteration of traditional society. The near-monopoly that the Christian missionary, the Asian merchant, or the European administrator enjoyed with respect to the introduction of ideas related to modernization left little room for maneuvering on the part of domestic innovators. The major exception to this was the Muslim *mwalim* (teacher), but even he for the most part was substituting one form of traditional society for another. Indeed, it was the absence of positive encouragement to domestic innovators that was to provide one of the most serious problems in getting the Makonde to accept the notions of modernization as being relevant to their situation. External pressures may initiate change; but if the change is to be creatively sustained within the society rather than accepted in robot-fashion, one must create a pool of domestic talent which is committed to the idea of constant change being a virtue rather than something that must be tolerated to please a bothersome cadre of external innovators.

There were a number of stresses and strains which were only coming into sharp focus at the time of the Second World War, even though the pressures were there long before the ill-fated experiment in Indirect Rule. For convenience of analysis, the activities of several of the agents of innovation will be examined both in terms of their present-day significance and in terms of their relevance to the developing struggle for Tanganyikan independence.

## THE RELIGIOUS AGENTS OF CHANGE

The earliest of the external agents of change had been operating in the Makonde area long before the arrival of the European administrators and even before the writ of the Sultan of Zanzibar and Oman was more than a feeble whisper in the areas beyond the coast. I refer, of course, to the Arab traders, who during the greater part of the nineteenth century had contributed to the gradual change of traditional Makonde institutions and values. The most direct and intended impact of change was in the sphere of economic transactions. The quest for slaves, ivory, gold, and other forms of wealth had, by the nineteenth century, brought about the establishment of regular caravan routes between Central Africa and the southern coast of Tanganyika. Although most of the early trading was on a barter basis, with cloth, guns, and small manufactured items being brought to the mainland by the Zanzibari, the notion of an exchange economy gradually took root among the Makonde during the Arab period. It was the Arabs, too, who stimulated the gathering of rubber, gum copal, and other products and the planting of mango and coconuts, which became elements of legitimate trade when the institution of slavery was under attack. Hence, at least one of the germs of modernization – the acceptance of an exchange economy – was planted decades before the Germans arrived on the scene.

Less intentionally, the Arab trader contributed to the alteration of the religious belief system of the Makonde and thereby also affected the range of social and political institutions supported by religion. As noted previously, the early Arab traders were not interested in converting the Makonde to Islam. It may have been, as Livingstone's informant suggested to him, that the Makonde were not considered good material for conversion, since it was felt that

> [they] know nothing of a Deity, they pray to their mothers when in distress or dying, know nothing of a future state, nor have they any religion except a belief in medicine; and every headman is a doctor. No Arab has ever tried to convert them, but occasionally a slave taken to the Coast has been circumcised in order to be clean; some of them pray and say they know not the ordeal or *muavi* (witchcraft).[1]

More likely, since the tenets of Islam forbid the enslaving of fellow Muslims, the Arab traders appreciated that conversion would deprive them of a source of slaves. This situation was apparently realized by Yao and other middlemen who embraced Islam in order to avoid becoming the merchandise of those with whom they did business. Furthermore, Yao leaders like Machemba – particularly after the allegedly major role the Sultan of Zanzibar played in stopping the Ngoni raiders at the Makonde plateau in 1878 – accepted Islam as a device for shoring up their tenuous control over the Makonde and Makua. Ironically, following the suppression of the slave trade, the German and early British administrators were themselves instrumental in the spread of Islam in that they imposed

---

1. *Last Journals of David Livingstone in Central Africa from 1865 to his Death* (London: John Murray, 1874), pp. 24–28.

Muslim rulers upon the predominantly non-Muslim Makonde. Just as the British-imposed peace in Northern Nigeria provided an umbrella for Muslim expansion, colonial rule on the Makonde plateau permitted and even encouraged the Muslim traders and holy men to penetrate areas previously barred to them. The suppression of the slave trade removed a major objection on the part of the Arab or Arabized elite to active conversion, and indeed the German-appointed akidas and jumbes found it advantageous to increase the ranks of co-religionists in order to buttress their position vis-à-vis both the German administrators and the Makonde masses.

In the developing competition for Makonde souls, the Muslim proselytizer enjoyed many advantages over his Christian counterpart. First of all, the mwalim was usually regarded as an African. That is, he was a Makonde or Makua, or he was the son of an Arab father and a Makonde mother. In the latter case he enjoyed the best of two possible worlds and could enjoy the property inheritance and religion of his father and the protection, companionship, and land rights of his mother's brothers. By contrast, the agents of Christianity were usually Europeans or alien Africans — Nyasa, Makua, and other Africans who had in most instances been rescued from Arab slavers and educated at mission villages. If the African deacon or pastor had been born a Makonde, he was not permitted the luxury of sliding freely between two social systems. He was expected by his European mentors not only to alter his own relations with his kin but also to urge new converts to reduce their family obligations to monogamous nuclear groupings in which the fathers bore primary responsibility for the rearing of their biological offspring.

Unlike his Christian counterpart, moreover, the mwalim was not a hard taskmaster. A simple expression of belief, supported perhaps by some rudimentary exposure to the Koran, was usually all that was expected of the Muslim convert in order to be accepted as a full member of the faithful. Although the mwalim might admonish those who failed regularly to pray, to fast, or to observe the other obligations of the Islamic community, he would seldom dare resort to the extreme step of excommunication. The Muslim moral restraints upon the acquisition of more than four wives, consumption of alcohol, and other practices were frequently ignored even by those who claimed to be leaders of the Islamic group. As Livingstone noted, the Muslims he encountered at Mikindani "begged brandy and laughed when they remarked that they could drink it in secret, but not openly."[2] So permissive was the system that many Makonde were prepared to conceal their religious affiliation and even change the names of their children in order to have them admitted to mission schools. By contrast, the Makonde convert to Christianity found himself required to undergo a long and hard course of catechism—often in association with an even longer course of general education taken in isolation from his non-Christian relatives—before he could be accepted as a member in full standing of the Anglican or Roman Catholic fold. Once admitted, moreover, he found himself subject to a hierarchy of taskmasters who demanded that his life be exemplary or that he pay the penalty for his transgression in terms of confession, penance, and—in extreme cases—excommunication.

Despite the many advantages which Islam enjoyed vis-à-vis Christianity in winning converts, Islam remained largely a conservative force. The more innovative Muslim impact did not really take place until after the Second World War when the Aga Khan Community began to expand its commercial, educational, and charitable activities in the Southern Province. The impact, however, was limited largely to the coast and to the Asian community, even though Africans of whatever creed reaped some of the benefits of this activity. A number of Christian Makonde switched allegiance to the Ismaili sect as an overt sign of rejection of European colonial rule and all that was associated with it. The majority of the Makonde Muslims, however, belonged to the more conservative Sunni and Shiite sects.[3]

While Islam was conservative in its philosophy, it gradually became a factor of political consequence if for no other reason

2. He did, however, pay them the backhanded compliment of noting that "they have not, however, introduced it as an article of trade, as we Christians have done on the west coast" (*ibid.*, pp. 16–17).

3. For a discussion of the Ismaili sect, see H. S. Morris, "The Divine Kingship of the Aga Khan: A Study of Theocracy in East Africa," *Southwestern Journal of Anthropology*, XIV (1958), 454–72.

than that it was occasionally a source of conflict within Makonde society. At times the dissension within the ranks of the faithful was the most noticeable form of disruption. In Lindi District during 1934, for example, a dispute broke out between the more conservative and elderly sheiks and the younger followers of a highly educated and influential sheik who had advocated innovations in connection with the observance of the ceremony of *Zikri*.[4] The conflict over religious observances quickly became a vehicle for the airing of a wide range of grievances and for the sharpening of factional lines within the entire Muslim community of Makonde, Arabs, and persons of mixed ancestry. Ultimately the Kadi of Tanga was brought in as an arbitrator and the conflict was resolved without violence.

It was only in the postwar period that Muslim-Christian antagonism became overt. By the early 1950s Makonde Muslims had started their campaign to have the government provide support to Koranic schools to balance the subsidization provided to the missions, insisting that only in this way could Muslim children get an education without being the victims of Christian proselytizing. Although the colonial government was reluctant to support additional religious schools at a time when a more secular school system was being introduced, some concessions were made. The mission schools, for example, agreed that Muslim teachers in Newala could come to the Roman Catholic or Anglican (the Universities Mission to Central Africa, or UMCA) schools to tend to the spiritual needs of their flock. The mission authorities, moreover, were required to give a public accounting of the method whereby children were advanced from the primary to the middle and secondary schools in order to refute the charges of religious bias.

## The Special Impact of Christian Missionaries

The enormity of the task faced by Christian missionaries in winning converts among the Makonde was apparent to even the casual visitor to the area. As late as 1934,

4. Lindi Province, *Annual Report*, 1934 (TNA 11679). *Zikri*, or *dhikri*, is the Muslim ceremony in which one commemorates God by the repetition of

Mikindani was still the only district in the Trust Territory where missionary efforts had met with complete failure. In that year the first mission stations were established by Anglican priests of the UMCA at Mchuchu and by the Roman Catholic Benedictine Fathers at Nanyamba. Two decades later, the struggling priests were probably prepared to agree with the assessment of the local district commissioner, who stated to me that there was "little room for Christianity at present except among employed labour." Even in the Newala District, where Anglican and Roman Catholic efforts had a history going back to the last quarter of the nineteenth century, the most generous estimate was that no more than 10 per cent of the Makonde of the plateau were Christians.[5] Even this moderate success was attributed to the fact that the diocesan headquarters were in neighboring Masasi District. The Roman Catholic youths educated at Kitangari primary school could go on to secondary school at Ndanda, just as the children from Newala township went on to St. Joseph's College at Chidya, the UMCA secondary school in Masasi. The missionizing efforts of Anglicans and Roman Catholics in Lindi District were not much more successful than those in Mikindani despite the longer history of mission activity around Lindi township. Attempts in the Makonde area by other religious groups, such as the Seventh Day Adventists, who launched a mission along the Ruvuma River in Mikindani District in 1953, were ultimately frustrated either by the malaria which felled the missionaries or by the stonelike resistance of Muslim Makonde to conversion efforts.

Despite the paucity of its membership, the Makonde Christian minority was to have an influence far out of proportion to its numbers not only in the last days of colonial rule but also in the post-independence period. It was the Christian minority which enjoyed almost a complete monopoly of the single most

---

his name and attributes, coordinated with breathing and physical movements. It has both an individual and a collective form.

5. The first Newala mission was below the escarpment in the present-day Masasi District. It was moved to its present location in the 1880s following the last of the Ngoni raids. See *Journals and Papers of Chauncy Maples* (London: Longmans, Green, 1899), pp. 67 ff.

important requisite for modernization—a Western-type education. A literate education was essential to the establishment of
a rational, impersonal system of government and to the introduction of modern programs in the fields of health, welfare,
economic improvement, and the conservation of scarce resources. Some indication of the mission monopoly is revealed
in the figures on Christian and secular schools in Newala
during the colonial period. In 1926, at a time when there were
34 UMCA and 2 Roman Catholic "bush" and primary schools
in the district, there were no government schools at all. By 1955
the recognized primary schools consisted of 25 UMCA and 16
Roman Catholic institutions, while the government primary
schools numbered only 4. At the middle-school level the government effort in 1955 consisted of only 1 institution as opposed
to 3 UMCA and 1 Roman Catholic schools. The advantage
which Newala District in particular enjoyed over the other two
Makonde regions at the commencement of the independence
struggle is revealed in the primary-school enrollment figures
for the year 1951. At that time there were 746 children in
schools in Mikindani, 2,303 in Lindi, and 4,378 in Newala.
Although a policy of forced equalization of school facilities in
the region was conducted during the last days of colonial rule
and in the present period as well, the Makonde of Newala enjoyed an initial advantage which was to have a lasting effect
upon the kind of contribution they were to make not only
within their own district but throughout the Makonde area and
to the nation as a whole.[6] Certainly the mission effort was a
much more substantial one than that undertaken by the British government, despite the fact that district officers would
complain from time to time that the mission education was
totally impractical in that it emphasized mere literacy in the
Bible, catered only to the Christian minority, failed to attract
any female students, and found it difficult to sustain interest
in students who were enrolled. One of the Lindi officers who

6. The number of primary schools in Newala leveled off at 51 in 1957, whereas
the number of schools had risen to 46 in Lindi and to 23 in Mtwara (Mikindani).
Similarly, the enrollments in primary school between 1951 and 1956 had increased by 28 per cent in Newala (from 4,378 to 5,631), by 161 per cent in Lindi
(from 2,302 to 6,002), and by 313 per cent in Mtwara (from 746 to 3,077). See
Southern Province, *Annual Reports*, 1951–57.

complained in this fashion reported at the same time that the one government school at Lindi was closed in 1926 "due to a complete lack of support on the part of the people."[7]

Although the motivation of the Christian missionaries and educators was primarily religious conversion, the mission effort had an impact upon the entire social, economic, and political fabric of traditional Makonde society. In the political realm, it was the missions that were to provide both the colonial and nationalist regimes with the pool of manpower necessary to the introduction of a modern system of government; and the educational system provided by the missions did permit the Makonde youth to acquire a more scientific view of the world, which conflicted with the magico-religious bases of traditional political authority. The youth, moreover, who would be acquiring the new symbols of success and high status in the modernized sector would no longer show the same deference to the wakulungwa and village elders.

The transformation of traditional economic values and structures was also a by-product of the mission effort. Stemming from the early period when the Africans who had been rescued or purchased from the Arab and Yao slave-traders had to be provided with the means of economic survival, the missionaries were as effective as any other agent in the introduction of a cash economy. The needs of the missionaries to build schools, churches, and houses also demanded the creation of a pool of talent in the fields of carpentry, masonry, and other arts. One no longer had to be a cultivator in order to survive in Makonde society. The extent to which this occupational revolution had taken hold is evidenced in a survey I conducted on occupational preferences among boys who had completed Standard VIII education at the UMCA school in Newala in 1955. Only 1 of the 23 boys questioned was interested in agriculture, and in this case he was not interested in the traditional role of cultivator but rather in the tenant-farming scheme being conducted at Nachingwea, the site of the ill-fated Groundnut Scheme. The remaining 22 listed their job preferences as follows:

| Teacher | 5 | East African Navy | 1 |
| Rural medical aide, | 8 | Stock breeder | 1 |

7. *Annual Report,* 1926.

| male nurse | 8 | Mechanic | 1 |
| Policeman | 3 | Government clerk | 1 |
| Postal worker | 1 | Agricultural instructor | 1 |

The nonproselytizing efforts of the missionaries also contributed to altered views of what a Makonde should expect from his society in terms of dealing with the problems of poverty, disease, and malnutrition. In the process, these new expectations undermined the leadership of those persons in traditional society whose authority was based upon the practice of medicine. As is true of the field of education, the missionary medical effort even today surpasses the impact which government clinics and hospitals have been making upon health and sanitation in the Makonde districts. In Newala District in 1931, for example, the UMCA treated 21,251 cases of illness as opposed to 9,165 treated at the government or Native Authority facilities. By 1957 the missions, both Anglican and Catholic, were treating 147,000 cases annually while the government was treating 53,000. By contrast, in Mikindani, where the mission effort had been frustrated, the problems of securing adequate medical services for the Makonde were extremely acute.

It was in the area of social relationships, however, that Christianity was to make its most significant long-range impact upon traditional Makonde society. Reference has already been made to the impact that the Christian-organized family made upon the Makonde extended family, which was based upon matrilineal descent. There were also problems which the lessons of school and chapel posed to traditional social structures. In one instance, at least, the Anglican mission in Newala attempted to support the traditional position of the elders in their communities by inviting respected elders into the schools from time to time to discuss tribal customs and tribal history. Equally significant was the fact that both the Anglican and the Roman Catholic missionaries in the Southern Province attempted to soften the impact of the Christian experience by modifying the jando ceremonies and integrating the form of the traditional initiation rites with the Christian catechism. By 1935 the "Christianized" jando had become standard procedure in all stations in the Masasi Diocese of the UMCA, and a similar experiment was taking hold in the Roman Catholic Diocese of Ndanda. The modified version of the jando was held every two years instead of annually and was devoid of explicit sexual instruction, the "hazing" of the initiates, and the use of masked medicine men to frighten the youngsters. Instead, the instructors, who were usually the parish priests, mission teachers, and respected elders, concentrated upon religion, ethics for young people, and Christian morality. Attention was also paid to those elements of custom and tradition which were felt to be in accord with Christian principles, and neither mission was so strait-laced that it could object to the parents having their usual ngoma, or dances, following the release of the children from the jando.[8]

The impact of the Christianized jando was occasionally nullified by the parents taking the added precaution of sending their children to the traditional bush school once they had completed the Christian ceremonies. On balance, however, the experiment tended to disrupt the traditional social order, for it drove a sharper wedge between the Makonde convert and his fellows—especially in the case of the Muslims. Here again, this was only partially offset by the fact that several Muslim parents had encouraged their children to go through the Christian jando if they were enrolled in mission primary schools because, as one elder related to me,

> The fees are less than those charged in our village, and the children are only taken away from their duties for one month. The mission Fathers do not play pranks on the boys, such as putting bad medicine in their food, which makes them ill. Also, the priests do not permit the boys to use bad language or to forget to have respect for their mothers and their elders.

The influence which Christianity had upon the social role of women in Makonde society was slower to be realized than in the case of other types of social change. While it is true that both the Roman Catholic and the High Church Anglican com-

---

8. For a fuller discussion of the UMCA experiment, see Lyndon Harries, "The Initiation Rites of the Makonde Tribe," *Rhodes-Livingstone Institute Communications*, no. 3 (1944); and Denys W. T. Shropshire, *The Church and Primitive Peoples* (New York: Macmillan, 1938). The Roman Catholic experiment is described in A. M. Hokororo, "The Influence of the Church on Tribal Customs at Lukuledi," *TNR*, no. 54 (March, 1960), pp. 1–13.

munions placed a great emphasis upon the Virgin Mary and the importance of women in the Christian family, this did not lead to an automatic change in the general social role of the female members of society. Certainly the emancipation of women has not been characteristic of Latin America or of other countries where the Roman Catholic Church is dominant. The "Christianizing" of the Makonde ceremonies which were observed after a woman had given birth to her first child tended, like the Christian experiments with the jando, to ease the transition from traditional to modern society rather than to bring about a dramatic revolution. The educational effort, moreover, tended to concentrate almost exclusively upon boys until the last decade of colonial rule. Even following a concerted effort to enroll girls, the boys enrolled in schools in Newala and Lindi in 1957 outnumbered the girls by more than two to one, and in Mtwara (Mikindani) by more than three to one.

Christianity, nevertheless, was contributing to a change in status of Makonde women. The establishment of women's clubs was exposing young adults to new techniques in child care, homemaking, and crafts. The mission training programs had provided Makonde girls with new social roles as nuns, teachers, nurses, and other positions in the fields of health, education, and welfare. In villages where wakulungwa and other elders appreciated the goals of modernization, women were being permitted a voice in community affairs. However, it was also charged by some of the older people interviewed in the Makonde area in 1956 that Christianity was contributing to the corruption of women by loosening ties with their families and by undermining the traditional wifely duties. The Muslims and the traditionalists were incensed by the Native Authority Ordinance adopted in 1953, which required that "marriage shall have been agreed to by both parties to the marriage and that the woman freely consents to her marriage." They were also disturbed by the pressures of the Christian community to constantly raise the minimum age limit for marriage of young girls. Christianity, however, could not take all the praise or blame for the liberation of woman. One of the most vigorous complaints raised about the wayward ways of young women who refused marriage or abandoned their husbands came in Mikindani in 1929—a full five years before the first mission station had been established in that district.[9]

To the solitary European colonial administrator, the bickering within the ranks of the Christian community must have been a "heavy cross to bear." The comments of the district commissioner of Newala in 1933 had echoes throughout the colonial period as he complained:

> It is a pity that the Roman Catholic mission refuses unequivocally to come to any arrangement with the UMCA regarding spheres of activity. There results an overlapping and, to a layman, a waste of time and effort. However, there are no sufficiently strong reasons for refusing applications for any schools even when enroachment is obvious, and nothing can apparently be done to fix any boundary line between the two mission areas.[10]

On balance, however, the activities of the missionaries generated attitudes, created tools and skills, and developed organizational talents needed by the colonial administrator in the successful accomplishment of his tasks. Although Makonde society conceivably may have developed along these lines in response to internal dynamism, it must nevertheless be recognized that the Christian missionaries accelerated the transformation of Makonde society with respect to the notions of individualism, the idea of a market economy, the acceptance of scientific explanations of natural phenomena, and other aspects of modernization.

## THE EUROPEAN ADMINISTRATOR

The significance of the European administrator as the overseer of political, social, and economic change was only gradually realized by the Makonde cultivator. In the German period the commandant was a figure quite remote from the day-to-day affairs of the Makonde outside the coastal towns of Lindi and Mikindani, where the administrative and military staff was concentrated. As was noted previously, the Makonde

9. Lindi Province, *Annual Report*, 1929 (TNA 11679).
10. Newala District, *Annual Report*, 1933.

region was not regarded as economically attractive nor were the people of the hinterland particularly in need of "pacification." When Weule visited Newala in 1907, the district was under the authority of a single European administrator who had at his disposal a dozen or so African askaris, or soldiers.[11] The situation was not radically altered when the British displaced the Germans during the First World War, even though a few additional administrative officers had to be posted to the area to assist in the collection of taxes during the late 1920s and early 1930s. When technical officers in the fields of health, agriculture, and education were posted to the Southern Province, they invariably had responsibility for four or five districts and thus did not constitute an overwhelmingly visible European presence. Although Lindi and Mikindani were better staffed, for most purposes Newala was a one-man administrative post from the end of the First World War to the end of the Second World War. Indeed, there was even a stretch of six months in 1924 when the station was without the services of any European official.[12]

Aside from the members of his family, there were few other Europeans to provide companionship to district officers in remote stations of the Southern Province. Most of the non-official Europeans were missionaries, and their moral posture—as well as the interests they pursued that brought them into conflict with the administration—made them poor drinking partners indeed. Similarly, the controversies over labor-recruitment methods and other economic policies limited the kind of convivial relationship the British administrator could establish with sisal estate owners and other European entrepreneurs. Particularly diffident during the period between the two wars were the German settlers, who had begun to trickle back to East Africa after the diplomatic *rapprochement* between Britain and Germany. This group was regarded with increased suspicion after the rise of Hitler and the reassertion of German colonial claims to East Africa.

In view of the foregoing, it is not surprising that one of

11. K. Weule, *Native Life in East Africa*, trans. Alice Werner (London: Pitman, 1909), pp. 107 ff, 352 ff.

12. Lindi Province, *Annual Report*, 1924 (TNA 1733/15/94).

Governor Sir Donald Cameron's officers reported in 1929 that

> The Province feels rather neglected and out in the cold; in fact I overheard it referred to as "the penitentiary," which is a great pity, but there are certainly fewer of the ordinary amenities of life than in most other provinces.[13]

Sometimes the enormity of the responsibility of being His Majesty's Government in Newala, Lindi, or Mikindani was more than the overworked and isolated district administrator could take. Although I never saw this substantiated by actual figures, it was firmly believed by local administrators that the record of physical and even mental exhaustion among officials in the Southern Province was considerably higher than the territorial average. A district commissioner had to be, at one extreme, the supreme legislator, executive, and judge for over a hundred thousand charges, while at the same time he would have to descend to the menial tasks of selling postage stamps, exchanging rat-eaten shilling notes for new ones, and instructing Makonde in the art of digging latrines. The abstract of one Newala district commissioner's safari diary in 1936 reveals the range of problems with which he had to deal during a four-day meeting with Native Authorities:

1. *Tax collection* — that cloth could be seized as evidence that defaulter could pay;

2. *Tax assistants* — more able headmen objected to the council paying high wages to tax assistants since many do without any help;

3. *Headmen* — request that their salaries be increased;

4. *Court elders* — wanted their fees increased;

5. *Ruvuma Ferries* — complaint that fares are too high considering subsidies to operators;

6. *Duties of present generation to posterity* —
   (a) preserve timber, water supplies;
   (b) educate people — help build schools, be "polite in dealings with missions" — "no headman may reasonably object to a village elder having a school — no person may interfere with a religious instructor if he conducts himself becomingly";
   (c) protect children against contagious diseases, and strictly obey leprosy regulations;

13. Safari notes of P. E. Mitchell to Cameron, August 23, 1929 (TNA 13538).

7. *Increase local wealth* — only through increased cultivation will district have money for new services;

8. *Successful Native Administration requires* —
    (a) sound finance — taxes collected on time and balance expenditures properly because any deficit "will hit headmen first!" —
    (b) strong, but just executive — don't be afraid to govern and avoid parochialism and conflict with neighbors;
    (c) impartial and speedy justice — must make decisions in court — no others are binding.

9. *Review the new rules and ordinances enacted in 1935.*[14]

One can't ignore the fact that the presence of European administrators in the Makonde area between the two wars was perhaps the single most important element in bringing about what development did take place in road construction, sanitation, and the introduction of cash crops. This development, moreover, was often undertaken with only limited financial help and intermittent encouragement from the central government in Dar es Salaam. Significant though this side of the ledger is, however, it must nevertheless be appreciated that geographic isolation, the absence of the restraining influence of other Europeans, and other factors, all led to the emergence of attitudes on the part of administrators that were not, in the long run, conducive to development. One of these was the attitude of paternalism, which in an egocentric (albeit benevolent) way exaggerated the importance of Europeans in the survival of the Makonde people. It was an attitude of "empire-building" which undermined self-reliance and local initiative in bringing about modernization. It is succinctly reflected in the almost Kiplingesque tone of one Newala administrative officer in 1925 who wrote:

> In a lonely station such as Newala is, with absolutely no social life, the officer in charge cannot very often help, even in his off duty hours, allowing his thoughts to dwell on his every day work. Are the people happy, industrious and contented? Is anything left undone which might be

14. Newala District Book, "Native Administration," entry for June 4–8, 1936.

done for the welfare of the people under his charge? Have the people confidence that in continuing to reside in the Sub-district, they are assured of protection for life and property? [15]

It was this sort of paternalistic attitude which led to the constant intervention of officers in the political affairs of the Makonde and the constant manipulation of the economic, social, and political system. On occasion, paternalism extended to the desire to regulate even the most intimate detail of Makonde existence. The Annual Report of the district commissioner of Mtwara in 1954, for example, suggested the following:

> In order to increase agricultural production within the ability of the taxpayer, using only a hand hoe, orders were made requiring every married taxpayer to cultivate 6 acres per annum, of which one would be partly grown muhoga [cassava], and another would be a new planting of muhoga, the other 4 would be planted with whatever crops were found to grow best in the area, such as mtama [millet], mbaazi [pigeon peas], fiwi [lima beans], choroko [garden peas], kunde [beans], mbarika [castor beans], and possibly a little maize. . . . It was also agreed that each year each married taxpayer should open up 2 acres of new land and leave fallow 2 acres of land which had been cultivated for more than 3 years. This rotation would require an area of 18 acres for each married taxpayer. It was further agreed that an unmarried taxpayer need only cultivate half this acreage, and if he was only 18 years of age, his first year of paying tax, he would only be required to cultivate one acre in the first year, 2 acres in the second year and three acres in the third year. In order to make cultivators start early and cultivate their land in good time, before the rains in mid-December, it was decided that 2 acres should be cultivated by the end of September, 2 more by the end of October and the final two by the end of December, and that failure to carry out these orders would result in prosecution before the native courts. These decisions, although they may take a year or two to fully implement should be within the ability of all taxpayers, and should make a start to a very real increase in produce from the district, resulting in increasing wealth for the individual as well as the Treasury.

15. Lindi Province, *Annual Report*, 1925 (TNA 1733/10:75).

A more specific manifestation of this general attitude was the administrative behavior referred to by Africans as *wazimu wa mzungu*, or "white man's madness." This was the "disease" which seemed to compel each new district commissioner to make his own special imprint upon a district during his brief tenure in the area. The special "madness" of one man might be road construction, while that of his successor might be soil conservation. These in turn would be followed by a district commissioner with a penchant for getting the people to breed hybrid chickens, perhaps, or dig latrines, or dig wells. The arrival of a new European brought a period of uncertainty to a district until the people had ascertained what his particular "madness" was. Once this was discovered all energies could be directed to pleasing his idiosyncrasy and ignoring the pet projects of his predecessors. The elaborate network of paths and roads established by his predecessor could be surrendered to the jungle; the latrines could become chicken houses; and the hybrid chickens could revert to their primitive type. Although this certainly overstates the case, the behavior pattern can in fact be fairly well documented. In analyzing the court records regarding Native Authority Rules and Ordinances (which are themselves the inspiration of European officers rather than African Native Authorities), there is an infraction pattern which simply does not reflect human behavior in the mass. Neither does the infraction pattern reflect the occurrence of drought, epidemics, and other environmental situations which could account for the chaotic "curves" plotted in Figure 5, which indicates enforcement of Native Authority Rules and Orders in Mikindani District over a thirteen-year period. This constitutes a graphic documentation of the "white man's madness." (See Figure 5 following page 146.)

The absence of administrative restraints from the remote headquarters of Lindi or Dar es Salaam could leave the genuinely creative and empathetic district commissioner farther inland with sufficient scope to develop a positive relationship between himself and the people under his jurisdiction. Indeed, I was struck in 1955 by the intensely positive images which many Makonde—especially the older ones—retained with respect to former district commissioners. In Newala District, for example, J. W. Large, was remembered as "one who appreciated our history and our customs and the man who built our roads." [16] There was also remembered a Bwana Allen, who "was always fair and knew how to joke with us without making us feel bad." [17] There was also one district commissioner who "made us see the advantage of starting Native Authority schools so that Muslims would no longer be at the mercy of missionaries."

Equally vivid, however, were the recollections of several elders regarding district commissioners who were portrayed as having abused their trusts. One district commissioner who served in a coastal district during the 1930s was remembered as being "worse than the akidas in the German days. He hounded us for taxes when there was no food to sell. . . . He made us work long hours on the roads, and he was the only one who had a motorcar." A district commissioner in Newala in the early postwar period was alleged to have "made the people stand whenever he walked by. Even an old man would get a crack from his *kiboko* [a riding crop made of hippo hide] if he failed to show respect to this young man!" The abusiveness of some officers when on safari in the district is officially confirmed by Mitchell, an aide of Governor Cameron who inspected the Makonde districts in 1929 and commented:

> Officers still appear to think that, however poor and small a village, it is under an obligation to produce food for perhaps thirty porters and servants, if they elect to camp there. Moreover, very few officers take the trouble to see that the people, to whom the food belongs, receive the payment; the Headman collects from hut to hut a couple of fowl, a few baskets of flour and some sweet potatoes, and takes them to the officer who gives him a few shillings, which he appropriates for himself. The result can be seen in the very strong disinclination of natives to live on roads where there is porter travel. . . . One is constantly coming across

16. His interest in Makonde customs is reflected in the remarkable District Book which he started and which Sir Donald Cameron felt to be among the best in Tanganyika.

17. Although then known as I. W. T. Allen, this is the John W. T. Allen who has become one of the foremost authorities on the Swahili language. In 1967 he was still actively engaged in research at the University College, Dar es Salaam.

people who want to make rules about the sale of food to travellers, fix prices, and so on.[18]

In cases where Makonde were punished for failure to provide chickens, firewood, or laborers, Mitchell added:

> I do not suppose these officers were parties to the punishments; they probably do not realize the consequences of making a fuss over their personal matters. . . . It is a very great pity that nearly all cases, at any rate nearly all recorded cases, of unjustice, or which call for comment, arise from the performance of some service for a British officer, or for the Government.[19]

Staffing policies as well as environmental factors resulted in the extremes of underexposure or overexposure of British officers to the Makonde people. Official policy with respect to home leave and rotation in office resulted in a constant loss of continuity in programs and a loss of the kind of understanding and intimacy which would have made for more effective accomplishment of British goals in the Makonde area. New officers, since they bore the ultimate responsibility for the administration of their districts, were reluctant to delegate authority to the Native Authorities until they knew them well. Short tenure meant that the relationship seldom reached this stage, since invariably the first few months were devoted to settling-in and the last few months were spent in preparing for home leave. If the short tour covered the rainy season, there were five to six months in which it was either difficult or impossible to establish close contact between the district commissioner and the African authorities. The short tour, however, occurred with great frequency in the Makonde districts and was often justified because of hazardous health conditions. In Newala from 1919 to independence in 1962, there were 16 tours shorter than 18 months in duration, while in Mikindani there were 10 tours

18. P. E. Mitchell to Governor D. Cameron, August 23, 1929 (TNA 13538). Cameron's marginal notes indicated his clear annoyance with these practices. With regard to the direct payment to the owners of the produce, Cameron wrote: "They *must* do so!" At the end of the recitation, he noted: "Issue a strong warning about this to departmental officers, please."

19. *Ibid.* Cameron's concluding marginal note to this section was: "Put this in the next Memorandum II" (i.e., the Native Administration Memorandum on Courts").

that ranged from 3 to 16 months in length. The adjustment of the African authorities to changes in personnel of the British administrators was considerable, since there were 26 men who held the post of district commissioner in Newala during the 43-year period and 28 in Mikindani (later renamed Mtwara) District.

Long tenure, on the other hand, brought with it risks to the health of the officer as well as the possibility of the officer placing the interests of his district ahead of the overall territorial objectives of the British administration. On balance, however, it was those officers who served longer tours that were able to amass more impressive records of accomplishments and who were remembered with greater favor by the elder Makonde. J. W. Large had the longest tenure. In three separate tours in Newala, he served a total of 87 months, while four other officers served single tours ranging from 30 to 34 months. In Mikindani, C. P. Lyons served 61 months in four tours of duty; Mr. R. S. B. M. Hickson-Mahony accumulated 39 months of service in two tours; and three additional officers served single tours of 29 to 33 months in duration. Thus very few officers got to know the Makonde and their problems with any degree of intimacy. (See Figures 6 and 7 for details.)

On a day-to-day basis as well, other factors limited the possibility of close administration that might have led to a more effective relationship between the colonial administrator and the African officials with whom he was to work. The automobile and an improved system of roads, ironically enough, were factors in the breakdown of intimacy. In the safari records for the 1920s and 1930s, one is struck by the fact that British district commissioners spent roughly one-third of each year on tour within the district—a great percentage of it on foot safaris with porters. In 1951, at a time when head porterage was becoming almost a matter of legend, the provincial commissioner of the Southern Province, writing in his annual report, was urging its continuance on the grounds that it was

> on these foot safaris that contact is made with the local population in their own homes and much can be done to eliminate or remedy those small difficulties that arise which can cause great unrest if not attended to.

These sentiments were echoed in the comments of Rashidi

FIGURE 5

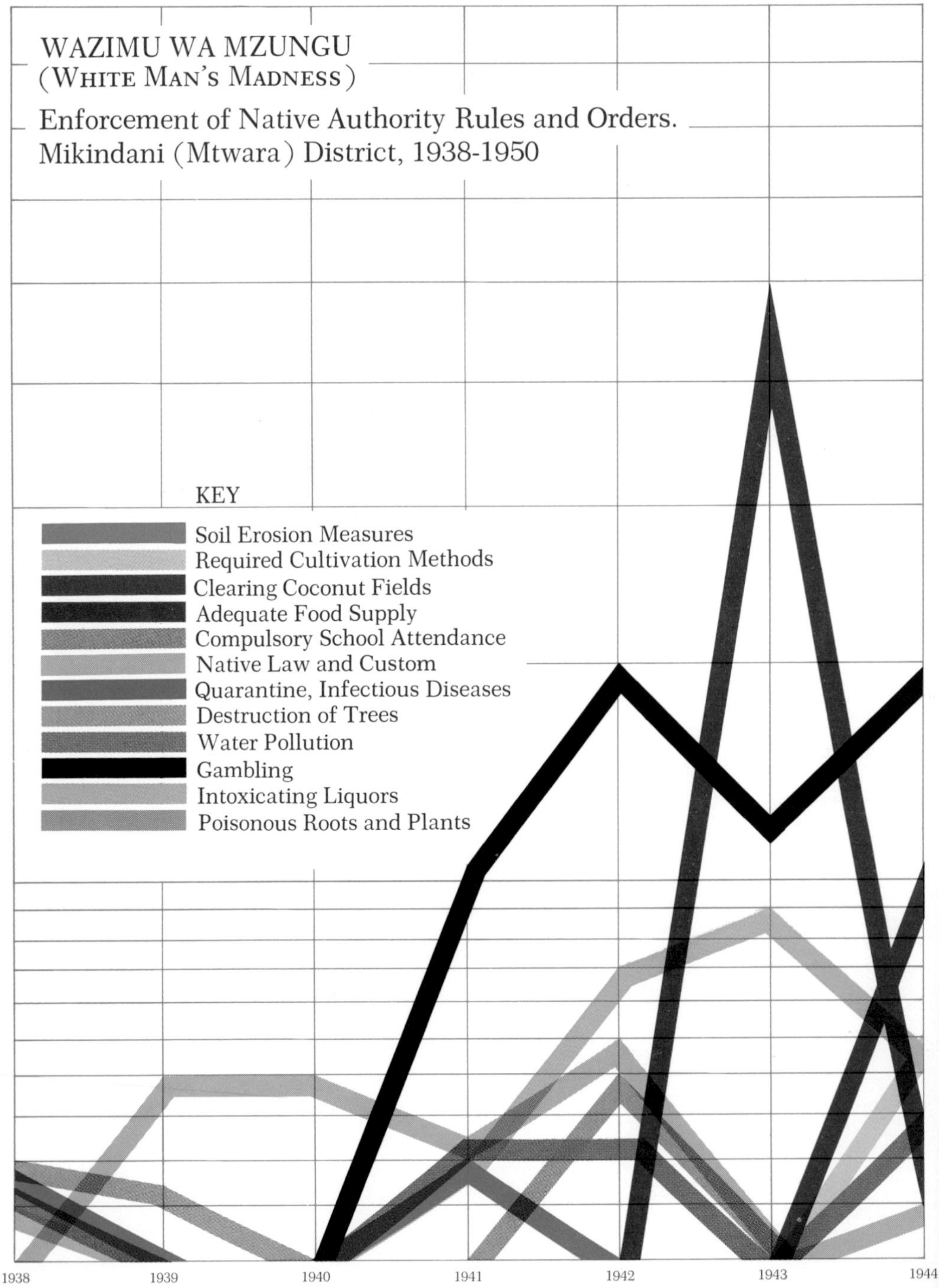

WAZIMU WA MZUNGU
(WHITE MAN'S MADNESS)

Enforcement of Native Authority Rules and Orders.
Mikindani (Mtwara) District, 1938-1950

KEY

Soil Erosion Measures
Required Cultivation Methods
Clearing Coconut Fields
Adequate Food Supply
Compulsory School Attendance
Native Law and Custom
Quarantine, Infectious Diseases
Destruction of Trees
Water Pollution
Gambling
Intoxicating Liquors
Poisonous Roots and Plants

1938    1939    1940    1941    1942    1943    1944

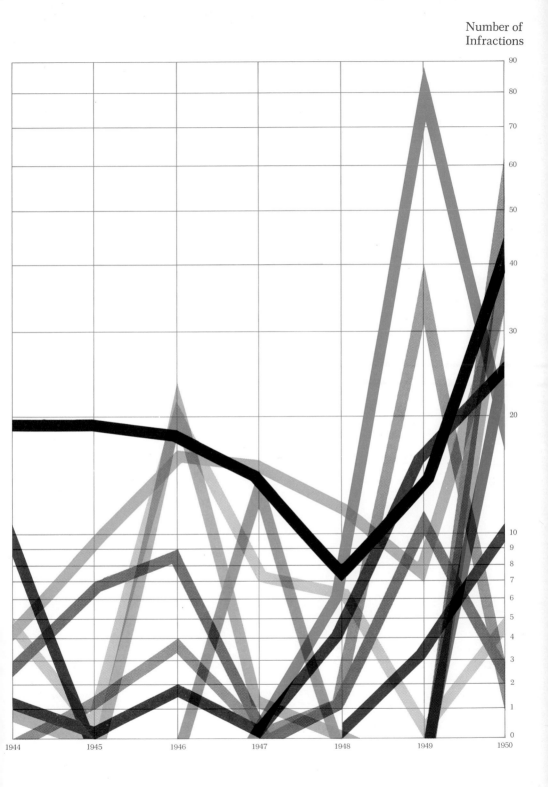

Number of
Infractions

Mtalika, the former mkulungwa mkuu of Newala, as he reminisced with me in 1956 about the situation in the early days of British rule:

> The people seldom saw the D.C., but when he came to a village he sat down for several days and listened to our problems and told us what government expected from us. They didn't push the people around so much and treat us like their monkeys. If the mkulungwa told the D.C. that things must be done slowly, the D.C. took his advice. Now all these young men are in a hurry and want everything done all at once. They don't really stay long enough to see whether we do these things. They are in a hurry to jump in their cars and get back to the boma.

In other ways as well the intimacy of the administrative relations was being eroded as the technology of the twentieth century caught up with Newala, Mikindani, and Lindi districts. With refrigeration, canning, and improved merchandising, the European officer no longer had to depend upon the African community for food, furniture, and the other necessities of life. The improved living conditions, moreover, made it possible for a British officer's wife and children to accompany him to a remote station, and thus the officer was no longer obliged to rely upon the indigenous community for his social contacts. In the process, valuable channels of information regarding the state of the district and the popularity of programs were closed to the administrators.

Large-scale economic and social development also contained its own self-defeating aspects. The influx of large numbers of European technicians in the employ of the Departments of Agriculture, Water Development, Public Works, Cooperatives, and Health not only further diminished the reliance of the district commissioner upon the African community but also brought to the district people with problems that took an increasingly larger proportion of the administrator's time. From a handful of Europeans in the 1920s, by 1957 the European population stood at 209 in Mtwara (formerly Mikindani) District, 189 in Lindi, and 71 in Newala. Moreover, the development planning and other aspects of the work associated with the rise in number of European technical personnel meant a sharp increase in the amount of time the district commissioner

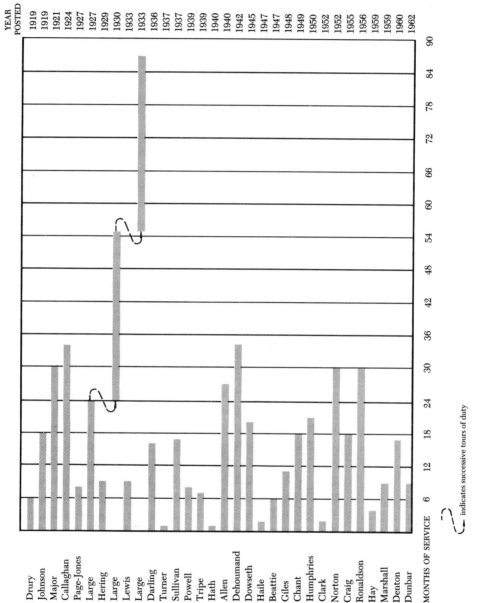

FIGURE 6: TENURE OF DISTRICT COMMISSIONERS, NEWALA, 1919–1962

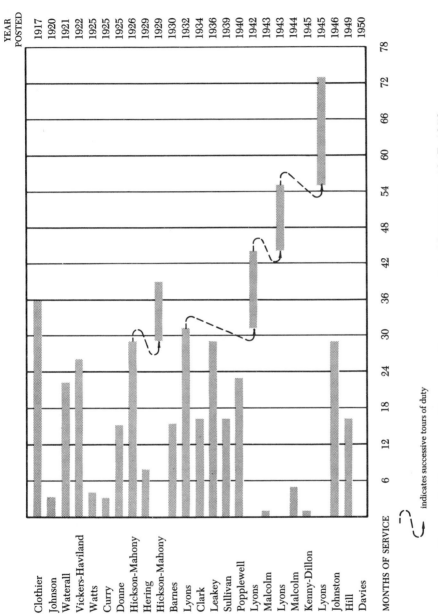

FIGURE 7: TENURE OF DISTRICT COMMISSIONERS, MIKINDANI, 1917–1950

had to spend at his desk drawing up estimates, keeping accounts, and writing regular and special reports. D. S. Troup, the provincial commissioner of the Southern Province, stated to me in 1956, only half in jest, that "British rule in Tanganyika is not going to be toppled by UNO, TANU, or any other human force; it will be ultimately crushed under the weight of its own paper." [20]

## THE ASIANS

Arabs and Europeans were not the only external agents of change within Makonde society. Indians—including Hindus, Roman Catholic Goans, and Muslims who were later to identify with Pakistan or the Ismaili community—became a force of increasing importance in the Southern Province. As was noted previously, the earliest references to the Indian presence in southern Tanzania indicated the use which the Omani Arabs made of "Banyans" to assist them in the collection of revenues and the stimulation of trade at the coast. The number of Indians increased under both German and British rule as the Europeans appreciated that the Asians were literate, were interested in the expansion of a cash economy, and possessed some of the skills in banking, carpentry, masonry, and tailoring which were essential to the European colonial effort. The Asians thus thrived on the lack of interest of European settlers and merchants in the area and on the absence of Africans with craft, commercial, and other skills. The number of Asians grew steadily, quickly outpacing both the Arabs and the Europeans in the three Makonde districts. By 1957, on the eve of independence, their numbers had risen as shown in Table 1.

The Asians were concentrated for the most part in the three coastal towns of Lindi, Mtwara, and Mikindani, but gradually they extended their influence inland. The Asian population of

20. For a leisurely account of life in Mikindani District in 1954, read J. C. Cairns, *Bush and Boma* (London: John Murray, 1959), pp. 54–119; although the book has little to commend it by way of literary style, it does catch the flavor of a district officer's life in a Makonde district.

TABLE 1:
ASIAN POPULATION IN MAKONDE DISTRICTS, 1957

| District | Indians | Goans | Pakistanis | Arabs |
|----------|---------|-------|------------|-------|
| Lindi  | 2,160 | 71 | 83 | 37 |
| Mtwara | 791 | 62 | 110 | 45 |
| Newala | 284 | – | 93 | – |

SOURCE: East African Statistical Department, *Tanganyika Census of Population* (Nairobi, 1958).

Newala township, for example, grew from 4 in 1930 to 377 by 1957. Indeed, in every instance where a minor settlement was in the process of developing, one could expect the ubiquitous Indian shopkeeper to begin peddling his hoes, cloth, kerosene lamps, and tinned goods. It was actually the Asian, rather than the European, who brought the material culture of the West to the Makonde and in the process offered a more positive incentive to the acceptance of a money economy than that provided by the European tax collector.

While the role of the Asians was predominantly commercial in character, the vital role they played in administration was revealed in these ambivalent comments of the senior administrator of Lindi Province in 1924:

> At the present time for the more important work Asiatic clerks are employed at all the stations in this [province]. For some years to come they will continue to be employed at the coast stations. . . . [In Newala, however,] there is firstly the trouble of getting them there. On arrival at the station they get lonely, as they have no friends to talk to. Frequently they get sick and there is nobody to nurse them, and eventually they apply to be moved somewhere else.[21]

Recognizing their importance in the colonial scheme, the Asians felt frustrated by the situation in which they found themselves. On the one hand, they resented the British administrators and attempted to translate the struggle for Indian

21. *Annual Report*, 1924 (TNA 1733/15/94).

liberation from Asia to the African continent, as evidenced by
the abortive passive-resistance campaign of 1922 in Lindi.
On the other hand, they demanded equality with the Europeans
in regard to the ownership and leasing of land, the representation of their interests at the territorial level, and in the making
of economic policy for the Southern Province. The Indian Association was a constant source of antagonism for British
administrators during the 1920s, leading to the expulsion of
the Lindi branch secretary from Tanganyika. There was a constant flow of petitions from Lindi to Dar es Salaam, ranging
from major policy questions to complaints that the European
officer at the boma treated Asian petitioners "no better than
Africans." [22] It was only the Goan community, which consisted for the most part of Roman Catholics and of persons with
special clerical and professional talents, who found themselves
being admitted to the two unassailable sanctuaries of British
snobbery—the European club and the European cemetery.

Rejected generally by Europeans, the Asians also found
themselves resented by the Africans. Africans were assumed
to have more intimate bonds with Asians than they did with
Europeans, because the few contacts the Makonde had with
Europeans were limited largely to the payment of fines, taxes,
and fees. Makonde leaders also stated that they felt that in
commercial transactions the better-financed and literate Asian
shopkeeper invariably outwitted his less sophisticated African
customer. Although occasionally an Asian shopkeeper would
assist a budding African businessman by permitting the latter
to rent a truck, for the most part the Asian community took
both overt and covert action to immobilize African competition
in the commercial sector. Moreover, since the Hindu Asians
were not concerned about proselytizing, and inasmuch as the
Pakistani and Indian Mulims were for the most part either
Ismaili or members of the once-heretical Shi-ite sect—rather
than Sunni, or orthodox Muslim—there were few bonds which
could put them into a single camp in opposing the European
colonial system.

22. Lindi District, *Annual Report,* 1923 (TNA 1733/13); and "Complaints of
the Indian Association against District Officer Fryer," 1927 (TNA 10575).

## The Cumulative Impact
## of Economic Change

Although reference has already been made to the roles which the European administrator, the missionary, and the Asian merchant played in the economic transformation of Makonde society, it will be useful to single out several facets of the change for more detailed analysis. One of the most significant elements in this respect was the introduction of cash crops, which was largely attributable to the colonial administrators. Recognition, however, has to be made of the incentive which the Arabs had earlier provided in getting the Makonde to sell crude latex, gum copal, simsim, and rice. The European administrator, in contrast to the Arab trader, was much more systematic in securing the introduction and extension of production in a variety of areas. His prime reason for doing so was to secure tax revenues to finance the services of local government and the system of administration which the Europeans had imposed upon the area. The early practice of accepting subsistence produce or service in lieu of cash soon proved cumbersome and unwieldy once the scope of the administrative enterprise had been enlarged. It was thus necessary to find a series of crops which would have ready markets outside the southern districts, and thereby provide a monetary base for tax purposes.

The second reason for the direct intervention of European administrators in the area of cultivation was to deal with the problems of recurrent famine, which hit the Southern Province every sixth or seventh year. In 1967, for example, the southeastern sector of Tanzania was facing its second year of underaverage rainfall, and the specter of famine once more loomed large. In view of this, the coercive measures of colonial officers requiring the planting of cassava and other crops in Newala came to mean not only the survival of the people of that district but also the relief of people in adjoining districts who imported cassava from Newala. Indeed, from 1949 to 1954 cassava was the leading cash crop of the district, and in one of the best years, 1952, cassava accounted for 80 per cent of Newala's exports.[23]

In the absence of a large cadre of agricultural officers (the majority of whom had to be shared among three or four districts), the district commissioners were limited in the kind of economic changes they could effect. For the most part, they simply encouraged the planting of cassava, sorghum, and other subsistence crops, with the surplus being offered for sale. New crops could only be introduced where the administration was convinced that the people would be receptive to some measure of innovation. Thus, in 1933 – during the peak of the world-wide economic depression – the Newala Native Treasury purchased simsim and groundnut seeds and distributed them to over 2,000 cultivators, who agreed to follow instructions in planting. It was another matter, however, to sustain interest in a cash crop when the threat of famine was negligible or the opportunities for sale were limited. Reliance upon the whim and varied fortunes of the Asian or African itinerant trader could hardly provide a sound base for a market economy. It was only with the establishment of Native Authority markets in each of the minor settlements in Newala, Lindi, and Mikindani districts in 1945 that the situation was radically altered. The local government markets not only gave the African grower a better price for his commodities but also stimulated a system of internal exchanges within the districts instead of having all crops leave the area on Asian trucks. It is perhaps understandable why the Asian merchants sent letters of protest to the governor of Tanganyika objecting to the interference of the district administration with the operations of the "natural" economy. The impact which the Native Authority markets made upon the Makonde economy is indicated by the increase, for example, in the tonnage of marketable crops from Newala District between 1950 and 1959. During this period production rose from 3,438 tons to 20,732 tons and came to include a great diversity of crops: sesame, maize, sorghum, groundnuts, pulses, castor beans, sunflower, paddy, rice, mambara nuts, millet, and beeswax. The two dominant crops during this period, however,

23. Cassava requires less care and rainfall than many other subsistence crops and is also less destructive of the soil than maize, which many Tanzanians have come to prefer as a staple.

were cassava—which had earned Newala the local title of the "granary" of the south—and cashew nuts.

Increasingly, it was cashew production that was to provide the mainstay not only of an economic revolution in the Makonde area but of a social revolution as well. By 1965, although there was a greater tonnage of cassava in Newala, the value of the cassava crop was only Shs. 1,103,040 (U.S. $132,365), whereas cashew nuts brought in Shs. 12,260,000 (U.S. $1,471,200). Surprisingly, the economic revolution which cashews brought was a long time in developing. Although the crop is indigenous to Central America, Bishop Chauncy Maples in 1881 noted that the area in northern Portuguese East Africa was "indeed a land of plenty . . . and notable for cashew apple trees everywhere." [24] It was not until the period after the Second World War that production in southern Tanzania was encouraged, as a consequence of several factors—the need for new crops to make the port of Mtwara a paying proposition; the Portuguese dispute with India over the ownership of Goa, which deprived Mozambique of its traditional market for cashews in India; and the development of new uses for cashew oil in plastics and other modern industries. To the British administrator, cashew trees provided a fairly steady source of wealth for the Makonde, and, in addition, tree cultivation broke the rotation cycle of agriculture, which was becoming wasteful as population pressure increased.

The impact of cashew production upon social stratification within Makonde society was apparent almost as soon as the first trees began to provide significant yields in the early 1950s. The earnings to the present cultivators eliminated rather quickly whatever higher economic status had been enjoyed by the Native Authorities, the government clerks, the mission teachers, and the returned workers from the northern sisal estates. Suddenly it had become reasonably respectable for the semiliterate Makonde male to stay at home and engage in agriculture instead of feeling obliged to migrate to the urban centers for economic improvement. Moreover, the expansion of cashew groves shattered the last vestige of economic prerogatives which had been retained by the wakulungwa and the

24. *Journals and Papers*, pp. 27–29.

heads of the litawa—namely, the reassignment of land within the community. Although technically the land under the trees belonged to the village and could be reassigned if left vacant, in fact the land became the "private" property of the man whose trees were planted on the land. The planter, under the traditional rules of land tenure, enjoyed his rights to the trees in perpetuity and could bequeath them to his heirs.

A future social and political consequence of the expansion of cashew production was that it provided the younger, modernized Makonde with a crop whose production and sale could be organized along cooperative lines. The Makonde saw that those tribal groups in Tanganyika which had organized marketing cooperatives were regarded as the most progressive in the territory. Thus it was argued that, if the Makonde hoped to have the schools, clinics, and other material prosperity of the Chagga, Nyakyusa, Sukuma, and Haya, they had to organize their economy along cooperative lines. It was only in this way, the younger Makonde insisted, that they could break both the parochialism of their area and the tight control which the Asian community had over the Makonde economy. The remarks made by one young Makonde sounded remarkably similar to the complaint of Paul Bomani and other Tanzanians who had, at an earlier date, organized the cotton growers in the area south of Lake Victoria. The Makonde leader noted:

> After we spend years of planting cashew nuts and weeding the shambas, we turn everything over to the Asians. It is an Asian lorry that comes to my village and charges me not only a fare for myself but freight as well to carry the bag of nuts to Newala. There an Asian buyer gives us a miserable Shs. 1/10 per kilo and transports them to Lindi or Mtwara for consignment to another Asian. Eventually they are sent to India [actually, Goa] where they make them into nuts. They return to Africa where we can see them in little tins on the shelves in the Indian duka. Since that tin costs Shs. 6, no African can afford to buy it. So who gets all that profit? The Asians! And what do I and my family get for our sweat? Those shoddy things they sell in the dukas and money for taxes!

As will be noted subsequently, it was not until the eve of independence that the British government finally acceded to the request by the Makonde to establish cooperative societies.

The British argued that it was wasteful to start cooperatives without "proper" (that is, European) supervision. What was not stated was the fact that cooperative societies had a curious way, in colonial Africa, of becoming effective vehicles for making political demands upon the British administration.

One final aspect of the economic transformation of Makonde society began to take explicit shape in the period between the two world wars. This was the emergence of a class of Makonde migratory workers, which was to have several indirect—but nonetheless significant—impacts upon the Makonde economic, social, and political order. The extent of involvement of Makonde—as opposed to Maconde from Mozambique—in migratory labor is impossible to state with any degree of accuracy. The enumerators who conducted the 1957 census for Tanganyika did provide for a separate "Mawia" category, but undoubtedly many of the 6,000 Makonde reported for Tanga Province and the 3,000 listed in the Eastern Province were in fact Maconde from across the Ruvuma River. These suspicions are based partly on my own observations of returnees in 1956 and on the writings of early administrators, who indicated a reluctance on the part of the Makonde to engage in migratory labor. J. W. Large in 1929, for example, reported in the *Newala District Book* that

> as a whole the Makonde objects strongly to seeking steady work for good pay at the coast. He takes food for about half a month, reluctantly engages to clean a coast native's garden, and either comes back because his food is finished or remains working haphazardly or irregularly. He comes back with Shs. 3/-. Later he sells a fowl or two. Perhaps later he works again for a few shillings, and from first to last he has worked three or four months.

This was also confirmed by a district officer in Lindi three years earlier, who noted:

> Employers in Lindi District appear to find the Makonde natives generally lazy and unsatisfactory as workers, and prefer to employ Yao Natives from Portuguese territory and Tunduru. . . . . They complain, too, that the demeanour of the Makonde leaves much to be desired and that they are intolerant of discipline. [25]

25. Lindi Province, *Annual Report*, 1926 (TNA 1733/6/59).

Whether it was the stereotyped prejudice of the European or the problems of transportation, the fact is that the Makonde were not regarded as one of the significant migratory labor groups in the period before the Second World War.[26]

Two situations contributed to a gradual change in the Makonde attitude toward migratory labor. The first was the sanctions that were applied to Makonde who failed to have cash to pay their hut and poll tax. Working off one's taxes by constructing and maintaining roads was regarded by many Makonde males as a far greater penalty than leaving one's family for extended periods to secure money for the tax collector. The second incentive, more positive in character, was the realization by Makonde that the wage economy could provide them with enough cash not only to pay their taxes but also to acquire the cloth, cheap pots and pans, and other items which were becoming more readily available in the Asian shops. Although attachments to home might deter one from easily leaving his wife, family, and friends, the Makonde proved during several periods that they were willing to respond to a favorable wage differential. The first response came with respect to the wage disparity between the sisal estates of Lindi and Mikindani and those of Tanga and other places farther north. At a time when the estate managers in Lindi were complaining about the shortage of Makonde labor, Makonde were appearing in increasing numbers at the estates in Dar es Salaam and Tanga. The second response came during the short-lived Groundnut Scheme of the Overseas Food Corporation. In 1948, for example, it was estimated that over 5,000 laborers had left Newala District to seek employment with the Groundnut Scheme at Nachingwea. Generally, however, the Makonde do prefer—all other things being equal—to remain at home. Fairly refined statistics collected in 1955 confirmed that of the 4,280 persons who were professionally recruited in Newala for labor outside the district, only 1,172 were Makonde from the district; the remainder were "alien" Africans—that is, Maconde and Makua from Mozambique. Of the 1,172 Makonde laborers, roughly one-third went

26. See E. C. Baker, *Report on Social and Economic Conditions in the Tanga Province* (Dar es Salaam: Government Printer, 1934); and F. Longland, "Labour Matters in Sisal Areas, No. 1, Tanga," March 29, 1936 (MS.).

no further than Lindi and Mtwara in seeking employment.[27]

However few in number at any one time, the Makonde who were absent from their home districts were nonetheless a significant factor in the economic, social, and political transformation of the Makonde areas. Even the short-term migratory laborer created problems for the community he left behind. It was apparent, for example, that the imbalance of females to males in the Makonde districts left the women with greater responsibilities in sustaining the agricultural economy of the area and in the rearing of children. It also provided females with greater opportunities for sexual license, and the incidence of reported cases of adultery and other sexual offenses was almost as great in rural Liteho and Kitangari divisions of Newala District as it was in the urban centers of Mtwara and Lindi. The inability of the village elders to restrain the "safari widows" was a recurrent complaint heard during my inquiries in 1956.

In terms of economic development schemes, moreover, the short- or long-term withdrawal of the most productive members of the society from the district creates problems of the first magnitude. During the Groundnut Scheme, for example, the district commissioner of Newala complained bitterly that the demands for labor from every railway and development camp between Mtwara and Nachingwea gave the Makonde a wide choice of seasonal employment, with the result that it was difficult to find either laborers or sufficient funds for work within the district itself.[28]

Equally disruptive of the traditional social and economic order was the return of the worldly wise and slightly wealthier migrant to his home village. Although the bolts of cloth, utensils, and other forms of wealth might be quickly dissipated in gifts to his elders and extended family, the giving of gifts also provided the returned worker with a new element of prestige rivaling that of the traditional holders of power. His prosperity and boastings also whetted the appetites of other young men to venture forth from the parochial village to partake of

27. Southern Province, *Annual Report*, 1955.
28. Newala District, *Annual Report*, 1948.

the material pleasures of Dar es Salaam, Tanga, or even Lindi or Mtwara. Occasionally, of course, the returning migrant might enlarge the pool of economic skills in the community, particularly if he had saved well and had acquired a sewing machine or a bicycle. For the most part, however, the Makonde had a reputation for not staying long enough at his external job to acquire any skills which would radically speed the process of modernization within the Makonde village. He was usually too eager to return home for fear that his claim to land would have been forfeited or that his wife would have been unfaithful.

The political impact of the returnee was also an important factor. The elders of several villages echoed the remarks of the jumbe of Mnolela in Kitangari, who complained that the migratory workers not only came back with smart new clothes, but also

> [they] feel that they are much smarter than the rest of the people and are constantly criticizing the elders and saying disrespectful things to them. When we threaten to bring them to court, they say that only Government can tell them what to do. Since they can get work outside the village, they tell us they can leave whenever we try to bring them into line.

In addition to his role as an underminer of traditional authority, however, the returning migrant was to become perhaps the most effective political communicator of the new order that the emergent elite in Tanzania would be constructing in the postwar period. Cut off as the Southern Province was for six months of every year, it was the returnee from the sisal estates in Dar es Salaam and Tanga who would assist in stirring the Makonde villagers to respond to Julius Nyerere and the Tanganyika African National Union in the mid-1950s.

## THE SECOND WORLD WAR

Much of the writing on African politics which appeared during and immediately after the Second World War assumed that the events of the war and the widened horizons of the returning veterans would be among the most significant factors in a developing anticolonial struggle. It was assumed implicitly that the veterans would be a vital force not only in the contest between Africans and European colonial administrators but also in the internal struggle between the elite that had received support from the colonialists and the emergent elite of teachers, workers, and successful cash farmers. Admittedly, the war situation and the returning veterans contributed to the general ferment which made it possible for African nationalist leaders to press their claims against the colonial regime. The actual contribution of the veterans as a class, however, has not been properly assessed. In many instances the veterans were quickly reabsorbed into their rural communities or became lost in the urban milieu. Their experience may have been a very limited one after all, or it may have been no more transforming in character than other kinds of experiences, such as education, migration, urbanization, or government service.

The difficulty of assessing the veterans' impact is certainly evident in the case of the Makonde. The actual number involved was relatively small. Using as an estimate the number of service medals that were distributed at the end of the war, approximately 770 Makonde from Newala District had served during the six-year period from 1939 to 1945. Figures for the two coastal districts were only slightly higher. Apparently the Makonde took to military service with even less relish than to employment as migratory laborers, where it was at least possible for one to break the contract and return home if he became homesick, tired of the regimentation, or worried about his family and fields. The aversion of the Makonde to conscription is revealed in the rather remarkable comments of the district commissioner of Newala in 1943:

> Conscription has had to develop into a cunning procedure on the part of both the hunter and the hunted. A date is fixed with the Liwalis and any signs of the impending action, such as the ordering of lorries for the transport of recruits to Lindi and preparation of notices of selection, must be kept secret. The Liwalis give the Jumbes the shortest notice possible so that stray words or demeanour may not cause suspicion. Then in the night preceding the fatal day a swoop is made and a few of the weak, meek, and slow are gathered. Relatives and friends have previously been warned or are "missed." On the other hand, the hunted,

after a certain period, begin to feel it is time attention was paid to them and so, in order to baffle the Jumbes at night they go to sleep in the huts of the persons who are not likely to be bothered on account of conscription (widows, old people) or make themselves scarce until the danger is past. It is useless to be shocked at such procedures. It is this or nothing. The Wamakonde in fact accept the procedure as natural.[29]

So unconcerned were the Makonde with the defeats and victories of the Allied troops that the district commissioner of Newala eventually gave up distributing weekly news bulletins on the progress of the war.

Not having sought military service in the first place, the returning veteran found that his status was not noticeably higher as a consequence of his experience. Several district commissioners in the postwar period commented that the status of the veteran as a "Big Man" in his community was dissipated almost as quickly as the funds in his postal savings account had been exhausted and distributed as gifts to his friends and relatives. As an organizer for the Tanganyika African National Union remarked in 1956: "It is impossible to tell an ex-askari from any other person. They went into the army as illiterates and they remained 'empty-headed,' forgetting everything but how to give a snappy salute and say '*Ndio, Bwana*' [Yes, Master]." Despite the absence of ex-askari among the ranks of either the Native Authorities or the burgeoning political leadership, one can't help but feel, nevertheless, that the wartime experience contributed in its own small way to the alteration of the traditional Makonde way of life.

29. *Annual Report.*

# 7:
# Return to
# Direct Rule:
# The Liwali System

The stresses and strains which became evident in the Makonde districts by the eve of the Second World War and in its aftermath had their counterparts in other regions of Tanzania. Indeed, a more intense and even broader spectrum of change was apparent in the Chagga, Sukuma, Hehe, Nyakyusa, and other areas where the missionary efforts in education and the pace of economic development made the changes in the Makonde region seem almost imperceptible by contrast. In certain respects, however, British officers in the Makonde area were better prepared to deal with the problems of postwar reform in local government that were plaguing British administrators throughout the Trust Territory. I observed that, in districts farther north, European officers were still sentimentally committed to the perpetuation of the spirit, if not the form, of Indirect Rule despite the constant complaints regarding the multiplicity of tribal units, the inability of hereditary chiefs to carry out programs of modern government, and the constant drain upon both the time and energy of British officers in introducing economic and social change through inappropriate semitraditional structures. Several British officers admitted frankly that they felt much more comfortable in the presence of elderly but illiterate chiefs than in the presence of younger, educated

Africans. The latter, undoubtedly sensing the lack of ease in their relationships with European colonial officers, inevitably resorted to stances of either outright belligerence or self-conscious servility—neither of which was conducive to the vital reform of local government the British were ostensibly seeking. Ultimately, too, administrators would have to overcome the nostalgia for the "good old days," that is, the period before five-year development plans, visiting missions from the United Nations, and modern communications facilities had intruded upon the tranquillity of the feudal fiefs over which many of the district commissioners reigned.

Indirect Rule had been abandoned in the Makonde districts a full decade before failure was acknowledged in other areas of Tanzania. Thus the officers in Newala, Lindi, and Mikindani during the postwar period were spared from going through what must have been for them the burdensome and occasionally disheartening task of whittling away the prerogatives of traditional rulers. In the Makonde area, the task had already been accomplished. What was needed in the postwar period was the securing of popular acceptance of the objectives of modern local government; the delineation of more rational territorial units within which the services of local government were to be provided; the designation of appropriate personnel to carry out modern programs in health, education, agriculture, and natural-resource development; and the improvement of procedures for making the benefits of these programs available to the people.

## POPULAR ACCEPTANCE OF THE LIWALI SYSTEM

In contrast to the mkulungwa system, the introduction of the liwali system was viewed by the British as a move toward more efficient administration, which would permit British officers to engage in more meaningful economic planning. The manner in which the liwali system was introduced, however, left grave doubts about its ultimate popular acceptance by the Makonde. In Mikindani District, for example, as was discussed briefly in Chapter 5, the provincial commissioner convened a meeting of headmen, elders, and notables on March 31, 1937, and informed them "at some length but not in minatory terms" that the Native Authority system had failed. The commissioner was apparently so impressed with the lack of dissent from his audience, and with the good humor in which the criticism was taken, that he abandoned his explicit agreement with the governor that changes would take place gradually and only after the notables had had the opportunity to discuss the new developments with their constituents. He moved immediately to a discussion of the new plan for local government that British officials had already fashioned. Thus all pretense of popular consultation on the new form of local government was dropped.[1]

In Newala District as well, informants in various parts of the district indicated that there had been no prior consultation with the people regarding the abandonment of the mkulungwa system in 1942. Although several wakulungwa were retained as jumbes under the new system, there were many who were merely dismissed without compensation and without even a ceremony thanking them for their loyal services. As one ex-mkulungwa told me: "We kept quiet because we all feared government; but we shall never forget this injustice. The people were annoyed, but there was little they could do. Not even the wazee were consulted." And again, there were the comments from a group of elders I interviewed in one village to the effect that the term "mkulungwa"

> has a history with us: it means a "big man." The wakulungwa were "big men" because they were selected by the people as their leaders, and they held office because they had our respect and confidence. The liwalis are "big men" only because the *Serikali* [Government] says they are or because they think themselves better because of their education. They are not "big men." As of old, we show respect to our leaders; but our respect today is only on the surface and is given in fear.

Although the stance of supporting the wakulungwa was not entirely consistent with the subsequent posture of the Tanganyika African National Union (TANU), one young TANU leader complained to me that the abandonment of the wakulungwa

---

1. Confidential letter of A. E. Kitching to Chief Secretary, September 6, 1937 (TNA Vol. 21, 26752).

in Newala was the choice of the district commissioner alone. The post of liwali was the creation of the commissioner, and "the men he chose owe nothing to the people but everything to government. Must we doubt whose side they are on? We are like stones. The only men the D.C. talks to are the liwalis, and they only talk to their relatives and friends."

In the selection, moreover, of liwalis, wakilis, and jumbes, the "intervention syndrome" became much more blatant and open than it had been under the mkulungwa system. Under Indirect Rule an attempt at least was made by British officials to give the appearance that traditional norms and procedures were being observed in the designation of Native Authorities, even though manipulation—in the name of greater efficiency of administration—was occasionally even openly admitted. The manipulation, however, was justified on traditional grounds, and, given the flexibility of the traditional system of succession, it was possible to do so in most instances.

The shift from a political and administrative system based upon tradition to one which seeks modernization as its goal, however, signals a change in the qualities sought in recruiting officials for the new or revitalized institutions. Traditional systems rely largely upon ascriptive qualifications—that is, upon characteristics such as sex, age, race, physical attributes, birth into a particular family or class, and other factors over which the individual has no control. Modernizing institutions tend to rely upon achievement qualifications. They seek those who have demonstrated their intellectual or physical claims to leadership by having been exposed to a more rigorous and specialized form of education than that available to the masses of society; by having accumulated wealth through one's own ingenuity; by demonstrating skill in the use of words or in the manipulation of other men; or through manifesting administrative or military organizational talents.

The above is, of course, an oversimplification of the case. Traditional societies often protect themselves against the rigid application of ascriptive rules which might deny them the talent needed for survival or prosperity. Mechanisms exist for encouraging upward status mobility. Thus, a first son or nephew may be passed over (or actually killed to simplify the question of legitimacy) so that political office may go to younger siblings who possess the talents needed to face recurrent challenges to that society. Slaves are occasionally adopted as members of a ruling family; and women are sometimes chosen as chiefs. In each case, however, the fiction of ascription is maintained through avoiding public reference to the original slave status of the new nobleman and through giving the female chief all the prerogatives of a male, including the right to "marry" a series of wives. Conversely, a modernizing society frequently finds that officials who succeed are those who not only possess educational or administrative talents but who can also demonstrate the proper lineage or claims to having participated in some historic event associated with the survival or the greatness of that society.

In shifting from a traditional to a modern system of politics, the central question remains that of legitimacy. Will the masses of society accept the decisions of those who lack the traditional claims to leadership? In introducing the liwali system the British administrative officers at the provincial and district level placed a greater emphasis upon finding individuals who possessed the proper modernizing qualifications than they did upon the question of popular support—although the latter issue was certainly not ignored. They had little confidence in the Makonde making the right choices, and hence the intervention of British officers in the selection of liwalis was manifest from the outset of the experiment in Mikindani District in October, 1937. Although the opinions of the elders were solicited at that time regarding suitable candidates for the five posts of liwali, ultimately the district officer felt obliged to make four of the five choices himself. In three of these cases he insisted he did so because "the leaders stated that there was nobody whom they wished to nominate as a candidate and that they wished to leave the matter in the hands of the District Officer." In the fourth case, the elders of Nanguruwe "nominated a very aged and decrepit 'mwalim' as liwali," and the British officer told them that their choice was unacceptable to the government. In the one instance where an element of popular choice was involved, the elders had suggested that the liwali of Mikindani town (an area not covered by the previous mkulungwa system) be asked to extend his authority over the adjacent hinterland area.[2]

Indeed, neither in the available documents nor in my interviews was I able to discover many instances in which popular approval was regarded as an essential factor in the designation of individuals as liwalis, wakilis, or even jumbes, the lowest rung of the local government ladder. One of the most interesting cases of popular involvement came in the rejection by a group of elders of the nominee for the post of wakili, or deputy liwali, of Kitangari in Newala District. In this instance the people seemed to resent not merely the fact that the nominee had been brought back from Dar es Salaam after an extended absence from the area but also that he was regarded as being too closely identified with the incumbent liwali, who was in turn too closely identified with the European presence in Newala. It is perhaps one of those ironies of Tanzanian politics that if this candidate had actually been named wakili in the early 1950s, he would not in 1967 be one of the more influential and respected ministers of Julius Nyerere's government! The "spurned" candidate for the post of wakili was Lawi Sijaona, who served since 1961 as a member of Parliament (originally from Lindi, later from one of the two constituencies in Newala) and in 1967 was Minister of State in President Nyerere's government. The case of Lawi Sijaona is instructive, however, for it points to the basic dilemma faced by all liwalis when they accepted the nomination of the government. As government appointees, were they representatives of the people and interests in their areas, or were they solely the spokesmen of the British government in the conduct of local affairs? It was a dilemma which found men of good will and talent sharply divided with respect to how they could best serve their people.

## THE LIWALIATE

The delineation of the administrative units of local government under Indirect Rule had provided one of the most vexing problems for colonial administrators in the Makonde

2. *Ibid.*

districts. Clearly the virambo were too small for effective economic planning, and the British insistence on clearly defined boundaries undermined the very role of the chirambo as an effective social and economic unit whose membership and geographic jurisdiction changed in response to other situations. In establishing the liwaliates, the British administration had to deal with fewer—but larger and more efficient—administrative units, and in the process they reduced the many boundary disputes to the level of insignificance.

In delineating the boundaries of liwaliates, various factors were taken into account, including many which were ascriptive in character. In Lindi, for example, ethnicity was a significant consideration, and care was taken to separate the Makonde from the more numerous Mwera of that district. In Sudi, Nyangamara, and Nangaru divisions, the Makonde constituted 86, 78, and 69 per cent of the population, respectively. In Mingoyo liwaliate they were the largest (49 per cent) of several tribal groups in that division. In Mikindani District, which was overwhelmingly Makonde in membership, the major considerations were geographic continuity, density of population, and ease of access by all villagers to the liwaliate headquarters. The original five liwalis were increased by 1940 to eight, including one for the township of Mikindani with judicial rather than executive functions.

Only in Newala did the British administration attempt to create liwaliates which had some economic rationale—however imprecise. The five units in Newala were organized around the various sources of water available to the people on the plateau. Thus, the Kitangari, Namikupa, and Newala rivers, the Liteho pool, and the Mahuta wells formed the cores around which the administrative units were organized. In view of the important role water has played in the lives of the plateau Makonde, and considering the subsequent political significance of the quest for cheap and reliable supplies of water, the criterion of boundary delineation in Newala was a rational one.

Although the new units of administration in Lindi, Mikindani, and Newala might have added a measure of efficiency which was lacking in the preceding system, something else was lost in the process. This was the proximity of government to the needs and wishes of the people. By contrast with the mkulungwa system, the new form of government was remote. A Makonde cultivator with a problem often had to spend the better part of a day traveling to the liwali headquarters, only to discover upon arrival that the liwali was off on safari in another part of the liwaliate. If the cultivator did find the liwali at his headquarters, the chances were that the new executive was a stranger to the area, to its people, and to the day-to-day problems of survival. As one old man said to me in a small village of Kitangari liwaliate:

> I hate to go to Kitangari. We have to stand a long time when
> we reach the baraza, and when they do look at us, I must
> answer silly questions about who I am related to. Being
> old, we deserve to be known by those who will judge us.

The foregoing problem was only partially offset by the fact that the liwaliates were further divided into jumbeates, each under the jurisdiction of a village headman, or jumbe. Clearly, the jumbe commanded neither the respect nor the authority of the retired mkulungwa. Even where the jumbe had served under the previous system, he was now subordinated to a liwali, his jumbeate was not necessarily coterminous with the former chirambo, and his claim to office was not based upon tradition but upon the convenience of the British administration.


## RECRUITMENT OF LIWALIS

The transition from the mkulungwa to the liwali system did not immediately bring to office individuals possessing all the modern qualities desired by the British administrators. There was a paucity of educational facilities in the Makonde areas and only limited opportunities for Makonde to gain experience in government, commerce, and agriculture. Hence, in order for British administrators to secure a form of local government which had both a broad base of implicit popular support and a reasonably high level of efficiency, they unavoidably had to rely upon individuals whose qualifications were partially ascriptive in character. (See Figure 8 for details on the attributes of Makonde Native Authorities in the year 1956.)

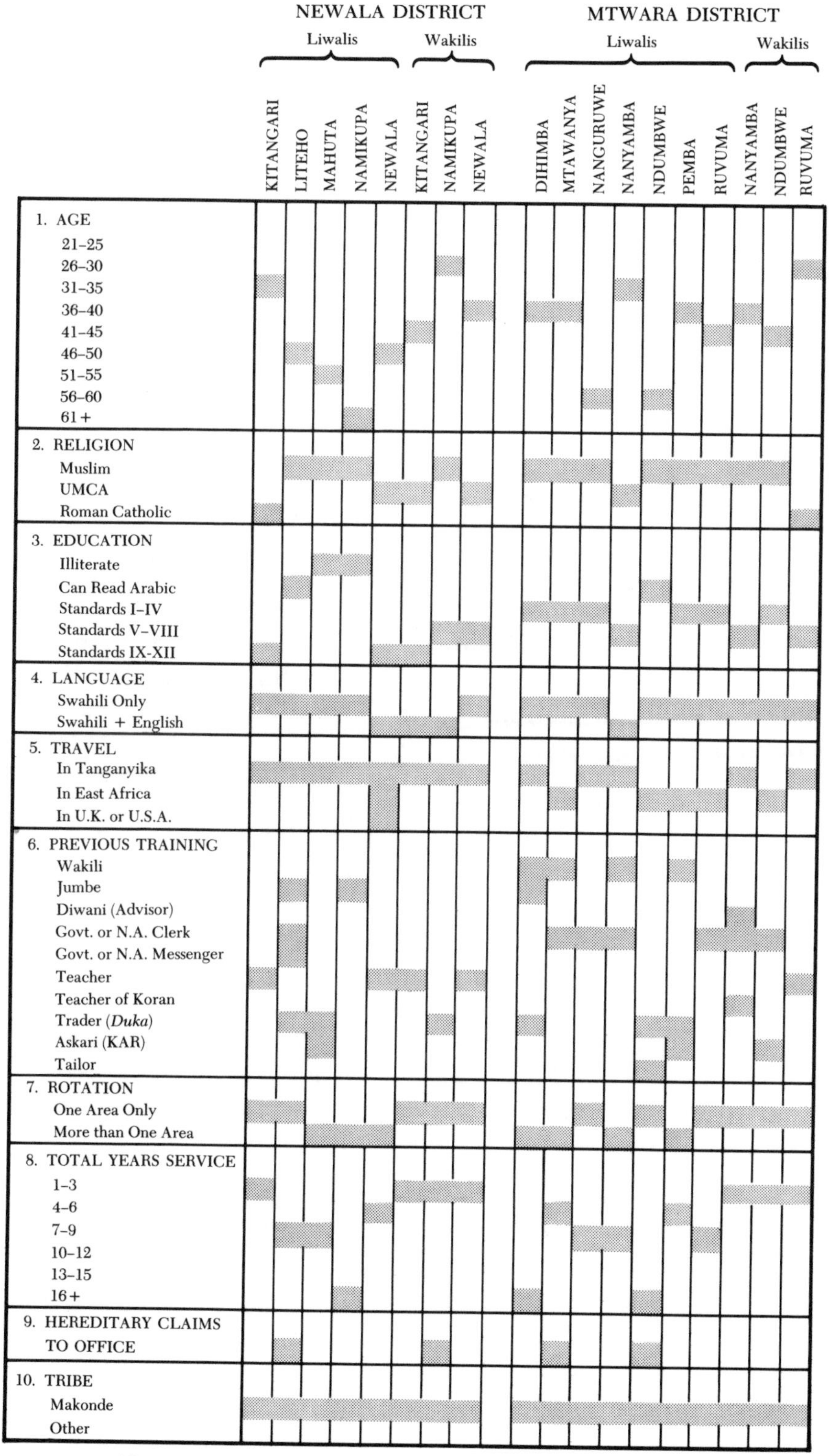

**NEWALA DISTRICT**  **MTWARA DISTRICT**

Liwalis | Wakilis (Newala) — Liwalis | Wakilis (Mtwara)

Columns (left to right):
KITANGARI, LITEHO, MAHUTA, NAMIKUPA, NEWALA | KITANGARI, NAMIKUPA, NEWALA | DIHIMBA, MTAWANYA, NANGURUWE, NANYAMBA, NDUMBWE, PEMBA, RUVUMA | NANYAMBA, NDUMBWE, RUVUMA

1. AGE
   21–25
   26–30
   31–35
   36–40
   41–45
   46–50
   51–55
   56–60
   61 +

2. RELIGION
   Muslim
   UMCA
   Roman Catholic

3. EDUCATION
   Illiterate
   Can Read Arabic
   Standards I–IV
   Standards V–VIII
   Standards IX–XII

4. LANGUAGE
   Swahili Only
   Swahili + English

5. TRAVEL
   In Tanganyika
   In East Africa
   In U.K. or U.S.A.

6. PREVIOUS TRAINING
   Wakili
   Jumbe
   Diwani (Advisor)
   Govt. or N.A. Clerk
   Govt. or N.A. Messenger
   Teacher
   Teacher of Koran
   Trader (*Duka*)
   Askari (KAR)
   Tailor

7. ROTATION
   One Area Only
   More than One Area

8. TOTAL YEARS SERVICE
   1–3
   4–6
   7–9
   10–12
   13–15
   16 +

9. HEREDITARY CLAIMS TO OFFICE

10. TRIBE
    Makonde
    Other

FIGURE 8:
MAKONDE NATIVE AUTHORITIES, 1956

One of the ascriptive criteria was hereditary descent. Despite the apparent rejection of this as a factor in political success when the liwali system was launched, it persisted until after independence. This was true even for Lindi and Mikindani districts, where in the initial designation of liwalis the incumbent wakulungwa were completely ignored.[3] In subsequent years the heirs of several of the former wakulungwa in Lindi were designated as liwalis. In 1956 two of the seven rural liwalis in Mtwara—the new name for Mikindani District— were related to former wakulungwa or jumbes. In Newala the link with the past remained a strong consideration throughout the liwali period 1942–1962. Three of the initial five liwalis in 1942 were former wakulungwa—including the former mkulungwa mkuu, Rashidi Mtalika. During my inquiries in 1956 I found one liwali and one wakili related to former wakulungwa. This persistence of hereditary qualifications is not too startling in view of the fact that educational opportunities were more readily available to the families of wakulungwa. Nevertheless, it was a factor of significance in Makonde politics. It was reported by many informants that liwalis and wakilis having "royal" credentials did emphasize these in dealings with their constituents even though they may have found these attributes embarrassing in their relations with their fellow liwalis.

A second ascriptive factor in the recruitment of liwalis and wakilis—religion—ultimately proved to be a source of bitter contention in the coastal districts. It had been the view of A. E. Kitching, the provincial commissioner who in 1938 had urged the governor to abandon the wakulungwa system in the Makonde area, that Islam should be given some sort of official recognition. In this regard, he was no doubt echoing the words of E. K. Lumley, the district officer in charge of Lindi in 1937. Lumley felt that Islamic religion and law should be

> cemented into the fabric of any system of native administration which seeks to serve the interests of a Mohamedan people. On these grounds I consider that it may be necessary to incorporate some of the Sheiks, Khadis, and other notables of the Moslem community into our scheme. These

3. Letter of A. E. Kitching to Chief Secretary, November 7, 1938 (TNA 12800/II).

persons would play their part not as teachers of a particular faith, but as advisers and councillors in the native courts and other representative gatherings of the villages. It is of serious administrative importance that the suspicion which exists in some areas that Government looks askance at the Mohamedan religion should be removed.[4]

To implement his point of view, Mr. Lumley, in nominating candidates for the ten liwaliates in the Makonde and Mwera areas of Lindi District, largely ignored the village headmen, suggesting that they were incapable of coming up with the names of qualified candidates. Instead he only consulted the "leaders of native life and Mohammedism" in the district, hoping thereby to find individuals who were well versed in Islamic law. Not unexpectedly, five of the ten persons the district officers ultimately recommended as liwalis had been Muslim *mwalimu* (advisers on Koranic law), Koranic teachers, or akidas or khadis under the Germans, where one of their primary responsibilities had been the enforcement of Muslim law of marriage and property.[5]

In announcing the change in local government in 1938, Mr. Lumley stressed in each baraza that the liwali system of government was based upon the *Utawala wa Mohamadia* ("Rule of Islam") and the *Hukumu ya Mungu* ("Authority of God"). It was perhaps inevitable that such pronouncements would arouse the Roman Catholic missionaries, who were having a difficult time in making headway among the Makonde of the coast. The Bishop of Ndana himself addressed a letter of complaint to Governor Sir Mark Aitchison Young stressing that the Christian minority was bound to be discriminated against if the new system was based upon authority within the religious, rather than the tribal, community of Lindi District. The provincial commissioner was clearly embarrassed by the unnecessary and tactless behavior of Mr. Lumley, and he conducted a formal inquiry. In January, 1939, the provincial commissioner held several barazas in which he renounced all previous

4. Letter to Provincial Commissioner of Lindi, October 21, 1937 (TNA 26753).
5. Letter of Mr. Foster, Acting Provincial Commissioner of Lindi, to Chief Secretary, April 7, 1938 (TNA 12800/II).

statements regarding the religious character of the liwali system. He stressed that only the governor, and not the Muslim community, could appoint liwalis. He urged any Christian or pagan who felt discriminated against because of his religion to bring the matter to the immediate attention of the administration.[6]

Although the incident in Lindi in 1938 probably discouraged future British administrators in the Makonde region from overtly employing religion as a factor in the recruitment of Native Authorities, the matter of religious affiliation of the liwali or wakili continued to be a vexatious problem throughout the colonial period. This was obviously the case where the search for a man of talent produced a candidate who was Roman Catholic or Anglican. In 1956 two Christian liwalis in Newala and one in Mtwara, as well as a Christian wakili in Newala, found themselves governing areas which were predominantly Muslim in background. In view of the paucity of Makonde Muslims who possessed secondary-school training, this trend may have continued had not the colonial system come abruptly to an end. For both Muslim and Christian officials, however, a further religious complication developed in that the religion of the liwali in one out of five cases in Newala and in six out of seven cases in Mtwara differed from that of a majority of his staff. Some of the implications of this will become apparent subsequently in the discussion of the Newala Local Council.

The issue of tribal affiliation as an ascriptive criterion for recruitment to the post of liwali was sidestepped in the early stages of the transition from the mkulungwa system. In Mikindani District in 1937, it was almost a matter of coincidence that four of the five original liwalis (the number was subsequently raised to seven) were Makonde and the fifth a son of a mixed Makonde-Yao union.[7] In Lindi District the quest of Mr. Lumley for individuals having a knowledge of Islamic law and custom led almost to a return to the akida system. The liwalis selected for the Makonde and Mwera areas of Lindi were, as the provincial commissioner stated, "for the most part of the

6. Letter of Bishop of Ndanda, September 12, 1938; letters of A. E. Kitching to Chief Secretary, November 7, 1938, and January 9, 1939 (TNA 12800/II).
7. Letter of A. E. Kitching to Chief Secretary, September 6, 1937 (TNA Vol. 21, 26752).

type of Arab found on the coast; this is inevitable under the circumstances." [8] Five of the ten were Arabs, including one whose home was at Lamu in Kenya. One of those listed as a Makonde in fact had an Indian father, although it was insisted that he had been reared by his Makonde mother and uncles. A second liwali had an Arab father. Of the two liwalis whose parents were both Makonde, one had served as an akida under both the Germans and the British.

In view of the above, it is understandable why the chief secretary feared that the officers in the Southern Province were attempting to return to the akida system. The selection of Arab liwalis could be, he commented, "a case where a cut-and-dried scheme has been put up for approval as being the wish of the people. It . . . makes me a little suspicious." [9] He was not entirely satisfied with the explanation that those who called themselves Arabs were really Makonde of mixed parentage who felt that their identification with the Arab community gave them added prestige—an "attitude of racial superiority which commanded respect." [10] Ultimately the provincial commissioner, Mr. Kitching, was compelled to conduct an inquiry in which it was admitted that "the persons appointed to be liwalis have few associations with the areas in which they are stationed, [and] a more determined effort should have been made to find local candidates." [11] Despite this admission, however, the situation in Lindi was not immediately altered.

Gradually, the principle of ethnicity—which had been adhered to from the outset in Newala District—became the pattern in the other two districts. By 1945 the Arabs in Lindi had been replaced by Makonde of proven ability in government, and Mikindani had achieved the same status by the time of my inquiries in 1956.[12] Although ethnicity was accepted as a requisite for office, residence in the locality was not. On the contrary, in hopes of putting the posts of liwali and wakili on a

8. Letter of Mr. Foster, Acting Provincial Commissioner of Lindi, to Chief Secretary, April 7, 1938 (TNA 12800/II).
9. Marginal comments by Mr. Sayre, Chief Secretary, to *ibid.*
10. Letter of Mr. Foster, May 25, 1938 (TNA 12800/II).
11. Letter to Chief Secretary, November 7, 1938 (TNA 12800/II).
12. Ethnicity can also make life uncomfortable for a Makonde liwali in areas where Makonde have only a tenuous majority or only a plurality, as was the

professional basis, the British from the outset adhered to a policy of rotation. Many of the smaller and less important liwaliates served either as apprenticeship posts for new liwalis before they moved on, or as semiretirement stations for less active liwalis who did not yet merit dismissal from the service. Hence, in 1956, of the five liwalis in Newala and seven in Mtwara, seven had had experience in at least two liwaliates. In addition to serving the above purposes of professionalism, rotation served to prevent the emergence of conflict-of-interest situations, which seemed to arise with long tenure.

Finally, two further criteria which may be considered ascriptive in character—sex and age—limited recruitment to the posts of liwali and wakili. The dissatisfaction of the British administrators in both Mikindani and Lindi districts with the performance of several female wakulungwa convinced them that women should be excluded from posts in the new system of local administration. The male ego in a predominantly Muslim society apparently could not cope with a female executive. There were many duties to which women simply could not attend.

The factor of age as a criterion for political office under the new system was in many ways the reverse of that which prevailed in traditional Makonde politics. Youth in the new administration was more highly regarded than old age, on the assumption that young men would have been exposed to European education and perhaps have modern experience which would better adapt them to the needs of contemporary local government. Hence it is difficult to label the factor of age as being strictly ascriptive in character. Regardless of the purpose, the annual reports of the district commissioners indicate a steady procession of liwalis being retired for old age. The comments of the district commissioner for Mtwara in 1954 are perhaps typical:

> During the course of the year two Liwalis resigned. They were both elderly men with many years service in the Na-

---

case in several liwaliates in Lindi. Even in Newala, however, an ex-mkulungwa of the Matambwe minority in Namikupa attempted to oust a Makonde liwali in 1949. Only intervention by the district commissioner thwarted the rebellion.

tive Administration, and their usefulness, which had doubtless been great in the past, had become but little. The opportunity was taken to appoint two younger men, both with experience in Local Government.[13]

The campaign to find qualified young men for the posts of liwali and wakili was a difficult one. The information obtained for Newala and Mtwara districts in 1956 indicated that of the eighteen Native Authorities involved (twelve liwalis and six wakilis), nine (50 per cent) were past the age of 41, and four (22 per cent) were over 51 years of age. On the other hand, four (22 per cent) were less than 35 years of age.

The primary achievement criterion in the selection process was education. It is not entirely accurate to state that the general level of education of the liwalis and wakilis in the Makonde areas in 1956 was superior to that of the general mass, for the level in that mass was low, reflecting the general absence of educational facilities. Moreover, the schools were largely in the hands of Christian missionaries, and Muslim parents were frequently reluctant to expose their youth to a Christian environment. In view of this, it is not surprising that of the eighteen liwalis and wakilis interviewed in Newala and Mtwara, there were four (22 per cent) who had no formal education in either Swahili or English or were only literate in Arabic, that is, had attended Koranic schools. Taking a middle-school education (Standards V through VIII) as being the minimum requisite for administering programs in education, health, agriculture, and other facets of local government, ten of the eighteen (56 per cent) lacked this minimum exposure to formal education. At the opposite end of the scale, only three of the officials (17 per cent) had completed secondary school. An indicator of change, however, was the fact that the individuals with the best educational credentials were those who were appointed most recently, suggesting a general upgrading of the qualifications of liwalis and wakilis.

Whether education brought the desired improvement in local administration, however, was a matter of debate within

13. *Annual Report,* 1954.

administrative circles. As the provincial commissioner, A. H. Pike, commented in his annual report for 1951:

> In the appointment of Liwalis generally there is a continu-
> ing dilemma about the educated and the uneducated. The
> men of character seem to lack education and the men of
> education seem to lack character, but in some of the recent
> appointments it has been possible to get men of both edu-
> cation and character who have been acceptable to the
> populace.

Often it was the older, less educated men who brought experience to the office of liwali which was lacking by the young
man fresh out of middle or secondary school. In all, the accumulated experience of the eighteen liwalis and wakilis of
Newala and Mtwara as primary- or secondary-school teachers
(five), traders (six), minor local government officials (six),
Government or Native Authority clerks (seven), askaris with
the military or the police (three), a Koranic teacher (one), and
a tailor (one) represented a pool of talent considerably above
the level of the Makonde population as a whole, where the majority were either cultivators or gatherers.


## LIWALIS OF NEWALA DISTRICT, 1956

Perhaps a better appreciation of the system of recruitment to office can be obtained from a more detailed biographi-
cal sketch of three liwalis from Newala District, representing
a wide range of personality and experience.

At one extreme in 1956 stood Liwali Nangololo Namaleche
of Liteho, who was at that time 46 years of age. Inasmuch as
he came from a Muslim family, his parents refused to send
him to either the UMCA or Roman Catholic schools, even
though they certainly could have afforded the fees. He was the
grandson of a Makonde who had served first as a jumbe under
the Germans and then as an mkulungwa when Indirect Rule
was introduced by the British. The grandfather was succeeded
by his son, the uncle of Liwali Nangololo. The uncle was also
called Nangololo, and it was he who became the first mkulungwa mkuu of the Newala Makonde. Thus, in terms of family

reputation, Liwali Nangololo felt that his credentials to govern were much more substantial than those of his fellow liwalis.

Despite his lack of formal education, Nangololo Namaleche managed to acquire reading and writing ability in Swahili as well as a moderate ability to speak English. He came up the administrative ladder the hard way, serving for six years as a court messenger, seven years as a public works supervisor for the central government, and three years as the jumbe of Kitangari Township. Along the way he had also spent two years as a shopkeeper in Kitangari. On the basis of his experience as well as his family position as a descendant of the famous Nangololo, he fully expected to be named liwali of Kitangari when that post became vacant in 1949. To Nangololo's dismay, the district commissioner brought in Justino Mponda, the headmaster of a secondary school in neighboring Masasi District, to serve in that capacity.

It was not until two years later that another district commissioner recognized Nangololo's talents and named him the liwali of the less important Liteho division. Subsequent district commissioners, however, did not have the same regard for his abilities as a "clever person"; they imposed upon Nangololo a deputy liwali, or wakili, who had a Standard VIII education and was expected to carry the primary burden in court work and administration. The pill was a bitter one for Nangololo to swallow, as the wakili was not only a Christian but also a relative of Justino Mponda! In the appointment of his staff, moreover, Nangololo found himself outshone by a cadre of five clerks who were far better educated (a Standard VII average) and included at least two Christians.

Nangololo's antagonist, Justino Mponda, represented the opposite end of the spectrum in terms of the expectations British administrators had with respect to the ideal qualifications of a liwali. He was a Makonde, still comparatively young—he was 39 at the time of his appointment—and with the proper educational background and experience. He had received a Standard XII education at St. Andrew's (Minaki), outside Dar es Salaam, and returned in 1935 to become a teacher at the UMCA school at Chidya in Masasi District, which he had attended as a young boy. After three years he became the headmaster, a position he held until 1949 when the district commissioner of

Newala recruited him for the post of liwali of Kitangari. After serving with distinction there he was elevated to the more important liwaliate of Newala in 1954, where he became a sort of unofficial adviser to several district commissioners.

As was true of other African leaders who had demonstrated a capacity for leadership at the local level, the British administrators provided Justino Mponda with a larger arena for his talents. From 1952 to 1958 he served two terms in the territorial Legislative Council as the African representative for the Southern Province. In 1952 he was also included in the Tanganyikan delegation at the coronation of Elizabeth II and as a member of the Tanganyikan delegation to the United Nations in New York, where he helped provide countertestimony to that of Julius Nyerere. Later he was sent to Britain for a three-month course on local government, which in many respects he regarded as being the turning point in his career. He returned from his trip to Britain fired with enthusiasm for putting the knowledge he had gained regarding community development into action in his own liwaliate.

To the people of Kitangari and Newala liwaliates, Justino Mponda was a source of mixed blessings. He was clearly anathema to many of the older Makonde, especially those who felt that his UMCA background worked to the detriment of Muslim interests in the appointment of local government personnel and the expansion of school facilities. The elders clearly resented the way he appeared to lecture them in the fashion he had found so successful in dealing with schoolboys. The younger element, on the other hand, were equivocal. They applauded his stands on modernization, expanding opportunities in education, and his emphasis on self-help. They admired his ability to debate Europeans in public on their own terms. Several young teachers had gone so far as to suggest to me in 1956 that Justino Mponda should be named the paramount chief of the Makonde, giving him a status equal to that of Thomas Marealle among the Chagga of Kilimanjaro. Yet, there were many of the younger element who resented his close identification with the overall purposes of the British administration, and they later came to hold him responsible for the inclusion of Europeans and Asians in the governing of Newala under the multiracial Local Council.

Justino Mponda himself tended to view his role in the political development of the Makonde as having the quality of a sacred mission. He had, he explained to me, long urged his schoolboys to take a more active role in governing themselves and improving their economic and social positions. Hence, when he was offered the post of liwali, he felt he could not in conscience refuse even though he recognized that his superior educational qualifications might be resented by many of the Makonde cultivators. Nevertheless, he felt that an example of hard work might spur his people on to greater things. If the Makonde did not have leaders who were articulate and prepared to stand up to European demands, he argued, they would continue to be governed by illiterate jumbes who could only bow, scrape, and say "Ndio, bwana" to the every command of the European for fear of losing their jobs.

Intermediate to the extremes of Nangololo Namaleche and Justino Mponda was Liwali Manzi Matumula of Mahuta. In many respects he typified the kind of personality and possessed the qualities which combined a high measure of talent with a fairly broad base of popular support. Like Nangololo, Liwali Manzi was a Muslim whose family decided not to send him to a mission school. He became literate in Swahili largely through his own efforts. Despite the generally conservative posture of his co-religionists, however, Manzi was determined to improve himself by becoming a merchant. In doing so, he found it necessary to compete with the better-financed Asians in the sale of cloth, pots, pans, and other commodities throughout the Southern Province. So successful was he as a trader that in the postwar period he became the founder and later manager of the African Traders Association, which had members throughout the area between Lake Nyasa and the Indian Ocean. It was his talents as a trader that first brought him to the attention of the British administration. During the war, when many commodities were in short supply, Manzi seemed to be able to provide many of the scarce items needed by the provincial administration. A European officer indicated to me that no questions were ever asked about the "methods" of supply.

In addition to the modern qualities he demonstrated in the field of self-help and economic improvement, Manzi Matumula was a strong advocate of schooling for the Muslim people of his area. His own sons had attended school, and during my earlier investigations one son had been accepted for a commercial course at Makerere University. Liwali Manzi was also instrumental in the establishment of a series of government schools throughout the district, thereby undercutting the fears that Muslim parents had when they sent their children to mission schools.

It was evident from my inquiries that Liwali Manzi enjoyed both the respect and the affection which neither Nangololo Namaleche or Justino Mponda had from their constituents. Religion, age (he was 55 at the time of my research in 1956), and experience as an askari in the German army gave him the respect of the elders comparable to the respect accorded him by the younger element because of his progressive ideas toward education and economic improvement. I asked people from various divisions to rank their own and neighboring liwalis, and Manzi came off with the best cumulative rating. The respondents felt that he was "kind"; "welcomed everyone to come to his baraza to voice their complaints"; "listened fully to everyone and heard all sides before making a decision"; "did not show favoritism to his own relatives or even other Muslims"; and "helped us stand on our own feet instead of always waiting for the Serikali [Government] to pass out our food and water." Manzi's own estimate of his success was that the Makonde wanted to be governed by one of their own— "someone with whom they can joke." Perhaps the best index of his ability to please the administration without losing popular support is the fact that from 1949 to 1956 his liwaliate was always the first to get its tax money collected.

## STAFFING THE LIWALIATE

Perhaps the real test of the liwali system of administration came in the quality of the men recruited for staff positions at the liwali headquarters and for the post of jumbe. With respect to staff members, the results were somewhat unclear. In terms of education, there was little doubt that the wakilis and the various court, tax, and market clerks had attained a generally higher level of education than that achieved by the liwalis as a group. The majority of the clerks possessed a Standard VII or VIII education, and in no instance did a clerk have less than Standard IV.

Offsetting the factor of education, however, was the very high incidence of dismissal for peculation and other offenses among the clerical class. Equally disturbing to those who were concerned about the adherence to modern criteria of selection was the frequency with which religion, family ties, and friendship were relevant factors in the recruitment of staff for the liwaliates. In the two liwaliates of Newala District in which the liwalis were Christian, all of the staff in Newala division, including the wakili and the court clerks, were Christian, as were the wakili and five of the seven court clerks in Kitangari. In the latter liwaliate two of the Roman Catholic (as opposed to the UMCA) clerks were added only after a Roman Catholic liwali had been appointed. On the other hand, in the liwaliate of Manzi Matumula six of his staff of eight were Muslims like himself. In the two liwaliates where Muslim liwalis presided over staffs which were predominantly Christian in character, intrigue over religious matters was a constant source of difficulty.

Although only fragmentary evidence was available on the extent to which kinship was a factor in recruitment, there were sufficient indications that it was as common under the liwali system as it had been under Indirect Rule. One of the most outstanding examples of kin and friendship ties being a factor in recruitment was the network of support which Liwali Justino Mponda had developed throughout Newala District. The wakili of Newala was his nephew; the wakili of Kitangari was from the same village and had been a classmate at Chidya and St. Andrew's (Minaki); the liwali of Kitangari had been appointed by the district commissioner upon the personal recommendation of Justino Mponda; the wakili of Namikupa was alleged to be a relative; and the clerk of the Local Council in 1955 and several other members of the district staff had been recruited by the peripatetic Liwali Justino from among his relatives, friends, former classmates, and former students.

## THE RECRUITMENT OF JUMBES

It was at the grassroots level that the liwali system met its severest test. The performance of the jumbes, who operated under the jurisdiction of the liwalis, were generally regarded as being the weakest element in the system of local government in the Makonde area. As the district commissioner of Newala in 1944 remarked:

> The jumbe, the teeth of the administrative saw, have had to undergo a fair amount of continual resetting and sharpening but their resilience has been up to the strain. Why does a jumbe remain a jumbe is a question which it would perhaps be just as unwise as inexpedient to solve.[14]

His successor five years later was even more pessimistic about the performance of the jumbes, noting:

> [They] seem hardly capable of summoning up enough energy to come to collect their pay. . . . the more effete and supine the headman, the more popular he is, and "parochialism" continues to be the most besetting problem among the Makonde.[15]

The administration, in the absence of an educated pool upon which to draw, was content to let tradition and local custom play a greater role in the recruitment of new jumbes. In the transition from the mkulungwa to the liwali system a more concerted effort was made to integrate the more efficient wakulungwa into the new system as jumbes, if for no other reason — said one official — than to obviate future discontent. Thus, in Mikindani District in 1937, only 13 of the 66 wakulungwa were forced to resign, and this included several women, old men, and a few who were regarded as manifestly unfit for office.[16] Later, as younger jumbes replaced the wakulungwa-*cum*-jumbe, an attempt was made to retain their services in one form or another. In Mikindani, for example, they were paid a small remuneration in the form of court sitting fees to encourage them to associate with the new local government officials. In Newala

---

14. Newala District, *Annual Report*, 1944.
15. *Ibid.*, 1949.
16. Letter of A. E. Kitching to Chief Secretary, September 6, 1937 (TNA Vol. 21, 26752).

District they were still regarded as useful in 1956 in assisting the tax collectors, helping to allocate land and solving land disputes, and in soliciting opinions regarding popular reactions to new programs. Thus, the legitimizing value of the wakulungwa as traditional authorities was not lost upon the district commissioners or the liwalis.[17]

The prevalence of the hereditary factor in the recruitment of Makonde jumbes was still apparent in 1956. In Newala District, 6 of the 73 jumbes were former wakulungwa, and a total of 46 of the 73 had hereditary qualifications of one sort or another. In Mtwara the hereditary factor had been substantially reduced as a result of the mass retirement of a number of elderly jumbes in 1955. Nevertheless, even there 17 jumbes (including 6 former wakulungwa) had traditional claims to office. In nearly every case examined, the succession was matrilineal, with a jumbe succeeding his brother, his maternal uncle, or his maternal grandfather. Indeed, the persistence of the notion of matrilineal succession had compelled a number of otherwise efficient jumbes to resign, being no longer able to cope with the constant challenges to authority emanating from the brothers and nephews of the former jumbes.

Recognition of the hereditary principle, however, did not mean that the people necessarily had a free hand in the selection of jumbes. In a few cases a strong jumbe might be able to indicate his choice of a successor prior to his death or retirement. In other cases the liwali might canvass the whole range of possible choices before indicating his preference. One liwali, to counter the weight of the wazee wa vijiji (the elders), would include some of the brighter young men in the decision-making, "even though," as he said, "the young people themselves are not suited for the post of jumbe." Since the poor performance of a jumbe was a reflection upon the liwali, the liwalis intervened fairly frequently to prevent the choice of a candidate with an unsavory reputation or one who was totally unqualified for the task.

Whatever the criteria employed, the level of competence of the jumbes in Newala and Mtwara districts in 1956 was rather

17. Discussions with former mkulungwa mkuu Rashidi Mtalika; see also Provincial Commissioner, Southern Province, *Annual Report*, 1945, p. 65.

low. In Newala District, 37 of the 73 jumbes were completely illiterate, and only 5 had any exposure whatever to a European-type education. In between were 6 who had taught themselves Swahili, plus an additional 25 who had attended Koranic schools and could read simple Arabic prose. Since Arabic was not one of the languages of administration, this did little by way of preparing the jumbes for the tasks of modern government although it may have been of prestige value in establishing their legitimacy within a predominantly Muslim society. It might also be added that several of them were much better versed in Islamic law than the liwalis and wakilis, especially where the latter were Christians. In terms of general experience, an overwhelming number of jumbes—59 of 73 (or 81 per cent) possessed at the time of their appointment talents which were no worse but certainly no better than those of their fellow citizens. That is, they were cultivators. Although 18 had an additional political or occupational role, the knowledge of local government problems gained by a road foreman, a policeman, or a court messenger is not very substantial. The 6 who had previously been wakulungwa and the 6 who had been traders or shopkeepers perhaps had a better appreciation of the problems of modern government and a money economy. Ultimately, however, age might have been the most significant factor in their lack of vigor. Only 14 of the 73 (19 per cent) were under 40 years of age, whereas 29 of the 73 (39 per cent) were 50 or older. Included in the latter figure were 11 (15 per cent) who were over 60.

If Mtwara District in 1956 seemed to be more promising than Newala, this was because of the mass replacement of elderly jumbes with younger men the year previously. Twenty-one of the 65 jumbes (32 per cent) were under 40 years of age, and only 9 (14 per cent) were past the age of 50. In each district the majority of jumbes were between 40 and 50 years of age. In terms of educational experience the jumbes of Mtwara were roughly in the same category: 4 (6 per cent) had some exposure to European education; another 4 had taught themselves to read Swahili; 30 (45 per cent) could read simple Arabic; and 27 (42 per cent) were completely illiterate. A higher number, 24 of the 65 jumbes (37 per cent) brought to their posts talents other than those of simple cultivators. Of this latter group, however, only the 6 former wakulungwa, the ex-teacher, the dhow captain, four fishermen, and the two traders had experience which might have proved useful in the administration of a jumbeate.

Given the limited talents of the jumbes of Newala and Mtwara, it is not surprising that the liwalis and district commissioners rated them most effective only with respect to two tasks: tax collection and the enforcement of Native Authority ordinances relating to peace and order. In the more complicated tasks, especially those relating to the introduction of new agricultural techniques, programs in health and sanitation, and cooperation with the primary-school officials, the jumbes lacked either the interest or the understanding to be very effective local government administrators.

In 1956 it was the jumbe who was the most frustrated of all the local government officials in the Makonde region. He was invariably berated at every turn—and frequently in public— by the liwali or the district commissioner for his poor performance. He was constantly being challenged by the various litawa heads in his jumbeate, who still jealously guarded kinship prerogatives and attempted to deprive him of his meager fees by settling minor disputes among themselves. His life was especially difficult if he had several ex-wakulungwa living in his area, for they continued to wield a considerable amount of influence behind the scene. And the most recent challenge came from the "Standard IV boys," who would not themselves consent to serve as jumbes since they found the pay too low and the work insufficiently interesting. Moreover, being somewhat versed in the ways of the world, the young unemployed insisted that their cases and problems be taken directly to the liwali or the district commissioner instead of having to "waste time with illiterate old men."

## THE ASSESSMENT

The measures which the British officials took in the Makonde districts to establish more rational units of local government and to staff the administrative machinery with men having achievement rather than ascriptive qualities for

governing were undoubtedly acceptable to the current leadership of TANU in its efforts to establish a modernized bureaucracy throughout Tanzania. The British efforts, however, were
largely half-measures rather than vigorous frontal assaults on
the old order. One serious obstacle was the lack of African
personnel with the requisite education and experience who
were willing to undertake, at very low pay and with few psychic
rewards, the hard task of transforming a traditional society. The
lack of schools and other modern structures of society would
leave the area short of qualified personnel for some years to
come.

Equally obstructive to the goals of modernization were the
attitudes of two groups whose transformation was essential
to the success of the experiment. The first, perhaps obviously,
comprised the Makonde masses who still attached great
importance to the traditional claims to rulership made by the
wakulungwa as well as to the unofficial and often unrecognized
structures through which the Makonde continued to resolve
their various social, economic, and even political problems.
Religion, family ties, and other social linkages, as well as
deeply rooted attitudes toward traditional ways of earning a
living, made even the best-qualified liwali and the best-inten-
tioned British officer ineffective agents of modernization.

The second group obstructing modernization was perhaps
less obvious. This was the British administrative class itself,
which suffered a deep ambivalence. On the one hand, rotation
in office constantly brought to the area men who were either
sentimentally or by dint of experience elsewhere, committed
to the retention and strengthening of tribal affiliations, traditional values, and even Islam. The commitment to the foregoing hampered the creation of an African administrative class
that was secular in outlook and prepared to make decisions on
the basis of rationality rather than upon primordial attachments.
On the other hand, when the British administrators did place
men with modern talents in positions of responsibility in local
government, the Europeans were reluctant to "let go of the
leash." Minor sins of omission and commission might lead to
public rebukes or outright dismissal from office. The European
presence was always there, seemingly undercutting any attempts on the part of the liwalis to establish genuine popular

bases of support. Thus, Africans of talent who did accept posts in local government ran the almost certain risk of being labeled tools of the British government.

Finally, as in the preceding periods of European rule, there was a continued reliance upon coercion as the most effective means for altering human behavior rather than the encouragement of more positive approaches. Instead of demonstration plots and widespread distribution of improved seed, a series of Native Authority rules and ordinances carrying various kinds of penalties for violating measures regarding soil conservation or famine planting constituted the agricultural program for the area. Similarly lacking in educational approaches to social change were the "programs" in health, natural-resource conservation, and moral improvement.

# 8:
# Encouragement
# to Tribalism

One of the briefest and least formalized of the British experiments with administrative reform of the Makonde political system illustrates in sharp perspective the capricious character of colonial rule. This was the tentative planning between 1949 and 1954 designed to bring the Makonde of Newala and Mtwara districts (and presumably those of Lindi District as well at a later time) into a single administrative unit. The experiment was referred to as *Umakonde Umoja,* or "Unity of the Makonde People" — a name chosen perhaps with the intent of giving the move a popular base of support.

Viewed from the standpoint of administrative efficiency, the idea of consolidating the two districts could be regarded as both progressive and modern. It took into account the fact that the boundaries drawn in the early part of the century were purely arbitrary and designed for the administrative convenience of the understaffed European colonial service. Now, in the days of large-scale planning in the fields of health, education, and economic development, it was necessary to go beyond the village and the district and use larger regional units for making more rational decisions about sources of revenue, road planning, market networks, water development, secondary-school locations, and antimalaria campaigns. Since the people of

Mtwara and Newala were predominantly Kimakonde speakers, there were no real problems of communication. Despite the head start, moreover, that the Makonde of Newala had in educational facilities and production of cash crops, the level of development in the two districts was regarded as a "natural" outgrowth of an idea which had been advocated intermittently ever since the tenuous administrative union of Newala and Mikindani (the former name of Mtwara) had been tried in 1926 and quickly abandoned. A. M. J. Turnbull, provincial commissioner of the southern region, recorded in 1928 that

> The ultimate aim is to secure a tribal amalgamation when practicable, but it is clear that it cannot be rushed, and that all must obtain first a better idea of the principles of indirect rule and of the benefits of the tribe being united as one unit.[1]

Viewed from another perspective, however, the idea of Umakonde Umoja was retrogressive. Oddly enough, it emphasized ethnic exclusivism at a time when the budding African nationalist leadership was attempting to forge a political movement which was nontribal in character and when the European colonial administration in Dar es Salaam was itself on the brink of launching a series of political experiments emphasizing multiracial cooperation rather than ethnic exclusivism. It was retrogressive, too, in that it seemed calculated to recapture part of the spirit of Indirect Rule that was lost when the mkulungwa system of local administration was abandoned. The tribe was still a "romantic" unit of administration for some of the old-time colonial administrators, just as the tribe still has a very romantic appeal to anthropologists and other social scientists who work in Africa. Finally, the idea of Umakonde Umoja can be regarded as retrogressive since it did not take into account the rights of, or the contribution that could be made by, the non-Makonde minorities within the two districts. Reference has already been made to the British penchant for classificatory neatness, which resulted in the "elimination" of tribal groups to suit the convenience of the census-taker. There was also the minority discontent stemming from Matambwe and Makua headmen having to participate in a tribal

1. Lindi Province, Provincial Book.

council consisting largely of Makonde. Umakonde Umoja would make the position of the non-Makonde minorities even more unbearable than it had been under the mkulungwa system.

My investigations in 1955 and 1956 convinced me that the origin of the experiment in district consolidation was European in inspiration, despite the fact that the secretariat in Dar es Salaam had for two decades stoutly resisted efforts on the part of administrators in the Southern Province to translate Commissioner Turnbull's goal of tribal consolidation into reality. It is difficult to believe that the isolated and parochial Makonde could suddenly have put aside their local jealousies and come up with the idea that the Makonde people must be united. It is easier to believe that the administrators in the Makonde area were impressed by the progress of tribal amalgamation in the Lake Province, where the Sukuma Federal Council had brought together into a single political system more than one million Sukuma tribesmen who had previously been divided among more than fifty chiefdoms and five administrative districts.[2] The move for Umakonde Umoja, moreover, coincided with the plans to launch a county form of local government in Tanganyika — a project which was ultimately recommended by the constitutional commission headed by Professor W. J. M. Mackenzie in 1951 and took legal form in the Local Government Ordinance of 1953. As in the case of the launching of Indirect Rule in 1927, the British officers in the remote Southern Province saw no reason why they should not be permitted to participate in, or even anticipate, major changes in territorial administrative policy.

The change in official attitude in the Southern Province must have occurred during 1949, and it constituted an abrupt change indeed. Only three years previously, for example, the provincial commissioner had written:

> In Umakonde the Native Authorities of the Districts of Newala and Mikindani have functioned so adequately as

2. See J. Gus Liebenow, "Responses to Planned Political Change in a Tanganyika Tribal Group," *American Political Science Review*, L (June, 1956), 442–61.

> to warrant no comments, the Native Authority of Newala being as perfect a set-up as one can expect.[3]

His successor, A. H. Pike, commented two years later that in the Makonde districts

> the local population is more parochially than politically conscious. There is no demand for a democratic council — in fact the people are uninterested in councils, but they dislike any outsider being employed in any of the local Native Administrations.[4]

By 1949, however, Mr. Pike dramatically reversed his ground and concluded that Makonde parochialism had now been

> turned to good account by creating a joint Makonde Council for [Newala and Mikindani]. This has already functioned with great success and shows signs of developing that political consciousness now so obviously lacking. . . . [This council] shows every sign of dealing with the local problems in an able and energetic way.[5]

The only suggestion I had that the idea was African rather than European in origin came from a liwali from Mtwara District who indicated that the district commissioners were responding to complaints from the plateau Makonde, who were distressed by the rude treatment that they received when they went to Lindi, Mtwara, or Mikindani. The plateau Makonde felt that their coastal cousins regarded themselves as superior because of their contact with Arabs. Since the plateau Makonde had had a better exposure to Westernized education, they saw no reason why they should have to tolerate such abuse. It was to overcome this misunderstanding, the liwali insisted, that the idea of Umakonde Umoja was launched.

The primary structural form that Umakonde Umoja took during the period from 1949 to 1953 was the semiannual meetings of the liwalis, *diwanis* (councilors), and European administrative officers of Newala and Mtwara districts. Although the meetings were informal, rather than legally constituted gatherings, it was assumed at the outset that the body

3. J. Rooke-Johnston, *Annual Report*, 1946, p. 48.
4. Southern Province, *Annual Report*, 1948, p. 68.
5. *Ibid.*, 1949, p. 93.

would achieve constitutional status and have authority to take common action in formulating legislation and programs for the region as a whole. During its lifetime the joint council was considered a useful forum for the discussion of common problems. In May, 1953, for example, the council considered the launching of a joint ploughing scheme for the Ruvuma Valley, the marketing of produce within the region, the employment of a game scout to keep hippopotamuses and other marauding animals under control, the joint operation of the Mkunya Leprosarium in Newala District, the formation of a joint educational committee to meet the needs of the entire Makonde region, the feasibility of employing joint personnel as supervisors of dispensaries within the two districts, and the organization of all welfare activities (such as sports, mass literacy, and youth activities) on a Makonde-wide basis.

The level of enthusiasm on the part of the liwalis of Newala District in particular was quite high. Early in the history of the joint discussions, two liwalis from each district were sent to Sukumaland to observe the operations of the Federal Council there. Upon hearing their report the liwalis were unanimous in their recommendation to move ahead quickly to the stage of framing a charter of federation. Even prior to this, however, the liwalis requested that the services of a government sociologist be made available to them so that there could be a codification of Makonde customary law, unifying all Native Authority rulings with regard to marriage, divorce, inheritance, and other traditional matters.[6] Moreover, to bring the idea of Umakonde Umoja to the masses and thereby popularize the notion, a monthly newspaper was published for each of the two districts to publicize local government programs, events of interest to all Makonde, and other items which might further the idea of tribal solidarity.[7]

The enthusiasm of the liwalis seemed to be matched by that of the British administrators. H. S. Senior, provincial commissioner in 1950, was convinced that the joint meetings had

6. The government sociologist was Wilfred Whitely, who met with the council in 1951. He retired from government service shortly thereafter to pursue an academic career.

7. The newspaper in Newala was called *Uchele* (Dawn Has Come), and the one in Mtwara was entitled *Katapala* (Thing Which Pleases).

"proved the forum for much useful discussion of matters of common interest."[8] His successor, A. H. Pike, was almost euphoric in his comments the following year:

> [There is] undoubtedly a sense of unity arising between the Makonde of Newala and Mikindani, which should form a useful base for future political developments. The minor difficulty that the Mikindani Makonde are mostly Moham- medan and the Newala Makonde tend to be Christian does not seem to have adversely affected these meetings; at the moment a common tribal bond seems to be a greater unifying factor than the division caused by different religions.[9]

Just as abruptly as it had been started, the experiment in Umakonde Umoja came to a halt in 1953. Indeed, several of the liwalis interviewed in 1956 were not sure that the idea of interdistrict meetings had been abandoned; they were just aware that no meetings had taken place during the previous two years. The official explanation was given by the provincial commissioner in 1953:

> Neither [Newala nor Mikindani] was ready for it; Newala being progressive, industrious, and wealthy had little, except tribal name in common with a more apathetic coastal Mikindani. It was finally decided that, for the time being, both should develop independently.[10]

This may indeed have been at least a part of the actual truth, for the minutes of the final meeting, held in August, 1953, indicated that the Newala liwalis had expressed fears that the prosperity of their district might be threatened if they had to share their revenue with the less developed Mtwara District. Liwali Justino Mponda expressed the view that the average Makonde peasant farmer hardly understood the functioning of his own liwaliate or district; how could he be expected to understand the functioning of a larger regional grouping of Makonde? Apparently all that they desired at this stage was informal cooperation in social and economic matters. The interviews with liwalis from both districts also confirms the opinion that jealousy, animosity, and ill-will were much in

8. Southern Province, *Annual Report*, 1950, p. 107.
9. *Ibid.*, 1951, p. 108.
10. S. D. Troup, Southern Province, *Annual Report*, 1953, p. 97.

evidence during the joint meetings. A liwali from Mtwara interviewed in 1956 stated, for example, that "the liwalis of Newala had spoiled the idea of Umakonde Umoja. They had lots of money for their council and they feared that the people of Mtwara would steal it from them." On the other hand, several Newala liwalis pointed out that the Mtwara group had always managed to shy away from cooperation when it meant that they would be expected to contribute funds to a project such as the Chiumo Tractor Scheme for developing the Ruvuma Valley. As one Newala liwali angrily stated: "We got tired of the arrogance of those coastal people, especially when we all know that their people are too lazy to work and pay taxes and that they are lacking in any ideas of progress." Another suggested that the notion of Umakonde Umoja failed because "some of the Mtwara liwalis are really Arabs; what would they care about Makonde unity?"

While the antagonism indicated above may in fact have been an element in the termination of the experiment, it can hardly be considered a sufficient reason. Indeed, the animosity between the plateau Makonde and their coastal brethren had been known for generations. In 1928, for example, Commissioner Turnbull recorded in the *Southern Province Book:*

> The Makonde of the Plateau have maintained tribal law and custom to a far greater extent than those in the coastal regions, and they look down on the latter, who in turn regard the Makonde of the Plateau as people of the [bush].

More likely explanations are that the British enthusiasm toward the idea of Umakonde Umoja cooled as a result of two developments. The first was the peculiar kind of tribal nationalism that was generated by the joint meetings of liwalis. As was true elsewhere in the territory, the British were prepared to encourage tribal cooperation, but they shied away from movements to establish paramount chieftainships. The mood of the day favored modern secular councils over traditional vestiges of authority. Hence, the British in Newala and Mikindani viewed as retrogressive the demands made by several divisional councils in 1951 and 1952 that a *Liwali Mkuu,* or "King of the Makonde," be elected to govern a united Makonde people. Fearing a recurrence of the situation which had developed among the Chagga and Nyakyusa in which the

British ultimately had to accede to demands for the establishment of paramount chieftainships, the British in the Southern Province decided to dampen the enthusiasm for Umakonde Umoja.[11] They were also disturbed by the ethnic parochialism which found the councils of both districts insisting that only Makonde be permitted to hold posts in local government. The absurdity of this position was pointed out to the liwalis by the district commissioner of Mikindani in 1951 when he noted that there were only 23 Makonde boys who were then enrolled in Standard V or better, and that only a very few Makonde had reached even that standard in the past. In the face of tribal nationalism, the government began to emphasize that the joint council of liwalis should create machinery needed for developing the two districts "primarily economically and only secondarily politically."[12]

The British were also concerned by the fact that the tribal nationalism generated by the idea of Umakonde Umoja had taken shape in a popular association which attempted to operate outside the framework of the established local government system. During this period, the predecessors of the Tanganyika African National Union and other political associations based upon tribal membership (e.g., the Sukuma and Haya unions) were having difficulties surmounting the various legal and practical hurdles placed in their paths, for the British administration in Tanganyika was not interested in encouraging the growth of popular political organizations in the Southern Province. And yet the brief appearance of the Wamakonde Union in 1953 seemed to be in direct response to the idea of Umakonde Umoja. Oddly enough, however, its main base of operation seemed to be in Lindi District, an area which had not been included in the joint deliberations. In a petition sent by four officers of the Wamakonde Union to the district commissioner of Lindi, an attempt was made to emphasize the supremacy of the Makonde within Lindi District.[13]

11. See J. Gus Liebenow, "Tribalism, Traditionalism, and Modernism in Chagga Local Government," *Journal of African Administration,* X (April, 1958), 71–82.

12. Mikindani District, *Annual Report,* 1951.

13. Letter of August 8, 1953, written in Swahili by Ismaili Mussa Ndiseze, Hassani Omari, Isse Masudi, and Alli Bwankuu of Kitala (Lukumbi) Mingoyo, Lindi District.

The essence of the letter was contained in this statement:

> We strongly oppose the claim by the Wamwera that part of Lindi is their property, and we say emphatically the truth which is clear shows that not even one section of Lindi District is theirs. All parts are the property of the Wamakonde alone, and it is they who came upon us and we welcomed them.

Asserting that the Mwera had a long history of trouble-making among all their neighbors as well as with the Arabs and later with the Germans during the Maji Maji Rebellion, the leaders of the Wamakonde Union insisted that the Mwera "must be under our authority or they must return to their homeland" in Mozambique. This outburst of Makonde tribal nationalism certainly complicated the tasks of British administrators in Lindi, who were attempting to move rapidly to a more efficient, non-tribal form of local government. Inasmuch as the leading candidate for the post of presiding officer of the Lindi council of liwalis was of the Mwera tribal group, the reaction of the Makonde should not have been surprising. Like many of the tribal-based associations which emerged during the last phases of colonial rule, the Wamakonde Union sputtered briefly and then failed.

In addition to British concern over the development of Makonde tribal nationalism, the second unstated reason for British abandonment of Umakonde Umoja is that it conflicted with the notion of multiracialism, which in certain respects was the "religion" of Governor Sir Edward Twining's administration, just as Indirect Rule had been the "religion" of the disciples of Sir Donald Cameron.[14] It apparently mattered little that the Southern Province was not typically multiracial in composition. The latest tergiversation in colonial policy had to be tested in Newala, as the next chapter will discuss.

Despite its very brief existence, the idea of Umakonde Umoja did manage to excite the enthusiasm of the Makonde throughout Mtwara and Newala districts. For a time it brought both the traditionalists and the modernists in the younger generation of Makonde into a common camp. The traditionalists saw

14. See Cranford Pratt, " 'Multi-racialism' and Local Government in Tanganyika," *Race*, II (November, 1960), 33–49.

Umakonde Umoja as a device for shoring up tribal values, especially those which emphasized respect for the elders. The notion of a liwali mkuu hearkened back, in Newala District at least, to the period of the mkulungwa mkuu, when the strengthening of tribal bonds had coincided with a reinforcing of traditional structures and values.

Although by 1968 the younger Makonde were to condemn Umakonde Umoja as being unprogressive because it emphasized tribal parochialism at the expense of loyalties to a greater Tanzania, in 1956 the small nucleus of educated Makonde supported the notion of Makonde unity. Unappreciative of the many economic, educational, and historic considerations involved, they erroneously assumed that the prosperity of the Chagga, Nyakyusa, Sukuma, and Nyamwezi was attributable almost exclusively to their recent achievement of unity. Since the most advanced—the Chagga—had achieved unity under a paramount chief, the younger Makonde assumed that this then must be the appropriate course for them to follow. Only in this way, it was assumed, would the Makonde have a leader who could successfully challenge the European administrators and resist unpopular programs. This group felt betrayed when the semiannual joint councils were allowed to lapse, and especially so when the next stage of administrative innovation found Europeans and Asians being associated with the liwalis in the planning of the Makonde future.

# 9:
# The Experiment
# in Multiracialism

The introduction of the liwali system between 1937 and 1942 placed the transformation of local government in the Makonde area a decade or more ahead of other districts of Tanganyika in which the philosophy of Indirect Rule continued to be followed slavishly. The abandonment of traditional rulership, however, was only one aspect of the transformation of local government which the British sought to accomplish in the postwar period. Clearly the British reformers were seeking larger units of local government which would be more efficient in providing services in the fields of health, education, social development, and natural-resource utilization. Efficiency, however, was related to responsibility, and the reformers were seeking meaningful ways of incorporating teachers, businessmen, successful farmers, and other members of the emergent African elite into the structure of local planning. Only by securing the active support of the newly educated, it was argued, could the progress toward self-government and modernization be both creative and orderly.

The crux of the modernization of local government was the conciliar system, which was embodied in the Local Government

Ordinance of 1953.[1] Even prior to the enactment of the ordinance, a series of local councils had already been established in many villages, chiefdoms, divisions, and even several districts in the territory. Where feasible, it was planned that two or more of Tanganyika's fifty-four districts could be amalgamated into larger units called counties. Following the reforms of local governments which were going on in Britain itself during this same period, the councils at each level of authority were to be multipurpose bodies with standing committees having responsibility for local programs in the fields of health, education, community development, and resource utilization. While the central government still supervised the operation of the system and bore the major responsibility for financing, the councils increasingly were to share in the responsibilities for planning, executing, and financing programs through locally levied rates, fees, and cesses. The councils at each level were to be "popular," with both indirectly and directly elected members, even though the British administration might control the major membership of these bodies through appointment. Finally, to ensure that the system functioned as an integrated whole, some of the membership of each council above the village level consisted partly of persons who had been co-opted from councils at the level immediately below.

The postwar changes were to alter not only the structure of local government but also the quality of participation, by raising the vision of the African beyond his village and even beyond his tribe. Wherever possible the units of local government were to be nontribal or at least multitribal in jurisdiction. Furthermore, it had become increasingly obvious from 1949 onward that government at all levels in Tanganyika was to be multiracial in character, with Europeans and Asians being given significant roles in the development of national policy and local services. Multiracialism was to be pursued even though non-African minorities constituted less than 2 per cent of the total population of Tanganyika and despite the fact that Africans in Kenya and Central Africa at that time were rejecting the idea of a greater political role for Europeans and Asians

---

1. See J. Gus Liebenow, "Some Problems in Introducing Local Government Reform in Tanganyika," *Journal of African Administration*, VIII (July, 1956), 132–39.

in their countries. Governor Sir Edward Twining, nevertheless, persisted because he believed that an extraordinary voice had to be given to an unusually small minority in order to utilize and retain the ideas and services they alone at that time could contribute to the development of Tanganyika.[2] Finally, the new councils were to be secular in character. That is, the approach to the problems of the environment was to be rational and scientific rather than based upon tradition or the performance of magic and ritual. Increasingly, moreover, the membership of the councils was to be based upon achievement criteria with the role of traditional authorities being substantially reduced. Traditional personages might serve as local administrators, but their legislative and executive roles were to be shared with persons having modern experiences and their judicial roles were to be surrendered entirely to independent magistrates.

## THE MOVE TOWARD A LOCAL COUNCIL IN NEWALA

The popularization of district councils in the Makonde area of Tanganyika preceded the introduction of the Local Government Ordinance by four years. In 1949 a token number of diwanis, or councilors, were nominated to assist the liwalis and jumbes in their deliberation of affairs within the districts. The following year, councils were established at the village and divisional (liwaliate) levels. In Newala District, change proceeded more rapidly than in the other Makonde districts with the addition of a significant number of unofficial members at each level. At the divisional level, for example, the liwali presided over a council consisting of all the jumbes within the liwaliate as well as one diwani for each jumbeate within the division.[3] At the same time the district council's membership was broadened so that the district commissioner heard not only from the five liwalis but from others as well.

2. See Cranford Pratt, "'Multi-racialism' and Local Government in Tanganyika," *Race*, II (November, 1960), 33–49.
3. See Ian H. Norton, "An Inter-racial Local Council in Tanganyika," *Journal of African Administration*, VIII (January, 1956), 26–32, an article written by the district commissioner in charge of Newala during its most critical period of administrative change.

Each divisional council was permitted to elect one of its un-official members and one jumbe to represent it at the district level. Finally, to give the unofficial side an equal voice, six diwanis were selected by the district commissioner to ensure that teachers, progressive farmers, deacons, African business-men, and others would have a voice in the district's affairs.

In line with Governor Twining's desire for multiracialism, the next "reform" in local government in Newala included the addition of three Europeans and two Asians as co-opted members of the council, even though Newala District was perhaps one of the least likely candidates for multiracialism in the whole of Tanganyika. It contained only 400 Asian merchants and their families and 50 Europeans, as opposed to 175,000 Africans! Missionaries, administrators, and their families dominated the European population, and there was only one permanent European resident—a sisal grower and labor re-cruiter, who eventually ran afoul of the law on a morals charge.

Inasmuch as there was no legal authority for the inclusion of non-Africans as members of a Native Authority, the en-larged body functioned as an advisory council for two years. Early in 1954, District Commissioner Ian Norton requested the central government to reconstitute the district council as a multiracial Local Council under the provisions of the 1953 Ordinance. In a manner reminiscent of earlier manipulation of the Makonde political system, Mr. Norton insisted that there was a "widespread desire of the Wamakonde that such an interracial council should be formed and should have power to enact orders which would be binding over people of all races in the district." [4] Since there was no other precedent to guide the central government, a "shadow" local council was estab-lished for the purposes of experimentation.

The "shadow" council, under the chairmanship of the dis-trict commissioner, was a broad mix of racial representatives, women as well as men, Native Authorities and popular repre-sentatives, and a scattering of commercial, educational, and other constituency interests. The "shadow" council was con-stituted into committees on finance, natural-resource develop-ment, social services, staff and general services, and education.

4. *Ibid.*, p. 28.

Although the council and its committees met quarterly, the finance committee met more frequently in order to prepare the annual budget, or estimates. To provide further continuity the council selected a clerk to conduct the day-to-day affairs of the council and to keep its members informed of new developments.

On the assumption that the "shadow" council had functioned well during most of 1954, the central government in December issued the instrument which created Newala as the first multiracial Local Council in Tanganyika. Subsequent events almost made it the *only* multiracial council created at the district level, since only Mafia District emulated the experiment. That, however, was not foreseen in 1954 when Commissioner Norton heralded what he thought was the dawn of a new era in multiracialism. The new Local Council became the successor to the Native Authority, and all previous acts which were not racially discriminatory were considered bye-laws of the new body. The only exception permitted liwalis to handle cases dealing exclusively with Africans where customary rules of law could be observed and when all parties were agreed. The liwalis and jumbes now became servants of the Local Council in the exercise of administrative and judicial duties.

## Makonde Responses
## to the Local Council

The Makonde responses to the reforms in local government can best be appreciated by considering the reaction of Africans generally to the proposals of the British government to develop self-government in its colonies in West, East, and Central Africa in the postwar period. The policy statement to which most African nationalists reacted was the speech of Colonial Secretary Arthur Creech Jones to Parliament in July, 1947:

> The encouragement of local political interest and the building up of a system of efficient and democratic local government is a cardinal feature of British policy in Africa. It is now recognized that the political progress of the territories is dependent on the development of responsibility

in local government, that without sound local government a democratic political system at the centre is not possible, and that, if social services are to be built up and expanded, there must be efficient organs of local government directly representative of the people to operate and control them.

African nationalists did not object to the reforms in local government per se; indeed, they too regarded the reliance upon traditional authorities as obsolete. They did reject the notion that local government should serve as a substitute for self-government at the territorial level. Without reform at the center, local government reform would have the effect of strengthening rather than weakening the colonial system of administration, making it increasingly difficult for the emergent elites to form broad alliances for the ultimate smashing of the colonial machine. They rejected, too, as nonhistorical even for Britain the assumption that local government institutions were training grounds for participation in national politics.

In view of the statements of District Commissioner Norton and Liwali Justino Mponda that the idea for a multiracial Local Council arose from the ranks of the liwalis and their people, one might at least have expected general enthusiasm for the experiment from this sector of African opinion. On the contrary, of eight officials (five liwalis and three wakilis) interviewed on the subject, four had explicit or implicit reservations about the popular basis of the idea. One stated quite bluntly that he first heard about the idea of a Local Council when he attended a meeting of liwalis in Newala. A second commented resignedly: "Who were we to question the District Commissioner? People never made noises about the dismissal of the wakulungwa. Why object to this? Government is the affair of the Europeans. Is it our lot to complain?" Still a third liwali stated that the district commissioner had simply informed him that the people of Newala were going to have a new type of local government. When this liwali indicated that he would like to know more about it, he received a response from the district commissioner which was reminiscent of the advice given by the witch to Hansel and Gretel as she invited them to investigate the interior of her oven: "The D.C. told us that the best way to see what it was all about would be to try to work with it."

As I moved about the district in 1955 and 1956, interviewing jumbes or attending village councils and gatherings of elders, the criticism was not only much more vociferous but also much more specific in its indictment of the Local Council. An almost universal complaint, which has particular relevance in the African context of justice and fair play, was the statement of one jumbe: "The D.C. got us all to attend a baraza at Kitangari because he said he very badly wanted our advice. When we got there he told us we were going to have a new kind of council. He didn't have time to hear our advice."

A second form of criticism stated that the new Local Council really changed nothing. Although the council was supposed to hear the opinions of the people through their diwani, or councilors, many cultivators complained that they didn't know who their diwani were, how they were chosen, or what they were supposed to do. There was a strong feeling that the district commissioner and the liwalis decided all the important matters before the meeting and that the council itself only had the power to talk, and not the power to alter affairs. An African teacher at the Roman Catholic school near Kitangari stated: "Do they really think we are foolish enough to believe that we could do something that might displease the D.C.? If we can't do what *we* want, why call it a 'local' council?"

The most intense criticism, however, was reserved for the multiracial character of the new district body. Far from bringing about the kind of racial harmony for which Governor Twining was hoping, the establishment of the Newala Local Council had the effect of bringing to the surface antagonisms which had remained latent until this point or had not even existed before. The specter of non-African intervention in affairs which involved only Africans served to prejudice the entire experiment in modern local government based upon British lines.

While recognizing that the European ancestry of the researcher may have distorted the interview, it seemed to be correct that the major criticism was directed against the inclusion of Asians on the council. Inasmuch as contacts with Asians had been confined largely to commercial transactions, African relations with Asians were hardly cordial. Being the weaker party in a monetary negotiation, the Makonde felt that he was at the mercy of the Asian shopkeeper in buying cloth or hoes and at the mercy of the Asian transporter in getting his cashew nuts and other produce to the markets at the coast. Those Makonde who had visited Lindi and Mtwara returned with stories regarding the disparity in prices between Newala and the coastal towns, and the conviction was widespread that the Asians were defrauding the Makonde. Most Makonde, moreover, remarked during interviews that they were convinced that eventually the Asians would leave, taking all their wealth to India and leaving nothing behind. As one skeptical jumbe stated: "Now that the Asians are on our council, will they teach us the ways of good business as the European missionaries have taught our children how to read? I doubt it!"

Although the Makonde were accustomed to having European district commissioners and technical officers intervening in their affairs, the inclusion of nonofficial Europeans in the government of the Makonde did not go completely without comment. A number of people expressed fears that the new political role for Europeans might bring an influx of European settlers. This seemed to be confirmed by the sudden appearance of European surveyors who were putting in wooden stakes near the southern edge of the plateau. Many Makonde remained skeptical despite the assurance of the district commissioner that the surveyors were there in behalf of the Makonde Water Development Corporation, which was to pump water from the Ruvuma valley to the plateau.

Several of the African teachers at mission schools were particularly critical of the inclusion of European missionaries on the council. A caustic critic noted: "The priests have been very generous in letting us participate in the running of the churches and schools; but while we play with those things, behind our backs they take over our government!" Generally, however, the criticism of the European missionaries was muted by the fact that many Makonde—including even Muslim informants—had a high regard for the labors of both the Catholic Benedictine fathers and the Anglican sisters and priests of the UMCA. Unlike certain well-endowed missions elsewhere in Tanganyika, the missionaries in Newala lived a fairly frugal existence. They enjoyed a good record with respect to the early Africanization of their schools, churches, and clinics. One young Makonde, who was highly critical of British administrators and Asian shopkeepers, said: "The missionaries are different. They only came here to teach, not to take our land and our money. We are not treated as their stones, to be moved about from here to there without any feeling for our thoughts. We give them our respect because we love them, not because we fear them." It was widely conceded that the Europeans had, for the most part, come as teachers or doctors and that the Makonde still had much that they could learn from them before the Europeans voluntarily withdrew. As an ex-mkulungwa in Mahuta remarked: "We never kill a goat while it is still giving milk."

## LINES OF DISCORD WITHIN THE COUNCIL

In many respects, the observation of the Local Council in action provided a useful index not only with regard to the substantive issues stimulating people within the district but also with regard to the lines of discord being fashioned among various competing political groups. The physical setting for the council meetings was ideal in this respect, for the council chamber, or baraza, was a pavilion open on three sides. Throughout the proceedings, the interested and the curious could congregate along the outer railings. Although Ian Norton's successor as district commissioner, Mr. Ernest Craig, discouraged "audience participation," inevitably the public intervened from time to time. The old women in particular voiced their approval of statements by making the traditional high-pitched tongue-wagging sound expressing joy. Occasionally, too, the sounds of the market place or of passing trucks intruded on the deliberations to remind one of the active and real world outside the chamber.

A further characteristic of the council deliberations which made them useful for observation of political behavior was the tendency for each topic of interest to be discussed until it, and the council members as well, had been thoroughly exhausted. Despite the overlap and repetition, Commissioner Craig made no effort to stifle comments, on the assumption – as he explained later – that the Makonde would "accept even the most bitter pill if they had had sufficient chance to discuss it before having to swallow it." In many respects this may have been sound practice in terms of getting the Makonde to accept innovation through a traditional mechanism. Decision-making in the pre-European era and well into the present century in Umakonde has been based upon a striving for consensus in the face of crises which disturbed the established equilibrium. One came to accept change not because an idea was new, but because discussion had managed to call forth precedents and whittle away some of the more disturbing features of a new idea until it could be made acceptable to the dominant conflicting forces in the community. A bipolarization of issues and forces, characteristic of Western society, was to be avoided at all costs. All parties to the discussion were to leave feeling either that they had won or that at least the justice of their position had been appreciated by the other sides to the controversy, and this would restrain them from pressing their victory too far. While the district commissioner's attitude toward traditional debate may have had a cathartic effect, it also had its negative consequences. Many of the topics on the agenda which were really crucial to development, but which would not necessarily arouse public passions, were dispatched with relatively little discussion or referred to a committee because of "lack of time." Since the committee meetings were dominated by the district commissioner, in effect this reserved important matters for his decision.

Despite criticisms of the way in which the membership of the council was formulated, the discussions in the meetings were not pro forma. In fact, there was a lively exchange not only between the African and non-African members of the council but between the liwalis and the elected councilors as well. It is true, as was charged by some of the young men who were attempting to organize a branch of TANU in Newala, that the majority of the diwanis were uneducated and were handpicked for their jobs by the liwalis and jumbes. Nevertheless, given the opportunity of voicing their opinions in public, the men councilors spared no one in expressing themselves. Unfortunately, one of the most persistent themes pursued was the matter of the compensation they were to receive for serving on the council, but they did address themselves to more critical problems as well. The female diwanis, on the other hand, did not noticeably enhance the intellectual quality of the proceedings, with the exception of one young Makonde nurse who had some very perceptive comments to make with regard to health, education, and marriage payments. Undoubtedly the caustic comments made by several male diwanis—both Christian and Muslim—made it obvious that they regarded the inclusion of women as a radical departure from Makonde tradition.

A second group whose members appeared to be aware of the hostility regarding their presence was the Asian bloc. During the first day of a three-day session, the Asian members literally spoke only when spoken to. During the remaining days, however, Mr. Hirji, a businessman from Mahuta, commented quite regularly on issues, particularly as they related to the economic progress of Newala. Although his points of view were frequently challenged by the African members, the bantering was in good humor on all sides. I subsequently discovered that Mr. Hirji had a reputation in Mahuta of being a "progressive" Indian; that is, he frequently gave assistance to his African competitors in the trading center by transporting commodities to and from the coast without charge. His presence on the council undoubtedly prevented explicit slurs being made against the Asian community.

By contrast with the Makonde women and the Asian members, the European presence on the council was very much in evidence. The district commissioner, for example, tended to dominate the proceedings despite his very apparent efforts to remain neutral during much of the discussion. It was he, however, who ultimately decided questions regarding the order of the agenda, when to terminate debate, what matters would be referred to committees, and the membership of the *ad hoc* and regular committees. In an effort, however, to give the council deliberations an African flavor, he very pointedly deferred to the advice and assistance of one of its members—Liwali Justino Mponda.

The missionary members felt obliged to comment on practically every item under consideration except where it was patently of concern only to the African members. One of the most interesting missionaries was Miss B. M. East, an elderly "no-nonsense" Englishwoman, who had served many long years in the district as a teacher and supervisor of the UMCA schools. The countless miles she had spent cycling through sand or mud along the bush roads of the district had made her a living legend to many Makonde. In 1954 she received the Member of the British Empire award for her services to the people of Newala. Several of the Makonde members of the council had been her students years before, and this perhaps accounted for the didactic tone she employed in speaking to the liwalis and diwanis.

Perhaps the performances which were most revealing in terms of the future development of local government in Newala District, however, were those of the liwalis and wakilis. Although they were nominally part of the official side of the council, they frequently challenged the district commissioner and the other European officials who were invited to participate in the council's debates. Liwali Justino Mponda, in fact, often assumed the posture of "leader of the opposition" and managed to speak out on practically every item on the agenda. By virtue of his membership on the territorial Legislative Council and his trips abroad (both of which points he constantly brought to the attention of his audience), he appeared to the African diwanis to be able to compete with the Europeans on equal terms. The contribution of the other liwalis and wakilis, however, bore a strong relationship to their friendship with, or antagonism toward, Liwali Justino. Thus he became a constant focal point in the deliberations of the council. The other strong center was Liwali Manzi of Mahuta, who frequently supported the European position on very rational grounds while Liwali Justino was busily backtracking on a position which he had initially taken only to find that it lacked general support among the diwanis.

## THE SUBSTANTIVE ISSUES

One method for analyzing the lines of discord within the multiracial Local Council is the consideration of the manner in which it dealt with substantive issues in the fields of education, health, and natural-resource utilization. Action in these areas was, of course, related to the fiscal competence of the council. As Table 2 for the year 1955 indicates, the major revenue available to the Newala council was the proceeds from the local rates, which was the new form which the central government Native Hut and Poll Tax assumed under the 1953

Ordinance. The remainder of the revenues were more local in character, but often the cost of collection equaled the revenue yield. The costs of local administration and marketing activities as shown in Table 3, for example, consumed more than half of the total expenditures and roughly equaled the revenues from court fines and fees, licenses, market receipts, and other fees and dues.

TABLE 2:
NEWALA DISTRICT REVENUE RECEIPTS, 1955

| | | |
|---|---|---:|
| I. | Taxes – local rate | £16,086 |
| II. | Court revenues | |
| | a. Fees and fines | 1,018 |
| | b. Marriage and divorce | 262 |
| III. | Licenses | |
| | a. Liquor | 627 |
| | b. Arms | 166 |
| | c. Game | 1 |
| IV. | Market Receipts | |
| | a. Produce | 6,609 |
| | b. Rental of booths | 6,589 |
| V. | Fees and Dues | |
| | a. School fees | 719 |
| | b. Government grants to middle schools | 1,379 |
| | c. Minor settlements and trading centers, rates | 37 |
| | d. Agency for Makonde Water Corporation | 394 |
| VI. | Revenue from property and Reimbursements | |
| | a. Motor vehicle receipts | 330 |
| | b. Garage receipts | 10 |
| | c. Sale, Local Council Gazette | 6 |
| | d. Education grant, school equipment | 260 |
| | e. Sale of seeds | 16 |
| | f. Sale of gunpowder, caps | 486 |
| VII. | Interest | |
| | a. Local Council bond | 686 |
| VIII. | Contribution and Grant-in-aid, education; primary schools | 80 |
| IX. | Miscellaneous receipts | 1,277 |
| | Total Revenues | £37,038 |

TABLE 3:
NEWALA DISTRICT EXPENDITURES, 1955

| | | |
|---|---|---:|
| I. | Local Administration | £12,990 |
| II. | Marketing | 2,126 |
| III. | Communications (roads) | 1,501 |
| IV. | Health | 2,333 |
| V. | Education | 4,772 |
| VI. | Agriculture | 772 |
| VII. | Veterinary | 37 |
| VIII. | Forests | 172 |
| IX. | Game | 854 |
| X. | Water | 325 |
| XI. | Miscellaneous | 965 |
| XII. | Contributions to Development | 1,000 |
| | Total Expenditures | £27,847 |

## Education

In terms of revenues expended, time spent, and the level of enthusiasm generated by the subject, educational affairs was the most important single concern of the council. Nevertheless, the impact which any unit of local government was permitted to make upon the colonial educational system was relatively slight. The curriculum, the placement of new schools, and even the employment of teachers and the setting of salaries were under the jurisdiction of the central government, with some involvement of the missionaries. Almost in defiance of its lack of ability to exercise real control over education, the Newala Local Council spent hours discussing matters such as school attendance, the opening of the new school year, the level of fees required of parents, and other peripheral problems relating to education. With respect to each of these items, however, some revealing points were made. It had been widely assumed, for example, that enthusiasm among the Makonde for education was quite high. This was particularly the case among the Muslim community, who had complained that the role of the Christian missionaries in the educational system of the district had denied Muslim children the opportunity of going to school. At one point in the council's deliberations, however, the Muslim liwali of Mahuta apologized for the poor attendance at the new Native Authority primary school at Mnyawa. He explained, quite simply, that the previous jumbe had recently died and his successor was ill; hence, "there was no one who could arrest parents for not sending their children to school." Thus, resort to coercion as a means for "educating" people with regard to their own welfare was a difficult habit to break.

Another predominant attitude in the council's discussion of educational matters was the notion that education should be free throughout the district. No amount of argument from the district commissioners, the missionaries, and even several of the Makonde on the council seemed to convince the diwanis and jumbes that money was not available to build schools, pay teachers, and purchase equipment. There was a decided sentiment indicating that the colonial government "owed" at least this much to the Makonde people. Indeed, this sentiment was to become a recurrent theme in Makonde politics, which had echoes elsewhere in the continent. In part this expression may have been the means whereby the nationalist leadership built up a following by severing the bonds that united the European administrator or missionary and those who materially benefited from their presence. Instead of feeling a debt of gratitude the latter were encouraged to feel that it was the outsiders who were the indebted class, since they had come uninvited and had taken possession of the country and its resources or had taken its sons and daughters for labor on the sisal estates or in government offices. In part, too, the attitude of indebtedness may have arisen from the fact that modern government and schooling were essentially affairs of the Europeans, who had monopolized the initiative and had undertaken changes in government without really involving the Africans. Consequently, if Africans were expected to participate in these European games, they should be paid for doing so. Finally, there is the suggestion of the French psychologist, O. Mannoni, that there had developed a "dependence syndrome" between the European colonialist, who suffered from an inferiority complex and needed subordinated people to satisfy his ego, and the dominated African, who had had his race and culture demeaned and had been

forced to sacrifice the security of the tribe, and therefore expected his detractor to assume a protective role as a reward
for the African showing him deference.[5]

In other respects as well, the issue of payment of school fees
had struck a sensitive spot in the social fabric. Inasmuch as
the Makonde social system was undergoing a basic change in
its pattern of family organization, there was an element of conflict over parental obligations. The older men on the council
stated that they did not feel that they should be responsible for
the school fees of their children inasmuch as under the matrilineal system of responsibility they were required to look
after the needs of their sisters' children. They complained that
many of the younger men wanted the best of two worlds: they
wanted to bequeath their property to their offspring and yet
insist that the maternal uncle of their children had responsibilities for school fees and other forms of assistance. The same
sort of nether world was developing, incidentally, with respect
to the matter of responsibility for disciplining wayward youngsters.

A further change in the social system was exposed during
the discussion of educational opportunities for Makonde girls.
Religion and the traditional Muslim attitude regarding the low
status of women appeared to be only part of the reason accounting for the reluctance of Makonde to enroll girls in mission and
government schools. Education of young girls not only accelerated the abandonment of the matrilineal kinship relations
but also altered the bridewealth system, which had become
based on money and was now regarded as a fairly lucrative
source of income for Makonde fathers. The missionaries on
the Newala council bore the major responsibility in arguing
the case for female education, with little apparent support
from the Makonde males—or even the females, for that matter.

The conflict between educational objectives and traditional
practices was also revealed in the discussion regarding the
school year. The missionaries in particular were distressed by
the fact that the beginning of the school year was frequently

5. *Prospero and Caliban: A Study of the Psychology of Colonisation*, trans.
Pamela Powesland (New York: Praeger, 1956).

delayed by the prolongation of the jando ceremonies. Although the colonial administration had been successful in reducing the period of the initiation rites, the timing of the rites was related to the agricultural cycle rather than to the more regular and precise calendar year.

The discussion of educational problems that revealed the deepest social cleavages within the Newala community, however, came with respect to complaints regarding the lack of government support for Islamic schools and the charges of religious discrimination in mission schools. The former was a recurrent issue. Inasmuch as 90 per cent of the taxpayers in Newala were Muslim, it seemed illogical that the Christian minority should receive government subsidies for their schools while the needs of the Muslim majority went unattended. The device, moreover, of permitting Koranic teachers to visit both government and mission schools to minister to the needs of the Muslim children was regarded as a sham. The time set aside for instruction in the Koran was very early in the morning when the students were still drowsy. The district commissioner and the Christian liwalis on the council insisted that mission schools were only supported because they taught subjects other than religion, whereas the Koranic teachers were concerned almost exclusively with religion. It was apparent, however, that the older diwanis were not placated by this response.

On the matter of religious discrimination the missionaries themselves took a much more active stance in challenging the allegation that favoritism was given to Christians in advancing students from the primary to the middle schools. One of the more interesting vignettes on an otherwise lethargic session of the council was the exchange between Miss East and a Muslim liwali who had complained that Muslim students who had completed work in the primary grades were denied space in the UMCA middle school at Newala. Rising to the challenge, Miss East demanded chapter and verse. Upon receiving the list of alleged victims of religious discrimination, she left the council chambers and cycled off through town. Half an hour later she returned and read off each name on the list, followed by the statement: "Failed the Standard IV examinations." By the time she had reached the last name on the roster, the baraza was roaring with laughter, and no one was laughing harder than the liwali who had made the charges. He had been "caught out" and took his medicine like the "naughty schoolboy" that Miss East took him to be.

It was apparent, nevertheless, that there was indeed a remarkably close correlation between failure on the examination and Islamic background. And oddly enough there was a tacit admission by the missionaries that religion did serve as an indirect factor in ultimate failure in school. The Muslim children, for example, missed many days of school during Islamic holidays, whereas the schools were closed during Christian holidays. During the month of Ramadan, moreover, the Muslim children who fasted from sunup to sundown were at an obvious disadvantage in competing with Christian children. Finally, the incidence of withdrawal of girls from school was much higher among Muslim families than it was among Christian families.

## Health

The matter of health and sanitation was also very high on the list of concerns for the Newala council. Here was clearly an aspect of the European presence that was regarded by the Makonde leaders as a positive contribution. The evidence that people had been cured of certain illnesses or had reduced the frequency of certain kinds of diseases by using Western medical care had been demonstrated during the several decades of mission activity in Newala. The solution to the health problem, to many of the councilors, was thus simply a matter of constructing more hospitals and dispensaries and employing more nurses and doctors. It was apparent that, in this segment of Newala society at least, the battle between traditional and modern medical practices was being won by the latter, even though—as will subsequently be indicated—the campaign was far from over. Discussion in the Newala Local Council was directed to such issues as establishing maternity clinics, convincing the people that paludrin and nivaquin were more effective than herbs in dealing with malaria, launching a yaws campaign similar to those launched elsewhere in East Africa, establishing a roving dispensary to meet the needs of areas away from the liwaliate headquarters, dealing with abortionists, encouraging young women to enter nursing, and insisting that the schools devote more time to instruction in personal hygiene.

The one area in the field of health which caused the most discussion was the treatment of leprosy, which is endemic in southern Tanzania.[6] The BELRA (British Empire Leprosy Relief Association) staff which managed the Mkunya Leprosarium were most realistic in appreciating not only some of the traditional hostilities and fears surrounding leprosy but also some of the traditional family and other social patterns which had to be taken into account if the disease was to be controlled. Thus, they not only permitted outpatient treatment by itinerant employees of the noncontagious cases, but also encouraged whole families to move to the leprosarium. Thus, it was possible to detect leprosy in the children at an early stage, and the continuation of traditional family patterns and cooking arrangements encouraged the patients to stay until their treatments had been completed. The leprosarium had land for garden plots and farm labor. It also had woodcarving and other crafts which provided both the mental and the physical therapy needed to prevent the atrophying of limbs. The testimony of people who had been cured or whose case was arrested helped ensure the continued success of the operation, but credit was also to be given to the members of the Newala council who pressured their constituents to seek aid at the leprosarium or the clinics.

There was one area in the field of health where the medical staff in the district and members of the Newala Local Council parted company. This was the matter of fee payments for treatment of leprosy. The doctor on the council and others insisted that the modest fee of five shillings (seventy cents in 1955) at the time of the initial treatment not only helped defray the costs of the out-clinics but was also an effective device for keeping the patient regular in his treatments inasmuch as he had a financial investment in his own cure. To counter this argument, several African members of the Newala council insisted that

6. James Ross Innes, "Leprosy in Tanganyika: A Survey in the Southern Province," *East African Medical Journal*, XXVII (December, 1950), 459–65.

the people who had leprosy were frequently the least able to pay the fees. Despite the insistence of the leprosarium staff that the sickest and poorest patients at the hospital were excused from the payment of fees and that others could earn the money for the fees by performing chores at the hospital, it was obvious that the liwalis and others felt obliged to press a popular cause — free medical service.

## Agriculture and Economic Development

Given the nature of the economy and the insistence by the central government that local services in the future were to be supported largely at the local level, the relatively low priority given to the discussion of agricultural and economic development matters by the council was somewhat surprising. The gap between the traditionalists and the modernists, moreover, was readily apparent. The older diwanis, for example, were concerned about the same problems that had beset their ancestors: "What," they asked, "was being done about marauding pigs, baboons, and other vermin that raided the crops?" "Was it still illegal to make 'native guns'?" "Why did government insist that a fee be paid to the Native Authority when timber was cut in the forest instead of the mkulungwa receiving his traditional gift of a chicken?" "And why were people prevented from cutting timber as the need arose — since everyone realized that there had always been enough wood for everyone?"

The younger members of the council (in particular the Christian liwalis) seemed more disposed to address themselves to the question of innovation in the agricultural sector. Nevertheless, several themes persisted during the discussion of development matters that indicated a depth of despair over the prospects of improving the economic lot of the Makonde of Newala District. Inevitably, for example, discussion of any development proposal returned to the problem of credit for the expansion and diversification of agricultural production. Since land was communally owned it could not be mortgaged by the individual tenant, and the central government had objected to the extension of credit based upon cashew nuts and other crops serving as security. The lack of reserve capital, by the way, affected not only the peasant cultivator; it also threatened the success of government-sponsored improvement schemes. One of the major problems in the rice-mechanization scheme at Chiumo in the Ruvuma Valley, for example, was the lack of sufficient capital to carry the participants through the first growing season. The tenants adopted the posture that "since government wanted this scheme, they owed it to us to pay for the seed, equipment, and family needs required to make the project succeed."

It was obvious, too, that the "white man's madness" discussed in Chapter 6 had taken its toll and had left the Makonde with a measure of skepticism regarding the wisdom of agricultural innovation. Frequently, during sessions of the council, the jumbes and diwanis were scolded by both the Europeans and the liwalis because the people had failed to use the new experimental seed, to employ more effective techniques in planting and weeding cashew farms, and to practice soil-conservation measures. Innovation which had been unsuited to the environment of the Makonde plateau had in the past brought the risk of starvation and financial disaster, and the Makonde were not interested in experimentation for its own sake. This skepticism had been dramatically reinforced in 1954 when some of the small savings of Makonde peasants had been wiped out in an ill-conceived chicken scheme. Although the hothouse-bred chickens flown in from Mpwapwa might have been fatter and produced larger eggs, they lacked one important quality that the domestic chickens possessed—the ability to survive.

Inevitably the question of agricultural innovation was resolved by the suggestion that more attention ought to be paid to the school children—assuming that the older generation was a lost cause. Great stress was to be placed upon revision of the school curriculum, with a heavier emphasis being placed upon agricultural education. The school garden plots were to be the primary arenas for changing not only agricultural techniques but also the attitudes of the younger generation with respect to the dignity of farming as a way of life. No one asked the really embarrassing question of how one first changed the attitudes and the technology of the teachers.

### Water Development

The lack of water on the Makonde plateau has been one of the major areas of concern to European administrators during the seventy years of colonial rule in the area. Although the ban on intertribal warfare had eliminated one of the major barriers to Makonde settlement in the river valleys, the Makonde still preferred to live on the plateau and send their women down to the rivers and wells in search of water during the long dry season. Efforts to dig deeper wells had failed to tap the very low water table. Ultimately, in the early 1950s, the government launched a scheme to have the water pumped from springs in the valley and distributed by pipe throughout the plateau. The capital for the company—the Makonde Water Development Corporation—was to be secured through the mandatory membership of every adult resident of the district in the corporation. In addition to the ten-shilling membership fee, moreover, a charge of ten to fifteen cents per container was to be made at the water kiosks.

The discussion regarding the progress of the scheme in the period of my research revealed some of the difficulties which European administrators created for themselves in introducing new institutions for development. In the first place, for a people who did not even have banks and who had only recently been drawn into a money economy, the idea of a modern corporation was almost beyond comprehension. No sensible Makonde would have even considered walking into an Asian shop and giving the proprietor ten shillings on the understanding that the shopkeeper would give him a piece of cloth in two or three years. And yet the government was asking the Makonde cultivator to become a member of a corporation which would not provide him water for perhaps four or five years—and no guarantee even of that. Moreover, since the officers of the government corporation were the same European officials and the same liwalis who ran the Local Council, it was difficult to convey the idea that the corporation was a different entity. The local government officials helped publicize the corporation and helped in the collection of its subscriptions. The jumbes and elders, moreover, were required to assist the surveyors and other employees of the corporation in their work.

Finally, the fiction of the distinction between local government and the corporation was obscured by the fact that the ban on government employees joining political parties was extended to cover the employees of the Makonde Water Development Corporation as well.

The rules governing the operation of the corporation were often classic illustrations of the European disease of over-planning. It was reasoned by the planners of the scheme that, in order for the project to be effective, it had to have 100 per cent membership and competing sources of water had to be eliminated. This led them to the assertion that all the water runoff from the plateau was to be considered the property of the corporation. Hence the collection and storage of rain water in large pots (a traditional Makonde method for coping with water shortage) was declared to be illegal. It was obvious that such overplanning was bound to be ignored and lead to law-lessness. Even more important, it taxed the credulity of the Makonde peasant, who was convinced that the Europeans had lost their minds.

## Problems of Social Change

It was apparent to me, after attending several sessions of the Newala Local Council, that it had taken on the task of regulating the rate of social change in the district in addition to trying to cope with the problems of social maladjustment. Being largely a rural district, Newala did not have the same experience of social disruption as Lindi or Mtwara. The town of Newala in 1955 was still largely a collection of government offices, Indian shops, and the mission compound of the UMCA, which included the primary and middle schools. The aban-doned European hotel was an indication that the dreams had exceeded reality. A decade or more later the urban sprawl would begin to cause serious social problems, but in 1955 control over the mixed Makonde, Mwera, Yao, and Maconde inhabitants of the town area was still a manageable proposition.

One of the areas of social concern which absorbed the at-tention of the council during several of its meetings was the conduct of the younger generation. In many respects this was related to the issue of education. Even a modicum of education placed the young boys a measure above their elders. Hence they either treated adults with disrespect or they left the district and gravitated to the large towns where they could escape the control of their parents or uncles. Unlike the traditional migrant worker, as one jumbe said, "when these Standard IV boys return home, they cause trouble and they bring nothing back to their families to show their respect." One of the teachers on the council complained that it was not simply the Standard IV boys who caused problems:

> What about the boy who did well through Standard VIII only to find that there is no job for him in the district? Have we not cheated him? What good does it do to tell him now about the dignity of farm work when we have taken him away from the farm and taught him to be a leader? Did he spend eight years in school only to go back to his kerosene lamp in the village and work beside his illiterate brothers?

Clearly, the school system was educating the youth of Newala out of their environment.

Of almost equal concern to the councilors was the problem of emancipated women in the district. The elder Muslims clearly resented the elevation of women to a status of equality with men. The requirement that women pay the hut taxes of their absent husbands was regarded as the thin edge of an entering wedge, even though the administration at first insisted that it was only going to collect the taxes from women who were in business selling *pombe* (beer) or vegetables. There was another type of woman, however, who was of even greater concern – the woman who engaged in prostitution while her husband was absent in Tanga or Lindi on the sisal estates. Indeed, some of the opposition to the Makonde water development scheme came from the traditionalists, who feared that liberating women from the task of spending twelve hours a day gathering water during the dry season would leave them with too much idle time, so that they would engage in prostitution or cause trouble for their husbands. The more general question of female emancipation arose in connection with the suggestion that women be hired as clerks in the market and at the liwaliate headquarters. Here the basic conservatism of the Muslim community manifested itself. The only Makonde female leader who seemed to command the respect of both men and women during the period of my research in 1955 was Mrs. Thekla Mchauru, who was running a nursing program in the district. Perhaps her success stemmed from the fact that she was a Christian (and thus could be expected to be emancipated in her actions) and related to a family that had enjoyed high status in the district for many decades.

## Traditionalism and Makonde Nationalism

The British creators of the local council system in Tanganyika had intended that the councils would concern themselves with very practical matters and largely limit their discussion to problems of revenue and the provision of local services. Since the reforms of 1953 were thought to be a radical departure from the system of Indirect Rule, it was not intended that the new councils should become vehicles for the expression of tribal or traditional values. Nevertheless, some of the most emotional discussion during several sessions of the Newala Local Council revolved around such issues.

There was, for example, the extended debate over the responsibility of the council in honoring the grave of Nangololo, the first mkulungwa mkuu of the Makonde, who died in 1937. Although the district commissioner, Ernest Craig, attempted to rule the matter out of order, it was obvious that the councilors wanted to discuss it. The arguments revealed many of the cleavages within the Makonde community. Surprisingly, it was Justino Mponda—the most modern of the liwalis—who introduced the topic by suggesting that the council have a sign put on the grave of Nangololo. Throughout the discussion the other liwalis were ranged against him, asserting that the Makonde never had a paramount chief and that Nangololo was merely the chairman of the Newala council of wakulungwa. Significantly, the group opposing Mponda included Liwali Nangololo of Liteho, the nephew of the deceased mkulungwa mkuu. The liwali said that he had refused to do anything about the grave because he was afraid that people would think he was claiming the office of mkulungwa mkuu for himself, since he was the first heir of the late ruler.

Throughout the argument, however, it was clear that jumbes and diwanis, who represented the more traditional element in the district, felt that something should be done to honor Nangololo. As one jumbe said: "Even if he was not the leader of all the Makonde, certainly he was one who during his life had worked hard in behalf of all of us." Ultimately it was the traditionalists, with Mponda in the lead, who carried the day. A committee was established to collect money for the building of a proper grave, so that Nangololo could be honored in the same way as Matola I and Matola II, whose graves can still be seen in Newala. It was only later, incidentally, that a disgruntled liwali suggested to me that Mponda's role in the argument was probably personal, inasmuch as he hoped to have the office of paramount leader reestablished for his own occupancy.

A second item, which also found Liwali Mponda at the center of the discussion, was the question of writing a history of the Makonde. In 1954 the liwali had taken this task upon himself with the object of including it in the civics instruction given in the schools. Although the traditionalists were enthusiastic about the idea, there were several who resented having Liwali Justino project himself once more to the center of the stage. The Muslim liwalis suggested that a history written by a Christian would tend to slight the role of Islam in Makonde society.

The final item of a traditional nature which absorbed the council was the presence within the district of one Chikonda, a native witch-finder. It was obvious from the discussion that there was a division among the councilors about whether Chikonda's presence was desired and indeed whether he ought to be employed by the Newala council to drive Makonde witch doctors out of the district by exposing them. Some felt that it was Chikonda himself who was the greater threat to the security of the district. The self-righteous indignation expressed by the European members of the council with regard to the suggestion that Chikonda be "employed" by the council was rather amusing. Just three months previously I had traveled through Kilwa District with the district commissioner, who readily admitted that one of the more powerful witch-finders in southern Tanganyika—Nguvu Mali—had been hired by the government to root out the local practitioners of magic.

SUMMARY

It was apparent that the Newala Local Council did serve a vital function in terms of educating the liwalis and a select few jumbes and councilors about the functions of modern government. It was a place, too, in which various cleavages within the social fabric were brought out into the open and aired, if not resolved. It was largely a fiction, however, that the multiracial character of the Newala Local Council was a response to African suggestions. It was questionable, too, whether the majority of the citizens desired that the traditional wakulungwa be excluded from active participation in the affairs of modern government. Modern local government was still largely an affair of Europeans and of the district commissioner in particular. The forced development of modern local government in advance of genuine popular demand was destined to lead to disaster. The lack of experience of liwalis and councilors guaranteed the continued intervention on the part of the district commissioner if the services of local government were to be effectively provided. As I have indicated elsewhere, the dominant role of the district commissioner, especially in fiscal affairs, made

> the conciliar system vulnerable to the charges made by leaders of the Tanganyika African National Union and other political bodies that the new system is really "just more of the same, with a few of the chiefs' cooks and houseboys thrown in for appearance sake." By keeping the newly formed councils as advisory organs for a number of years, the administration might have avoided the new system becoming the target for the discontented element.[7]

Although the European administrators seemed to take pride in the pioneering effort of Newala District in launching the first multiracial council, the experiment did not meet with enthusiasm elsewhere in the territory. Mafia District – which was even less multiracial than Newala – became the only other district which would emulate Newala District.

7. Liebenow, "Local Government Reform in Tanganyika," p. 134.

# 10:
# The Grouping
## of Forces,
## 1956-1958

The year 1956 represents the high-water mark in terms of British political and administrative control in Tanganyika. Although its representative on the Trusteeship Council was still talking bravely about the lack of realism in the suggestion that Tanganyika could possibly achieve independence even in 25 years, the actions of administrators on the spot revealed a certain sense of urgency if not desperation. Governor Sir Edward Twining obviously recognized the very real challenge which a revitalized TANU presented to the British government. This was evident in June, 1956, when his government decided to sound out the chiefs and other more conservative elements within Tanganyika to see whether a counterbalance could be established to the growing power of Julius Nyerere and other leaders of TANU. At that point the battle that had been slowly gathering form was joined. What had been a loosely organized, quadrangular struggle among the British government, the Native Authorities, the leaders of TANU, and the organizers of other popular associations (tribal unions, cooperatives, and trade unions) tended increasingly to become a two-sided struggle between TANU and the British government. It was indeed the moment of truth for chiefs, union leaders, and others who had to decide which way to jump. The middle ground was rapidly becoming quicksand.

The dynamism, however, which infected the political process throughout most of Tanganyika in the early 1950s took a longer time to reach the Makonde region. Geographic isolation and the low level of economic development accounted in part for this lethargy. In any event, as late as 1949 the provincial commissioner of the Southern Province, Mr. Pike, could write with confidence that the Makonde were still "more parochially than politically conscious." [1] Political change in contemporary Africa, however, has a remarkable way of skipping stages or of telescoping for one area those developments which were spread out over a longer period in other regions. By June, 1956, the political dynamism which was sweeping other parts of Tanganyika became faintly perceptible among the Makonde as well. For Newala District in particular, June, 1956, constituted the moment of awakening. During that month an amorphous and largely inert political mass was transformed into a series of fairly-well-defined political camps—competing and yet overlapping. The factor that brought about this reshaping of the Makonde political system was the appearance in Newala of Julius Nyerere. At that point the few, but determined, adherents of TANU in the district took on a new vitality and became contenders for political power.

The occasion of Mr. Nyerere's visit to Newala was his first major recruitment drive through the Southern Province, where membership of TANU had remained almost miniscule. The British administrators in the Makonde area were convinced that the demonstrated conservatism of the Makonde was a sufficient barrier to Nyerere's success. Indeed, the district commissioner went out of his way to comment to me that he wasn't even taking the standard precaution of stationing extra police in the town of Newala during Nyerere's political rally. "Who," he asked, "would bother to come hear that unknown little rabble-rouser? Why send police—it would only give him an audience!"

How wrong the district commissioner was became increasingly obvious as more than six hundred people streamed into

1. *Annual Reports of the Provincial Commissioners*, 1949, p. 93.

the township from all over Newala and adjoining districts. Nyerere's fame as a defender of African interests, and especially his appearance at the United Nations in New York the year previously, had apparently been well publicized. (What made the United Nations trip so significant is that the TANU leader confronted not only the British at New York but also challenged Liwali Justino Mponda, who was sent to champion the colonial point of view.) This was my first exposure to Julius Nyerere's charisma, and I was entranced with the magnetic rapport he established with his audience during the speech and in a question period that lasted nearly three hours. It was a dialogue in which the speaker never departed from his audience. His sense of timing and dramatic skill were almost flawless as he varied his pace between clowning and mimicry of his political opponents at one moment and a sober, carefully reasoned sermon at the next. Perhaps what made the performance all the more remarkable was the manner in which he "scolded" his audience and failed to sympathize with their self-pitying comments about the lack of economic development in Newala District. A theme which eleven years later crystallized in the Arusha Declaration on Socialism and Self-Reliance was driven home hard that day in Newala. In the presence of several local Asians who had come to listen to him, Nyerere chided his audience by saying:

> Do you ever see Asians, who come all the way from India, remain poor? No! They may come barefoot, but after they have been here a little while they are riding around in fancy cars. Why? Because they can always rely upon their brothers to help them get a start in business instead of everyone having to fend for himself. And then, instead of spending their little money on *pombe* [beer], fine clothing, and soft chairs, they pinch themselves even further until they are really able to afford their fancy cars. While you are out dancing at an *ngoma* or drinking beer, the Asians are burning their lights in the back of their shops, improving themselves. If you got together and bought a lorry instead of bicycles, you could all be as rich as Indians.

He was well on the way to earning his ultimate title of *mwalimu,* or teacher, that day in Newala.

In one respect, Julius Nyerere's impact on the Makonde political system was immediate. Prior to his appearance in the district it had been indicated to me by one of the organizers for TANU, Mr. Leopold Pallahani, that the membership drive was proceeding very slowly. Although the leaders publicly boasted that they had enlisted five hundred members between November, 1955, and June, 1956, the number of paid members was much closer to one hundred. During Nyerere's visit and in the week following it, the number of membership subscriptions had risen by more than three hundred. TANU's changed fortunes in the district did not immediately sweep everything else before it, however. What it did was to add to the scene another significant political contender and help to crystallize in a dramatic fashion the political cleavages within the rest of Makonde society.

In a crude sort of way, the grouping of political forces that emerged in 1956 reflected the series of manipulations to which Makonde society had been subjected during the eighty or more years of subordination to Arab, German, and British rule. Political legitimacy was not the monopoly of any single group of Makonde leaders. Leadership was factionalized, with each politician claiming to represent the interests of the total society but having in fact only a limited mass appeal. Thus, despite the popularity of the Umakonde Umoja movement, the authority system of the Makonde people was in certain respects as polycentric in 1956 as it had been in 1885, although admittedly the quality of the polycentrism had been radically altered in the intervening period. Cleavages did not polarize neatly around such factors as traditionalism versus modernism, the old versus the young, Christians versus Muslims and "pagans," parochialism versus cosmopolitanism, or rural versus urbanized population. Nor was polycentrism clearly traceable to the historic loyalties based upon kinship or residence. It was a complex mixture of all of these factors. For purposes of analysis, however, five fairly coherent groupings were discernible. For convenience I have labeled these groups parochial traditionalists, tribal nationalists (with both traditionalist and modernist factions), accommodating modernists, dissenting modernists, and pivotal modernists.

## The Parochial Traditionalists

In terms of sheer numbers it was undoubtedly the parochial traditionalists who were predominant within Makonde society in 1956. In terms of leadership and political acumen, however, they were the least dynamic of the various competing forces within Newala District. Their leaders, the former wakulungwa, constituted only a potential rather than an organized elite, since their individual claims to authority were based upon the legitimacy of the parochial virambo. The chirambo as a functioning unit of government had been rejected by the colonial administration more than a dozen years earlier, and the wakulungwa—much to the lingering chagrin of the parochial traditionalists—were turned out of office in 1942 without even so much as a medal, let alone a pension, for their good work. The few wakulungwa who had been retained under the liwali system as jumbes had sided with the accommodating modernists (that is, those educated Makonde who cooperated with the colonial administration) and were in one way or another contributing to the transformation of traditional values. The complete rejection of the wakulungwa by the British administrators was revealed in the plaintive remarks of one ex-mkulungwa near Mkunya, who complained that in the olden days, when the government wanted to build a road, the district commissioner himself would come and ask the mkulungwa's advice. The mkulungwa would then say prayers to his ancestor to ensure the success of the venture. Now, as in the case of the Makonde Water Corporation's road, he commented: "They cut through my *shamba* (field) without even asking my permission. I like the new road," he said. "I and all my people use it. But the government today is lacking in respect. Respect is more important than roads."

The parochial traditionalists also felt themselves to be the target of abuse from another quarter, the young educated and semieducated men who were to provide the mainstay of the dissenting modernists (the educated Makonde who most vigorously opposed the colonial system). As the informant quoted above stated:

> The young men of today are better off than we are because they can read. But they have lost all their manners. They

are too proud. They would never think of helping an old
man with his load or helping him repair his house. They
do not even help each other.

Why is this so? Because so many have gone off to Lindi
or Dar es Salaam and see the way those "children of slave
people" misbehave, and they try to imitate them.

Today the young men never go to see their elders before
they start off on a journey. They never go to prayers. They
say that they fast during Ramadan, but it is not true.

The elders of one village in Kitangari felt that in the olden days
the elders had the respect of the young men. If a young man
stole or used bad language (*matusi*) or sat on the mats of the
elders, he could be punished. When I asked them what the
punishment was, the leader responded, almost nostalgically,

If the man was very bad, we could tie fire in his hands; or
we could tie him at the throat to a very big tree or pole.
When he got tired he would have to stand up or hang himself. If his offense was not a serious one, we would just beat
him or give him nothing to eat.

Today we can't even touch a youth who is wrong because
he will bring a case against the elders. They complain about
the injustice of the liwalis, but they never fail to use the
liwali's court in bringing cases against their elders.

Among the values that the elders of the Kitangari village felt
to be most threatened by the changes in Newala District were
the unity of the family, respect for the elders, the sacred
character of land, respect for customs perpetuated in the initiation rites, prayer, and respect for women. Respect for
women apparently meant keeping women in their "proper
place" in society. The elders strongly objected to the inclusion of
women in the new village councils (including their own) and
on the Local Council in Newala. The elders also opposed the
new Native Authority rules which outlawed prepuberty marriage contracts. Even the Makonde Water Corporation was
attacked because it liberated women from the task of gathering
water during the dry season. "With all that time on their hands,"
one old man said, "our women will engage in intrigue, and our
lives will be miserable. The women will be slipping off to take
lovers. Today, if a woman returns with an empty water-pot, we
know that she has been up to mischief."

## THE TRIBAL NATIONALISTS

The second discernible faction within Newala District was substantially smaller in numbers than the preceding group. This faction, the tribal nationalists, looked to an enlarged Makonde polity as a means for achieving goals which were threatened by the colonial administrators and the Tanganyikan nationalists alike. The more conservative wing of the tribal-nationalist faction saw the emphasis upon Makonde ethnicity as a means for preserving and revitalizing traditional customs and values. Rather than shoring up the authority of the wakulungwa, however, this group looked back to the brief "golden age" of Newala politics under the two wakulungwa wakuu. It made its voice heard in the form of demands that respect be paid to the grave of the first mkulungwa mkuu, Nangololo, and that the second paramount ruler, Rashidi Mtalika Mfaume, be given the respect which was due him by an ungrateful colonial government. This latter objective, incidentally, was partially achieved in 1958 when Rashidi was awarded the Queen's Badge of Honour for his past services. The conservative tribal nationalists took an exclusivist attitude with regard to African participation in the affairs of Newala District. Indeed, they not only sought the exclusion of all non-Makonde from employment by the Local Council and the Makonde Water Development Corporation but also wanted to restrict the opportunities open to coastal Makonde within Newala District.

The second wing of the tribal-nationalist camp differed in two essential respects from the conservative wing. In terms of membership, first of all, it sought the inclusion of all Makonde within a single unit of local government – an idea which had been encouraged during the Umakonde Umoja movement of the early 1950s. Second, it sought an enlarged Makonde polity in order to bring about the more rapid modernization of Tanganyika's third-largest tribal group. Many Makonde leaders thought that it was more than coincidental that the tribal groups which had achieved a measure of unity under British colonial rule – the Chagga, Nyakyusa, and the Sukuma, for example – were also those which had a disproportionate share of the territory's schools, clinics, and producers' cooperative societies. Thus the modernist wing of the tribal-nationalist faction pressed for a Makonde County Council, joint meetings of the education committees for Newala and Mtwara districts, and the formation of a Makonde cooperative society for the marketing of cashew nuts. Only through unity, it was argued, could the Makonde achieve their just share of the good life.

Whether the orientation of the tribal nationalists was to the past or to the future, the group as a whole was anathema to the dissenting modernists, who made up the core of TANU. In this stage of Tanganyikan nationalism, tribalism constituted one of the more serious threats to the achievement of independence and tended to frustrate the full utilization of the country's limited resources for development. TANU recognized that the appeasement of tribal sentiments by the colonial administration not only strengthened the hand of the traditionalists but also siphoned off the talents of many of the educated youth who saw the short-run opportunities of a revitalized tribalism far outweighing the vague promises of a Tanganyikan nationalism. TANU thus pitted itself against the formation of tribal political unions, and it rejected the notion of a political party being formed on the basis of inter-ethnic affiliation, such as Nnamdi Azikiwe had done in Nigeria.

## THE ACCOMMODATING MODERNISTS

At the outset of the developing struggle for influence and authority in Newala District in 1956, it was the accommodating modernists who monopolized the formal positions of power within the area. This group included a majority of the liwalis and jumbes as well as their respective relatives and friends who occupied the subordinate patronage posts within the local administration. This group was accommodating with respect to the demands of the British colonial administration, and it assumed that dissent could only lead to dismissal from office and the loss of privilege. It was modernist not so much from commitment to the notion that new roads, schools, clinics, and the other trappings of modernization were good in themselves; rather, it was modernist because this was the current mood of the British administrators in Newala and because modernization had brought distinct material and psychic rewards to this group in particular.

It would be unjust to impugn the motives of all who co-operated with the British administration. It would be equally naïve, however, to deny that the rewards of cooperation were numerous. The salary of a liwali in Newala District ranged from Shs. 500 to Shs. 600 per month at a time when an un-skilled laborer was paid one shilling a day and the entire harvest from several acres of cashew trees would bring the peasant farmer about Shs. 90 for his effort. The liwali, moreover, had a measure of influence in controlling the appointments to other highly remunerative jobs in the native administration, such as those of medical assistants, market inspectors, and drivers, where the monthly salaries ranged from Shs. 120 to Shs. 200, as well as the posts of tax and market clerks, road foremen, mid-wives, and agricultural inspectors, where the salaries averaged between Shs. 90 and Shs. 100 per month. Even the lowest-paying jobs in the native administration — market sweepers, messengers, and headmen (between Shs. 30 and Shs. 50 per month) — were normally reserved for the relatives and friends of the liwalis and jumbes. Economic opportunities outside the native administration, moreover, were extremely limited in 1956. A few independent tradesmen (having incomes of Shs. 80 to Shs. 150 during the post-harvest season), mission teachers (an average monthly salary of Shs. 300), and the drivers and mechanics employed by Asian merchants were the only African competitors for high economic status in Newala District.

Although he enjoyed considerably higher prestige than most Makonde in Newala District, Liwali Justino Mponda repre-sented many of the qualities typical of the accomodating mod-ernist. He had acquired his education in UMCA schools in Newala and Masasi districts at a time when the privilege had come to very few Makonde. Mponda had been an energetic and exacting teacher, and his elevation to a position of responsi-bility at the secondary school in Chidya was prima facie evi-dence in the 1940s and the 1950s that he had come to accept a European outlook. Indeed, the eagerness with which he presented European ideas such as the multiracial Local Council and the Makonde Water Development Corporation as examples of "African self-help" earned him the contempt of the dissenting modernists, who knew the origin of these projects. The British administration, on the other hand, rewarded him in many ways for his expressions of support. He was, for example, sent to the United Kingdom in 1953 for a course in community development. The following year he was selected to help present the British case for Tanganyika before the United Nations Trusteeship Council. His activity in the Territorial Legislative Council earned him the admiration of Governor Twining as one of the most "responsible" Africans in the territory, and he was invariably praised by European officials during their tours of the province. He was awarded the Queen's Medal for Chiefs in 1955, and in the following year was made a Member of the British Empire.[2]

The commitment of Liwali Justino Mponda and other liwalis to the path of accommodation was clearly revealed by their participation in a last-ditch effort by the British to create a conservative counterforce to TANU. Paralleling similar moves in Ghana, Western Nigeria, and other colonies on the eve of independence, the governor of Tanganyika called a Convention of Representative Chiefs. The convention, which met periodically between 1957 and 1960, was to be a precursor of an upper house in the Legislative Council where traditional prerogatives could be preserved. The participation of liwalis from Newala and Mtwara—at a time when TANU was pressing for a popularly elected majority in the Legislative Council—was a strategic blunder, for it associated them with chiefs, representing dynasties of long standing, who had no legitimate traditional claim whatever to a role in territorial politics.[3] The collaboration of Makonde liwalis with traditional chiefs substantially undermined their own popular base of support at home.

2. Other Makonde liwalis were similarly "seduced" in the Queen's Birthday Honours List. Liwali Manzi Matamula of Mahuta received the Queen's Medal for Chiefs in 1955, and Liwali Masudi Namwete of Kitangari got the Queen's Certificate in 1958.

3. Tanganyika, Convention of Representative Chiefs of Tanganyika, Minutes of the First Meeting, May 14–16, 1957; Third Meeting, June 24–26, 1958; Fourth Meeting, December 17–20, 1958; Fifth Meeting, March 5–7, 1959; and Sixth Meeting, November 16–19, 1959.

## THE DISSENTING MODERNISTS

Western-educated Makonde who rebelled against the colonial or traditional systems of politics were not a significant political force in Newala until roughly the 1950s. Partly this was a problem of economic survival. There were really only two avenues of employment open to the educated Makonde who desired to apply his talents in his home district: government or the missions. In both instances the employers were not interested in a radical overturning of the status quo. A Makonde clerk, teacher, or hospital orderly who was not content with economic security and the prestige which his education gave him, and who insisted upon hurrying the pace of change, was labeled "cheeky," and his tenure was liable to be limited.

The prospects of an educated Makonde becoming an independent entrepreneur in his home district were not very bright. As a potential businessman he not only lacked the initial capital but also found himself hopelessly defeated by the competition of more highly organized Asian and Arab traders. Agriculture also had limited appeal. If the classic curriculum of the school system and the quarantinelike environment of the middle- and secondary-school compounds had not made the educated Makonde hostile toward a career as a farmer, other factors would have done so. The restrictive nature of the traditional land-tenure system, for one thing, made it difficult (though not impossible) for an enterprising Makonde to secure an economically efficient farm. The marketing facilities in the district and even at the coast, moreover, were either poorly developed or almost entirely controlled by the Asians, Arabs, and Europeans. Finally, the industrious and efficient cultivator would soon find himself faced with the fate of other moderately prosperous Africans. This was the prospect that the ever expanding ranks of his extended family would make demands upon his new wealth, wiping out his economic gains and providing a constant drain on his resources.

The foregoing discussion assumes that the educated Makonde had an economic choice. In fact, he did not. Of the twenty-four boys at Kitangari Middle School whom I interviewed in 1955, twelve were still without jobs six months after completing their eighth year of schooling. Four of the youths had been employed locally by the Roman Catholic mission as carpenters or clerks; the remainder had to leave the district for further training as teachers, medical technicians, and natural-resource instructors. The chances of the latter group returning to Newala upon completion of their training were remote. Thus, they would follow the lead of their seniors in gravitating to Dar es Salaam, Tabora, or possibly the Makonde coastal towns of Lindi and Mtwara. If they were to be apostles of dissent, rebelling against the traditional and colonial orders, their voices would be heard largely in districts away from home.

This is not to say that dissenting modernists were entirely absent from Newala District prior to the 1950s; it was only that their numbers were few and their voices weak. Indeed, however feeble they were, expressions of discontent had been detected by the colonial administration as much as two decades previously. In 1931 the provincial commissioner of Lindi Province, C. H. Grierson, had remarked that during a safari through Newala he had noted that

> In one part of the District small plots had been cleared and fenced under a tree, and [I] ascertained that some youths were in the habit of meeting together and holding junior Parliaments. Careful watch was kept over this innovation, which seems to have died a natural death; it is considered to have been more in the nature of a pastime, with no special significance. The younger generation are always encouraged to attend official court and council meetings, and a fair proportion of the more experienced and sophisticated young men of decent repute, take their recognized place among the Elders on their special mats.[4]

These "rump parliaments" did not immediately disappear, as the officer had assumed. The Newala district commissioner noted three years later that these gatherings – going under the name of *chama* (plural: *vyama*), *umoja*, *ushirika*, and other terms meaning "partnership" or "cooperative venture" – were still actively functioning. He noted that they were a frustrated response on the part of the young and early-middle-aged men who had been to the coast, had come into contact with other tribes, and had become disenchanted with their lot. The D.C.

4. *Annual Report*, 1931.

did not regard the action as a rejection of the authority of the wakalungwa but rather as resentment of the inability of the elders to adapt to changing conditions of life and disappointment with the slow course of justice under senile or lazy headmen. Despite the fact that these vyama had occasionally threatened the judicial roles of the wakalungwa, the British officer felt that their positive value as informal self-help organizations in the clearance of bush, payment of taxes, care for the sick, and other community projects far outweighed their potential for mischief:

> They serve as a point of contact with the expanding ideas of the more thoughtful Africans, exercising, as they must, some stimulus among the very conservative Makonde families. These societies are not met with in many parts of the District, and are nowhere beyond the experimental stage.[5]

As long as the dissenting modernists were small in number and limited in their objectives, the British administration in Tanganyika was prepared to be responsive in its attitude toward the formation of popular associations. The official attitude in the prewar period is best summarized by the confidential letter of the chief secretary to all provincial commissioners in 1940.[6] The chief secretary felt that freedom of association was as necessary to the development of a democratic Bantu society as it was for other nationalities. He argued that traditional African society seldom gave its leaders the power to forbid meetings that were not secretive, conspiratorial, or subversive in character. Moreover, central government's legislative powers were adequate for dealing with the problems of subversion. "Government is not," the chief secretary stated, "prepared to support the general proposition that under Native Law and Custom, a meeting of natives is unlawful merely by reason only of the fact that it has not [had] the prior approval of the chief."[7]

After the Second World War, nationalist agitation in many parts of Africa became more effective in its challenge to British

---

5. Newala District, *Annual Report*, 1934.
6. L. B. Freeston, March 21, 1940 (TNA 4/464). This was prompted by the inquiry into disturbances in Upare and Tanga in 1939.
7. *Ibid.*

rule. At this point the attitude of British administrators in Tanganyika became less sanguine regarding political dissent. The new accord that transferred Tanganyika from the mandate system of the League of Nations to the United Nations trustee-ship system did pledge the British to bring the people of Tanganyika to either self-government or independence. The form and pace of political development, however, was left largely to the discretion of the colonial administration. And British officials had no intention of breaking radically with previous policies and practices. The Native Authorities, for example, were to remain the chosen instruments for evolutionary growth even though they would be required to act with the advice of representative councils. Legal and administrative obstacles were erected to make it difficult for these new councils to come under the sway of popular political associations.

The most significant weapon in retarding the growth of a nationalist movement was the battery of extraordinary powers given to the registrar of societies under the Societies Ordinance of 1954. The registrar enjoyed exclusive authority to grant or deny recognition to any group attempting to constitute itself as an association, and his decision to deny or withdraw recognition could not be appealed through the courts. A group which was not officially recognized was regarded as an illegal society, and its leaders and members risked various penalties if they solicited for new members, held meetings, collected dues, or engaged in other activities. It was impossible, moreover, for a society to achieve recognition on a territorial basis; recognition had to be applied for, on a piecemeal basis, in each district or subarea of a district where the society wanted to operate. For at least two reasons this proved to be an unintended advantage to TANU. In the first place it compelled Nyerere and other leaders to make TANU a genuinely nationalist movement instead of letting it remain—as many African political parties had done—the plaything of the urban elite. If TANU claimed to speak for Tanganyika as a whole, it had to have the organization and membership to prove it. Second, since a society could not be registered nationally, it could not be dis-mantled nationally. A political indiscretion or violation of a law by the leaders of a local branch of TANU could lead to the withdrawal of recognition for that branch, but it did not affect other branches of the association.

Achieving recognition was only the first hurdle for TANU and other dissenting modernists. Continued recognition required that the leaders of an association operate within narrowly prescribed limits in holding public meetings, keeping accounts, distributing literature, and presenting petitions. Where the rules themselves were not unduly restrictive, the arbitrary whims of the local district commissioners could provide even more effective harassment to political dissenters. Especially crippling was the governor's circular letter of August 1, 1953, which prohibited government employees from joining any association of a political nature while continuing in Her Majesty's Service. Inasmuch as government was the most significant employer of educated talent in Tanganyika, the order attempted to deny political movements a broad-based leadership. The application of the letter, moreover, not only denied membership to civil servants in security and policy-making positions (which might have been reasonable); it was applied as well to the lowliest dispensary workers and market sweepers. Indeed, even many of the mission teachers I interviewed in Newala felt that they were not legally permitted to join TANU. They suspected that the subsidies granted to the Roman Catholic and UMCA missions made them *de facto* civil servants. If the district commissioner didn't interpret it that way, at least some of the church fathers might. They were very much aware of the action taken against Julius Nyerere in 1954 by the European supervisors of St. Francis College (Pugu) near Dar es Salaam. Following Nyerere's appearance at the United Nations in New York, he was required to make a choice between his teaching and his political careers.

Finally, there was the limitation that political movements in Tanganyika prior to 1958 were not permitted to carry on the normal activities of political parties. At the territorial level, for example, membership on the Legislative Council did not come as a result of a popularly contested election. Nominations were made by the governor, and it was apparent that representation was based upon race, geography, personal qualities, and factors other than political affiliation. At the local level as well, the district commissioners did everything possible to prevent the emergence of a political party system in the contests over elected seats for the village, chiefdom, and district councils.

The only societies which operated in the Makonde region prior to the 1950s were trading associations, teachers' organizations, and other groups which were nonpolitical in orientation. As far as I could ascertain, the Makonde Union had applied for registration at Lindi in 1951 but was denied recognition. The government also resisted all overtures from the Makonde cashew growers and other farmers who wanted cooperative societies introduced to the area. The cultivators were convinced that cooperative societies had been the key factor in the prosperity of the Sukuma, Chagga, and other wealthy tribal groups in Tanganyika. British officials, on the other hand, were mindful of the fact that the cotton cooperatives in the Mwanza area had provided a vehicle for political expression at a time when various branches of TANU had been banned in the Lake Province.[8] The government's public explanation was that cooperatives could not be introduced without adequate supervisory personnel in order to protect the rank-and-file membership against mismanagement by untrained leaders. Indeed, it was not until 1959 that the British administration felt compelled to establish producers' cooperatives in the Ruvuma Valley, and then only after the unregistered Makonde Collective Marketing Union had been suppressed by the police for illegally engaging in trading and for misallocating funds.[9]

The national leadership of TANU decided to organize in the Makonde area in 1955, despite the administrative obstacles and the pessimistic assessment given to Nyerere by a young educated Makonde who in later years was to become a leading member of the Tanzanian government. The young teacher had warned Nyerere that the Makonde cultivators were lethargic, fearful of government reprisals if they joined TANU, and incapable of understanding even the depth of their own misery let alone that of the people of Tanganyika as a whole. The peasants, he informed me shortly after his meeting with

8. See J. Gus Liebenow, "Responses to Planned Political Change in a Tanganyika Tribal Group," *American Political Science Review*, L (June, 1956), 442–61.

9. Southern Province, *Annual Report*, 1959, p. 143.

Nyerere, would resist parting with the two shillings for membership in exchange for the promise of a better future. The educated youth, moreover, felt intimidated by the inclusion of the Makonde Water Development Corporation within the ban on civil servants joining political movements.

Initially the pessimistic assessment appeared to be painfully correct. TANU recruiters whom I interviewed in late 1955 had succeeded in making minor progress in only two liwaliates. One of the liwaliates was Namikupa, where the wakili had secretly joined TANU and had encouraged others to do the same. The wakili enjoyed great respect because of his Standard VIII education and his years of success as a timber contractor and trader in the area. He was an example of self-reliance at work and was responsible for much of the progress made in a midwife program, economic betterment schemes, a sanitation campaign, and other activities in his liwaliate. Inasmuch as the liwali under whom he worked was both old and uninterested in his work, the people of the liwaliate had started coming to the wakili with questions ranging from the proper price they should get from the Indian merchants for their cashew nuts to how they could borrow money to pay school fees. The second area in which the recruiters made some headway was Mahuta. Although the liwali had not joined TANU, his previous experience (and that of two of his jumbes) as organizer of the African Traders Association made him at least tacitly sympathetic to TANU's cause.

Generally, however, the initial attempt to gather a following proved rather disappointing throughout Newala District as a whole. Several of the early leaders such as Abdallah Hassan Uzzy, the district secretary, encountered the usual hostility which Makonde afford Africans from other districts who attempt to regulate their lives.[10] He and Martin Kalemaga, the first district chairman, witnessed the Makonde lethargy to which they had been alerted. What was required was more dynamic leadership provided by one who had already won a measure of confidence among the Makonde.

10. Mr. Uzzy has nevertheless continued to be a major political force in the area, serving as area commissioner of Lindi, TANU district secretary in Newala, and in other roles. He was born in Kilwa in 1931, attended Songea Secondary School, and traveled to Israel and Moscow as a representative of TANU.

It was one of the ironies of Newala politics that the man who ultimately provided the challenge to the accommodating modernists had been induced to return to Newala by Liwali Justino Mponda himself. That man was Lawi Sijaona, a native of Newala, who, following his mission education, took a job editing a Swahili newspaper in Dar es Salaam for the Tanganyika Public Relations Department. Mponda recognized Sijaona as a man of talent and, with the approval of Ian Norton, the district commissioner, induced Sijaona to return with him to Kitangari where he was to be appointed Mponda's deputy, or wakili. The event was noteworthy both for the future development of Newala politics and because it provided one of the few instances when popular objection caused a district commissioner to reverse a nomination. While not objecting to the qualifications of Lawi Sijaona (indeed, they hardly knew him), the jumbes and elders of Kitangari objected strenuously to the highhanded tactics of Justino Mponda in hiring Sijaona without consulting the people of the liwaliate. Ian Norton was obliged to withdraw the nomination of Sijaona and to devise another strategy for utilizing the considerable talents of the man and for bolstering the sagging prestige of Mponda. These objectives were accomplished by promoting Mponda to the more significant Newala liwaliate and naming Sijaona as the clerk of the embryonic Local Council.

Under Ian Norton the post of clerk of the Newala council was a key office in the developing system of local government. The arrival of Ernest Craig as the new district commissioner in 1954 dramatically altered the situation, and by early 1955 the signs of strain between Sijaona and Craig became pronounced. The new commissioner was used to running "his" district in a more autocratic fashion, and his public criticism of Sijaona's work undermined the latter's effectiveness in dealing with the liwalis, jumbes, and members of the council. By the end of 1955 it was apparent to Sijaona that the local government reforms under Craig constituted a façade for the continuation of British paternalism. He therefore resigned as clerk and immediately joined forces with the small nucleus of TANU adherents in the district. In recognition of his education and experience, he was quickly made chairman of the local branch of TANU and began to provide the organizational talents so badly needed. He possessed the qualities of leadership required at that point in time: a reputation for being able to stand up and challenge European officials, inside information on the operations of local government in the district, and good relations with TANU leaders in Dar es Salaam. It was Sijaona who convinced Julius Nyerere that a successful recruitment drive through the Southern Province—regarded as the most backward of the territory—would strengthen TANU's claims that it was a national movement. Nyerere's trip was indeed a success, and it was undoubtedly this action that started Lawi Sijaona on the pathway to national prominence in the 1960s, when he held a number of important legislative and executive positions. For the year 1956 in Newala, however, he epitomized the dissenting modernist in the developing political drama of that area.[11]

## The Pivotal Modernists

The group that was to play the strategic role in determining the outcome of the many-sided struggle within Newala District was the pivotal modernists. These were the young, recently educated Makonde who had not in 1956 directly committed themselves to any faction in the contest for power and influence. Many in this group had interests which were so predominantly economic, religious, or educational in character that they rejected a political role. Others, such as the mission teachers and even employees of the central and local governments, felt that their own job security prevented them from becoming political activists. There were some as well who were genuinely convinced that economic and social development were necessary preconditions for any meaningful and lasting change in the political order. It was felt that a widening of the political controversy at that stage was not only premature but would jeopardize the slight material and psychological

11. Mr. Sijaona has represented Lindi and Newala Pachoto in the National Assembly, and has held the following posts: parliamentary secretary for the Ministries of Local Government (1961) and the Treasury (1962); minister for National Culture and Youth (1962); minister for Lands, Settlement and Water Development (1964); minister for Home Affairs (1966); minister of State in Second Vice President's Office (1967); and chairman of the Tanzanian Youth League Central Committee (1968).

advantages that the members of this group enjoyed over the less-educated and less-enterprising Makonde. Finally, the pivotal-modernist camp included a number of the non-Makonde Africans resident in the district. These were the clerks and teachers who were influential in the modernization process of the district but who nevertheless recognized that the extreme parochialism of the Makonde made it difficult for Ngoni, Nyam-wezi, or other "alien" Africans to become involved in the political affairs of the area.

Despite the lack of political commitment in 1956, it was the pivotal modernists who had the choice of throwing their weight to the dissenting modernists or remaining silent and thereby giving tacit support to the accommodating modernists. Although remaining politically detached until this point in time, the pivotal modernists did constitute distinct interest groups in Makonde society, and they were not even averse to organizing for the achievement of their primary goals. There were several identifiable categories of pivotal modernists in Newala in 1956.

## Economic Entrepreneurs

Although a decade later the cashew growers were to constitute the most significant economic entrepreneurs among the Makonde, in 1956 they were just beginning to prosper and still had to overcome administrative resistance to the formation of cooperative societies. The most significant of the economic entrepreneurs in this earlier period were the traders of Lindi, Mtwara, Mahuta, and the other minor settlements. One of the former leaders of the trading group was Manzi Matamula, who demonstrated the weakness and the strength of the pivotal modernist group. In 1948 Matamula had organized the shopkeepers and small itinerant traders of the Southern Province in order to defend themselves against the Asians, who attempted to monopolize the wholesaling and retailing of commodities in the province. Matamula traveled regularly from Lindi to Songea — a distance of more than five hundred miles — collecting produce orders, making bulk purchases at the coast, and delivering the produce in vehicles rented from sympathetic Asian businessmen. Most Asians, however, were antagonistic to this threat to their near-monopoly, and they even appealed to the Economic Control Board in Dar es Salaam in an effort to have the African trade association banned. Manzi Matamula, however, had the support of the provincial commissioner in Mtwara as well as that of the British administration in Newala. In the long run, Matamula's success may have been the undoing of the association, for the struggle brought Manzi Matamula to the attention of the district commissioner, who was looking for new Makonde administrative talent. In 1948 Matamula accepted the position of liwali of Liteho—thus giving the appearance of accommodation to British goals. In fact he continued to be a thorn in the side of the established order by attacking mission educational policies and the monopolistic practices of the Asian merchants and also by publicly pressing the British administrators to deliver on their promises of economic development. The introduction of the mechanical ploughing scheme in the Ruvuma Valley, for example, can be credited to Matamula. The success, moreover, of TANU in Mahuta (to which Matamula was later posted) was attributed by TANU leaders to the permissive attitude of Liwali Manzi with respect to the party's recruitment drives. Thus, this pivotal modernist was prepared to incur the displeasure of the British administration in furthering the development of his people.

## *Teachers*

An even larger segment of the pivotal-modernist camp, and one with more generalized goals than the traders, were the Makonde teachers. Most were in the employ of the UMCA and Roman Catholic missions, but an increasing number taught in central and local government schools. Very cautiously this group attempted to steer a tenuous and tortuous course among the missionaries, government officials, the emerging political leaders, and the uneducated masses. Protest on their part against the existing social and political order was to be very carefully weighed against the possible loss of the material and psychological security which education had provided them. It was clear that they were generally discontented with the state of affairs in the Makonde region and with their own lot in particular, but it was equally clear that they were not always interested in making common cause with all classes to correct the ills of Tanganyikan society. As one teacher stated:

> If I joined TANU now I would find myself the only educated man among a horde of ignorant tribal people. If trouble develops, the government would hold me responsible. It would not matter that the president or secretary of TANU or its chapters are well-intentioned people who really stand for the material progress of the Africans. If the rank-and-file uneducated member misinterprets the programs of the leaders, the whole movement is discredited.

His elitist remarks were echoed by another mission teacher who insisted that court cases involving teachers should be heard by the same magistrates who dealt with Europeans and Asians although "people of the third class" should continue to secure justice from the liwalis. In their self-estimation of where they stood on the prestige scale, they were outranked by liwalis, government teachers, rural medical aides, clerks, traders, and jumbes. Only semiskilled laborers, farmers, and court messengers ranked lower in prestige. The concern about the lack of *heshima,* or respect, was frequently voiced, as in the complaints of one mission teacher:

> Even our former students merely greet us with "Jambo, bwana." This is the same as they would greet their chums. With government teachers there is respect because the people fear them, feeling that the power of the D.C. and the liwali is behind them. The people know that the missionaries cannot put people in jail.

Although the government teachers in 1956 felt that the strictures of civil service employment prevented them from forming any type of association, the mission teachers had elected to brave the possible wrath of both the government and the missionaries and had joined the already thriving associations which had been formed in adjacent districts — the Masasi Diocese African Teachers Union, for the UMCA teachers; and the St. Augustine Teachers Association, for Roman Catholic teachers. In attending meetings of the Newala and Kitangari chapters of these two groups and in perusing their minutes, I was struck by the marked job-orientation of the mission teachers. The meetings were devoted almost entirely to the questions of better salaries, housing, medical services, and further training for the teachers.[12] They expressed resentment of the paternalism of the missionaries and of efforts to regulate their morals and social life (while at the same time indicating that the priests and nuns were "loved as fathers and mothers of us all"). They felt, too, that African teachers should have a more active hand in the planning of curricula and in the discussion of discipline codes, school fee payments, and other broad education issues.

It was only outside the formal meetings that teachers expressed to me an interest in the political, economic, and social problems of the district or of Tanganyika as a whole. Their comments, however, largely reinforced the notion of elitism referred to previously. One of their greatest concerns with the current system of local government, for example, was the fact that too few teachers had been selected to serve as liwalis and even fewer as jumbes and unoffical members of the Local Council. This means, said one, "that educated people must suffer the indignity of taking orders from illiterates." Another insisted that "We are the natural leaders in this community because we know how to talk with the people about their problems. We use simple psychology in putting things across." Although several teachers did question the wisdom of having Europeans and Asians on the Local Council, their concern was more material than political: "Would the Asians have an equal role in competing for educational scholarships and building sites?" "Does equality mean we will all pay the same taxes?"

On the issue of the relationship between education and economic development, the mission teachers displayed ambivalence. On the one hand, they insisted that the school curriculum was much too narrow and was not providing Tanganyika with the engineers, carpenters, masons, and bank clerks that it needed. Yet, in the one area where the colonial government had been attempting to deal more realistically with the most pressing problems of economic development, the teachers were patently unhappy: this was the insistence that the middle-school

12. Grade I teachers in 1956 made between Shs. 300 and Shs. 583 per month, which put them subordinate only to the liwalis and some of the top clerks. Grade II teachers were also relatively well paid, receiving Shs. 180 to Shs. 300 per month.

curriculum assume an agricultural bias. Clearly, the teachers' own classically oriented education had not prepared them to deal with the problems of agricultural instruction. It seemed, too, that their own view of their status – which was low enough – prevented them from being enthusiastic about glorifying the role of the farmer. Although on this issue the teachers seemed to be making common cause with TANU leadership elsewhere in the territory, it was apparent that the latter opposed the British government as a political issue. The Newala teachers in 1955–56 were not yet prepared to add their weight to the nationalist cause. Thus, some of the most articulate and best-educated members of Makonde society were playing a waiting game.

## Students

The student group may also be considered part of the pivotal modernists in 1956. The Standard VI to VIII boys whom I interviewed in Newala differed substantially in their political outlook from others of their generation who either had remained with the traditionally oriented majority or who had failed in school at some prior stage and had become part of the dissenting-modernist group. They were modernist insofar as success in the school system was reserved to those who had demonstrated at least an outward acceptance of modernity by embracing Christianity and its moral values, adhering to new standards of dress and hygiene, being able to read and write, and accepting scientific rather than magical explanations of natural phenomena.

Their insulation from their parents and peer group in the rural area was obvious in their lack of accurate knowledge regarding the system of local government in the district. They most strongly identified with, and understood the roles of, the district commissioner, the social development officer, the agricultural officer, and the liwali – in that order. They knew very little about the work of the jumbes, and what they did know was essentially negative. That is, the jumbe was regarded as one who dealt with minor disturbances of the peace, helped collect taxes, and enforced cultivation orders. Even less knowledge existed regarding the activities of the wakalungwa, and generally the traditional headmen were regarded with a measure of disdain.

The position of the schoolboy was essentially pivotal in character even though while in school he could have been classified as an accommodating modernist. That is, he had to conform by passing examinations, attending chapel, doing his chores in the compound, and avoiding infraction of other rules which would lead to a summary dismissal. On the other hand, departure from the school system would compel him to face the real world without the paternalism of the church fathers. The choice of returning to the village and assuming the role of a cultivator was apparently not a realistic one. Not only did the hothouse environment of the mission school poorly prepare him both psychologically and technically for such a role, but apparently the parents and other relatives who had paid his school fees would not hear of such a waste of their "investment." The job preference of the Newala schoolboys referred to in a previous chapter indicated that only one of the twenty-three questioned was interested in agriculture, and a second was interested in stock breeding – an occupation which had little relevance to the Makonde region at that time. Oddly enough, when I talked to the boys *as a group*, they placed a very high value on agriculture and indicated that improvement of agriculture was the most pressing problem facing Tanganyika and the Makonde in particular. The idealization of the situation, however, was merely a parroting of the then-current European sermons on the subject. The schoolboys realized only too well that government assistance to farmers in the form of loans and low-cost mechanical equipment was not forthcoming, and therefore an educated man could not expect either high income or high prestige.

The same sort of ambivalence was evident in their attitude toward government employment. In indicating job preference and in their group discussion beforehand, there was a great deal of interest in teaching, becoming a rural medical aide, or applying for work with the social welfare department. Only three expressed an interest in police work, one wanted to become a government clerk, and none considered attractive the posts of liwali, district officer (a position they knew was at that

time being filled by Africans in other districts), or other positions associated with enforcement aspects of government. Yet
at the time of job placement a few months later, more than
half of the boys I had interviewed informed the school authorities that they wanted to become government clerks, recognizing
that this was still the quickest and easiest way to higher income
and prestige.

## Development Officers

The final group of Makonde in the pivotal-modernist
camp was the small cadre of African officials engaged in
development work. As employees of the central government or
the Newala Local Council, they had much in common with the
accommodating modernists in terms of educational background, source of income, and restrictions on overt political
activity. Nevertheless, being associated with the more positive
aspects of government operations they were viewed by others,
and they perceived themselves, in a different light. They were
associated with the future rather than with a maintenance of
the status quo; with education and persuasion rather than
with coercion; with the increases in income and prestige rather
than with tax collection and the more demeaning aspects of
colonial rule; and with Makonde self-help rather than with
alien enforcement of scarcely understood rules.

Not all the development officers fit these prescriptions. There
was, for example, the agricultural officer, Abdullah Fundikira,
who was subsequently to achieve a national reputation as a
prominent chief among the Nyamwezi. Although he later broke
with Nyerere following independence, he was one of the
earliest of the traditional chiefs to identify with TANU. Being
a Makerere University graduate with significant government
experience (including a trip to the United Kingdom for an
agriculture course), his support was regarded as crucial for
Nyerere in the independence movement. At the time of my
studies in 1955-56, he was serving as the first African agricultural officer in the territory. In general the African reaction
to his program and performance was favorable. Fundikira's
responsibilities differed substantially from the agricultural
work of the liwalis and jumbes, who were concerned with en-
forcing soil-conservation measures, fining people for failing

to plant famine-relief plots, and other punitive measures. Fundikira was credited by various informants, both illiterate and educated, with many positive advancements in Makonde methods of farming. He had urged the people to use hybrid seed, to enlarge their stands of cashew trees as well as their cassava and millet fields, and to participate in rice-mechanization schemes in the Ruvuma Valley. His approach was educational rather than coercive. Nevertheless, the compliments of my informants were invariably hedged with such comments as: "Of course, he is not a Makonde"; "the Nyamwezi do not cultivate as we do, so we must be cautious"; "he is a very wealthy man, so he does not understand how we poor people do things"; or "we have heard these 'new' things before but they did not always work."

It was clear that the more effective development officers were those who were Makonde residents of Newala, and it was they who provided a favorable climate for the subsequent recruitment efforts of TANU. Some, such as Leopold Pallahani, a young health officer who is today a leading official in NUTA (National Union of Tanganyika Workers), were quite bold in their support for TANU. Others, such as Frederick Mchauru, the social development officer, advanced TANU's objectives while keeping their political views muted. Mchauru, who by 1968 had risen to the post of principal secretary to the Ministry of Home Affairs, came from a much-respected family of the district. His father, the Reverend E. T. Mchauru, was the first Makonde to become an Anglican priest and was instrumental in getting the Makonde clan leaders to accept mission education for their youngsters despite very strong fears that the children would be served pork at school. Reverend Mchauru's father had been an important headman in the German period, and thus the children of Reverend Mchauru had respected credentials among both the traditionalists and the modernists. Frederick Mchauru's young brother, Albert, had opted for a career in administration, and at the time of my investigations in 1955 he was serving as the liwali of Nanyamba—the only Christian among the seven liwalis of Mtwara District. Frederick, who had been educated at St. Joseph's (Chidya) and St. Andrew's College (Minaki) before going to the United Kingdom for a diploma course in the social sciences at the London School of Economics, felt that he could make a more positive contribution to development by joining the Social Welfare Department.

In 1955 and 1956, Frederick Mchauru and his wife, Thekla, proved to be a very effective team working in the area of community development. Thekla Mchauru was a trained nurse and her father had been the liwali of Mchauru in neighboring Masasi District. It was her responsibility to establish midwives' programs and to organize the women of the district into clubs where they could receive instruction regarding proper family nutrition, child rearing, and home management. Over six hundred women in 1956 participated in the clubs. Frederick Mchauru at the same time sought the cooperation of the jumbes and other leaders in getting each village to organize a *chama cha maendeleo*, or progressive society dedicated to the principle of self-help. The vyama, which included both men and women, were making a noticeable impact in the direction of modernization and were forerunners of the TANU village schemes introduced a decade later.

Mnolela village in Kitangari liwaliate constituted a model community in Mchauru's program. The jumbe, Saidi Nantanje, had only a Standard I education, but he committed himself and his people fully to the concept of the chama cha maendeleo. It was an idea, he said, which the Makonde had long ago accepted but which was dying out under colonial rule. Nantanje divided his jumbeate into eleven wards, with a village elder as head of each ward. The village chama met twice weekly and considered a range of issues; the whole jumbeate met once a month. The following is a brief résumé of items discussed during a jumbeate meeting I attended in May, 1956:

1. Problems of boys stealing clothes, money, food.
2. Necessity of having every person, women and children included, plant a food crop.
3. Obligation of every person, whether Muslim or Christian, to know his religion.
4. Need of every parent to raise the money to send his children to school.
5. Finding out whether Makonde land is good for new crops.

6. People must go to the hospital when they are sick; otherwise they cannot work their fields and they will spread the illness to others.
7. No one is too old to read, and only by reading can you prevent others from cheating you.
8. The area must be kept clean; people should dig latrines and garbage pits.
9. It is wrong for mothers not to take better care of their babies.
10. Women have a duty to learn better ways of keeping house.

The chama cha maendeleo, however, was not merely a talking shop. The society was given a concrete form of action to bind its members through the organization of a farming guild, to which each member of the jumbeate belonged. From 1954 to 1956 the guild realized a profit of over Shs. 400 from the sale of cassava, millet, and maize which the members had cultivated and harvested in common. The profits were used to purchase insecticides, fertilizers, storage bins, and farm implements. The new techniques of cultivation and of spacing fruit and cashew trees employed on the common plot were soon copied by the individual members on their own farms. Thus experimentation took hold because the initial risk was a community rather than an individual one.

Despite the fact that the farm guild brought an individual profit as well as providing funds to establish a medical aid station and a community shop (selling soap, cigarettes, kerosene, and other commodities) for the benefit of all, it was apparent that the road to progress was not free of obstacles. Many of the villagers resented the time that had to be spent in the common effort and regarded the persuasion of the jumbe as carrying with it the force of authority. Hence, it was impossible to predict that the scheme would be continued if the existing jumbe were replaced or retired. Even the supposedly more enlightened ward leaders indicated that they had not completely accepted the idea of voluntary community participation. There was apparently much grumbling about the fact that the councilors were not paid for their attendance at the meetings of the chama cha maendeleo.

## SUMMARY

The Makonde on the eve of Tanganyika's independence were very much a divided people. The divisions were in most instances traceable to the constant political and social manipulation to which the people of southeastern Tanganyika had been subjected during sixty to seventy years of alien rule. Whether or not the dissenting modernist could convert the overwhelming majority who were still wedded to some form of traditionalism was a moot question. The essential struggle for power, however, was one which pitted the dissenting modernists against the educated Makonde who cooperated with the British colonial rulers. The decisive factor at the local level, at least, appeared to be those modernists who had not yet made up their minds regarding which way to jump politically. The struggle at the local level, however, was to be determined in an arena far from the Makonde homeland.

# 11:
# The Triumph
## of TANU

The Makonde played only a peripheral role during the Maji Maji uprising as the first great intertribal struggle against European colonial rule swept the southern part of Tanganyika in 1905. The tribal group seemed destined to remain a minor actor when the final drama in the anti-European struggle was enacted half a century later. The great confrontations of the 1950s between the British government and TANU did not take place in Lindi, Mtwara, or Newala. The main centers of TANU strength and action were Dar es Salaam, Mwanza, Tabora, Arusha, and other towns in the north. Geographic isolation, compounded by lethargy and the political fractionalization of Makonde leadership, had relegated the Makonde to the role of passive responder to vital decisions made elsewhere in the territory.

TANU did manage, nevertheless, during the period from 1956 onward, to dominate the political scene in the Makonde districts. It is open to question, however, whether it succeeded because of the organizational talents of its local leadership or because the issues it espoused and the grievances it exploited were sufficient to undermine loyalty to the liwalis and waku-lungwa. In certain respects the British administrators, through sins of omission and commission, had managed to weaken popular confidence in the systems of local government they had created. The emphasis on multiracialism, for example, was viewed with great suspicion, and Makonde fears were confirmed by reports that Asian merchants had made inquiries of the provincial administration regarding the acquisition of land on a freehold basis. The Makonde of Newala were also irritated over the water tax and impatient that the Makonde Water Corporation had not immediately brought water to all sectors of the plateau when the corporation came into operation in 1956. There were, moreover, grievances on the part of cashew growers over delays in launching producers' cooperatives and over the failure of government to control Asian purchases of their crops. The Muslim parents, furthermore, were irritated with the slow growth of a secular school system, and many parents as well as their youngsters objected strenuously to the agricultural bias of the middle-school curriculum.

TANU was ultimately successful in its campaign in the Makonde districts because it was able to convince many traditionalists, pivotal modernists, and even some accommodating modernists that TANU was on the verge of displacing the British government *in Dar es Salaam*. It was not an easy task initially. One major obstacle was the district commissioner's veiled suggestions that TANU was an illicit organization (despite the fact that it had complied with registration procedures for Newala District) and that the ban on joining political movements extended to employees of the Makonde Water Development Corporation (which it did not). Another obstacle was the reluctance of Makonde cultivators to part with the two shillings required for membership. And, finally, there was the frequently voiced fear of the police, who were from other tribal groups and would, as one informant said, "swoop down on a village and terrorize us all."

Despite the odds, the local TANU leaders persisted in their campaign to enlist the support of the Newala peasantry. The fact that Sijaona, Martin Kalemaga, and Abdallah Hassan Uzzy could attack the British administration and colonialism and not be arrested for their words was not lost upon the Makonde cultivators. Word spread, too, that the wakili of Namikupa had joined TANU and that many prominent employees of both the central government and the Local Council were beginning to talk openly of their membership in the party. Indeed, some

TANU adherents were so confident they could act with impunity that by mid-1956 several government employees had started recruiting for TANU on government time.

I accompanied one officer, Leopold Pallahani, who at that time was a social-development assistant and exemplified the pivotal modernist position, on safari near Malatu. I found that Mr. Pallahani had been educated through Standard IX at Ndanda mission school and had originally intended becoming a Roman Catholic priest. When that option was closed to him, he became in turn an agricultural instructor, then a market master, and eventually he was picked by the administration to work with Frederick Mchauru in various development schemes in Newala District. I discovered, during our safari, that only a portion of his time was spent discussing adult-literacy and sports programs, new cash crops, and the need for better training of midwives. He seemed to be equally concerned in his public meetings with urging people to join TANU, with criticism of the multi-racial composition of the Local Council, and with advocating policies and programs which had not as yet been sanctioned by the British government for the Newala area. He suggested, for example, that the people of Malatu force the government's hand on the issue of producers' cooperatives by banding together and selling their cashews and cassava in bulk at Mtwara. He insisted that "people should stop thinking that all things are impossible. Only the fear of government prevents people from realizing a better life; and this fear is often mistaken. TANU will teach us the way to get the good things of life."

The crucial factor in turning the tide in TANU's favor was—as indicated previously—the visit of Julius Nyerere to Newala in July, 1956. Within a matter of weeks the small nucleus of stalwarts around Lawi Sijaona had grown to between five and six hundred. The appearance of the national leader, making speeches which were manifestly critical of colonial rule, gave the local leadership of TANU the kind of support that was needed. From that point forward the campaign of harassing the British administrators and their appointed local officials began to produce the desired effect. By 1958 the provincial commissioner, S. R. Tubbs, was complaining that

> It is a matter of concern to the [liwalis] that many of the people now pay more attention to political leaders than to

traditional or appointed local authorities. The chiefs have no quarrel with the basic nationalist desire for self-government, but only too often nationalism is interpreted locally as opposition to all established authority and development schemes.[1]

The consolidation of TANU's position within the Makonde area did not become fully apparent until February, 1959, and once again the action at the local level was a response to more significant developments on the national plane: the parliamentary elections which TANU had pressured the British government to call. The elections came in two stages, with half of the provinces voting in September, 1958, and the Southern Province and four others balloting in February, 1959. In order to fully appreciate the significance of developments at the micropolitical level, it is necessary to shift the focus of analysis momentarily to the macro level.

## THE PRESSURE FOR SELF-GOVERNMENT

The concession made by the colonial administration in scheduling popular elections for the Legislative Council was a remarkable victory for Julius Nyerere and TANU. In the four years following TANU's birth in July, 1954, Nyerere had reorganized the old Tanganyika African Association and converted it into a vigorous political instrument which could effectively challenge a wide range of opponents: the colonial government, the Asian and European settlers, the traditional chiefs, and the modernizing tribalists. What made this feat all the more remarkable was that at the time of TANU's second birth in 1954 the British government was still adamantly opposed to discussing even a twenty-five-year timetable for Tanganyikan independence. What, then, were the factors that brought about this dramatic change of attitude in the brief space of four years?

While students of international organization generally overestimate the role of the United Nations in terminating colonial rule in Africa and Asia, the Trusteeship System was a vital factor in the independence movement in Tanganyika at least.[2]

1. Southern Province, *Annual Report*, 1958.
2. There are a number of studies on the progress of Tanganyika toward in-

The recommendations of the triennial visiting missions, the presentation of petitions on a range of issues from political parties to prostitution, and the personal appearances of Julius Nyerere and other leaders at U.N. sessions in New York did keep the colonial government accountable for many of its failures and shortcomings. United Nations action, coupled with the examples of successful drives for independence in India, Ghana, and elsewhere, forced the British to address themselves to the question of "Why not Tanganyikan independence?"

When the colonial administration finally acceded to the demands for constitutional reform, Tanganyika was to follow a path which had been blazed by Lord Durham for Canada in 1837 and had been used in turn by the "white" dominions, India and Ceylon, and more recently by Nigeria and other African dependencies. In this pattern of constitutional development, there were two critical institutions – the legislative and executive councils – which were to serve as training grounds for the acceptance by colonial peoples of full responsibility for the management of their own affairs. These two institutions were the embryonic parliament and cabinet of the future independent state. Although the details of development and the timing of stages varied for each territory, several general principles emerged. First, devolution of authority to local leadership was to be gradual and yet at the same time to steadily progress toward the heart of the governmental process. Second, to ensure both broad representation as well as "responsible" action, a variety of devices were employed in constituting the membership of the councils. In the initial stages the governor and other senior members of his administration outnumbered the unofficial members who represented the colonial public. The membership on the unofficial side, moreover, went through a gradual

---

dependence. I refer the reader to several of the more outstanding works on this period. See William H. Friedland, "The Evolution of Tanganyika's Political System," in *The Transformation of East Africa,* ed. Stanley Diamond and Fred G. Burke (New York: Basic Books, 1966), pp. 241–311; J. Clagett Taylor, *The Political Development of Tanganyika* (Stanford: Stanford University Press, 1963); Margaret L. Bates, "Tanganyika," in *African One-Party States,* ed. Gwendolen M. Carter (Ithaca: Cornell University Press, 1962), pp. 395–483; and Henry Bienen, *Tanzania: Party Transformation and Economic Development* (Princeton: Princeton University Press, 1967).

transition from being entirely nominated by the governor to being partially nominated and partially elected and, ultimately, to being almost entirely elected. Concomitant with changes in the means of selection, the representation of interests was broadened. Initially British missionaries, settlers, and business-men dominated—and sometimes monopolized—the unofficial side. As membership was broadened to include indigenous in-habitants, care was taken to guarantee representation of a wide variety of religious, ideological, economic, and other interests—usually far out of proportion to their numbers in society.

As the demands of independence became more vocal or as the British administrators anticipated such demands, critical changes would be made in both the legislative and executive councils. On the eve of independence the legislative council would consist almost entirely of elected, unofficial members representing political parties rather than other types of inter-ests. The elected leaders of the legislative council, in the mean-time, had come to assume a majority on the executive council as the governor and his senior officials withdrew. The accept-ance by the unofficial leadership of minor portfolios, such as tourism, was gradually succeeded by the surrendering of the ministries of education, agriculture, industry, and other domes-tic departments of consequence. At the final stage the leader of the unofficial majority in the legislative council was named prime minister, and he and his fellow cabinet officials assumed responsibility for the key ministries of finance, justice, defense, and foreign affairs. As the Union Jack was lowered, the governor assumed the figurehead role of governor-general, and a sover-eign independent state was born.

## The Pattern of Development in Tanganyika

At the time of TANU's formation in 1954, only the most dedicated believer could have convinced himself that Tanganyika would achieve independence in slightly more than seven years. In 1954 the Europeans not only monopolized the official majority membership in the Legislative Council; they held seven of the thirteen nominated seats on the unofficial side as well. Africans—until an additional seat was added later in the year—divided the remaining six nominated seats with Asians. Reforms in 1955 modified the situation somewhat in favor of the Africans on the unofficial side, but the best that Governor Sir Edward Twining's policy of "multiracialism" could offer Tanganyika's eight million Africans was parity of representation with the territory's 20,000 Europeans and its 60,000 Asians. Under the Twining program, each of the provinces and Dar es Salaam had three representatives, nominated from among the three major racial groups. An additional three persons were selected to represent general interests, bringing the council to thirty members. To ensure control over the Legislative Council, however, thirty-one officials were included, giving the government a majority of one. Since all of the officials were Europeans, the African members were outnumbered by more than five to one.

Numbers were not the only problem facing TANU in its effort to capture this vital institution. The governor, in nominating Africans to the council, showed a decided preference for those who represented traditional values and tribal points of view. He appeared to be particularly hostile toward political party leaders who attempted to organize movements on a territorial basis. Reference was made in a previous chapter to the role of the registrar of societies in frustrating political party development in Tanganyika. On a number of occasions between 1954 and 1958 the power of the registrar was employed in denying recognition to prospective branches of TANU and in suspending existing branches whose leaders were charged with various disturbances of peace and order. Administrative harassment, moreover, took the form of occasional bans on outdoor speeches by Nyerere and of costly and time-consuming libel suits.

In the long run, TANU seemed to thrive on British hostility. Although it lost some of the more conservative members from the old Tanganyika African Association, and although the government had placed a ban on African civil servants joining parties, it nevertheless grew from an estimated 100,000 members in 1955 to roughly twice that number in 1957. While the character of the Legislative Council did not permit TANU to

prove itself on the national plane, it did manage during this
period to win a few significant victories at the village, chiefdom, and district levels. In several contests over seats on the
newly formed local councils, TANU adherents won out over
traditionalists as well as candidates of tribal-based political
parties. Its campaign of harassment against the chiefs, moreover, was beginning to win some reluctant—but nonetheless
significant—converts from that quarter.

Nyerere's strategy for TANU was to form a coalition among
the educated, the urban workers and unemployed, the discontented cash farmers, and a few enlightened chiefs. By mid-1958
there were only two groups—aside from the British government
itself—which were assumed to be strong enough to oppose
TANU in its quest for popular loyalty. The first was the United
Tanganyika Party, which had been formed in February, 1956,
with the full blessing of Governor Twining. The leaders of the
UTP were the nominated members of the Legislative Council,
who were committed to the idea of multiracial parity and cooperation in developing Tanganyika. The second challenger to
TANU was the African National Congress (ANC), a group which
had splintered off from TANU. Its leader, Zuberi Mtemvu, advocated the immediate independence of Tanganyika, a policy
of noncooperation with Europeans and Asians in the territory,
and a more radical approach to economic and social development.

In pressing for a rapid termination of the trusteeship arrangement, TANU's leaders did not reject cooperation among the
three races since they recognized that Tanganyika would need
the talents and the investment of Europeans and Asians. Their
goal, however, was not a multiracial state but a nonracial one.
If multiracial parity had to be accepted during the transitional
stage, then it should be parity between the African and non-
African communities rather than equality among all three
races. Moreover, if the members of the Legislative Council
were to be truly representative, they must be elected by the
people rather than nominated by the governor.

Ultimately the British administration agreed to further constitutional reform. One of the last acts of Governor Sir Edward
Twining in 1958 was to schedule new elections for the Legislative Council. While acquiescing to the demands for election

rather than nomination of members, Twining did not capitulate entirely to TANU, which he stubbornly insisted lacked popular support. Thus, although there was to be a common nonracial voters roll, candidates were to stand for racially designated seats, and the tripartite racial representation for each province and Dar es Salaam remained in effect. Since each voter marked his ballot for three candidates, in theory the African majority could select not only the African candidate but the European and Asian as well. To avoid this eventuality, the franchise for the common roll was to be restricted to those persons who were twenty-five years of age or older and who either had an income of at least £150 a year and a Standard VIII education or were serving as a chief, liwali, or other official of local government. By most interpretations civil servants who possessed these qualifications were assumed to be denied not only the right to stand for office but also the right to vote. In any case, only 59,317 out of a population of more than eight million registered for the elections. Candidates' requirements, moreover, limited the campaign to those with a Standard XII education, Shs. 4000 a year income, or previous service on the council. The English-language requirement further limited the field of eligible Africans.

## The Elections of 1958–59

The flaw in the Twining plan for achieving a conservative multiracial victory was the ability of TANU to organize and dominate the African sector of the electorate while the Asian and European communities found themselves hopelessly divided by religious, ethnic, and ideological considerations. The non-Africans spread their votes over a wide range of candidates standing for the European and Asian seats, whereas TANU in each constituency endorsed a single European and a single Asian candidate when it was determined that they were sympathetic to TANU's point of view. In several instances the Asian and European candidates were not aware of the fact that they were being considered for endorsement and had not even met Nyerere or the other principal TANU leaders.

In the months preceding the September election, TANU was transformed from a political faction into a nationalist movement. To the alarm of British officials, TANU organized a Youth League, adopted a flag, colors, and ritual, and even began to usurp the authority of local chiefs on the assumption that the concession on holding elections signified the capitulation of the colonial regime. The administration overreacted to TANU audacity and in July charged Nyerere with criminal libel for comments made by him in the party's house organ, *Sauti ya TANU*. The arrest and subsequent trial of Nyerere undoubtedly added to the stature of TANU's leader—for the role of prison graduate is an honorable one among nationalist leaders in British Africa. It was only because of the intervention of the new governor, Sir Richard Turnbull, that Nyerere was fined rather than imprisoned. Despite the fears of TANU's leadership, the elections were not postponed.

The results of the first group of elections, in September, 1958, came as a complete shock to the British administration. TANU not only won the five African seats, but it made a clean sweep of the European and Asian contests as well. The UTP was annihilated by wide margins, and the African National Congress and Mtemvu himself found almost no ground for encouragement. Thus, Nyerere and TANU's credentials in speaking for Tanganyika as a whole could not be denied. The colonial government conceded in good style and advanced the second stage of the parliamentary elections from September, 1959, to February of that year.

The outcome of the second stage of the electoral process was predictable, and the developments in the Southern Province roughly paralleled those in the remaining four provinces. The UTP choice, Justino Mponda, who had represented the province during the period of nominated African membership on the Legislative Council, decided not to stand for office. He pleaded that his new appointment as chairman of the Newala Local Council would make such heavy demands on his time that he would not be able to devote adequate attention to territorial problems. Others speculated, however, that his frequent visits to Dar es Salaam had convinced him that the handwriting was on the wall for those accommodating modernists who had too eagerly collaborated with the colonial administration. By an odd twist of fate this left the field clear for TANU's candidate, Lawi Sijaona, who had once been a protégé of Mponda. No independent candidate felt sufficiently strong to oppose Sijaona.

The European seat similarly went without contest and was claimed by a missionary having TANU backing. The Asians, on the other hand, found themselves split along religious and ethnic lines. The two Asian candidates, J. A. G. Versi and A. Thanki, were Lindi merchants; however, the former was a Muslim and the latter a Hindu. On purely religious grounds, the Arabs and the Muslim Makonde in Mtwara and Lindi districts might have been expected to support Versi. Like Mponda, however, Versi had previously served as a nominated member of the Legislative Council and thus was tainted with the charge of open cooperation with the British regime. Thanki, on the other hand, had established a sound reputation with African merchants and consumers. Sensing that TANU was gaining strength in the Southern Province, Thanki sought and received TANU backing. In the ensuing election he won a decisive victory over his opponent.

The accomplishment of TANU in the south was duplicated elsewhere in the territory, and from that point forward Tanganyikan independence was no longer the central issue; it was rather the question of when and under what conditions this goal was to be realized. TANU elected members, with the full blessing of Nyerere, who chose to remain as the leader of the unofficial side of the council, cooperated with Governor Turnbull and the British administration in working out the details for further constitutional reform. Lawi Sijaona was among the members of a committee which proposed a radical transformation of the Legislative Council and of electoral requirements and procedures.[3]

The committee's proposals—most of which were ultimately accepted by the colonial government—included an expansion of the size and authority of the council; an elected unofficial majority; the elimination of racial designation for all but

3. See Tanganyika, *Report of the Post Elections (Ramage) Committee, 1959* (Dar es Salaam: Government Printer, 1959).

twenty-one of the seventy-one elected seats (eleven reserved for Asians, ten for Europeans); and a broadening of the franchise on a common electoral roll. On the last item TANU lost its bid for universal franchise but did get the educational and financial requirements considerably eased. A potential registrant had to satisfy one of the following conditions: literacy in Swahili or English; an income of £75, as evidenced by the payment of certain taxes; the holder or former holder of a recognized office in local government. It was estimated that the new provisions would extend the suffrage to over 800,000 residents of Tanganyika. Finally, the government concurred in the positive stance taken by the elections committee in rejecting both the establishment of an upper house of the legislature for traditional authorities and the idea of reserving seats on the Legislative Council for chiefs.

## THE CONFRONTATION OF 1959–60

The victory of TANU in the 1958–59 elections and the administration's acceptance of further constitutional reform led to a certain amount of confusion in many parts of Tanganyika regarding the significance of these events. The Makonde area was no exception. One of the immediate features of this confusion was the calling of a tax strike by some of the younger members of TANU in Newala District who had assumed that the impending demise of the colonial regime would mean an end to various forms of taxations. While some of their elders appreciated that even an African-run government would require revenue, they went along with the Youth League on the tax strike, suggesting that people withhold their taxes from the colonial government so that they could pay them to the TANU government, which would take over shortly. The harassment of the TANU Youth League succeeded, moreover, because the liwalis and jumbes were unwilling to risk further unpopularity over the issue of tax collection, in the hopes that inactivity now might secure their positions under the new TANU government.

In addition to the tax strike there were other millennial expectations voiced by TANU youth in the Makonde area which made the lot of the liwalis and jumbes difficult during the first half of 1959. Rumors were rampant that the agricultural bias of the middle-school curriculum would be dropped, that co-operatives would be established immediately, that the water fees would be discontinued, and that the Asians were leaving the province. At one point in 1959, local-government operations came to a virtual standstill. A special point of contention was the multiracial character of the Newala Local Council. Liwali Justino Mponda, who in 1959 had become the first African chairman of a district or local council in Tanganyika, had a very difficult time maintaining the façade of multiracial cooperation. Many of the councilors failed to appear for meetings of the council or its committees, and the councilors and even several of the liwalis and jumbes were becoming publicly hostile to the advice given by European officials. A movement was initiated to convert the Local Council to a District Council, in the hopes of excluding Europeans and Asians from participation. Parallel developments had already taken place in Lindi and Mtwara districts where the Makonde and Mwera successfully resisted the idea of establishing multiracial local councils.

Once again the local situation in the Makonde area responded to more significant action on the territorial plane. The crisis in Newala District ended when Julius Nyerere and other TANU leaders in the Legislative Council urged people throughout Tanganyika to support the British government during the transition period. With this signal from Nyerere the Makonde youth relaxed their campaign against the liwalis, and in both Newala and Mtwara districts there were monthly meetings between the officers of TANU and the liwalis in an effort to resolve a number of the impasses. In a remarkable about-face, TANU Youth League members began assisting the liwalis and jumbes in collecting the taxes, and by the end of 1959 Newala had collected 85 per cent of its local rates and Mtwara 61 per cent.[4] It was soon apparent, however, that the cooperation during this period was merely a marriage of convenience. By 1960 the conflict between the dissenting modernists (represented by TANU) and the accommodating modernists

4. S. R. Tubbs, *Annual Report of the Provincial Commissioner, Southern Province*, 1959.

(represented by Justino Mponda and the other liwalis) erupted in two separate arenas.

The first clash came over the composition of the Newala Local Council. The elections at the village and jumbeate level for councilors to the Newala council in 1960 for the first time took on a decidedly partisan flavor, with TANU actively supporting diwanis who were sympathetic to its program and policies. Raphael Saidi, TANU district secretary, conducted a vigorous campaign in behalf of TANU candidates, making the Makonde Water Development Corporation his primary target. He hit a very popular chord in demanding not only that the scheme be extended to cover the entire Makonde plateau but that free water should be provided at the kiosks and that the water rate should either be abolished or included as part of the Local Council's general rate. He proposed, moreover, that the structure of the Makonde Water Corporation be altered to permit unofficial Makonde representation, in order to convince the people that they—rather than the British government and the liwalis—owned the scheme.

TANU carried most of its candidates to victory, and this set the stage for the next round—a challenge to Justino Mponda in his bid for a third term as chairman of the Local Council. Undoubtedly the long-smoldering resentment of the other liwalis and the jumbes was a major factor in the first-ballot success of Raphael Saidi over Mponda. This action not only placed a hostile critic of British colonial rule at the head of local-government operations in Newala but also signaled the demise of Tanganyika's first experiment in multiracial government at the district level. By the end of 1960 the Newala Local Council had opted for the district council system, which was nonracial in character and thus gave a much more effective role to African residents. The reconstitution of the council, moreover, gave Saidi the opportunity of undermining traditional authority, since the thirty-five new wards, from which councilors were to be elected, did not conform to the traditional jumbeate boundaries. The elected unofficial membership far outnumbered the seven ex-officio members (the five liwalis and two wakilis) and six special members co-opted to represent interests which might be passed over in a purely electoral system. In the ensuing elections, TANU candidates won in each of the thirty-five wards, standing without opposition.

The second major confrontation in the Makonde area during 1960 came with respect to the elections for the Legislative Council under the procedures recommended by the electoral commission in 1959. The constituencies for the new assembly roughly paralleled district boundaries, and thus the Makonde were divided into three electoral units. In Mtwara and Lindi, TANU faced only mild opposition. Lawi Sijaona, in particular, won handily in Lindi and was ensured of continued influence in the Nyerere leadership group. In Newala, however, the controversy between TANU and its opposition became very heated. In a rerun of previous action, Raphael Saidi was pitted against Justino Mponda in the contest over the Newala seat. In this instance, however, there was a curious reversal of roles and postures.[5] Saidi, the former dissenting modernist, suddenly became an accommodating modernist, who insisted that everyone – African, European, and Asian – give generously of their time and talents in building a new Tanganyika. That new Tanganyika, of course, would be guided to its destiny by TANU leadership. Mponda, on the other hand, feeling rejected by the British administrators he had long served so faithfully, joined the African National Congress. Thus Mponda, in one of the two constituencies contested by ANC, found himself echoing Zuberi Mtemvu's demands that Africans must cease cooperation with Europeans and Asians, who were the exploiters of Tanganyika. Apparently Mtemvu's defeat in 1958 by TANU had only made him more vitriolic in his advocacy of a policy of "Africa for Africans,"[6] and Mponda had his own special cause for dissatisfaction. Mponda's attacks on Europeans, Asians, and multiracialism, however, were greeted with derision by TANU campaigners, who were quick to point out that it was the European teachers, doctors, and others who had provided

5. Some of the material contained here appeared in a third-year honors paper in political science written by Anverali S. Dhalla, "Newala District – A Political History" (University College, Dar es Salaam, 1967, mimeo.). I acknowledge my debt to this young scholar.

6. See George Bennett, "An Outline History of TANU," *Makerere Journal*, no. 7 (1963), pp. 15–29.

Mponda with the experience he paraded as his major qualification for leadership.

Mponda also attempted to out-radical TANU on the matter of the timing of independence. Although he had previously agreed with the British government in rejecting a twenty-five-year United Nations timetable for Tanganyikan independence, Mponda now accepted the ANC line that colonial rule should come to an immediate end—regardless of the consequences. TANU leaders, seeing independence within their grasp, insisted that a prosperous future demanded that colonial rule be phased out in an orderly fashion. Indeed, it was even acknowledged that many of the enlightened colonial officers would be asked to stay on after independence to assist the new nation in its development planning.

The difference in ideological stance was not the only thing that made the electoral campaign in Newala an interesting one. It was significant for the organizational growth which TANU underwent within the district. Leopold Omari, the district secretary (and brother of two men who were to achieve notable reputations as leaders in Tanzania and East Africa), relied heavily on the TANU Youth League in getting eligible voters to register, to contribute to the campaign, and to vote.[7] With the tables now somewhat turned, TANU leaders felt no compunction about using the instrumentality of the Local Council in helping win the election for them. Over the strenuous objections of the territorial chairman of the ANC, Local Council employees campaigned in behalf of TANU, and the council's Land Rover and other equipment were used by Raphael Saidi, who did not distinguish between his roles as chairman of the Local Council and candidate for office. Saidi refused to resign from the post during the campaign, and the district commissioner ignored the charges of intimidation and fraud made by ANC against TANU.

The election results of August 30, 1960, demonstrated that the TANU could capture the sympathies of those who were entitled to vote under the restricted franchise prevailing in 1960. The TANU Youth League had very effectively identified Raphael Saidi with Julius Nyerere and the slogan *Uhuru na*

7. Dhalla, "Newala District," pp. 31–33.

*Kazi,* "Freedom and Work." Raphael Saidi amassed 4,846 votes, drawing upon a wide spectrum of central- and local-government clerks, teachers, domestic servants, mechanics, drivers, the more prosperous cultivators, and the unemployed school-leavers. He literally swamped Justino Mponda, who could rally only 209 teachers, medical aides, and other members of the semiprofessional class to his side. Indeed, under the rules of the election, Mponda's poor showing compelled him to surrender his Shs. 500 deposit, which had been posted as evidence of the seriousness of his candidacy.[8] What the election did not demonstrate, however (since there was no way of recording it), was the magnitude of TANU's popularity among the illiterate cultivators who made up the overwhelming majority of Newala's citizenry. The 5,265 voters in the 1960 election represented only 3 per cent of the total population of the district and certainly no more than 7 per cent of the estimated adult population of the district. TANU's influence with the Makonde masses would have to be measured by other means.

## THE "HOME STRETCH"

The election results in Newala followed a national trend. In the contests for the 71 seats in the new Legislative Council, TANU candidates won 58 without opposition from any quarter. In the remaining 13 contests TANU candidates were pitted against independents and two ANC candidates (including Mponda). TANU was victorious in all but one of these races, where an independent-TANU candidate won. TANU not only won; it received over 82 per cent of the territorial vote. ANC, the sole organized opposition party, captured only 0.3 per cent of the total vote.

If there had been any lingering doubts before the election regarding the ability of TANU to speak for the more articulate and less apathetic citizens of the Trust Territory, they were certainly dispelled. The British government did not even bother to make a point of the fact that the poor turnout (roughly 7

8. There were 210 spoiled ballots. The balloting represented 82 per cent of the 6,220 registered voters in the district.

per cent of the estimated eligible voters) indicated a general
political apathy on the part of even the literate and more af-
fluent Tanganyikans as well as organizational weakness on the
part of TANU. Rather, the British government seemed weary
of the struggle and, indeed, eager to liquidate as quickly as
possible its remaining political and administrative responsibilities in Tanganyika. Within two months the new Legislative
Council was convened and the territory was set on the path of
*madaraka,* or responsible government. Nyerere was named
chief minister, and he presided over a cabinet consisting of
Africans, Europeans, and Asians, including a number of civil
service ministers. Since there was an elected majority in the
council, Nyerere had complete maneuverability in setting domestic policy as well as in laying the groundwork for future
relations with foreign states.

Wishing to convince the British government (and indeed
the outside world) that TANU could govern responsibly,
Nyerere moved cautiously but deliberately toward his goal of
*Uhuru.* Complete internal self-government came in May, 1961,
following the recommendations of a constitutional conference.
On December 9 of that year the Union Jack was lowered in
Dar es Salaam, and seventy-six years of European colonial
rule in Tanganyika came to an end.

# 12:
# The New Political Order
# in Tanzania

A trend which had been emerging at the conclusion of my first period of field work in Umakonde (1955–56) had become a pronounced feature of Makonde politics by the end of the 1960s. This was the *expectation*, at least, that developments within the Makonde area—and indeed within every region of Tanzania (as Tanganyika had now come to be called)— were to be integrated into a national plan for political, economic, and social growth. In fact, the geographic isolation, the shortage of both human and material resources, and other factors tended to leave the Tanzanian official in Umakonde pretty much to his own devices, as had been the case with his British predecessor under the colonial regime. The difference today, however, is that administrative autonomy no longer enjoys legal, ideological, or even practical sanction, and one who radically deviates today from the directives of the central government cannot do so with impunity. Even if the local administrator cannot perform according to national expectations, he is to be constantly mindful of the overall scheme for national development and should be prepared for a more persistent intrusion of the external political and economic environment into the day-to-day lives of the Makonde people. For this reason an analysis of the political process at the micro level in Uma-konde in the late 1960s cannot proceed without some attention being given to those structural and procedural changes at the macro level which have set new limits for legitimate activity in the more parochial unit and provide a new set of imperatives which either stimulate or inhibit dynamic internal responses to local problems.

When I again picked up the thread of field research in 1967, much had changed within the country as a whole as well as within the region. Tanzania had enjoyed over five years of inde-pendence. The politics of the nation-in-being continued to be dominated by the dynamic personality of Julius Nyerere and his lieutenants in TANU who sought to weld the peoples of more than 120 ethnic groups into a common political com-munity. As the instrument of nation-building, TANU had been considerably rejuvenated since the days when its primary ob-jective was the termination of colonial rule. Indeed, a few months after the achievement of independence, Nyerere – in a dramatic and initially enigmatic act – resigned as prime min-ister in order to strengthen TANU at the grass-roots. The plans which he set in motion during those months "in the wilder-ness," as well as the subsequent reorganization of TANU into an ever extending network of cells, have made TANU one of the most effective and genuinely participatory political parties on the African continent.

Nyerere returned to power in December, 1962, on the first anniversary of independence. He did so on the strength of a referendum which had converted Tanganyika into a republic and an election which overwhelmingly endorsed Nyerere as the first president. Even with a revitalized TANU, however, the task of nation-building has not been an easy one. Nyerere has had to face challenges to his regime from a variety of quarters. One struggle had been joined long before independ-ence. This was the confrontation between TANU and a series of both traditional and modernized Africans who had attempted to emphasize the tribe – rather than the nation – as the legiti-mate vehicle for development. Two significant landmarks in TANU's ultimate triumph over the tribalists were the pre-independence ban on political parties based on tribes and the 1962 legislation which abolished the post of traditional chief and turned the power of the Native Authorities over to elected district councils. These two acts effectively terminated the threat of tribalism at the central government level, even though tribal parochialism continued to manifest itself in local affairs. In a number of areas the deposed chiefs continued to have influence in local political decision-making after 1962, and tribalism continues to present obstacles to large-scale development planning.[1]

In addition to the issue of the scale of the new society, Nyerere and TANU have also had to struggle for power against modern competitors who have sought to secure a privileged and sanctified role for special interest groups within the developing nation. In its advocacy of the general interest, TANU has successfully met the challenge of special privilege posed by its erstwhile allies in the anticolonial struggle—the trade-union leadership.[2] Similarly Nyerere has had to wrestle with the demands for economic autonomy made by the leaders of the cooperative societies who wanted a freer role in setting prices and other marketing conditions.[3] Still a third source of concern has been the student groups, whose causes for restiveness have run the gamut from demands for greater privileges for the educated elite to insistence that the pace of radical transformation of social and economic institutions be accelerated. By far the most crucial of the particularist threats was posed in January, 1964, when army troops in Tanganyika mutinied against their officers (most of whom were still European) and brought the TANU government to the verge of collapse.[4] With the assistance of British commandos the situation was quickly brought under control, and a program of reform was launched, creating a citizen-army under the control of the

1. See Norman N. Miller, "Village Leadership and Modernization in Tanzania: Rural Politics among the Nyamwezi People of Tabora Region" (Ph.D. diss., Indiana University, 1966).

2. See William H. Friedland, *Vuta Kamba: Trade Unions in Tanganyika* (Stanford: Stanford University Press, 1969).

3. See Tanzania, *Report of the Presidential Special Committee of Enquiry into the Cooperative Movement and Marketing Boards* (Dar es Salaam: Government Printer, 1966).

4. Henry Bienen, *Tanzania: Party Transformation and Economic Development* (Princeton: Princeton University Press, 1967), pp. 363–81.

TANU Youth League. Another direct result of the mutiny—which had been sparked by the Zanzibar revolution earlier in January—was the proclamation in April, 1964, of a political union between Tanganyika and Zanzibar. Thus Tanzania was born.

In the pursuit of nation-building, it has often been difficult to separate internal from external policies of the Tanzanian government. Certainly Nyerere's role within his own country has been strengthened as he has courageously pressed for such supranational objectives as the East African Common Market, to link still further the economies of Tanzania with Uganda, Kenya, and perhaps other East African states as well. Similarly, Nyerere has reconfirmed his legitimacy with TANU's more militant left as Dar es Salaam has become—as one pundit has expressed it—not only the "haven of peace" but the haven as well for FRELIMO (the Mozambique liberation movement) and refugee organizations from Zimbabwe, Malawi, South Africa, and Namibia. Equally significant have been Nyerere's efforts to strengthen the ties between his country and Zambia during the prolonged crisis with the Rhodesian whites—even at the expense of financial and other ties with Great Britain. In that crisis, Nyerere has insisted, as he has in his differences with the United States and West Germany, that the pursuit of an independent foreign policy takes priority over the need for external economic aid. Hence, he has been prepared to seek aid from Communist China and the West, from Israel and the Arab states, from both East and West Germany, and from other apparently mutually hostile sources. He has been prepared to pursue ideological objectives abroad, even if it means that the border areas of Tanzania itself are threatened—as indeed they have been along the Ruvuma River.

It is Nyerere and TANU's domestic policies, however, which will be more crucial in determining the ability of the regime to maintain the loyalties of the modernizing elite and the peasant masses. The problems of "status" and "stomach" have had to be attacked simultaneously; and often action on one problem has negated the advantages gained in pursuit of other goals. As an example, Africanization of the administration, the economy, the school system, and other sectors of society was pursued somewhat gingerly during the first two or three years

of independence for fear of losing the talents and capital of
Europeans and Asians – whether residents or expatriates. Once
it had become apparent, however, that the regime was suffering
a crisis of confidence because it had downgraded the question
of status, the Africanization of Tanzanian society proceeded
at a dizzying pace, endangering at times some vital long-range
development programs. This placed such a strain on the limited
pool of educated African talent that it was virtually impossible
to maintain programs at both the central and local levels of
government, with the latter invariably having to suffer. In any
event the young educated and semieducated who had chaffed
at being unemployed or denied higher status now became enthusiastic supporters of the regime.

Similarly, the Arusha Declaration of February, 1967, in
which Nyerere presented his and TANU's program for socialist
development, represents a careful balancing of objectives.
Feeding, clothing, and housing the people of Tanzania are
high-priority objectives of a government in a developing society. Nyerere, however, rejects the notion that to accomplish
these goals one must sacrifice freedom and self-respect. Thus,
Nyerere has insisted that his nation's sights must be set lower,
relying primarily on what can be produced out of its own resources and talents rather than mortgaging control over the
political and economic destinies of the new state in return for
"instant prosperity." It is for this reason that Nyerere has insisted that development for Tanzania means *rural* development, since that is where over 90 per cent of the people live.
And people – more than minerals and machines – he insists,
are the real source of a nation's wealth.

A parallel juxtaposing of objectives has come with respect
to the responsibilities that officials at the center are to share
with local government officers. Given the nature of the anti-
colonial struggle and the antipathy of tribal leadership, it is
understandable why TANU – like most other African governing
parties – has tended to favor the centralization of governmental authority. The anticolonial struggle had been concentrated on smashing the power of the British government at the
center, and the belated efforts in the postwar period to encourage popular participation in local government had been
regarded as a ruse to distract the modern elite from the more

significant arena of power. In practical terms, as well, the preference was for utilizing the limited pool of educated talent at the vital center for fear that spreading that talent over the entire country would deprive the nation of the wisdom and energy needed to mobilize its scarce resources. Moreover, the trend during several decades had been for the modernized elite to gravitate to the urban areas or to employment in the central administration, inasmuch as the rural area was dominated by the traditional forces and job opportunities there were limited indeed.

Despite the urban predilection of the elite and the lingering threat of tribal resistance in certain areas, TANU was convinced that nation-building and sustained economic development required genuine popular involvement of the rural masses. It thus became mandatory to strike a more equitable balance between the powers of the central and local governments.[5] The difficulties of accomplishing the latter have in most instances led to a certain ambivalence in the maturing of local government institutions. One difficulty, for example, has come with regard to the political role of local government administrators. The British had almost a fetish about the separation of the civil service from politics and took somewhat extreme steps to insulate the former from the latter. TANU, on the other hand, regarded this divorce as working to the disadvantage of the political forces seeking to shape a new society. Thus to ensure that the local government administration and local political leadership did not work at cross-purposes or lose sight of the national objectives, the machinery of local government had to undergo a drastic overhaul.

One of the first steps in the reform was launched by the Nyerere government in June, 1961 — six months before independence. This divested the liwalis and other nontraditional chiefs of all executive functions within their areas, although

5. See William Tordoff, "Regional Administration in Tanzania," *Journal of Modern African Studies,* III (May, 1965), 63–89; W. J. Warrell-Bowring, "The Reorganization of the Administration in Tanganyika," *Journal of Local Administration Overseas,* II (October, 1963), 188–94; Stanley Dryden, "Local Government Reform in Tanzania," *TNR,* no. 66 (December, 1966), pp. 147, 154; and William Tordoff, *Government and Politics in Tanzania* (Nairobi: East African Publishing House, 1967).

headmen or jumbes could remain as executives within their previous spheres of authority. This action was followed quickly by the assault (previously referred to) on the power of the traditional chiefs, which officially terminated their administrative authority and political status on December 31, 1962. In the meantime, Chief Abdullah Fundikira, who had become the minister of justice in the Nyerere and Kawawa governments, announced in July, 1962, that the judicial authority of the chiefs and liwalis was to be terminated, and they were to be replaced by independent magistrates appointed by the minister of justice. In the long run, although many difficulties lay ahead, the law administered by these professionally trained magistrates was to be unified without respect to differences in tribal custom.

The full penetration of TANU into the affairs of local government throughout the country came in a series of measures introduced between 1961 and 1965. Although some of the features of local government reform introduced under the British as well as the formal relationships between central government and field administration were retained, there were substantial changes made in the character of these institutions and how they related to the party. Thus, the changes in titles of provincial and district commissioners to regional and area commissioners were more than symbolic (although this was a significant factor in itself). Under the new system the area commissioners had considerably less authority than their British predecessors in making decisions which would be ratified by their superiors. Much of the effective planning of economic and social growth was to take place at the regional level, with the understanding that the district and village development committees would play an exceedingly active role in implementing the plans of the regional development committee. Moreover, to ensure the coordination of policy-making by the party and implementation by the bureaucracy, a new pattern of responsibility emerged which both politicized the bureaucratic pyramid and bureaucratized the party structure. This came through the assignment of multiple roles to persons at various levels of the system. Although this particular facet of the scheme was subsequently dropped, at one stage the secretary-general of TANU also served as minister for regional administration. The government has, however, continued the practice of having the regional and area commissioners double as TANU secretaries within their respective administrative units. To further link the regional commissioners directly with the political and governmental apparatus at the national level, they have been named ex-officio members of the National Assembly and are also required to participate in the deliberations of the TANU national conference.

At the district level, TANU has retained at least that aspect of the British reforms of 1953 which established multipurpose district councils. It rejected, of course, the idea of the multiracial Local Councils along the lines of those established in Newala and Mafia, and it has rescinded as well the steps taken to create supradistrict county councils. The district councils under TANU quickly became fully elected bodies. TANU, despite opposition in some areas of the country, has exercised control over the councils by requiring that only TANU members who have received the approval of the TANU district executive committees may stand for election. To ensure coordination between government and party, the TANU district chairman normally serves as ex-officio chairman of the district council. Again, for the purpose of coordination and to emphasize the importance attached to rural development, the TANU district secretary (who is also the area commissioner) serves as the chairman of the District Development Committee.

The area commissioner under the new system has assumed many—but certainly not all—of the responsibilities of the British district commissioners in maintaining law and order, promoting development planning, and coordinating the activities of the central government technical officers operating in his district. His primary staff assistant, the area secretary, tends to be a civil servant rather than a party official. He normally has longer tenure in the area and hence acquires greater knowledge of the legal, administrative, and practical limits of authority.

The district councils under the TANU regime have less financial autonomy than they had in the past and certainly less control over the appointment and dismissal of staff, now that the latter function has been largely assumed by the Local Government Services Commission in Dar es Salaam. District councils feel the pull equally from the area commissioner and the regional commissioner (whose predecessor under the colonial system was somewhat remote). The officers of the central government ministries, moreover, tend to regard themselves as much more subject to direction from Dar es Salaam than from the district headquarters, thereby reversing the pattern existing under the colonial regime. Each of these situations does lead to conflicts among officials at every level in the system.

The districts, as in the past, continue to be broken into smaller units, called divisions, under the administration of divisional executive officers (formerly the liwalis). The latter are employees of the district council, but to ensure coordination with TANU they work closely with the TANU divisional chairmen. The village executives (the former jumbes) in turn relate to the divisional executive officers administratively and to the TANU branch chairman for political purposes. The latter serves as the chairman of the village development committees.

The bottom layer of the party structure is the one upon which Julius Nyerere relies to keep TANU a vital institution of change. The scheme for the establishment of a cell system for the party structure came shortly after independence. Each cell consists of ten houses, under the leadership of a popularly elected leader, or *balozi*. The cell system was viewed as the most effective way for keeping the top and the bottom of the party pyramid informed regarding the substance of government policies, on the one hand, and the reaction of the people to these policies, on the other. All the balozi within a ward (the next highest political unit) are members of the village development committees of that area.

As the subsequent discussion will indicate, control of the new political and administrative apparatus by the TANU leadership has not automatically ensured the commitment of the Tanzanian masses to the new system of government, nor has it instantly projected Tanzanians at the grass-roots along the path to modernity in the spirit of self-reliance. Indeed, my revisit to Umakonde in 1967 provided ample evidence that the patterns of resistance which the Makonde had developed in response to the capricious manipulation of Makonde society during the colonial period had not disappeared simply because Africans were now in control of Tanzania. More disquieting perhaps was the reaction of Tanzanian officials to this resistance.

# 13:
# Post-Independence
## Social Change
## in Umakonde

When I returned to the Makonde region in 1967, it was apparent that much had been altered in the eleven years since I had last visited Mtwara, Newala, and Lindi districts. The most striking change, perhaps, was a human one. It was readily evident that the people in charge were Africans. The displacement of Europeans from positions of governmental authority was virtually complete, although a number of British, Scandinavian, Canadian, and American technicians had been employed to advise on medical, construction, financial, transportation, and other matters. What was surprising, however, was the systematic reduction of Europeans in the private sector as well. Early in 1967 the trade-union organization (NUTA) had taken over the last European-owned hotel in the Mtwara Region, following the deportation of the manager for discriminatory remarks. European businessmen in Mtwara and Lindi were few in number, although Lindi during the last two decades of British rule had been regarded as a lively recreation town by the Europeans who came in from the port and from the sisal estates on weekends. Even the Christian missions were rapidly being Africanized. Both the Catholic Order of Saint Benedict and the former UMCA (now styled the Church Province of

East Africa) in Newala were phasing out the activities of European priests and nuns and replacing them with Africans.

Although the visibility of Europeans was extremely low, the
same was not true for the Asians. Indeed, they were more
numerous in 1967 than they had been a decade earlier, when
many had expressed to me fears that their days in the area were
numbered. The operations of the cooperative societies (discussed below) and the Tanganyika Transport Company were
gradually removing Asians from the more lucrative economic
activities, and they were finding it difficult to diversify their
interests to keep pace with the Africanization of the economy.
Only the members of the Aga Khan Community appeared to
be optimistic about their prospects for continued residence.
Although their proselytizing efforts had not borne fruit, they
had nevertheless persevered in such projects as building
schools and clinics, which would be of use to the entire Tanzanian community.

The spirit of change was also very noticeable in the physical
environment. Feverish activity at the Mtwara airport was being
devoted to the expansion of the airstrip to handle jet cargo from
Central Africa and Europe, while harbor facilities at the port
were being enlarged to accommodate double berthing. In
Mtwara town, what had previously been a scattering of Asian
shops throughout an abandoned sisal field was now a fairly
impressive commercial block, with two-story buildings and
crowded walks and streets. Parks and a sports field were under
construction, and new schools, churches, and bars were beginning to fulfill the dreams of the English city-planner who laid
out Mtwara town two decades previously. The Israelis were
planning a new luxury hotel to attract tourists for the long-
delayed development of a deep-sea fishing industry. There
were several new cottage industries started in the town for the
manufacture of shirts, sandals, and coir fibre. There was even
discussion—also reminiscent of 1955—of a cannery and a
cashew-processing plant being established in the dock area.
The prosperity of the townspeople was apparent, as the fish
and vegetable markets were doing a brisk trade. Housing was
vastly improved over the shanty towns which had been spring-
ing up in 1955, and during 1966 alone the National Housing
Board had constructed sixty low-cost rental houses, with plans

for twice that many in 1967. Indeed, there was a wonderful feeling on the part of the African officials and merchants that "things were happening." Indeed the dynamism must have come close to approximating the spirit which had moved the employees of the Overseas Food Corporation in the early days of the Groundnut Scheme.

Inland, the impression of economic transformation was sustained. The number of African-driven trucks and taxis had risen dramatically, and even the people riding bicycles or merely walking along the roads displayed new cotton gowns (*kangas* or *shukas*) and many more were wearing shoes. Nanyamba, Kitama, Tandahimba, Nanhyanga, and Mahuta—which were only a series of small market centers along the main road in 1955—now qualified as towns, each with a significant cluster of shops, schools, clinics, government offices, and a church or mosque. The ubiquitous symbol of African prosperity—corrugated iron roofing—covered many of the new houses as well as other buildings. Sewing machines, grinding mills, and other wealth-producing instruments were very much in evidence. Some of the towns even had a cow or two, in spite of the scarcity of water, the presence of tsetse fly, and the high price of cattle.

Between the towns the cashew groves—planted initially during the colonial period as part of a soil conservation program on the plateau—were more numerous than in the past, marking a new kind of prestige symbol among the Makonde cultivators. Not only had the Makonde region within the past decade become the largest producer of cashews (46,000 tons in 1966), but cashews had become the fourth major export crop (after cotton, sisal, and coffee) of Tanzania.[1] The production of other export crops, such as cassava, rice, simsim, and castor beans, was also increasing. During 1966, close to 20,000 tons of cassava were produced in the Mtwara region (most of it in Newala, Mtwara, and Lindi districts), plus 7,000 tons of grains and other marketable crops. More than two-thirds of the £2,469,000 paid out by the Mtwara Region Co-operative Union Ltd. went to Makonde peasants. Furthermore, the surpluses in cassava and other

1. S. Jensen, *Regional Economic Atlas of Mainland Tanzania*, Bureau of Resource Assessment and Land Use Planning, Research Paper no. 1 (University College, Dar es Salaam, June, 1968), pp. 9–11.

crops were responsible for averting a major famine in neighboring Kilwa District during 1966 and 1967—a catastrophe
which led to the dismissal of the regional commissioner and
other officials who had failed to anticipate the crisis. Perhaps
the most promising feature of all, however, was the relative
absence of Makonde women carrying the large water-pots upon
their heads. The Makonde water scheme by 1967 had covered
over three-fourths of the plateau with water kiosks, and, since
TANU had delivered on its pre-independence promise to make
water available without charge, the use of water was increasing for a wide range of agricultural and domestic purposes.
There was even talk in 1967 of establishing fish ponds on the
plateau as a way of meeting the protein deficiency that plagued
most Makonde.

## Out of the Mainstream

Despite the many visible changes and the optimism of
officials with regard to development, it was apparent that the
Makonde area was still in the curious position that it had occupied during the long years of colonial rule: it was isolated from
the mainstream of territorial development and yet very much
subject to the whims of external events and interests.

Despite, for example, vast improvements in the Great North
Road and other arterial highways in Tanzania, the coastal road
linking Dar es Salaam with the Makonde districts still remains
closed during six months of every year. Moreover, the long
stretches of sandy road, as well as the ferry at the Rufiji River,
make the journey time-consuming even during the dry season.
The major east-west road, connecting the ports of Mtwara and
Lindi with Songea (and ultimately with Zambia), has been
improved, but—like the slave caravans in the nineteenth
century—it largely avoids the Makonde heartland by skirting
the northern perimeter of the Newala Plateau. The Mtwara–
Newala–Masasi road, which traverses the center of Makonde
settlement, has been given a lower priority in terms of maintenance and the routing of important motor-freight traffic.

The isolation of the Makonde districts from the country as a
whole is repeated at the micro level, with villages being in

many cases still inaccessible from the district headquarters. In Mtwara District only the two main roads are usable the year round, and Tanzanian officials complained of the costs and time involved in keeping the feeder roads cleared of the bamboo, wild rubber, and vine-covered thickets which constantly intrude upon any cleared area. They lamented, too, in 1967 that during the rainy season long detours were often necessary to reach remote areas cut off by floods and road washouts. This was further complicated by the severe shortage of petrol in the area due to the higher priority given to operations relating to the Zambian and Mozambique crises. As a consequence the petrol allowances of local officials were usually exhausted by the middle of each month, and touring came to a halt. The situation in Newala District was only a little better.

It was apparent, moreover, that much of the heightened activity in the Mtwara Region came not in response to the needs of the Makonde for development but rather in response to conditions elsewhere. The expansion of harbor facilities at Mtwara as well as the extension of the airfield might in the long run prove to be of great economic benefit to the area; they were undertaken, however, because of a crisis which had no direct relevance to the poverty and underdevelopment of the Makonde area: namely, the situation in Central Africa. The Unilateral Declaration of Independence (UDI) by the government of Ian Smith in Rhodesia had managed to draw the African leaders of Zambia and Tanzania closer together than they had ever been as members of a common British imperial system. The success of the oil and copper airlift which has been keeping the economy of Zambia functioning since 1965 gave new importance to the roads of southern Tanzania and to the port of Mtwara in particular. Whether or not the port and airfield were to continue to expand and become permanent features of the Zambian-Tanzanian trade, however, was a political rather than an economic question. A *rapprochement* between the Zambian and Rhodesian governments is not entirely out of the question, and this would immediately reduce or eliminate the importance of Mtwara as an outlet to the sea. Even if this were not to develop, it was obvious that the Tanzanian leadership preferred having the oil pipeline, the major road development, and the Tanzania-Zambia railroad terminate at Dar es Salaam rather than at any point to the south. Any other solution would deemphasize the crucial role of Dar es Salaam in the new political arrangements for East Africa as a whole, and it might raise the specter of "Katanga-ism" in any region which reaped undue benefits from the new Tanzanian-Zambian trade.

Similarly, the crisis in Mozambique, where FRELIMO (Frente de Liberação de Moçambique) was battling the Portuguese forces, had given the Makonde area a strategic importance which it would not otherwise have had. There was not only the disruption caused by the steady stream of Maconde refugees (numbering over 10,000 in 1966), who needed to be housed and fed in special camps, but Tanzanian troops had moved into the Makonde area, and the usual social problems arose. Starting in 1966, the conflict had actually spread to the Tanzanian side of the Ruvuma, and Portuguese commandos were accused of laying land mines and terrorizing Makonde villages in Tanzania.[2] The Makonde were prohibited from fishing in the river, and rice-cultivation schemes were seriously impeded. Many Makonde who had been persuaded during the past two decades to reside near the river's edge had to be evacuated to higher and safer ground. At one point in 1967 the situation became so serious that military reservists in the Mtwara Region were ordered to report to their area commissioners. Lawi Sijaona, who had become minister for home affairs, was dispatched by Nyerere to carry out an on-the-spot inspection of the situation. The prospect that the Makonde area would become a combat zone was heightened in May, 1967, when Second Vice President Rashidi Kawawa pledged that Tanzanian forces would be mobilized and sent into Mozambique should the FRELIMO liberation forces encounter extreme difficulties in their struggle to rid themselves of "the iron heel of imperialism."[3] Although an ultimate accommodation between Nyerere and the Portuguese seemed totally unrealistic—especially in view of the murder in 1969 of Dr. Eduardo Mondlane, FRELIMO's leader—it was possible that

2. United Nations High Commissioner for Refugees, "Refugees in Africa," *UNHCR Reports* (Switzerland: HCR Information Services, December, 1966), pp. 42–44.

3. *The Nationalist* (Dar es Salaam), May 26, 1967, p. 1.

the exasperation of Nyerere with FRELIMO's constant factionalism could lead to a reduction in overt support. In any
case, the crisis which had led to a further upheaval in the life
of the Makonde of Tanzania would either be intensified or resolved by actors and factors far removed from the Makonde
scene.

## THE "NEW ALIENS"

Although it was patently clear that the Makonde area
in 1967 was being governed by Tanzanians, it was not always
apparent that the alleged homogeneity of Tanzanian society
was appreciated either by the Makonde or by those governing
them. This is not to imply that the level of parochial nationalism
among the Makonde could be equated with that of the Chagga
or Haya areas, where the persistence of tribalism and the antagonism shown toward the central government and TANU has
been acute. It was, however, relatively easy to detect the kind
of negative attitude on the part of Makonde peasants toward
the new breed of African administrators that had previously
been evidenced toward British, German, and Arab officials.
Reciprocally, the attitudes of many non-Makonde Tanzanians
toward the people of the Ruvuma area resembled at times the
attitudes of colonial settlers and administrators.

This situation was perhaps unavoidable. The Makonde during
the many decades of colonial rule had remained relatively isolated from the mainstream of the developing Tanganyikan
society. The assault on ethnicity and traditional values associated with tribal particularism had been less severe in the
southeast than in perhaps any other region of the country. It
was, moreover, the commitment of Nyerere to eliminate as
rapidly as possible the major differences separating the 120 or
more tribal groups making up the new Tanzania. It was thus
consistent with his policy of nation-building that non-Makonde
should be posted to serve as officials in Newala, Mtwara, and
Lindi districts, even if the pool of local talent had been sufficiently large — which it certainly was not. Obviously the nation-
building process is accelerated if people of diverse backgrounds
readily come to accept advice from one another and to establish

economic, social, and political ties without taking ethnic differences into account. Moreover, given the uneven pace of
development under German and British rule—coupled with the
egalitarian posture of Julius Nyerere and TANU—it follows
that the leadership of Tanzania would require the more modernized Chagga, Nyakyusa, and Ngoni to share their abilities
to teach, organize cooperatives, and manage large-scale development schemes with people from neglected areas, such as
Umakonde. Nyerere's policy with respect to the posting of
civil servants on a national basis is consistent with his antipathy toward the establishment of tribal branches of TANU,
his policy on Swahili as a national language, and even his initial reluctance to have census-takers inquire about the tribal
origins of Tanzanians for the 1967 census.

I do not wish to suggest that Makonde have little to say in
their own development. Indeed, there was a *tendency* in the
Makonde districts to follow a pattern, common to other parts
of Tanzania, of permitting local tribesmen to dominate the
more manifestly political posts, such as member of parliament,
divisional executive officer, and many of the important offices
in TANU at the district and subdistrict levels. The Newala
Makonde were obviously better prepared to defend their ethnicity on this point than were the traditionally lethargic coastal
Makonde. The two M.P.s from Newala, for example, were Makonde, whereas the M.P.s from Mtwara and Lindi East were
not even long-term residents of their districts, let alone being
Makonde. At the divisional executive level, moreover, all five
of the successors to the liwalis in Newala were Makonde,
whereas in Mtwara four of the six divisional executive officers
in 1967 had been recruited from outside the district.[4]

The overall management of the political development of the
region as well as the supervision of economic and social services provided by both central government and district council,
however, found non-Makonde in charge. The area commissioner of Newala (who doubled as district secretary of TANU)

4. In Newala, one of the divisional executives (Albert Mchauru) had served
as a liwali under the colonial regime, and a second (B. S. Mnelemwana) came
from a family long respected in Newala for its work with the UMCA mission.
The divisional executives in both districts had a minimum of Standard VIII
education, and they averaged about 35 years of age.

was a native of Kilwa; the executive officers of both the Newala
and Mtwara district councils were Nyaturu from Singida District; the junior agricultural officer in Newala and the staff of
the cooperative union in Mtwara were Ngoni from Songea
District; the resident magistrate in Newala was a Sukuma
from Mwanza; the Mtwara town treasurer and the regional and
district educational officers were Chagga from Kilimanjaro
District; and the senior agricultural officer in Newala was a
Makua from neighboring Masasi District. This list is hardly
exhaustive.

The preponderance of alien administrators and their attitudes toward the Makonde were certainly factors in the kind of
response Makonde made to the new political and economic
order. I would hardly generalize from a single statement, but
I did in 1967 actually hear a Tanzanian official refer to "these
bloody Makonde"—in a manner quite reminiscent of the departed colonial administrator. Though less blatant, other
officers managed to express their exasperation with the slow
pace of Makonde development in more subtle ways. In Mtwara
town, for example, one official kept pointing out the differences
between the Chunu quarter, where many of the older Makonde
settlers lived, and Majengo quarter, which was populated
largely by Mwera, Ngoni, Yao, and others. It was the residents
of the latter, he noted, who insisted upon better schools for
their children and who filled all the new jobs at the port, the
airstrip, and the government headquarters. "The Makonde,"
he explained, "only know how to fish and farm." The frustration of agricultural officers, cooperative officials, and others
will be analyzed later in this chapter. One interesting commentary on the general disdain in which southeastern tribes are
held by other Tanzanians appeared in a letter to the editor of
the *Tanzania Standard*.[5] Having in mind the famine which
had recently afflicted parts of the Mtwara Region, a resident of
Tanga had a ready-made solution for the economic growth of
the area:

> As every production, including agricultural, follows the
> principle of supply and demand, the people of Mtwara were
> happy to grow only for themselves in the past. The lack of

5. (Dar es Salaam), July 13, 1967, p. 7.

incentive was due to bad and long communication between Mtwara and Dar es Salaam.

This area needs an injection of fresh blood. About 25 youths from each of the overcrowded areas of Usambara, Kilimanjaro, and Sukumaland should be sent there to take up vegetable farming, fruit farming, and cattle raising respectively.

. . . Settlement for these enterprising youths should be found at some distance from the coast where the land is higher up and full of water. This arrangement should be carried out by TANU with the assistance of the Mtwara M.P.s, who are well placed in the government.

"Operation Chakula" [Operation Food] — an appropriate name — should be carried out without any trumpets or fanfares. Shelter, tools, seed and subsistence allowance until crop production should be given to these settlers.

If the scheme in its humble stage works, then the number of these settlers should be increased. This process should gain momentum with the commensurate efforts of our coming closer with Zambia by the way of communications.

Who knows that one day, pioneers of this suggested scheme with their traditional initiative will be forerunners of the suppliers of essential commodities to Zambia and at the same time will establish a tradition, that every part should grow enough to meet its requirements!

There was also the frustrated magistrate in one district who felt that "the Makonde are reluctant to tell the truth in court. This applies equally to witnesses and to the police. They say in private that 'we must live with these people as neighbors, and thus we can't say everything that actually happened.' " Although knowing very little about the customary law of the Makonde (he was not even aware of some of the problems arising from matrilineal inheritance of property, for he came from an area in which the people follow patrilineal norms), the magistrate insisted that the Makonde do understand existing laws. "It's merely a case of not obeying them," he said, "or of misinterpreting one man's rights against another's." "Sometimes it is the officials themselves who do not understand the law. I had a village executive in court recently who had shaved a man's head because he had not paid his taxes." Under traditional practices, this was certainly a light enough penalty. In fairness to the judicial system through which

Nyerere hopes to bring the 120 disparate ethnic groups to-gether, it should be emphasized that the magistrate, who is not a native of the district, does work closely with the primary court officials, who are. The latter were selected on the basis of their knowledge of traditional law. Thus, a unified body of law is developing for Tanzania without ignoring entirely pa-rochial variations of rights and duties. It is the less mobile societies, which have not been affected by the great upheavals of the past two or three decades in Tanzania, that will suffer the most in this transition.

Experimentation by outsiders, who had only a casual knowl-edge of the human and physical environment, was an affliction suffered by the Makonde under colonial rule. There were a number of incidents I encountered in 1967 that convinced me that the "white man's madness" discussed in Chapter 6 is in fact color-blind. One case in particular might be singled out because the capital outlay was greater than it would have been for a new seed program or the many poultry schemes which failed in the 1950s. This was a project initiated by a Tan-zanian official who came from a cattle area in the north and who had lamented to me regarding the "backwardness" of the Ma-konde in not keeping cows. His plan, which had already been launched by the time of my arrival, was to bring 500 head of cattle into the Mtwara Region and sell them to Makonde peas-ants. In abstract terms, it is true that the Makonde do suffer a protein deficiency and that by-products from cattle produc-tion (manure for crops and leather for a shoe industry) could improve the economy. Cattle raising, however, is not an art that one acquires merely by having cows. Cattle require specific kinds of grasses and minerals in the soil. Inexpensive water is still a problem in certain parts of the Makonde plateau. No plans were under way for the establishment of veterinary serv-ices, and no thought was given to the presence of tsetse flies and other pests. Finally, the problem of social conflict that would arise if the cattle were not fenced in had not even been considered. Although, three years later, I have no word on the outcome of the experiment, it is probably safe to say that the official who broached the idea has been rotated to another dis-trict where he will not be able to see either the fruit or the failure of his innovation.

## Persuasion versus Coercion

One of the key weapons in TANU's campaign against the British in the 1950s was its opposition to the coercive character of colonial rule. TANU leadership rejected the notion that people had to be forced, under threat of fine or imprisonment, to pursue their own self-interests. The party acquired a considerable mass following largely on the basis of its opposition to such programs as the cattle-destocking campaign in Sukumaland, the compulsory planting ordinances in various districts, and the whole series of punitive rules and orders enacted under the Native Authorities Ordinance.[6] Nyerere and others insisted that once TANU came to power it would reconstitute the relationship of government to the people, emphasizing persuasion rather than coercion, encouraging community self-help projects rather than having all creative energy emanate from government, and instilling the notion of individual and collective self-reliance rather than having a distant and impersonal government serve as the constant conscience and guide to human development.

In the Makonde districts, TANU moved to implement its pledge even prior to independence. The pressure of the TANU Youth League had compelled the European government in 1960 to cease enforcement of compulsory agricultural and other natural-resource orders and to soft-pedal the punitive aspects of rules and orders dealing with sanitation, compulsory school attendance, and European-imposed standards of morality. When TANU assumed the reins of government, moreover, it moved quickly to expand the educational services of both the central and local governments in dealing with the problems of illiteracy, disease, and poverty. Thus, Newala District, which had its first agricultural officer posted to the area in 1952, had two officers in 1967. Officials for cooperative society development, which the colonial government had steadfastly failed to provide for the Makonde region, were numerous in each of the Mtwara Region districts in 1967. Moreover, rather than relying

6. See Lionel Cliffe, "Nationalism and the Reaction to Enforced Agricultural Change in Tanganyika during the Colonial Period," East African Institute of Social Research, Conference Papers (Makerere-University, December, 1964).

on the multiple talents of an overburdened district commissioner to carry the message of sanitation and proper care of the ill, each district now had its own health officer, who organized outpatient clinics, recruited midwives and assisted in their training, and attempted to avert smallpox and other kinds of epidemics. The positive character of government was also evidenced by the proliferation of marketing stalls in even the small villages, with supervisory staff being trained by the central government and employed by the district councils.

Despite the discernible posture tending toward persuasion rather than coercion, however, it was apparent in a number of respects that resort to the latter was once again manifesting itself. As suggested previously, resistance to new ideas may have stemmed from the fact that the advice came from non-Makonde. The legal and political integration of the Makonde into a new society under African control has not eroded the traditional Makonde distrust of strangers. During the colonial period, moreover, the Makonde had learned to react to innovative programs by going through the motions of acceptance, knowing that in due time the perpetrator of the newest "nuisance" would be posted to another district and old practices could be resumed. For the first time in their history, the Makonde were encountering outside innovators who persisted in their efforts to change both the Makonde social order and their technology. Almost inevitably, this persistence would produce a mixed record of persuasion and coercion, as the following will indicate.

## Agriculture

The greatest strides in modernization were being made in the agricultural sector, as the previous comments regarding cashew nut production indicated. The two agricultural officers in Newala District, with the help of nineteen assistants (each a local person who had received a formal course of training), fanned out across the district in an effort to improve the Makonde economy. Working through the village development committees, the agricultural staff was encountering a measure of success in introducing soy beans and other new cash crops, in expanding the use of fertilizers and chemical insect sprays, and in encouraging the thinning of cashew groves in order to allow for proper maturing of the trees. The staff spent a great deal of time working with the teachers and students at the primary and middle schools, each of which had their own fields.

Rather than providing radical solutions to agricultural problems, the Tanzanian officers in Newala had apparently profited from the mistakes of the British before them. New cultivation techniques were to supplement, rather than replace, the traditional stump farming and the bush-fallow system of soil rejuvenation. Unlike the cattle scheme introduced in Mtwara District, the officers in Newala were attempting to limit the impact of innovation in order not to raise false hopes. Thus, a poultry scheme was succeeding because the recipients of the hybrid hens were carefully selected and the project was designed to increase local consumption of meat and eggs rather than to launch a major export industry for the district.

Despite the great strides that had been made through persuasion, I detected the same sense of frustration on the part of Tanzanian officials that I had previously encountered a decade or more previously among the British officers. The agricultural staff was particularly disappointed over the failure of educated Makonde to return to farming, leaving only the illiterate peasant or the school-leaver to tend the major economic enterprise of the region. The relative absence of the modernized farmer was patently evident in a survey conducted by a Danish economist in Newala, Lindi, and Masasi districts during 1968. Of the 45 farmers interviewed, 42 indicated that they had not taken the trouble to avail themselves of the services of the agricultural extension division. Of the three who had, moreover, one indicated that he was unwilling to take the advice given.[7] There was also considerable resistance on the part of Makonde cultivators to mechanical cultivation. After almost a decade of spoon-feeding, the Chiumo rice scheme in the Ruvuma Valley had

7. Poul Westergaard, "Farm Surveys of Cashew Producers in Mtwara Region: Preliminary Results," Economic Research Bureau Paper 68.3 (University College, Dar es Salaam, January, 1968), p. 8.

placed only 5,000 acres under cultivation and was limited to a single crop. Despite inducements, such as charging only half a shilling an acre for mechanical ploughing, Makonde farmers still preferred to use the customary hoes and digging sticks on the plateau.

In many respects the failure to attract young educated Makonde into careers of farming can be laid at the doorstep of the overzealous TANU organizers of the 1950s who took such a vigorous stand against the agricultural bias of the middle-school curriculum. By 1967, TANU had found itself embracing the same policy it once attacked. Nyerere, in a new statement on educational policy, insisted that the school curriculum had to be revised to take into account the agricultural base of Tanzania's economy. School farm-plots were to become the order of the day, and the revised curriculum was to be heavily oriented to agricultural instruction as well as to training in crafts. A number of schools I visited in Mtwara and Newala in mid-1967 had embarked upon very ambitious gardening schemes, and a few had even engaged in auxiliary enterprises, such as fish ponds and the raising of short-haired sheep and a new breed of goat. The manual-training program not only glorified hard work (in contrast to the more rarefied atmosphere of the colonial-period schools) and encouraged students to take greater interest in agriculture, but the proceeds from the sale of crops provided additional revenues for the purchase of school equipment. The educational system was at last addressing itself to the restructuring of values beyond the slogan-mongering about "colonial mentality." Yet the innovation was resented not only by the parents of students, who saw their children's horizons limited to a rural environment, but also by the teachers, who were not equipped either by training or by self-perception for the new agricultural bias in the curriculum.

Perhaps the most disappointing retrogression, however, came with respect to compulsory agricultural rules and orders. Having rejected the idea of compulsion during the colonial period, agricultural officers in Newala in 1967 were talking seriously of reintroducing punitive soil-conservation methods. Once the enforcement of the Native Authority ordinances ceased, the Makonde farmers began once more to cultivate on slopes, and in many areas the erosion had reached alarming proportions. In neighboring Mtwara District, the matter of compulsory planting rules had already come full circle. During the disastrous coastal famine of 1966 the government felt that it had no alternative but to reintroduce the bye-laws which required every farmer to plant an acre of cash crops and an additional acre of food crops for his family.

## Health

A similar ambivalence between persuasion and coercion developed in the fields of health and sanitation. The health inspectors in Newala and Mtwara in 1967 were among the most energetic of the young officials interviewed. In Newala alone, over 9,870 persons had been vaccinated against smallpox in 1966, when an epidemic broke out among the Maconde and other refugees from Mozambique. The health inspectors were similarly aggressive in seeking the support of the balozi, or cell leaders, in carrying out various phases of the sanitation and health programs. The balozi were charged with the primary responsibility of getting latrines built, keeping their village compounds clean, reporting strange illnesses, and getting the members of their cells to use the services of the clinics. The health inspectors reinforced the action of the balozi with an educational campaign. One of the most effective tactics was the organization of health clubs among the young people, where the inspectors would give slide lectures on venereal disease, mosquito control, and the eradication of rats and other vermin.

Although one finds it difficult to be sympathetic on this point, it is apparent, nevertheless, that coercion is employed in getting the people to accept Western medicine. The balozi, for example, have been very hard pressed by the health inspectors to drive out the traditional medicine men and witch-finders. People who resort to the traditional medical arts instead of going to the modern clinics are severely fined. The witch doctors (as opposed to witch-finders) in 1967 were all in hiding, and they could practice their art with only the greatest difficulty. Another area of coercion came in the treatment of victims of leprosy, which under the colonial regime had been left largely to voluntary treatment. Under new bye-laws introduced in Mtwara in

1967, all persons with leprosy were required to register and submit themselves to treatment. Those who attempted to flee to the countryside were pursued and either hospitalized or required to attend the outpatient clinics.

## Residence and Population Movement

A further area in which coercion had reemerged was in the matter of residence and population movement. The British, it will be recalled, constantly sought to encourage the settlement of Makonde in compact villages for the purposes of providing governmental services in a more efficient and less expensive fashion. The TANU government continued the practice of concentrating schools, markets, water kiosks, clinics, shops, and government headquarters in what would eventually become minor settlements or towns. The fruits of that policy were evident on the road from Mtwara to Newala, where the small market centers of 1956 had been converted into urban clusters of considerable size by 1967.

It was readily admitted by the Tanzanian officers in 1967, however, that the urbanization of the Makonde had not been entirely voluntary. TANU had early decided that for tax and other purposes it was no longer deemed satisfactory for government and party officials to have to search the thicket for those citizens who had obligations to society or required government services. It was the organization of Makonde society into the ten-house cell system which ultimately broke the back of the dispersed settlement pattern of the Makonde. A potential balozi who needed constituents would go out and find them, with the full blessing of TANU and government. Now, neatly laid out clusters of houses appear along the main roads, marking future minor settlements. The house of the balozi—indicated by a green flag with a black diagonal—is frequently the site for adult literacy classes, vaccinations, and distribution of new seeds. Each ten-house unit assumes responsibility for keeping its area neatly cleaned and the village roads and paths in good repair. In Mtwara District each adult is required to give two days a month to road construction or other public services in his village.

The Makonde who did not have to be coerced into an urban way of life nevertheless encountered a measure of coercion when they took up residence in some of the established towns. Zoning regulations had finally caught up with the towns of Newala and Mtwara, and, in the latter town in particular, the government spent almost as much time tearing down the huts of squatters, who had come in and set up shanty villages, as they did in building low-cost housing. Moreover, what had been implicit in the move of the district headquarters to Mtwara in 1953 was realized in 1966 when the government decided that Mikindani township should cease to exist. Although it had been incorporated into the town of Mtwara seven miles away, there was to be a gradual curtailment of government services to the area in order to compel people to move to Mtwara. It was obvious during my visit to Mikindani in 1967 that the fishermen and shopkeepers of this historic town preferred to remain and could only be removed by force.

## Education

In the field of education, the Tanzanian government found itself pursuing diametrically opposite policies in Mtwara and Newala districts. Yet each, in its way, was inherently coercive. In Mtwara District, which had long lagged behind the rest of the country in terms of educational facilities, Muslim resistance to modern education persisted. Lethargy, objection to female emancipation, and religion were factors in this resistance. Although the Muslim parents could no longer complain of discrimination at the hands of mission teachers (since the schools were largely government-run), they nevertheless persisted in their pre-independence campaign to have Koranic teachers subsidized by the government. This the district council steadfastly refused to do. Despite an extensive building program and heroic efforts to staff the new schools, only 50 per cent of the places in primary schools in Mtwara were taken in 1966. To counter the parental resistance, the minister of education, S. N. Eliufoo, in 1966 took the drastic step of declaring Mtwara a compulsory-school-attendance district, with the provision that parents could be given stiff fines for failing to enroll and keep their children in school. The area commissioner and other local government officials in 1967 still regarded this to be their top-priority problem as they toured the district. Constant harassment, moreover, was finally yielding significant results with respect to female education. Despite the almost violent Muslim animosity of the past, the proportion of girls to boys in Mtwara schools had, by 1966, increased far more than it had in Newala, Lindi, and even neighboring Masasi District, which had a longer and more intensive experience with mission education. (See Table 4.)

In Newala District, coercion took another form. Here the TANU government was attempting to slow down somewhat the rate of growth of the educational system. In carrying out its overall territorial program in education, the government was concerned with achieving a more egalitarian stance, seeing that the limited number of teachers and funds for school construction was channeled to those areas – such as Mtwara – which lagged behind the rest of the country. The government was also concerned about having a more rational educational pyramid instead of funneling all its resources into a grossly expanded primary-school base when it was readily apparent that the middle- and secondary-school levels could not absorb the new inflow. To permit unbridled development of primary

TABLE 4:
SCHOOL ENROLLMENT IN MTWARA REGION, 1966

| District[a] | Standards I–IV | | Standards V–VIII | | | Number of Schools in District |
|---|---|---|---|---|---|---|
| | Boys | Girls | Boys | Girls | Total | |
| Newala (176,915) | 6,513 | 3,825 | 1,389 | 212 | 11,939 | 74 |
| Mtwara (94,715) | | | | | | |
| rural | 2,413 | 1,188 | 946 | 730 | 5,277 | 35 |
| town | 512 | 404 | 319 | 186 | 1,421 | |
| Lindi (160,000) | | | | | | |
| rural | 5,747 | 3,677 | 1,246 | 255 | 10,925 | 71 |
| town | 445 | 415 | 362 | 211 | 1,433 | |
| Masasi (150,339) | 8,175 | 7,360 | 1,308 | 414 | 17,257 | 122 |

[a](Population figures, 1957 census)

schools would merely aggravate the problem of school-leavers, and the political consequences of that situation would be too great to ignore. The government also wanted to achieve a broader balance in expenditures by the district councils. Unless restraints were imposed the district council would respond to popular demands and place most of its resources into primary education, to the neglect of roads, clinics, agricultural development, and other vital programs. Thus, self-reliance notwithstanding, TANU found itself actually discouraging self-help schemes in Newala which would throw the national educational program out of focus. The government was reluctant to have its hand forced by local initiative.

# 14:
# Political
# and Economic
# Institution-Building

The ambivalent response of the Makonde to modernization of their technology and transformation of their social
value system in the post-independence period was paralleled
by a mixed reaction to the new political and economic institutions which had been developing in Tanganyika since 1958.
Although some Makonde—such as Lawi Sijaona—had participated in TANU's reformulation of structures at both the national and local levels, the activity was conducted in areas
remote from the Ruvuma Region. The new system—however
meritorious in terms of democratic and modern values—had
not emerged from a spontaneous demand for change within
Makonde society itself. The new political and economic order
was shaped in terms of broader national objectives such as
nation-building, economic independence, and broadening the
base of political representation. Uniformity of institutional
structure and procedure throughout the entire political system
was regarded not only as more just but also as more efficient
considering the limited human and other resources available.
The system did not attempt at the local level to reflect the
variety of political traditions with respect to who should govern
and in what fashion.

## POLITICAL PARTICIPATION

The expansion in scale of the Tanganyikan political community was certainly an index of modernization. By expansion of scale we refer not only to the total numbers of individuals encompassed within the system but also to the number of central government transactions affecting individuals on a day-to-day basis. Where the overwhelming thrust for expansion comes from the center, however, there is normally a discontinuity in growth and acceptance of political institutions relating primarily to central government activities and those institutions which are concerned largely with local activities or with the integration of the peripheral units with the center. The discontinuity is marked by a decided decline in participation by modernizing individuals in political activities as the analysis shifts from the central to the peripheral institutions. The modernizing individuals recognize that the greatest rewards for their newly acquired talents will probably come through the more modernized sector of the political system. There may actually be a steady physical withdrawal of the modernizing individuals from the rural localities to the capital. The response of the transitional and the traditional elements in society parallels that of the modernizing individuals. That is, there may be an overwhelming participation of traditional and transitional men in referenda, elections, rallies, and other activities relating to the functioning of the central political institutions because the institutions may be viewed as remote and therefore not threatening to their vital interests. When it comes to more localized institutions of the new political system, the threats of modernization to entrenched traditional interests are more easily perceived. Thus there tends to be a withdrawal from participation, when this is possible, and even a reaction against modernization when the rules of participation permit a choice to be made respecting candidates or alternative policies. It may be that *sub rosa* informal traditional procedures continue to function in advance of the formal modern activity, making the latter less threatening to traditional values and interests.

## Party Membership

The general attitude of the Makonde peasantry with respect to the new political order is revealed through the analysis of various indices of political participation. Membership in TANU is one critical index, given the commitment of Nyerere and others to constitute TANU as a truly mass-based political party. Although records for the early period are not totally reliable, a student at University College, Dar es Salaam, Anverali S. Dhalla, has compiled a chart (Table 5) plotting the growth of TANU membership in Newala District during the decade 1955–65. The Newala Makonde took to TANU much more enthusiastically than did their fellow tribesmen in Mtwara and Lindi, who were characteristically more lethargic with respect to external innovation. Even in Newala, giving full credence to the above figures and to the method of calculating adults, the membership by 1963 had only risen to approximately 25 to 30 per cent of the adult population. The figures, however, are deceptive, for it was readily admitted that any post-puberty male who paid taxes was eligible for membership in TANU. Little distinction, moreover, was made in the early years of recruitment between new memberships and annual payment of dues by previous members. Members who had lost or could not produce their receipts were often "advised" to take out a new membership in order to bolster the reputation

TABLE 5:
TANU MEMBERSHIP IN NEWALA DISTRICT, 1955–1965

| Division | 1955–1963 | 1964 | 1965 | 1955–1965 |
|----------|-----------|------|------|-----------|
| Newala   | 5,996     | 842  | 1,215 | 8,053 |
| Mahuta   | 8,113     | 442  | 1,060 | 9,615 |
| Namikupa | 4,011     | 510  | 1,221 | 5,742 |
| Kitangari | 4,758    | 367  | 1,038 | 6,163 |
| Liteho   | 3,675     | 198  | 517  | 4,390 |
| Total    | 26,553    | 2,359 | 5,051 | 33,963 |

NOTE: Population according to 1957 census was 176,915.
SOURCE: Anverali S. Dhalla, "Newala District—A Political History," political science paper, University College, Dar es Salaam, 1967, p. 27.

of the recruiter. Indeed, following the tactics of the colonial government tax collectors, TANU recruiters would frequently lie in wait for Makonde farmers as they came into the minor settlements for commercial or governmental business. The greatest collections each year, Mr. Dhalla reported, were made at harvest time as the farmers came into the markets to sell their cashews and other produce. The doubling of new memberships between 1964 and 1965 was largely attributable to the assertion of the area commissioner that only bona fide TANU members could stand for election as balozi, or cell leaders, under the reorganization of TANU at the local level. The frequent chiding of the Makonde peasantry for their lack of patriotism indicated a great deal of dissatisfaction on the part of local TANU leaders with respect to the growth of the party in that region. The Makonde were extremely reluctant to part with their two shillings for membership in TANU or to cooperate in other party activities which required the outlay of even a token amount of money. In 1967, for example, the Makonde of Newala largely ignored the area commissioner's appeal that every cell member contribute 20 cents to an educational fund in connection with the celebration of *Saba Saba* (the Seventh of July, the birthday of TANU).[1]

## *Electoral Participation*

A second index of Makonde response to the new political order was their participation in the series of territorial or national elections from 1959 onward. The election of 1959 itself, however, was not very revealing on this point inasmuch as Lawi Sijaona and the European candidate for the Southern Province stood unopposed, with the only contest being between two candidates for the Asian seat. As previously indicated, moreover, the suffrage requirements were very high and severely discriminated against areas such as the Makonde region where educational opportunities were restricted.

The elections of 1960 and 1962, however, did provide some measure of the lack of Makonde enthusiasm for territorial

1. Anverali S. Dhalla, "Newala District—A Political History" (University College, Dar es Salaam, 1967, mimeo.), p. 27.

politics, at least in the early stages. In 1960, with an expanded electorate, and in one of the few contested elections for a seat in the Legislative Council, the turnout in Newala District was very low. Although the TANU candidate received 90 per cent of the votes in an election which pitted him against a former liwali who had presumably enjoyed a popular following, the total number of ballots cast amounted to only 5,265—less than 3 per cent of the adult population of the district. Even more disappointing to TANU leaders was the participation in the presidential election and republican referendum of 1962. In what was heralded as the real end of colonialism in Tanganyika and an awakening of a new national spirit, only 6,704 Makonde trooped to the polls in Newala District to endorse Julius Nyerere. An additional 293 voted for the African National Congress candidate, Mtemvu, and 435 ballots were spoiled. Considering that the suffrage had been broadened in the interval, this represented a serious indictment of TANU's effectiveness in winning mass support. Only a handful of people had taken the trouble to register and only 66 per cent of the registered voters cast their ballots.

TANU leadership in the Makonde area was determined to make a better showing in the parliamentary elections of 1965, the first to be held in Tanzania following the adoption of the single-party system. The first official statement of the one-party state came in the TANU Annual Conference of 1963, after which Nyerere and his lieutenants attempted to establish an electoral system which would indeed provide the voters with a democratic choice. In this respect TANU constitutes a refreshing contrast to Africa's other dominant parties, which have attempted to secure an almost machinelike unanimous ratification by the masses of the orthodox party candidates.

Under the electoral system launched in 1965, all candidates for office must be TANU adherents.[2] Any number of persons, however, may present their credentials to the TANU district conference in hopes of getting their names on the ballot. Each member of the conference, after questioning the candidates on their views and qualifications, casts a secret ballot, ranking

2. See Lionel Cliffe, ed., *One Party Democracy: The 1965 Tanzania General Elections* (Nairobi: East African Publishing House, 1967).

the candidates in order of preference. The list is then passed along to the National Executive of TANU. In the majority of cases in 1965, the National Executive endorsed the two leading candidates and required them to stand against each other in the subsequent election. The action, however, was not automatic. For reasons which were not always disclosed, the National Executive in certain cases ignored the district-level ranking. Candidates who had received few or no votes at all were permitted to stand against the first or second choice. Some candidates were permitted to stand without opposition. On the other hand, an unopposed candidate at the district level could be provided opposition by the National Executive. Regardless of the exceptions, the process constituted an effective experiment in combining local preference and national interests within a single system.

Perhaps realizing the international attention which was being given to the first openly contested election in Africa under a single-party system, TANU leadership left little to chance. Immediately after the dissolution of the old parliament on July 10, the full energy of the party organization was mobilized in getting people to register, in holding campaign rallies, and in publicizing the issues. The participation in the September elections ranged from less than 23 per cent in constituencies in the Mbeya Region, Masasi District, Mjombe North, and Morogoro North, to more than 88 per cent in Singida West. Considering the performance of voters in developed countries in the West, the overall national turnout of 46 per cent was very impressive. Even more startling, however, was the turnout of voters in the three Makonde constituencies having contested elections (A. K. E. Shaba ran unopposed in Mtwara). The percentages of adult voters who cast ballots in Newala Michila, Newala Pachoto, and Lindi East constituencies were 69.8, 58.6, and 81.8, respectively.[3] In the same election, the voters were asked on a simple yes-or-no basis to ratify Julius Nyerere as president of Tanzania. On this issue 60,543 voters in the two Newala constituencies, 37,411 in Mtwara, and 37,560 in Lindi East cast affirmative ballots. Thus, the election did demonstrate that the

3. The number of ballots cast was 30,698 for Newala Michila, 29,903 for Newala Pachoto, and 38,082 for Lindi East.

Makonde, by one means or another, could be stirred to participate in some activity related to the new political order.

In the next test of popular participation in the electoral system, the performance in the Makonde region fell off considerably, reflecting the discontinuity discussed previously. This
came in the local elections of 1966, when each of the districts
selected members for the district councils. The procedure followed was similar to that of the parliamentary elections of 1965.
In this case, however, the branch annual conference in each
ward winnowed out the various candidates and passed along
their preferences to the district executive committee, which
had the final say in listing the two final contestants or the unopposed candidate. Although I did not have access to data in
Mtwara or Lindi districts, the results in the more politically
alert Newala District are revealing. The combined balloting for
35 council seats brought out 17,200 voters. This was only slightly
more than one-fourth of the number participating in the parliamentary and presidential elections the year previously. Thus, in
the absence of the elaborate publicity and the overt and covert
inducements which accompanied the 1965 elections, the traditional Makonde lethargy seemed once more to manifest itself in
1966. Moreover, it is a curious commentary that the degree of
Makonde electoral participation varied inversely with the degree to which governmental operations affected them on a day-
to-day basis.

One further comment is in order regarding the electoral process under the single-party system. Although TANU attempts to
be broadly participatory and bring out a massive vote by providing the voters with a choice, the elitist nature of the operation is
still apparent. The masses have little control over the actual
choice of party leaders at the district and subdistrict levels. In
the 1965 parliamentary elections, moreover, the significant
winnowing-out process performed by TANU district conferences involved only 47 party leaders in Lindi East and 36 in
Newala (no vote was taken in Mtwara, where only one candidate
was considered).[4] Participation in the nomination procedures

4. The Newala District Conference included 5 TANU officeholders from the
district; 10 members of the District Executive Committee; 8 delegates selected
at the last District Annual Conference; 5 branch chairmen; representatives

for the 1966 local elections in Newala District was broader, since it involved 35 wards. The evaluation of credentials was performed by 1,560 — less than 1 per cent of the total population but almost 10 per cent of the number participating in the final election.

Some of the Makonde attitudes toward the modern political system imposed by TANU and toward modernization itself can be revealed through a more detailed analysis of the parliamentary elections of 1965 and the local elections of 1966.

## Parliamentary Elections of 1965

The four constituencies having Makonde majorities in the 1965 parliamentary elections were each interesting cases, revealing the differential response of the Makonde to the new political system. Mtwara District, which was regarded as having been the most politically lethargic under the colonial system, held true to form. It was one of only 5 constituencies (out of 107 for the country as a whole) which had its candidate run unopposed. Moreover, it deviated from the national pattern in which one or both of the candidates was a member of the dominant tribe of the district — a situation which reflected either strong tribal particularism at the one extreme, or the recognition by TANU that ethnicity could be instrumental in securing allegiance to the developing national political system. In Mtwara, however, the unopposed candidate, Austin Kapere Edward Shaba, had only recently established residence in the district. He was a Chinyanja-speaker whose parents were from Malawi but had emigrated to the Ufipa District of Tanganyika shortly before his birth. During the 1960 elections, when TANU was finding it difficult to recruit Makonde talent for organizing the party in Mtwara, TANU tapped Mr. Shaba — who had no strong attachments to any particular region of Tanganyika — to stand for parliament. He won by a considerable majority over his opponent and moved up the governmental ladder to become minister for housing at the time of the 1965 election. Local lethargy

---

from the TANU Youth League, the UWT (women's branch of TANU), NUTA (the trade-union organization), the cooperative union, and the elders; and 3 election supervisors.

was very evident, and it was the opinion of the analysts of the 1965 election that if Shaba had been "pitted against a local man in an open contest, he might have had a tough fight. Fortunately for him no other candidate materialized." [5]

The other constituency of coastal Makonde, Lindi East, also demonstrated the traditional lack of dynamism. Of the nine candidates presenting their credentials to the district conference, only two were Makonde residents of the district. The remaining candidates were Mwera, Comorian, Asian (2), Sukuma, Ngoni, and a newly arrived Makonde settler from an adjacent district. Moreover, properly calculating coastal Makonde lethargy, the National Executive of TANU was able to manipulate the preferences of the district conference in a fashion which would not have been tolerated in the Haya, Chagga, Sukuma, or other areas where tribalism was quite strong. The district conference balloted, giving the candidates the following numbers of votes:

| | |
|---|---|
| Ali Mogne-Halova Tambwe | 30 |
| Mohamed Salim Kampunga | 11 |
| Satchu Gulamali Abdulrajul | 3 |
| Mzee Selemani Masudi Mnoji | 1 |
| Bibi Ignasia Benedict Makota | 1 |
| Khamis Selemani Kharity | 1 |
| Imani Basil Bara | 0 |
| Kaisi Saidi | 0 |
| Kidaha Rashidi Mwinyimmadi | 0 |

Logically, A. M. Tambwe should have been the preferred candidate, with M. S. Kampunga as his opponent. Tambwe, however, was a Comorian, and despite his long years of service to TANU and his earlier political activity on Zanzibar he had managed to offend a number of important TANU leaders in Dar es Salaam during his tenure as junior minister of external affairs. In rejecting Tambwe, the National Executive also passed over the candidate with the third-highest number of votes, S. G. Abdulrajul, an Asian merchant of Lindi. The reasons for rejecting Abdulrajul were never made public, but it was speculated that the Asian community, which for decades had been politically

5. Cliffe, *One Party Democracy*, p. 386.

active in Lindi, might present a united front in support of Abdulrajul. These fears were perhaps well grounded, for in the Lindi West constituency an Asian lawyer-businessman presented a very respectable showing in the final elections after having put on a very halfhearted campaign. He captured more than one-third of the votes in a contest with a local farmer who had gained popularity while serving on the Lindi district council. In selecting an opponent for M. S. Kampunga in Lindi East, the National Executive chose a woman candidate, Bibi Makota, who had secured a single vote in a three-way tie for fourth place. To the surprise of many, Bibi Makota won a decisive victory in the election, winning 21,771 votes to Kampunga's 15,653. What made her victory all the more interesting is that she was neither a Makonde nor a resident of the constituency. Her home was in Nachingwea District. Moreover, she was a Roman Catholic running against a Muslim opponent in a tradition-oriented Muslim constituency. Thus she managed to overcome ethnic, religious, and antifeminist prejudices in forging her victory. Perhaps the most telling factor in the campaign, however, was the many years of service Bibi Makota had devoted to TANU adult literacy classes and community-development projects, which had brought her to the attention of Nyerere and of Rashidi Kawawa, whose home district was also Nachingwea. Kampunga, on the other hand, had remained largely aloof from active politics although he had long been a party member. Thus the implicit organizational sympathies were with Bibi Makota.

The performance of voters in the two Newala District constituencies contrasted sharply with that of the coastal Makonde. Although on various scales such as education, health, and economic change the Newala Makonde were more modernizing, they nevertheless had evidenced stronger traits of Makonde particularism during the last decade or more of colonial rule. Thus, although the Newala District conference of TANU considered a variety of candidates for both Newala Pachoto (embracing Newala and Mahuta divisions) and Newala Michila (including Liteho, Kitangari, and Namikupa divisions), each nominee was a Makonde with very strong ties in the district. The political patterns in the two Newala constituencies diverged, however, reflecting perhaps the manner in which TANU had established itself in the district.

In Newala Pachoto, the decision of Lawi Sijaona to give up his Lindi constituency and return to the region where he had early labored so hard and skillfully in developing a grass-roots organization was tantamount to election. During the days when few Makonde challenged Europeans openly, Sijaona had displayed his ability to debate with colonial officials on their own terms. His reputation was considerably enhanced in the region as he moved from one important post in Nyerere's government to another. He was clearly one of the men upon whom the president could rely implicitly. He had a touch of charisma despite his somber ways. Although his critics complained of his flashy Mercedes Benz and the lavish parades which gathered every time he came to Lindi or Newala, he clearly enjoyed the popular acclaim. Perhaps he was genuinely embarrassed when he had to scold the people of Lindi for disrupting business and wasting so much money and time on processions of vehicles and marchers.[6] On the other hand he did nothing to discourage the "cultism" evidenced by such things as permitting a new street in Newala township to be named after him.

Sijaona's experience, oratorical skill, intimate knowledge of the district, and organizational talent were more than a match for the only candidate who felt brave enough to oppose him— Anton Geonken Lilama. The opponent was an ex-soldier who had acquired land in the district and had become a wealthy cashew grower. His estate, the Kinombedo Farm, was the largest in the district. Lilama attempted to capitalize on the fact that he was a local man who had stayed behind and had come to know the problems of the farmers in the district—rather than having been educated and gone off to the big city to earn a handsome salary and a national reputation. By contrast with Sijaona, Lilama's experience in government had been that of a local magistrate and later the divisional executive officer in Newala. His major card, however, proved to be a double-edged sword. Lilama had stressed throughout the campaign that he had been instrumental in getting the cooperative movement established in Newala in 1962. He promised that if elected he would make the cooperatives even more useful tools of development by insisting that the marketing boards and the cooperatives pay

---

6. *Tanzania Standard* (Dar es Salaam), November 16, 1965, p. 3.

a higher price to the farmers for their cashews. Unfortunately for Lilama, his critics pointed out that he had not suffered as much as others from the pegged prices and that his profits under an uncontrolled system would be far greater than that of most Makonde. Moreover, as an officer of the cooperative union, he had been implicated in the loss of £500. Although he had never been convicted of wrongdoing, the issue was frequently alluded to by the supporters of Sijaona. It was undoubtedly a factor in Lilama's crushing defeat. He garnered only 2,107 votes to 27,650 for Sijaona.

The campaign in Newala Michila took a different turn. TANU had gotten a later start in Liteho, Namikupa, and Kitangari divisions, and the element of intimidation was frequently employed in getting Makonde peasants to join TANU and participate in its sponsored activities. The measure of resentment is perhaps attested to by the fact that this was one of the constituencies in which the sitting member of parliament was denied reelection.

From the outset of the campaign, developments in Newala Michila set it apart from Newala Pachoto. The candidates who presented themselves before the district conference represented the broad spectrum of political views discernible almost a decade previously, when TANU was just emerging in the district (see Chapter 10).[7] At the extreme right was Nangololo Namaleche (referred to as Namaleone), who represented the position of the tribal nationalists, as well as having appeal to the parochial traditionalists. He had served as liwali of Liteho during the colonial period and based his claim to leadership on his descent from the first mkulungwa mkuu of Newala District during the period of Indirect Rule.[8] Despite his advanced age and his lack of formal education, he seemed convinced that he had a broad following in the district. He attempted to ingratiate himself with the TANU leaders at the district conference by explaining that he had not joined TANU until August, 1964, because the "British government had colonized him." His political naïveté, however, was patently clear when he sug-

---

7. I am indebted to Anverali Dhalla's account of the minutes of the TANU annual conference contained in "Newala District," pp. 34–38.

8. See Chapters 5 and 10.

gested that the colonial government had done more and better things for the people of Newala than had TANU. After having heard his case, the conference unanimously concluded that Nangololo was a "useless" candidate.

The conference was much more sympathetic and gentle with a second candidate who had also served as a liwali under the colonial system and, in the context of 1956, had to be regarded as an accommodating modernist. Albert Mchauru, however, had distinguished himself as the liwali of Nanyamba in Mtwara District by introducing a number of progressive programs in the fields of health, education, and community development. With a Standard VIII education and membership in a family which had for decades been committed to modernization of Makonde society, he was not permanently condemned for his collaboration with the colonial regime. Indeed, following independence and the elimination of the liwali system, Albert Mchauru was retained by TANU as the divisional executive officer for Newala and later for Liteho (a post which he continued to hold in 1967). Like Nangololo, however, he had been stigmatized by many for his failure to join TANU until after independence. His explanation, that he had feared that he would have been dismissed from his civil-service position if he had joined a political movement, did not satisfy many at the conference. Although three of the delegates voted for Mchauru as a candidate, the secretary of the conference recorded that Mchauru was "proud" and that in any case his recent heart attack had disqualified him for candidacy.

The contest in Newala Michila ultimately centered on two candidates who had committed themselves to TANU almost a decade prior to the election of 1965. The first was the incumbent M.P. from Newala District, Raphael Saidi, who had been one of the original organizers of TANU in the district during my previous period of research. Since he had a Standard VII education, he was able to challenge the modernist credentials of Justino Mponda and eventually displace him as leader of the Local (later District) Council. He moved from his position as first elected chairman of the council to M.P. in the election of 1960. The grilling by the district conference indicated that his popularity was not beyond challenge. His absence from the local scene as well as his neglect of his duties as under–deputy regional secretary of TANU put him on the defensive with his Newala constituents. He was accused of having failed to cooperate with both TANU and government officials, of being unreliable, and of having refused to see his constituents who had pressing problems. Despite the very serious criticism, however, he garnered 21 of the 29 ballots and was obviously the preferred party candidate.

Saidi's principal opponent in the conference (and in the subsequent election) was Christopher Sadiki. The latter had modernist credentials in that he had been educated through Standard X and had, in addition, received two years of teacher training. He became the headmaster of Tandahimba Upper Primary School. At the risk of losing his job he joined TANU in 1956 and thus moved from the ranks of the pivotal modernists to those of the dissenting modernists. When TANU came out into the open as a political force before independence, Sadiki was elected to the Local (District) Council and served as vice-chairman for a number of years. Despite his popularity, the delegates to the conference were reluctant to embarrass Raphael Saidi, and Sadiki secured only 5 of the 29 votes.

Although the district conference could excuse Saidi for his neglect of constituency interests, the voters apparently could not. In the subsequent election Saidi lost to Sadiki by a vote of 17,538 to 12,553. Saidi, incidentally, was not the only incumbent M.P. to be penalized for that reason in the election of 1965. One of the casualties was Paul Bomani, Nyerere's minister of finance, who had not kept his fences mended in Sukumaland while being lionized at the national and international level. Lawi Sijaona in Newala Pachoto, however, had learned the lesson that Saidi had forgotten.

In the process, perhaps, the Newala Michila election reinforced the democratic quality of Nyerere's single-party electoral system. He had permitted the people to follow the maxim that "only the wearer of the shoe knows where it pinches," and they followed it. The defeat of Saidi could not be taken as an anti-TANU gesture, since Sadiki was also a strong TANU adherent. It could, however, be viewed as a general expression of distrust of a governmental system that had not yet demonstrated its capacity to satisfy the demands of its citizens.

## Newala District Council Elections of 1966

In view of the stronger attachments of Makonde to locally oriented political leadership during the precolonial and colonial periods, a revealing index of the response of Makonde to the new political order can perhaps be obtained from an analysis of the District Council elections of 1966. Here the discontinuity between the two levels of participation becomes evident. For a variety of reasons, I concentrated upon the elections in Newala District. This is the heartland of the Makonde area, containing over half the Makonde of Tanzania. It also has had a greater exposure to modern schools, clinics, and economic change. Its more active participation in political innovation under colonial rule as well as its latent nationalism made it a better case for analysis than either Mtwara or Lindi districts.

For the purposes of this election Newala was divided into 35 wards, the boundaries of which did not follow traditional jumbeate lines. Each ward had a branch annual conference of TANU, consisting of the various TANU leaders and other respected persons, who gathered to consider the qualifications of candidates who presented themselves for nomination.[9] The rankings of the candidates, based on secret balloting, were forwarded to the district executive committee, which had the ultimate responsibility for endorsing the two candidates from each ward who would oppose each other in the actual election. As in the 1965 elections, the reviewing body had the option of accepting the preference of the conference, adding other candidates, or making other changes deemed to be in the best interests of the district and TANU.

The election revealed some interesting things about Makonde responses to modernization and the new political system. For one thing, it showed that the election of Bibi Makota in Lindi in 1965 could not be taken as a sign that female emancipation had been achieved in Makonde society. Although women were participating in national politics, and despite the efforts of the Europeans to include women on the Newala Local Council in the 1950s, not one of the 35 branch annual conferences in 1966 considered a female candidate. Were it not for the fact that

9. Newala District Office, file "District Council Elections, Newala, 1966."

representation was specifically provided for a member of the
UWT (women's branch of TANU), it is doubtful whether any
women would have been included in the decision-making
process. Women did, however, vote in the election, and it was
stated by several informants that women had worked hard for
various candidates, spreading the word at the water kiosks.

The election also revealed a remarkable lack of interest on
the part of the educated, more modernized male sector of society to participate as candidates. The situation at the local
level thus contrasted sharply with the performance at the
national level in 1965. The leading contenders in each of the
Makonde constituencies in the parliamentary elections had had
seven or more years of formal schooling and a wide range of
experience in government, teaching, business, community
development, and other modern activities. In 24 of the 35 Newala wards in 1966, on the other hand, the only candidates
who presented themselves listed their occupation as "peasant,"
which was an indication of an absence of formal Western education. In the remaining 11 wards one or more of the candidates
indicated they had additional roles which might be classified
as modern. These included TANU branch chairmen, branch
secretaries, collectors, and monitors; cooperative society
chairmen or secretaries; village executive officers; and tailors.
Significantly, none of the roles which had been intentionally
represented on the Local Council in the colonial period—
teachers, deacons, medical aides, Koranic teachers, and the
like – were represented in the candidate pool of 1966. Admittedly
some of those who listed themselves as peasants may have had
some exposure to formal schooling, but this was not indicated
on the roster. Moreover, officials in Newala and Mtwara complained to me about the inability of councilors to comprehend
even elementary problems of government. The area secretary
in Mtwara thought they were quite fortunate in having a
"mayor" for Mtwara (actually chairman of the Mtwara town
council) who had a Standard IV education. It was clear that the
educated and semieducated looked elsewhere for prestigious
rewards for their talents.

The candidates with more modern roles associated with the
new political or economic order did not fare exceptionally well
in contests pitting them against "peasants." In 9 of the wards,

the branch annual conferences considered a mixture of peasant and "modern" candidates. In only three wards did a candidate or combination of candidates with modern credentials receive a majority over a candidate or combination of candidates listed as peasants. In 3 additional wards, "modern" candidates qualified for the election by virtue of having achieved a plurality at the conference stage, or because the procedures required that two names were to be considered in the election, or because the rankings were manipulated by the district executive committee. Although in the final election the modernists emerged victorious in 10 of the 35 wards, their victories were not altogether decisive endorsements of modernity. One ran unopposed; two others were declared winners by the district executive because of some confusion over the use of the hoe and house symbols on the ballot; and in two wards the modernists captured only 51 per cent of the votes. In only half of the contests did the candidates with modern roles win substantial victories over peasant opponents.

The performance of the TANU leadership in the election procedures was ambiguous. Although the leaders did attempt to provide an element of choice, they nevertheless wanted to exercise a firm hand over the options available to the electorate. In 5 of the 35 wards the district executive committee modified the recommendations of the branch annual conferences. In one ward the leading candidate was disqualified because he allegedly interfered with administrators when they were collecting membership fees for TANU. He had also served a 48-day jail sentence for showing disrepect to the president. He had apparently objected to a motion to have the people line the roads during a presidential visit, because the president "would not stand up and the citizens would be troubled needlessly." In a second case the district executive committee disqualified the second-ranking choice of the branch conference who had served three years as a member of the district council. It was alleged that he had once obstructed the nomination of TANU adherents as co-opted members of the district council and that he supported a non-TANU candidate for chairman of the council. It was stated, too, that he had been arrested by the police many times for smoking hemp and for gambling. In a third case the leadership removed from competition a Maconde from across the river who had defrauded Mozambique refugees by claiming that he was the leader of FRELIMO in the district. Previously he had been brought before the court on a number of occasions for deceiving people in his village regarding the manner of paying taxes. Finally, it was charged that he was not only morally corrupt but also had allegedly received support from the ANC in opposing TANU in earlier elections. Significantly, to replace the rejected nominee on the ballot the district executive selected the TANU branch chairman, who had run a poor third in the branch conference balloting. The TANU branch chairman went on to win in the subsequent election.

In two additional instances of manipulation by the district executive committee, TANU officials were victorious in the elections. Thus, in one ward, without any reasons having been offered, the TANU branch chairman (who had run a poor third, getting only 25 per cent of the conference votes) was substituted for a village executive officer who had run second. In the second case a peasant had been recommended by the branch conference without opposition. The district executive added a TANU collector, who had received no votes at the branch level, to oppose him. It should be noted that in two other wards the district executive committee had not felt obliged to provide challengers to candidates who had been recommended without opposition by their branch conferences.

In summary, the election did not constitute an overwhelming vote of approval for the new political system. Of the five TANU officials (two branch chairmen, one branch secretary, a monitor, and a collector) who were victorious over peasants or other modernists, three survived to the electoral stage only because of intervention by the district executive committee. Moreover, there was further antagonism evident toward the new political system in the treatment of incumbent members of the district council. Of thirteen incumbents, only five were renominated and reelected. One of the incumbents had been eliminated by the district executive committee, but the remaining seven were defeated at the polls. In one of the seven cases, the incumbent was defeated by a candidate provided by the district executive committee. Thus, the issue of grass-roots acceptance of TANU, or at least past performance of those associated with TANU, was not free from ambiguity.

## ECONOMIC PARTICIPATION

The hesitant response of the Makonde to the new political order was matched by a similar caution with respect to the new economic order. This can best be appreciated through an analysis of the reaction to the cooperative movement in the Makonde districts. Given both the depth of hostility of the Makonde toward the Asian traders as well as the optimism of a wide spectrum of the modernizing elite that cooperatives would lead to instant prosperity, the reaction of the Makonde in 1967 is interesting.

The initial Makonde reaction in 1962, at the time that cashew-marketing cooperatives were introduced, was one of apparent enthusiasm. Within a space of two or three years, 99 chapters were organized in the Mtwara Region, the bulk of them in the Makonde districts (24 in Newala, 12 in Mtwara, and 27 in Lindi). Membership soared, and by 1964 there were 42,100 subscribers in the region. By 1965 the Mtwara Region Cooperative Union moved beyond its exclusive concern with cashews and decided to buy cassava. The decision was a fortunate one, both for the farmers and the union, inasmuch as the drought that year brought in a very low yield of cashews without seriously affecting the usually high production of cassava. In the following years the activities of the Mtwara District cooperatives were expanded to cover the purchase of three additional crops — simsim, groundnuts, and castor beans. The branches in Newala covered the preceding five crops as well as maize, sunflower seeds, rice, and sorghum. In addition to the produce-marketing societies, other cooperatives, not affiliated with the Mtwara Region Cooperative Union, were organized in the region to cover timber and blackwood marketing (7), savings and credit (4), tailoring (2), fisheries (2), and building, carpentry, and the distributive trades (1 each).

Beyond transporting crops to exterior markets, providing gunny sacks for the produce, advancing credit for farm improvement, and providing a tractor service for members, there were a number of peripheral benefits which the cooperative societies extended to Makonde and other farmers in the region. It was apparent, too, that a highly vocal minority wanted the cooperatives to be even more aggressive and extend credit for mechanization, take all crops under the cooperative umbrella, serve as an agency for the sale of agricultural implements, undertake the introduction of new crops, and purchase motor vehicles instead of relying on the Tanganyika Transport Company. On a number of these issues, both the government and the cooperative union leadership refused to be persuaded. The introduction of new crops, for example, was – the cooperative officers insisted – the responsibility of the M.P. or the Agricultural Department. Government, moreover, opposed the outright purchase of vehicles, since it was not demonstrated that they would have a legitimate use between harvest seasons, and the cost of maintenance would more than offset any savings.

The optimism of 1962 had given way to pessimism by 1967. The Makonde were having second thoughts about the latest innovation devised for their economic improvement. Cooperative officers in Mtwara and Newala indicated to me that the people were beginning to suspect that the union was a device for permitting the government to check on earnings in order to levy higher taxes. Indeed, even the 12-shilling entrance fee and the 10 shillings a share were viewed as new forms of taxation, replacing the old water rate. What had been undertaken enthusiastically when the opportunity was optional became an object of resentment when the activity was made compulsory. The Makonde objected to the ruling that all crops that came under the jurisdiction of the district cooperatives could legally be sold only to the cooperatives, whether or not the farmer was a member. Moreover, since the prices for commodities were set in Dar es Salaam rather than in response to local conditions, the Makonde growers felt that low prices merely meant that money was being drained off to pay the salaries of officials. The fixed price, they insisted, gave them less freedom of choice than they had had under the old system of bargaining with the Asians.

The establishment of the cooperative monopoly also had the perhaps unintended consequence of driving the independent African traders out of business, since the crops they depended upon for their narrow margin of profit were those taken under the cooperatives' jurisdiction. The Asian traders, on the other hand, had sufficient capital to be able to diversify their operations when a crop was monopolized. Thus, Newala District, which in 1961 was already in the lowest category of having only one trader for every 300 inhabitants (the national ratio was one to 180 inhabitants), found one further avenue of economic modernization closed to the enterprising Makonde.[10]

Finally, there was the widespread feeling among the Makonde farmers, who had little genuine understanding of the cooperative objectives, that they were at the mercy of better-educated Tanzanians from outside the region. In the absence of very many local residents with experience in managing cooperative societies, the Mtwara Region had to rely upon leadership provided by Ngoni, Chagga, and others. Makonde fears of exploitation were partially reinforced in the latter part of 1966 when mismanagement and the loss of cash at both the union and individual societies level led to the dismissal of a number of officials and committee members. By 1968 conditions had become so bad that the committees for the Mtwara Region were suspended and the government assumed all decision-making powers. Fear that the Makonde economy was at the mercy of external forces was also voiced in connection with the absence of crop-processing industries in the Makonde area. Thus, much of the profits which could have gone back to the farmers went into transportation costs, and the area failed to realize the employment potential involved in crop processing.[11]

The Makonde expressed their strong reservations about the latest innovation in the economic order in a variety of ways. The most obvious was by withdrawing their membership in the unions. From a high of 42,100 members in 1964, the produce-marketing societies in the Mtwara Region dropped to 26,000 in 1966. Less than 10 per cent of the adult males in Newala joined local societies. Indeed, the only significant difference between members and nonmembers was that the former paid fees! The monopoly which the cooperatives enjoyed

10. See S. Jensen, *Regional Economic Atlas of Mainland Tanzania*, Bureau of Resource Assessment and Land Use Planning, Research Paper no. 1 (University College, Dar es Salaam, June, 1968), pp. 53–55.

11. The complaints were echoed elsewhere in Tanzania. See *Tanzania, Report of the Presidential Special Committee of Enquiry into the Cooperative Movement and Marketing Boards* (Dar es Salaam: Government Printer, 1966).

over certain crops eliminated the possibility of outside bargaining for better prices. Even the Makonde who continued as
members, moreover, evidenced a strong distrust of the cooperative system. Despite constant pleading of union officials that
continuity of leadership was essential for the success of the
movement, the membership used the occasion of the local
society's annual election to "throw the rascals out." Instead of
replacing only one-third of the committee membership each
year, in a number of cases the membership tried to replace all
nine committee members and the chairman. It was the incumbents who took the brunt of the blame for low prices, for failures to have sufficient cash on hand at the markets on buying
days, and even for crop failures. The officers of the local societies, moreover, continued to annoy the officers at the union
level by constantly shifting the location where crops were sold
so that it became difficult to plan transportation, cash outlays,
growing campaigns, and other aspects of the cooperative program. The officers of the local societies, who in most cases
had only functional literacy, tended to distrust the union officers, many of whom had had secondary-school education.

The difficulties faced by the produce-marketing societies
were apparent in the other societies as well. There was, for
example, a brightly painted sign along the beach at Mikindani
announcing the buying post of the Mtwara-Pemba Fishing
Cooperative. The society, however, remained stillborn in 1967
despite four years of government attempts to breathe life into
it. The fishermen were too individualistic in temperament to
go through the necessary steps leading to registration. Similarly, the tailoring, building, and consumer cooperatives remained paper organizations or did only negligible business
in the Makonde districts.[12] Only the carpenters' cooperative
in Mtwara was succeeding because of the building boom associated with the expansion of port facilities during the Zambian crisis.

In addition to the problems faced by cooperatives, there was
one other facet of the organization of production in 1967 which
seemed destined for difficulties: the emergence of a fairly extensive land "owning" class in Makonde society. Although, in

12. *Tanzania Standard* (Dar es Salaam), July 3, 1967, p. 3.

principle, Nyerere's government had made communally owned land part of the national domain, in fact traditional land-tenure rules and usages continued to prevail in many areas of the country. Traditional land tenure among the Makonde placed no limits upon the amount of land that an individual could have under cultivation, since it was presumed that his needs would expand and contract during his lifetime as his family responsibilities increased and diminished. Land not under use for a considerable period of time was considered forfeited and could be reassigned by the mwenye or the mkulungwa. An exception to the rule was that trees remained the property of the planter and his heirs even when the land beneath the trees had been reassigned. With the planting of cashew estates, however, a form of *de facto* private ownership emerged, since the trees were planted so closely that no other crops could be grown underneath them even if the land had been reassigned. Despite the pleadings of agricultural officers that the yield of cashews per acre was diminished by close planting, the Makonde farmers persisted in their habits without perhaps fully realizing the consequences for land holding. The planting of many trees gave a man added prestige and—fortuitously—close planting of trees cut down on his weeding problems.

Ironically, however, what had been undertaken by British colonial officers as a soil-conservation measure, rather than as simply an economic step, had transformed many aspects of Makonde culture and society. In the first place, the expanding cashew estates were gradually altering agricultural technology. Stump cultivation and plot rotation were no longer necessary in many parts of the district, and thus the area of cultivatable land was increased. Tree cropping permitted a greater stabilization of residence relative to one's place of work. Furthermore, the expansion of acreage under cashew cultivation gave rise to a new monied class that did not base its status either on traditional forms of wealth or upon the skills which were acquired through modern schooling (and which had to be employed largely outside the district, where the opportunities were greater). In several areas it was stated by agricultural and cooperative officers that some Makonde growers had fields of 150 to 200 acres of cashews, even though one- or two-acre plots were still more typical.[13] On the larger estates the family organization of labor was no longer adequate, and the landlord had to hire workers. The most readily available workers in 1967–68 were the Maconde refugees from across the Ruvuma River. Since the Maconde, under traditional land-tenure practices, were not permitted to plant perennials, they were not in competition with the Makonde as cashew growers. Thus the traditional castelike relationship between the two ethnic groups was reinstituted in a modern form.

It was apparent that this covert form of private ownership of land, the emergence of a "capitalist" class, and the employment of other Africans as laborers ran counter to the kind of development envisioned for Tanzania in the Arusha Declaration of February, 1967. For as Nyerere stated in his paper on *Socialism and Rural Development:*

> In the rural areas of Tanzania it is possible to produce enough crops to give an agricultural worker a decent life, with money for a good house and furniture, proper food, some reserve for old age, and so on. But the moment such a man extends his farm to the point where it is necessary for him to employ labourers in order to plant or harvest the full acreage, then the traditional system of ujamaa (communal cooperation and responsibility) has been killed. For he is not sharing with other people according to the work they do, but simply paying them in accordance with a laid-down minimum wage. The final output of the farm on which both employer and employees have worked is not being shared. The money obtained from all the crops goes to the owner; from that money he pays "his" workers. And the result is that the spirit of equality between all people working on the farm has gone—for the employees are the servants of the man who employs them. Thus we have the

13. In 1939, the average plot was estimated to be 2.69 acres under cultivation. In 1968, Poul Westergaard, a Danish economist, conducted a spot-check in two areas of Newala and estimated the average acreage of cashew under cultivation at 13 in Kitangari and 9 in Mahuta. For all crops, including maize, sorghum, cassava, and rice, the average was 17 acres in Kitangari and 9 in Mahuta. Although he recognized that his investigations were conducted during the rainy season, without local transport, he nevertheless managed to survey one farm with 35 acres of cashew trees and 2 acres of other crops. The annual income from cashews on this estate was Shs. 6,854. See "Farm Surveys of Cashew Producers in Mtwara Region: Preliminary Results," Economic Research Bureau Paper 68.3 (University College, Dar es Salaam, 1968).

beginnings of a class system in the rural areas. Also, the employees may well be paid for working during harvest or during weeding but get no money for the rest of the year. . . . The small-scale capitalist agriculture we now have is not really a danger; but our feet are on the wrong path, and if we continue to encourage or even help the development of agricultural capitalism, we shall never become a socialist state. On the contrary, we shall be continuing the break-up of the traditional concepts of human equality based on sharing all the necessities of life and on a universal obligation to work.[14]

The situation in the Makonde area presented a dilemma for TANU. On the one hand, TANU is committed to eliminating or reducing class stratifications within Tanzania. At the same time it is attempting to transform the economy and make it provide the basic requirements of life. The two are not inconsistent goals: a socialistic society cannot thrive if it stands at the margin of starvation. Yet, in the Makonde area, penalizing the larger and more enterprising cashew growers might lead to the further economic depression of the area and a further delay in the achievement of even minimal economic and social objectives. Ideology had already contributed to the elimination of the small African trader and transporter in the Makonde region as the cooperative unions monopolized both the purchase of key crops and the transporting of these crops in government-subsidized vehicles. Ideology might similarly undermine one of the most creative responses on the part of the Makonde to economic growth, for it had been demonstrated both that the cashew industry could provide the revenue for a vast program of local improvement and that the most successful producers (in terms of utilizing the advice of the agricultural extension service) were the large-scale farmers.[15]

14. (Dar es Salaam: Government Printer, 1967), pp. 7, 8.
15. See Poul Westergaard, "The Marketing Margin: An Analysis of Cashew Nut Marketing Costs," Economic Research Bureau Paper 68.13 (University College, Dar es Salaam, 1968). There were two further minor social consequences of the cashew industry. The major cashew producers tended to be Christian, since the Christians preferred to distribute land in major segments whereas the Muslims and tradition-oriented Makonde continued to divide land-holdings into smaller fragments. Second, the farming of trees rather than annual crops accelerated the practice of patrilocal over matrilocal residence, with the bride going off to live on her husband's farm rather than the reverse, since the husband had a fixed form of investment.

## GROWTH WITHOUT DEVELOPMENT

The material on economic transformation in Uma-konde presented in this and the preceding chapters fits the pattern of economic change which George Dalton, the economist, has referred to as "cash income growth without development." [16] That is, the transformation was not the consequence of a sudden and major disruption of traditional economic values and technology. Rather, the most significant innovation was the introduction of cash crops, the acceleration of wage-labor either within the area or through migration, and the establishment of other cash-earning activities. The monetized sector was largely an overlay that was loosely related to the traditional subsistence enterprises, which continued to absorb a considerable portion of human energies and productive resources. The type of economic growth described by Dalton could be accomplished without a radical change in technology, social customs, literacy rates, and other facets of traditional culture. On the other hand, the existence of money could generate changes in the social, political, and legal order which were quite far-reaching. The newly acquired cash income (and in some cases even the very means whereby the cash was acquired) has challenged traditional status rankings, prestige symbols, and political relationships. The new forms of production, moreover, provide novel sources of litigation over such matters as land boundaries, indebtedness, and gambling. Finally, this type of growth contributes to a breakdown of those traditional social and political relationships which had economic sanctions and gives rise to an emergence of individualism or of new and depersonalized forms of corporate groupings which weaken the village, age, and family corporate work arrangements.

The growth of the cash-income sector does broaden the horizons of the peasant even though he never strays far from his homestead. He is involved—however indirectly—with a world-wide money economy as his cashew nuts or labor is exchanged for European pots and pans, Asian printed cloth, or

16. For a recent statement, see his "Theoretical Issues in Economic Anthropology," *Current Anthropology*, (February, 1969), 63–80.

an admission ticket to an American film. Cash, being more easily convertible than labor or commodities, makes the social and political systems as well as the economy itself more dynamic and receptive to economic development. In themselves, however, the changes which take place as a consequence of the growth in the cash-income sector do not constitute development. Development only comes when there is *sustained* income growth through constant enlargement of — and integration and interdependence among — markets at the local, regional, national, and international levels. Sustained growth requires radical innovation in production technology, a willingness on the part of traditional groups to engage in risk-taking, and the establishment of institutions which can initiate and consolidate the benefits of change. In the late 1960s the people of Umakonde were still taking only the first steps toward genuine development.

# 15:

# Perspective

It would be erroneous to assume that the lack of a more positive response on the part of the Makonde to modernization in 1967 could be attributed solely to the existence of a colonial relationship during the period from the 1890s to 1962. Certainly there were other factors that contributed to the failure of the Makonde to marshal their human and physical resources by creating larger-scale political and economic systems and by employing more sophisticated technology in dealing with the problems of disease and poverty. The geographic isolation of the Makonde from other groups in East Africa, for example, as well as the obstacles which the physical terrain posed in terms of intratribal cohesion were not *created* by the alien dominators of the Makonde. They might be held accountable to the extent that they failed to make a major assault on the problems of transportation and communication in Umakonde similar to that made in the Chagga, Haya, Sukuma, and other tribal areas of Tanzania. The absence of an efficient road and rail network and of port facilities certainly reduced the possibility of innovative influences having a sustained impact upon Makonde society. But it was a policy decision of the colonial administrators, rather than colonialism itself, that was responsible for the isolation.

Furthermore, the parochialism of Makonde society today is at least in part attributable to conditions which existed prior to the imposition of Arab, German, and British influence in Umakonde. The dispersed patterns of settlement, which were a response to the problems of defense against Ngoni raiders, have persisted to plague even the contemporary rulers of Tanzania as they attempt to provide efficient services of modern government to the people of Newala and Mtwara. Loyalty to highly parochial leadership also continues despite the many innovations of the past eighty years leading to larger-scale political community. As recently as 1965, a Makonde student at University College reported that people in his area still regarded the wakulungwa as the "symbolic heads of their respective areas. They perform traditional rites for example during circumcision ceremonies. People in their areas respect them. On certain days of the year, they go to work in their *shambas* [fields] free of charge." If the British are at fault in this respect, it stems from their misguided efforts in employing what had once been regarded as the humanitarian policy of Indirect Rule and from having failed to be more ruthless in eradicating traditional loyalties once they had embarked upon a course of modernizing the political system. Similarly, the European administrators did not create the rudimentary technology which the Makonde employed in meeting their economic needs. Indeed, after trial and error, the European administrators found the extant technology to be the best adapted to the peculiar physical conditions of the plateau. In the absence of adequate financial, technological, and other resources for making a more systematic and massive attack upon the problems of production, this seemed to be the wisest course at the time.

Nor were the establishment of a superordinate-subordinate relationship and the application of force in themselves deterrents to modernization. Indeed, colonial rule in other quarters of the globe has actually been credited by the former subject people themselves with having facilitated the modernization of their societies. Colonial rule has done this both directly, by introducing intensive programs of economic development and administrative reform, and indirectly, by providing an umbrella under which other agents of innovation — traders, missionaries, and miners — have been able to intrude upon an area and conduct their activities in an orderly, albeit exploitative, fashion.

What then made colonial rule in the Makonda area counter-productive with respect to modernization? In the first place, the Arabs, the Germans, and even the British during most of their tenure as political suzerains employed a "dog-in-the-manger approach." That is, they insisted upon establishing a colonial "presence" which would exclude or regulate the kind of contact the Makonde could have with external innovators, but they were not prepared to establish an administratively efficient, dynamic system of modern government. Until well into the present century, there were many villages on the plateau and in the coastal districts as well that were only nominally part of a colonial system. There were others which were aware of the colonial relationship merely because of the incursions of tax collectors, labor recruiters, and others who upset the customary patterns of life. Far from providing positive services during most of the colonial period, the government acted as a restraining mechanism not only with respect to external innovative influences but also with respect to any internal dynamism within Makonde society which in any way challenged the European value system. The colonial regime was powerful enough to restrain, but it lacked the human, financial, and physical resources to be creative in any sustained fashion.

When colonial administrators did attempt to engage in creative innovation, their actions tended to be capricious. Indeed, it has been one of the principal themes of this book that *administrative caprice, more than any other factor, has been responsible for the failure of the Makonde to respond more positively to modern institutions and values.* There was constant manipulation by alien administrators and those associated with them of the social, economic, and political systems of the Makonde. Indeed, there was almost a monopolization of the initiative for modernizing innovation by persons who had no permanent or even long-term tenure in Makonde society. Innovation thus came to be viewed as an affair of the foreigner, which had to be endured, rather than as something which had demonstrable value to the Makonde peasant or leader. Modernization efforts were regarded as a series of meddling

acts without any patterns which were logical or meaningful to
the Makonde. If it indeed happened that some innovation did
have a discernible benefit, then one did not secure more of the
same by engaging in creative self-help; this might meet with
the displeasure of the administrator or his imminent successor.
Rather, one assumed the role of the supplicant and expected
further gifts from the innovator as the price he had to pay for
your deference and for having tolerated his foolish meddling.
Thus, the dependency syndrome, discussed in Chapter 9, was
a frequent manifestation in European-Makonde relationships.

The institutions, moreover, through which modernization
was to take place were subjected to constant caprice, and the
maturation needed to establish rational procedures and to
secure popular acceptance was never attained. Each institutional change called forth a new cadre of indigenous leadership, having different talents and constituencies than the
preceding groups of leaders, and with no greater assurances
than were given the previous groups that they would be permitted to display initiative in rational planning, and that they would
not in their turn be unceremoniously dismissed from office.
Thus, it was not that local leadership was uninvolved in European colonial administration; rather, it was that layer upon layer
of local leadership cadres were created, used, dismissed, and
expected to fade quietly away (which, of course, they did
not do).

The problems of administrative neglect and administrative
caprice arose in part because Umakonde was among the poorest
sections of a much larger colony, and Tanganyika in turn was
one of the poorest colonies of a much broader empire. Thus,
Umakonde was the victim of residual decision-making in which
higher priorities were given by colonial administrators to
European wars and depressions than to the welfare of colonial
peoples, and in which greater attention was given to the productive capacities of the Chagga area and the hostile attitudes
of the Hehe than to the quiescent, remote, and unpromising
area of Umakonde. The overall dictates of the colonial service,
moreover, were regarded as more important than the administrative needs of any particular region, and thus officers were
given short tenure and frequent rotation "for the good of the
service."

The colonial officer himself quickly came to have the same broader views of his superiors in Dar es Salaam, Berlin, or London. Recognizing, too, that his own transfer or promotion depended upon his making a significant mark upon a district, each officer attempted to engage in "creative" manipulation, often without regard to his predecessors' contributions. Acting for months on end without restraint from Dar es Salaam and yet vested with a wide range of authority to manipulate the structures and values of the subordinate society, the colonial official frequently assumed the role of a "benign meddler." He viewed himself as benign because the value system of his day left him convinced that he had indeed taken up the "white man's burden." Yet he was a meddler, since he could not possibly give his task the overview that was required for integrated and sustained change. Even if he appreciated the interrelated character of social phenomena and the fact that support for the acceptance of one norm depended upon the existence of other norms and social structures, there was little that he could do to control more than a fragment of the total picture. The best he could do, without divine wisdom, universal talents, and a full cadre of assistants, was to tinker. The appearance of success in tinkering with one facet of Makonde society seemed to give him license to manipulate all other aspects of the system. Although he lacked the overall plan establishing goals and limits, the European administrator was often as destructive of basic values as the totalitarian reformer. The masses under the jurisdiction of a colonial administrator literally did not know where next the ax would fall. Government consisted of "bugging the people" to pay taxes, to provide labor for road construction, and other coercive measures. And the people adjusted to and tolerated the colonial relationship by playing a waiting game.

Perhaps the most significant and destructive impact of the capricious innovation took place at the level of Makonde political leadership. The establishment of competing and overlapping leadership groups has been discussed above. Leadership tasks during the colonial period, moreover, were highly parochial in nature. Although a few Makonde, such as Justino Mponda, were consciously given territorial roles to perform, the opportunities of developing talents within a broader arena were limited. The British operated on the dubious assumption (certainly not borne out by circumstances within Great Britain itself) that experience in local government provided a natural training ground for participation in national government. The talents that were cultivated, moreover, were those of a general administrative character. With the exception of a few social-welfare positions, there was almost a studied failure to train Makonde for technical roles that would permit them to participate actively in economic development, improvement of sanitation, and environmental planning. Whether it was the introduction of a new crop, the provision of water to the plateau, or the planning of new road surveys, the Makonde were constantly in the position of relying upon the advice and orders of aliens. Thus, Makonde were never encouraged to take the risk of experimenting with the improvement of their condition. They had to rely upon alien personnel, whose motives were often patently materialistic and in any case suspect. When demands for technical innovation arose from within Makonde society itself — such as the demand for the establishment of cooperatives — the idea was either resisted or ignored.

Similarly, there was a calculated resistance to the development of Makonde political talents unless these were carefully nurtured by the colonial administrators themselves. The primary thrust of local government reform during the last decade of colonial rule took the form of imparting administrative skills to the Makonde rather than encouraging them to engage creatively in the decision-making process. Indeed, the greater the demands in Tanganyika generally for African involvement in politics, the more intent the British administration seemed to be on shifting decision-making outside the African community. They did this directly, by involving the non-African community (both Asian traders and European missionaries) in the politics of development, and indirectly, by attempting to select those Africans who were deemed sufficiently "responsible" to participate in the charade of decision-making. Thus, at a time when the rhetoric of the colonial administration insisted upon greater African acceptance of responsibility, the practice was to make them ever more dependent upon external stimuli and tutelage. The British administrators seemed unprepared to accept the idea that the success of modernization is as much a political as an administrative function, that there is a vital need to create political support for the actions of the new leadership in transforming the economic and social order. In the absence of accepted political mechanisms to make growth self-sustaining, the pre-independence reform constituted benign meddling on a vast scale.

The end of colonial rule in Tanganyika, as in other countries of Africa, has not spelled an end to poverty, disease, and illiteracy. In several countries, a combination of circumstances has actually decelerated the rate of economic growth, and the capacity of government to creatively control its human and physical resources has diminished. The lack of trained personnel, the mistaking of officials' private interests with the public interest, the loss of imperial subsidies coupled with the decline in prices for Africa's exports, and even civil war have been factors in this decline. Similarly, victory in the anti-colonial struggle has not always brought instant nationhood. The masses have not automatically identified with the nationalist elite. Indeed, in many states a fierce competition for the loyalties of the masses has developed between the national and the tribal elites. Despite the rhetoric of participatory democracy, open political systems have gradually given way to elite-dominated single-party systems and military coups. To the credit of Tanzania's political leadership, it has never promised that independence would be the end rather than the beginning of the struggle for modernization. Nyerere has consistently indicated that the future would, for some time to come, be a life of hard work and sacrifice. And he and his administrators have attempted to serve as exemplars of moral honesty and self-reliance.

There are undoubtedly many more criteria by which to judge the performance of Nyerere and TANU than the success or failure of modernization in the Makonde region. Given the limited personnel and the poverty of Tanganyika's development programs at the point of independence, it is remarkable indeed that Nyerere has been able to simultaneously maintain political stability, forge a creatively independent foreign policy, embark upon a daring and self-sacrificing program of economic development, introduce one of the few genuinely participatory political parties in Africa, and dramatically change an educational system rooted in the colonial past. Admirable though Nyerere's programs have been, however, they have not been without their economic, social, and political costs to severely neglected regions such as Umakonde. Rapid Africanization has diminished still further the limited pool of technical and administrative talent available for development. Ruptures in diplomatic ties with Great Britain, West Germany, and the United States have led to the depletion of sources for needed investment capital. Involvement in pan-African movements has diverted abroad scarce resources that might have been employed internally. And the daring attempt to bring about modernization via an agricultural rather than an industrial route is a gamble that has few historic precedents to support it. Nyerere is aware of these costs, and he would certainly not dismiss them as unimportant. However, he would insist that what is more important for a developing country is the *quality* of the society it is creating. Hence, instead of steel mills he desires a society in which distributive justice prevails; instead of being burdened with foreign debts, advisers, and political obligations, he wants a society in which the people accept responsibility for their own fate; instead of a frustrated political community in which expectations run beyond the limits of reality, he wants a society in which people understand that the task before them is hard but not impossible to achieve.

Whether or not Nyerere could accomplish for the Makonde area the same objectives he had set for Tanzania in general was still a matter of speculation during my return to Newala in 1967. Much would depend upon the stability of TANU leadership and the continuity of the development policies which Nyerere has enunciated in the Arusha Declaration and other statements on self-reliance. If the new village development committees, cooperative societies, and other institutions are given the time needed to mature and win the confidence of the Makonde peasantry, they may yet secure the creative energies and talents of that group. In 1967, the Makonde were still inured to the various attempts at external manipulation of their traditional political, economic, and social systems, and to the constant experimentation by outsiders who never stayed around long enough to witness its consequences. Having seen it all before, the Makonde peasant still tends to view each novel proposition with ennui or, at best, a spirit of sullen compliance.

Indeed, it may be that the transition from the present stage of "cash-income growth without development" to genuine development will come in areas where governmental action is less overt. The lesson of the ill-fated Groundnut Scheme in the colonial period seems to be that the best-laid plans often fail, whereas the improvement of infrastructure (roads, ports, market places, processing industries, and other facilities) in itself provides sufficient incentive for the expansion of peasant agriculture into new areas and new cash crops. In Umakonde, the most creative response to an economic challenge (increased taxation) has been the blossoming of the cashew industry. This was accomplished with relatively little prodding from either the colonial or the nationalist governments—indeed, the development came as a fortuitous by-product of a soil-conservation program. Similarly, the growth of the independent African trading community prior to independence took place largely without planning and in response to better prices, improvement in roads, and construction of market places. The enthusiasm of Makonde in the Newala District for modern education has also developed largely outside "the plan." It is undoubtedly within the spirit of a policy of self-reliance that the people should lead the way. Imaginative development planning incorporates the subjective desires on the part of the local community to modernize. Nyerere, however, is faced with a dilemma: he is committed to an egalitarian program for development in which there are no pockets of underdevelopment where the Gogo, Ha, or Makonde are neglected at the expense of the more economically advanced areas around Kilimanjaro and Lake Victoria. For a highly developed society to permit pockets of underdevelopment to exist in the midst of affluence (such as Appalachia or Harlem in the United States) is inexcusable; a government with a scarcity of human and material resources may have no other choice *for the time being*. Indeed, by marshaling its resources in the areas where there can be immediate and dramatic results, the demonstration effect in the neglected areas may bring swifter and more meaningful response than could have been obtained by direct planning—especially where direct planning is viewed with suspicion.

Finally, there is the matter of ethnicity and development. Modernization and nation-building alike stand opposed to the creation of parochial ethnicity. Ascriptive barriers which limit economic, social, and political interchange deny individuals the opportunity to fully develop their talents and condemn them to an existence where they are largely at the mercy of societies of expanding scale. Nevertheless (as the American commonwealth is coming to discover in its efforts to resolve its racial conflicts), a measure of self-pride is necessary before individuals can creatively relate to others in a developing society. In posting non-Makonde officials to the Ruvuma Region, Nyerere is acting not merely out of necessity (for there are not enough trained Makonde to fill the various positions in agriculture, cooperatives, health, and other development fields); he is aware as well of the positive value for both nation-building and development which can emerge from intimate contact between Makonde and non-Makonde. Only in this way, he could argue, can the Makonde overcome their perhaps understandable and justifiable fear of alien innovators. Ethnicity, however, will probably continue to remain an obstacle to Makonde development as long as there are relatively few Makonde who are visibly involved in the local planning of national policies. Without the latter development, the *self* in the objective of self-reliance will not have been realized for the people of Umakonde.

# Bibliography:

## OFFICIAL PUBLICATIONS
## GOVERNMENT AND PARTY

Many of the documents referred to in this study were originally scrutinized in the provincial (now regional) commissioner's office in Mtwara and in the district (now area) commissioners' offices in Newala, Mtwara, and Lindi. Following independence the bulk of these were transferred to the Tanzania National Archives, Dar es Salaam. Where possible I have cited the documents by the official numbering system employed by the colonial government and adhered to by the archives.

Considerable use was made of the political, economic, anthropological, and geographical data contained in the *District Books* for Newala, Lindi, and Mtwara (formerly Mikindani) districts. These were formerly kept in the district headquarters and contained the notes, both relevant and esoteric, on the developments of the district as perceived by the British district officers from the early 1920s to the time of independence in 1961. Microfilm copies have been obtained by Syracuse University.

In addition to the above, systematic perusal was made of the following documents:

1. Monthly and annual reports of the district commissioners of Lindi, Newala, Mtwara (Mikindani) districts to the provincial (or senior) commissioner at Mtwara (formerly at Lindi).

2. The annual reports of the senior commissioner, Lindi Province (1919–34), and the provincial commissioner, Southern Province (1935–61), to the chief secretary, Dar es Salaam.

3. Confidential correspondence between the governor and chief secretary, chief secretary and provincial commissioners, provincial commissioner and district commissioners.

4. Annual and monthly reports of the Departments (Ministries) of Local Government, Education, Public Works, Agriculture, Medical Services, and others as they related to the Makonde districts.

5. Special reports by *ad hoc* committees of inquiry or investigators such as F. W. Bampfylde, "Report on the Wamakonde and Wamwera Tribal Administration," July 12, 1929, Lindi District; and E. Craig, "Draft Agricultural Policy Framework, Newala District," 1956.

6. The following items by government committees or officials in Tanganyika (Tanzania) or East Africa:

Baker, E. C. *Report on Social and Economic Conditions in the Tanga Province*. Dar es Salaam: Government Printer, 1934.

Cameron, Sir Donald. *Principles of Native Administration and Their Application*. Native Administration Memorandum no. 1, rev. Dar es Salaam: Government Printer, 1930.

East African Statistical Department. *African Population of Tanganyika Territory: Geographic and Tribal Studies*. 1948 Census. Nairobi: EASD, rev., 1953.

_____. *Tanganyika, African Population Census, 1957*. Nairobi: EASD, 1958.

Gillman, Clement. *The Geography and Hydrography of the Tanganyika Territory Part of the Ruvuma Basin*. Dar es Salaam: Government Printer, 1943.

_____. *A Reconnaissance Survey of the Hydrology of Tanganyika Territory in Its Geographical Settings*. Dar es Salaam: Government Printer, 1943.

Nyerere, Julius K. *The Arusha Declaration and TANU's Policy on Socialism and Self-Reliance*. Dar es Salaam: TANU, 1967.

_____. *Socialism and Rural Development*. Dar es Salaam: Government Printer, 1967.

Tanganyika. *Administrative Conference, 27 Oct. to 7 Nov. 1924*. Dar es Salaam: Government Printer, 1924.

_____. *Local Government Memoranda, No. 1*. Parts I–II. Dar es Salaam: Government Printer, 1954.

_____. *Government Paper No. 2–1959: Government Proposals*. Dar es Salaam: Government Printer, 1959.

_____. *The Makonde Water Corporation: Report of Committee of Inquiry*. Dar es Salaam: Government Printer, 1959.

————. *Report of the Post Elections (Ramage) Committee, 1959.* Dar es Salaam: Government Printer, 1959.

Tanzania. *Report of the Presidential Special Committee of Enquiry into the Cooperative Movement and Marketing Boards.* Dar es Salaam: Government Printer, 1966.

## Published Secondary Sources

(Note: *Tanganyika* [later *Tanzania*] *Notes and Records* is abbreviated here as *TNR.*)

Abrahams, R. G. "Neighbourhood Organisation: A Major Sub-system among the Northern Nyamwezi." *Africa,* XXXV (April, 1965), 168–86.

Adam, Pater. *Lindi und sein Hinterland.* Berlin: Dietrich Reimer, 1902.

"The Ancient History of Lindi." "The History of Sudi." "The History of Mikindani." All in *Prosa und Poësie der Suaheli,* edited by C. Velten (Berlin, 1907), pp. 265–84. English translation of the first two in *The East African Coast: Select Documents from the First to the Earlier Nineteenth Century,* edited by G. S. P. Freeman-Grenville, pp. 227–32.

Anderson, J. N. D. *Islamic Law in Africa.* Colonial Research Publication, no. 16. London: H.M.S.O., 1954.

Anderson-Morshead, A. E. M. *The History of the Universities Mission to Central Africa,* Vol. I, 1859–1909. 6th ed. London: UMCA, 1955.

Bates, Margaret L. "Tanganyika." In *African One-Party States,* edited by Gwendolen M. Carter, pp. 395–483. Ithaca: Cornell University Press, 1962.

Bennett, George. "An Outline History of TANU." *Makerere Journal,* no. 7 (1963), pp. 15–29.

Bennett-Clark, M. S. "A Mask from the Makonde Tribe in the British Museum." *Man,* LVII (July, 1957), 97–98.

Bienen, Henry. *Tanzania: Party Transformation and Economic Development.* Princeton: Princeton University Press, 1967.

Bocarro, Antonio. "Gaspar Bocarro's Journey from Tete to Kilwa in 1616." In *The East African Coast: Select Documents from the First to the Earlier Nineteenth Century,* edited by G. S. P. Freeman-Grenville, pp. 165–68.

Bocarro, Gaspar. *Extractos da decada 13 da historia da India*. Lisbon, 1876.

Blood, A. G. *The History of the Universities Mission to Central Africa*, Vol. II, *1907–1932*. London: UMCA, 1957.

Boell, Ludwig. *Die Operationen in Ostafrika: Weltkrieg 1914–1918*. Hamburg: W. Dachert, 1951.

Bowie, D. F. "The Lip Plug, or 'Ndonya,' among the Tribes of the Southern Province." *TNR*, no. 27 (June, 1949), pp. 75–77.

Bridgman, Jon, and Clarke, David E., eds. *German Africa: A Select Annotated Bibliography*. Hoover Institution Bibliographical Series 19. Stanford: Hoover Institution, 1965.

Cairns, J. C. *Bush and Boma*. London: John Murray, 1959.

Cameron, Sir Donald. *My Tanganyika Experience and Some Nigeria*. London: Allen & Unwin, 1939.

Chubb, E. C. "East African Masks and an Ovambo Sheathed Knife." *Man*, XXIV (October, 1924), 145–46.

Cliffe, Lionel, ed. *One Party Democracy: The 1965 Tanzania General Elections*. Nairobi: East African Publishing House, 1967.

Collings, H. D. "Notes on the Makonde (Wamakonde) Tribe of Portuguese East Africa." *Man*, XXIX (February, 1929), 25–28.

Coupland, Reginald. *The Exploitation of East Africa, 1856–1890*. 1939. Reprint. Evanston, Ill.: Northwestern University Press, 1967.

Crosse-Upcutt, A. R. W. "The Origin of the Maji Maji Revolt." *Man*, LX (1960), article 98.

Dalton, George. "Theoretical Issues in Economic Anthropology." *Current Anthropology*, X (February, 1969), 63–80.

Dias, A. Jorge. "The Makonde People: History, Environment and Economy." "The Makonde People: Social Life." In *Portuguese Contributions to Cultural Anthropology*. Johannesburg: Witwatersrand University Press, 1961, pp. 21–61.

_____. *Os Macondes de Moçambique*, Vol. I, *Aspectos Históricos e Econômicos*. Lisbon: Centro de Estudos de Antropología Cultural, 1964.

Dias, A. Jorge, and Dias, Margot. *Os Macondes de Moçambique*, Vol. II, *Cultura Material*. Lisbon: Centro de Estudos de Antropología Cultural, 1964.

Dias, Margot. "Makonde-Topferei." *Baessler-Archiv*, n.s. IX (August, 1961), 95–126.

Dick-Read, Robert. *Sanamu—Adventure in Search of African Art*. London: Rupert Hart-Davis, 1964.

Douglas, Mary Tew. "Matriliny and Pawnship in Central Africa." *Africa*, XXXIV (October, 1964), 301–13.

[Douglas], Mary Tew. "Peoples of the Lake Nyasa Region." In *Ethnographic Survey of Africa,* Part 1, *East Central Africa.* London: Oxford University Press, 1950.

Dryden, Stanley. "Local Government Reform in Tanzania." *TNR,* no. 66 (December, 1966), pp. 147–54.

Dundas, Sir Charles. *History of German East Africa.* Dar es Salaam: Government Printer, 1923.

Fernando, Francisco A. "Mapico-dança dos Macondes." *Boletim da Museo da Nampula,* I (1960), 67–72.

Freeman-Grenville, G. S. P. "The Coast, 1489–1840." In *History of East Africa,* Vol. I, edited by Roland Oliver and Gervase Mathew, pp. 129–68.

_____. *The Medieval History of the Coast of Tanganyika.* London: Oxford University Press, 1962.

_____, ed. *The East African Coast: Select Documents from the First to the Earlier Nineteenth Century.* Oxford: Clarendon Press, 1962.

Friedland, William H. "The Evolution of Tanganyika's Political System." In *The Transformation of East Africa,* edited by Stanley Diamond and Fred G. Burke, pp. 241–312. New York: Basic Books, 1966.

_____. *Vuta Kamba: Trade Unions in Tanganyika.* Stanford: Stanford University Press, 1969.

Fülleborn, Friedrich. "Das Deutsche Njassa und Rovuma-Gebiet." In *Deutsch Ost-Afrika,* pp. 47–48. N.p., 1906.

Fundikira, Chief Abdallah. "The Reorganization of Courts in Tanganyika." *Journal of Local Administration Overseas,* I (October, 1962), 257–58.

Gardner, Brian. *German East: The Story of the First World War in East Africa.* London: Cassell, 1963.

Gillman, Harold. "Bush Fallowing on the Makonde Plateau." *TNR,* no. 19 (June, 1945), pp. 34–44.

Glickman, Harvey, "Traditional Pluralism and Democratic Processes in Mainland Tanzania." *Asian and African Studies,* V (1969), 165–201.

Gotzen, Gustav Adolf, Graf von. *Deutsch Ost-Afrika im Aufstand, 1905–1906.* Berlin: Dietrich Reimer, 1909.

Gray, Sir John. "A Journey by Land from Tete to Kilwa in 1616." *TNR,* no. 25 (June, 1948), pp. 37–47.

_____. "Mikindani Bay before 1887." *TNR,* no. 28 (January, 1950), pp. 29–37.

_____. "Zanzibar and the Coastal Belt, 1840–1884." In *History of East*

*Africa,* Vol. I, edited by Roland Oliver and Gervase Mathew, pp. 212–52.

Gulliver, Philip H. "A History of the Songea Ngoni." *TNR,* no. 41 (December, 1955), pp. 16–30.

Hailey, Baron William M. *Native Administration in the British African Territories,* Part 1, *East Africa.* London: H.M.S.O., 1950.

Hamilton, R. A. "The Route of Gaspar Bocarro from Tete to Kilwa in 1616." *Nyasaland Journal,* VII (July, 1954), 7–14.

Harlow, Vincent, Chilver, E. M., and Smith, Alison, eds. *History of East Africa,* Vol. II. London: Oxford University Press, 1965.

Harries, Lyndon. "The Initiation Rites of the Makonde Tribe." *Rhodes-Livingstone Institute Communications,* no. 3 (1944).

———. "Linguistic Notes from the Southern Province." *TNR,* no. 19 (June, 1945), pp. 45–48.

———. "Notes on the Mythology of the Bantu in the Ruvuma District." *TNR,* no. 12 (December, 1941), pp. 38–44.

———. "Outline of Maviha Grammar." *Bantu Studies,* XIV (1940), 91–146.

Hatchell, G. W. "The East African Campaign, 1914–1919." *TNR,* no. 21 (July, 1946), pp. 39–45.

Henderson, W. O. "German East Africa, 1884–1918." In *History of East Africa,* Vol. II, edited by Vincent Harlow, E. M. Chilver, and Alison Smith, pp. 123–62.

Hill, J. F. R., and Moffett, J. P., eds. *Tanganyika: A Review of Its Resources and Their Development.* Norwich, England: Jarrold and Sons, 1955.

Hokororo, A. M. "The Influence of the Church on Tribal Customs at Lukuledi." *TNR,* no. 54 (March, 1960), pp. 1–13.

Hornung, Chlodwig. "Die Religion der Bantu im Süden Tanganyikas." *Zeitschrift für Missionswissenschaft und Religionswissenschaft,* XLII (1958), 313–25.

Hurst, H. R. G. "A Survey of the Development of Facilities for Migrant Labour in Tanganyika during the Period 1926–59." *Bulletin of the Inter-African Labour Institute,* VI (July, 1959), 50–91.

Hyden, Goran. *TANU Yajenga Nchi: Political Development in Rural Tanzania.* Lund, Sweden: Scandinavian University Books, 1968.

Iliffe, John. "The Organization of the Maji Maji Rebellion." *Journal of African History,* VIII (1967), 495–512.

————. *Tanganyika under German Rule, 1905–1912*. Cambridge: At the University Press, 1969.

Jensen, S. *Regional Economic Atlas of Mainland Tanzania*. Bureau of Resource Assessment and Land Use Planning, Research Paper no. 1. Dar es Salaam: University College, June, 1968.

Johnson, Frederick. "Notes on Kimakonde." *Bulletin of the School of Oriental Studies, London Institution*, II (1922), 417–66.

Krapf, J. Lewis. *Travels, Researches, and Missionary Labours, during Eighteen Years' Residence in Eastern Africa*. London: Trübner, 1860.

Lang, Werner. "Makonde Masks in the Ethnological Collection of the Göttingen University." *Ethnology*, LXXXV (1960), 28–35.

Leslie, J. A. K. *A Survey of Dar es Salaam*. London: Oxford University Press, 1963.

LeVine, Robert, and Sangree, Walter. "The Diffusion of Age-Group Organization in East Africa: A Controlled Comparison." *Africa*, XXXII (April, 1962), 97–109.

Lewis, I. M. *Islam in Tropical Africa*. London: Oxford University Press, 1966.

Liebenow, J. Gus. "Legitimacy of Alien Relationship: The Nyaturu of Tanganyika." *Western Political Quarterly*, XIV (March, 1961), 64–86.

————. "Responses to Planned Political Change in a Tanganyika Tribal Group." *American Political Science Review*, L (June, 1956), 442–61.

————. "Some Problems in Introducing Local Government Reform in Tanganyika." *Journal of African Administration*, VIII (July, 1956), 132–39.

————. "Tribalism, Traditionalism, and Modernism in Chagga Local Government." *Journal of African Administration*, X (April, 1958), 71–82.

Listowel, Judith. *The Making of Tanganyika*. London: Chatto and Windus, 1965.

Livingstone, David. *Last Journals of David Livingstone in Central Africa from 1865 to His Death*, Vol. I. London: John Murray, 1874.

Maples, Bishop Chauncy. *Journals and Papers of Chauncy Maples*. London: Longmans, Green, 1899.

Martin, B. G. "Muslim Politics and Resistance to Colonial Rule: Shaykh Uways B. Muhammad Al-Barawi and the Qadiriya Brotherhood in East Africa." *Journal of African History*, X (1969), 471–86.

Mathew, Gervase. "The East African Coast until the Coming of the

Portuguese." In *History of East Africa*, Vol. I, edited by Roland Oliver and Gervase Mathew, pp. 94–128.

Morris, H. S. "The Divine Kingship of the Aga Khan: A Study of Theocracy in East Africa." *Southwestern Journal of Anthropology*, XIV (1958), 454–72.

Muller, Fritz F. *Deutschland-Zanzibar-Ostafrika: Geschichte einer deutschen Kolonialieroberung, 1884–1890*. Berlin: Rutten and Loening, 1959.

Norton, Ian H. "An Inter-racial Local Council in Tanganyika." *Journal of African Administration*, VIII (January, 1956), 26–32.

Nyerere, Julius K. "The Relationship between the Civil Service, Political Parties, and Members of Legislative Council." *Journal of African Administration*, XIII (April, 1961), 108–11.

Oliver, Roland. "Discernible Developments in the Interior, c. 1500–1840." In *History of East Africa*, Vol. I, edited by Roland Oliver and Gervase Mathew, pp. 169–211.

Oliver, Roland, and Mathew, Gervase, eds. *The History of East Africa*, Vol. I. Oxford: Clarendon Press, 1963.

O'Neill, H. E. "Journey in the District West of Cape Delgado Bay." *Proceedings of the Royal Geographical Society*, V (1883), 402.

Peters, Karl. *Die Grundung von Deutsch-Ostafrika*. Berlin: C. A. Schwetschke, 1906.

Pfeil, Joachim, Graf von. *Zur Erwerbung von Deutsch Ostafrika*. Berlin: K. Curtius, 1907.

Pratt, Cranford. " 'Multi-racialism' and Local Government in Tanganyika." *Race*, II (November, 1960), 33–49.

Rangeley, W. H. J. "Bocarro's Journey." *Nyasaland Journal*, VII (July, 1954), 15–23.

Raum, O. F. "German East Africa: Changes in African Tribal Life under German Administration, 1892–1914." In *History of East Africa*, Vol. II, edited by Vincent Harlow, E. M. Chilver, and Alison Smith, pp. 163–208.

Reis, Carlos Santos. "Contribuição para o estudo da robustez da raça Maconde." *Boletim Soc. Est. Colon.* (Mozambique), XXIV (July–August, 1954), 7–137.

Robinson, R. E. "Why 'Indirect Rule' Has Been Replaced by 'Local Government' in the Nomenclature of British Native Administration." *Journal of African Administration*, II (July, 1950), 12–15.

Scrivenor, T. V. "Some Notes on *Utani*, or the Vituperative Alliances Existing between Clans in the Masasi District." *TNR*, no. 4 (October, 1937), pp. 72–74.

Shepperson, George, ed. *David Livingstone and the Rovuma*. Edinburgh: Edinburgh University Press, 1965.

Shropshire, Denys W. T. *The Church and Primitive Peoples*. New York: Macmillan, 1938.

Smith, Alison. "The Southern Sector of the Interior, 1840–1884." In *History of East Africa*, Vol. I, edited by Roland Oliver and Gervase Mathew, pp. 253–96.

Steere, E. *A Walk to the Nyassa Country*. Zanzibar, 1876.

Stout, J. Anthony. *Modern Makonde Sculpture*. Nairobi: Kibo Art Gallery Publishers, 1966.

Taylor, J. Clagett. *The Political Development of Tanganyika*. Stanford: Stanford University Press, 1963.

Thomson, Joseph. "Notes on the Basin of the River Rovuma, East Africa." *Proceedings of the Royal Geographic Society*, n.s. IV (1882), 73–79.

Tordoff, William. *Government and Politics in Tanzania*. Nairobi: East African Publishing House, 1967.

United Nations High Commissioner for Refugees. "Refugees in Africa." *UNHCR Reports*. Switzerland: HCR Information Services, December, 1966.

Warrell-Bowring, W. J. "The Reorganization of the Administration in Tanganyika." *Journal of Local Administration Overseas*, II (October, 1963), 188–94.

Werner, Alice. "The Native Races of German East Africa." *Journal of the African Society*, 1910, pp. 53–63.

Weule, K. *Native Life in East Africa*. Translated by Alice Werner. London: Pitman, 1909. (Appeared originally as *Wissenschafliche Ergebnisse meiner ethnographischen Forschungsreise in den Sudosten Deutsch-Ostafrikas*. Berlin, 1908.)

*Who's Who in East Africa*. Nairobi: Marco Surveys, 1964.

Wilson, George Herbert. *The History of the Universities Mission to Central Africa*. London: UMCA, 1936.

Wilson, Gordon M. "The African Elite." In *The Transformation of East Africa*, edited by Stanley Diamond and Fred G. Burke, pp. 431–62. New York: Basic Books, 1966.

Wood, Alan. *The Groundnut Affair*. London: Bodley Head, 1950.

## Unpublished Secondary Sources

Alpers, Edward Alter. "The Role of the Yao in the Development of Trade in East-Central Africa, 1698–c.1850." Ph.D. dissertation, University of London, 1966.

Bennett, Norman R. "The Arab Power of Tanganyika in the Nineteenth Century." Ph.D. dissertation, Boston University, 1961.

Cliffe, Lionel. "Nationalism and the Reaction to Enforced Agricultural Change in Tanganyika during the Colonial Period." East African Institute of Social Research, Conference Papers. Makerere University, Kampala, December, 1964.

Dhalla, Anverali S. "Newala District—a Political History." Political Science Paper. Mimeographed. University College, Dar es Salaam, February, 1967.

Dryden, Stanley. "Local Government in Tanzania." Master's thesis, University of East Africa, 1966.

Gillman, Clement. "The Water Problems of the Makonde Plateau." Water Consultants Report, no. 4. Mimeographed. Newala District Headquarters, 1940.

Miller, Norman N. "Village Leadership and Modernization in Tanzania: Rural Politics among the Nyamwezi People of Tabora Region." Ph.D. dissertation, Indiana University, 1966.

Ranger, Terence O. "Witchcraft Eradication Movements in Central and Southern Tanzania and Their Connection with the Maji Maji Rising." History Seminar. University College, Dar es Salaam, November 30, 1966.

Rodemann, H. William. "Tanganyika, 1890–1914: Selected Aspects of German Administration." Ph.D. dissertation, University of Chicago, 1961.

Thomas, Gary. "An Inquiry into Makonde Shetani Carving." University College, Dar es Salaam, 1966.

Westergaard, Poul. "Cashew Nuts: The Quality Problem." Economic Research Bureau Paper 68.8. University College, Dar es Salaam, March, 1968.

———. "Farm Surveys of Cashew Producers in Mtwara Region: Preliminary Results." Economic Research Bureau Paper 68.3. University College, Dar es Salaam, June, 1968.

———. "The Marketing Margin: An Analysis of Cashew Nut Marketing Costs." Economic Research Bureau Paper 68.13. University College, Dar es Salaam, June, 1968.

# Index

"Accommodating modernists," 234–36
African Traders Association, 181
Aga Khan Community, 130, 286
Agriculture: African officials in, 252–53, 295, 297–98; bush fallow system of, 28, 43; compulsory innovation in, 142, 296, 299–300; loan credit for, 219–20; and school curriculum, 220, 299; voluntary innovations in, 220. *See also* Chiumo Tractor Scheme
*Akidas:* under Arab rule, 75; under British rule, 86, 89–92, 118, 173–75; under German rule, 83, 129
Allen, John (Iohn) W. T., 124, 144
ANC (African National Congress), 264, 266, 271–73, 309
Anglican Church. *See* Church Province of East Africa; UMCA
Arabs: as agents of British rule, 173–74; as agents of German rule, 82–83; and governing of the coast, 72–78; and Ngoni raiders, 29; and resistance to German rule, 80–81; and slave trade, 14–16, 23, 27, 68–70
Area commissioners, 281, 282
Arusha Declaration, 9–10, 279
Asians: as agents under British rule, 86, 151; as agents under German rule, 80; under Arab rule, 75; and land acquisitions, 258; in Mtwara, 286; political activities of, 151, 152, 206–7, 210, 263–69; population of, in Makonde area, 18, 150–52, 203. *See also* Aga Khan Community; Economy, Asian impact upon; Goans
Associations. *See* African Traders Association; Political parties; Popular associations; Teachers, associations of

*Balozi,* 283, 300, 301. *See also* TANU, cell system of
Baluchis, 75
*Banyans,* 75
BELRA (British Empire Leprosy Relief Association). *See* Leprosy
Benedictine Fathers. *See* Roman Catholic Church
Bocarro, Gaspar, 24
British rule, establishment of, 15–17, 86–92
Bülow, Baron von, 81
Bushiri. *See* Arabs, and resistance to German rule
Byatt, Governor Sir Horace, 86, 87

Cameron, Governor Sir Donald, 96 n, 121, 145 n; and philosophy of Indirect Rule, 93–94, 96–97
Cashew production, 155–57, 246, 287, 328 n, 329 n

Chagga, as cooperative society officers, 325

Chepepwa, Nangololo, 122, 123, 124, 178, 224, 225, 233

*Chihero*, 50. *See also* Makonde, religion

*Chirambo* (plural: *virambo*), 42. *See also* Makonde, political system

Chiumo Tractor Scheme, 196, 220, 247, 298–99

Christianity: and Islam, 16, 216–17; Makonde converts to, 129–30; and political factionalism, 138, 173–74, 216–17. *See also* Roman Catholic Church; Seventh Day Adventists; UMCA

Church Province of East Africa, 285–86. *See also* UMCA

Civil service, and politics, 241, 278–80

Clans. *See* Makonde, kinship

Class stratification. *See* Maconde; Slavery

Clitoredectomy, 50 n

Colonial rule: and constitutional change, 261–62; establishment of, in Makonde area, 14–17; and political development, 332–38; practice of, 10–11

Community development, 254–55

Convention of Representative Chiefs, 236

Cooperative societies, 287–88, 323–26; and conflict with TANU, 277; and effect on African traders, 324–25; introduction of, 12, 242, 246

Councils, local government, 202–3, 282–83

Courts, 57–58, 76, 77, 96 n, 109–12, 294–95. *See also* Makonde, law; *Mkulungwa,* judicial role of

Craig, Ernest, 208, 209, 244

Delimitations Commission (1886), 77

Dependency syndrome, 214–15

"Dissenting modernists," 237–45

District officers, British, 138–50; attitudes of Makonde toward, 143–45; and loss of popular contact, 145–47; and selection of liwalis, 163–66; and selection of wakulungwa, 99–100; tenure and rotation of, 145–46, 148–49

Economy: African entrepreneurs in, 246–47; Arab role in, 75, 78, 80, 127–29, 153; Asian impact upon, 150–52, 154, 156, 246–47; under British rule, 88, 153–59; under German rule, 16, 80; since independence, 286–88. *See also* Cashew production; Makonde, economy

Education: and Christian-Muslim conflict, 216–17; and compulsory school attendance, 302; and economic opportunities, 237–38; facilities in Makonde districts, 12, 133 n, 302–4; Islamic, 127, 129, 130; of liwalis and wakilis, 177–78; planned growth of, 303–4; problems of, in Newala District, 213–17. *See also* Christianity

Egalitarianism, in traditional Makonde society, 63–70

Elders, authority of, 51–52, 58–59

Elections: district council (1966), 311, 319–22; Makonde participation in, 308–12; parliamentary (1965), 308–18; presidential (1962), 309; presidential (1965), 310; and TANU membership, 282; territorial (1958–59), 265–68; territorial (1960), 271–73, 308–9

Europeans: and Newala Local Council, 207–8, 210–11; population of, in Makonde area, 18, 147, 203, 285–86; in territorial politics, 263–69. *See also* District officers; Settlers

Family. *See* Makonde, kinship

Famine, 26–27, 153, 154, 288, 293–94

Foreign policy, Tanzanian, 278
FRELIMO (Frente de Liberação de Moçambique), 278, 290–91. *See also* Mozambique; Portuguese rule
Fundikira, Abdullah, 252, 281

German East African Company, 79
German rule, 15–17, 72; and administration of Makonde area, 79–85; economic interests of, 17; establishment of, 79; resistance to, 80–82; termination of, 17, 33, 85. *See also* Maji Maji Rebellion
Goans, 151, 152. *See also* Asians
Groundnut Scheme, 18–19, 158–59

Harries, Lyndon, 32, 46
Health: facilities in Makonde districts, 12, 296–97, 300; mission contribution to, 135; problems before Newala Local Council, 217–19

Independence, achievement of, 9, 274
Indian Association, 152. *See also* Asians, political activities of
Indians. *See* Asians
Indirect Rule: abandonment of, at coast, 114–20; abandonment of, in Newala, 120–25; establishment of, in Makonde area, 72, 97–98; theory of, 94–95
Initiation rites, 49–51, 59, 135–36
Institution-building, in modernization process, 5–7
Iron-making, 64 n
Islam, 72–78; and Christianity, 130; and colonial rule, 118–19, 172–75; conversion of Makonde to, 76, 78, 128–31; as a source of factionalism, 130, 152; strength of, in Central Africa, 16. *See also* Arabs; Education; Zanzibar; *Zikri*

*Jando*, 49. *See also* Initiation rites
Jones, Arthur Creech, 204–5
*Jumbes:* during Arab period, 75; under British direct rule, 91–92; under German rule, 84, 85, 129; under liwali system, 184–87

Kalemaga, Martin, 243, 258
Kampunga, Mohamed S., 313–14
Kawawa, Rashidi, 290
Kilwa, 15, 21, 62, 73, 74
Kinship, alterations in, 215. *See also* Makonde, kinship
Kitching, A. E., 117, 120, 172, 175
Koranic law, 76, 84
Krapf, Rev. J. Lewis, 15–16, 23, 74

Labor: compulsory, 17, 82, 84; migratory, 17, 18, 38 n, 157, 160. *See also* Maconde
Land tenure, 42, 56, 66; affected by cashew production, 326–27
Large, J. W., 120–25, 144, 146
Leadership, Makonde, at national level, 12
League of Nations: Convention on Slavery, 87; Mandates System, 17, 86
Legislative Council: changes in, 263–65, 267–68; elections to, 265–68, 271–73
Leprosy, 218–19. *See also* Mkunya Leprosarium
Lichelo Hill, 20
Lilama, Anton G., 315–16
Lindi (port), 16, 17, 75, 76, 77, 81; founding of, 12 n, 21, 23; under German rule, 82; and Groundnut Scheme, 18; migration to, 29, 45, 74; and slave trade, 69, 73
*Litawa*, 41. *See also* Makonde, kinship
Livingstone, Dr. David, 16, 27, 68, 75, 128, 130
*Liwali Mkuu*, 196–99
*Liwali* system
—early period: under Arab rule,

75, 76, 77; under British direct
  rule, 89–92; under German
  rule, 83
—later period: clerical staff for,
  182–83; introduction of, 119–
  20, 124–25, 163–67; recruitment of liwalis for, 166–68,
  170–83; salaries under, 235;
  termination of, 280–81
Local Government Ordinance
  (1953), 200–202. *See also*
  Councils, local government
Lugard, Lord, 94
Lumley, E. K., 172–73

Machemba I, 29, 48, 81, 99 n,
  128
Machinga, 23 n, 97
Mackenzie, W. J. M., 192
MacMichael, Governor Sir
  Harold, 119
Maconde: art, 30 n, 35, 36; diet,
  34; kinship, 31; labor, 33, 37–
  38, 39 n, 157, 158, 328; language, 32–33; raiders, during
  World War I, 85; refugees, 37,
  290; witch-finding, 62. *See
  also* Makonde
Mafia District, 204
Magwangwara, 27, 28. *See also*
  Ngoni
Mahuta, founding of, 24–25
Maji Maji Rebellion, 17, 43,
  81, 82
Makonde: art, 35, 36, 60; body
  scarification, 36; defense,
  traditional, 42–43; diet, 34 n;
  economy, traditional, 26,
  55–56, 64–65, 67–70; inter-
  group hostility, 48; kinship,
  traditional, 20, 21, 31, 34, 41 n,
  42, 44–45, 53, 58–59, 63–65;
  language, 21 n, 32–33; law,
  traditional, 47, 48, 52; national
  leaders, 12 n; origins, 20–30;
  political system, traditional,
  41–71 passim; population, 12;
  relations with non-Makonde,
  30–39, 291–95; religion,
  traditional, 12 n, 54–55, 65–66;
  residence patterns of, 42, 43–
  44, 87, 301–2; resistance to

German rule, 81–82; slave
  trade, 23–24. *See also*
  Maconde
Makonde Collective Marketing
  Union, 242. *See also* Co-
  operative societies
Makonde plateau. *See* Newala
  Plateau
Makonde Water Development
  Corporation, 26, 207, 221,
  231, 232, 243, 258
Makota, Bibi Ignasia B.,
  313–14
Makua: converts to Christianity,
  129; marriage with Makonde,
  34; migrants, 158; residence
  in Masasi, 27; residence on
  Newala Plateau, 48, 66, 103
Malawi, Lake. *See* Nyasa, Lake
Maples, Bishop Chauncy, 155
Maraba, 21, 23, 97
Masasi District: migration of
  Makonde through, 20, 27; mis-
  sion activities in, 16, 17, 132
Mascarene Islands, 15
Matambwe, 97, 103, 112
Matamula, Manzi, 181–82, 211,
  243, 246–47
Matola I, 29, 48, 122
Matola II, 83, 122
Mauritius, 15, 23, 68
Mawia, 30. *See also* Maconde
*Mbepesi,* 54. *See also* Makonde,
  religion
Mbwemkuru River, 21
Mchauru, Albert, 253, 292 n, 317
Mchauru, Rev. E. T., 253
Mchauru, Frederick, 253–54, 259
Mchauru, Thekla (Mrs.
  Frederick), 224, 254
Mikindani: Arab governing of,
  75, 76, 77; decline of, 302;
  Livingstone's journey from,
  12 n, 16; Makonde migration
  to, 29; origins of, 23, 74; and
  slave trade, 15–16, 23, 24, 69
Military: and 1964 mutiny,
  277–78; and TANU Youth
  League, 277–78. *See also*
  World War I; World War II
Missionaries. *See* Education;
  Roman Catholic Church;

Seventh Day Adventists;
UMCA
Mkoto, Mkulungwa, 81
*Mkulungwa* (plural: *wakulungwa*)
— in indigenous traditional
society: control over land by,
42; economic authority of,
55–56, 65, 70; inter-village
influence of, 45–48; judicial
role of, 56, 57; recruitment
of, 52–54; religious role of,
42, 54; responses to European
rule, 84–85, 91
— under Indirect Rule: claims
to office of, 99–100; economic
rewards of, 103–4; executive
role of, 105–9; judicial role of,
109–12; legislative duties of,
112–14; performance of, 114–
20; reduction in number of,
100; reliance upon, by British,
97, 98
— under liwali system: 172,
184, 185
— in post-independence period,
231, 333
*Mkulungwa mkuu*, 34, 122–25,
224, 233. *See also* Chepepwa,
Nangololo; Mtalika, Rashidi
Mkunya Leprosarium, 194, 218
Mnima, 26, 28, 45
Mnolela, 26
Modernization, theories of, 3–11
Mondlane, Dr. Eduardo, 290.
*See also* FRELIMO
Mozambique: and German rule,
17, 81, 85; independence
movement in, 289, 290–91;
origins of Makonde in, 20–21,
30–39 passim, 68, 73
Mponda, Justino: career of,
179–81, 235–36; as historian,
47, 195; and legislative elections, 266–67, 271–73, 309;
and Newala Local Council,
205, 211, 224–25, 269–70;
relations of, with Lawi Sijaona, 244, 266–67; and
traditionalism, 224, 225
Mtalika, Rashidi, 123–25, 146–
47, 172, 233

Mtemvu, Zuberi, 264, 266, 271,
309
Mtwara: colonial development
of, 12, 13, 17, 18–19, 155;
post-independence develop-
ment of, 285–87, 289, 290, 302
Mtwara Region Cooperative
Union, 287, 323. *See also*
Cooperative societies
Multiracialism, policy of, in
Newala, 198–209
Muscat, 74
Muslims. *See* Islam
*Mwalim. See* Education,
Islamic
*Mwenyekaya*, 44. *See also*
Makonde, kinship
Mwera, 34, 62, 82, 198

Nachingwea, 18
Namaleche, Nangololo (Namale-
one), 178–79, 316–17
Native Authority Rules and
Ordinances, 143. *See also*
*Liwali* system; *Mkulungwa*
Ndanda Mission. *See* Roman
Catholic Church
Ndendeule, 103, 112
Ndonde, 20, 21, 26
Neighborhood bonds, 59–60
Newala District, during
World War I, 84–85
Newala Local Council, 202–26,
269–70
Newala Plateau, 24–27, 28
Newala township, 222
Ngindo, 62
Ngoni: and Arab caravans, 77;
attitudes toward Makonde,
14 n; as cooperative officers,
325; as German agents, 83;
and raids on Makonde, 27–29,
48; and slave trade, 42, 67–68,
72
Nguvu Mali, 62, 225
Norton, Ian, 203, 204, 205, 244
NUTA (National Union of
Tanganyika Workers), 253
Nyasa (tribal group), 129
Nyasa, Lake, 15–16, 23, 70, 73
Nyerere, Julius: anti-colonial
struggle of, 266, 267, 269, 274;

career of, 241; development
policies of, 8–11, 229, 279–80,
338–41; electoral campaigns
of, 276, 309, 310; and FRE-
LIMO, 290–91; views of, on
Maji Maji Rebellion, 81–82;
views of, on wage labor, 328–
29; visit of, to Newala, 228–
30, 245, 259; visit of, to
United Nations, 261

Oman, 74–75
Omari, Leopold, 272
Orde-Brown, Captain George
St. J., 90
Order of Saint Benedict, 285.
See also Roman Catholic
Church
Overseas Food Corporation. See
Groundnut Scheme

Pakistanis, 151, 152. See also
Asians
Pallahani, Leopold, 230, 253, 259
"Parochial traditionalists,"
231–32
Pawning, 67. See also Slavery
Pemba. See Zanzibar
Peters, Karl, 79
"Pivotal modernists," 245–55
Pogoro, 62, 81
Political parties, ban on tribal-
based, 277. See also ANC;
TAA; TANU; UTP; Wama-
konde Union
Polycentrism. See Makonde,
political system
Popular associations, 238–39,
240–42. See also Cooperative
societies; Political parties;
Teachers, associations of
Population. See Asians; Euro-
peans; Makonde
Portuguese rule, 33–34, 85, 290

Railroads, 13, 18, 19
Regional administration, 281–
82
Registrar of Societies, 240–41
Religion. See Aga Khan Community; Islam; Makonde,
religion; Roman Catholic

Church; Seventh Day
Adventists; UMCA
Réunion, 15, 23
Revenue. See Taxes
Rhodesian crisis, 278, 289. See
also Zambia
Roads, 13, 17, 78, 287, 288
Roman Catholic Church: alterations of jando by, 135–36; conversion of Makonde to, 130;
educational efforts of, 131–33,
135, 137–38, 207–8, 247–50;
and Islam, 173–74. See also
Order of Saint Benedict
Ruvuma Valley: as migration
route, 23; and slave trade,
15–16

Sadiki, Christopher, 318
Saidi, Raphael, 270, 271–73,
317–18
Saint Joseph's College, Chidya,
132
Sauti ya TANU (Dar es Salaam),
266
Sayyid Barghash, 75, 77, 78, 87,
128
Sayyid Said, 74, 77, 78
Scott, Acting Governor John, 93
Sefu, Akida, 89
Settlers, European, 139
Seventh Day Adventists, 132
Shaba, Austin K. E., 310–12
Shariʿa, 76. See also Koranic
law
Sijaona, Lawi: career of, 245 n;
as clerk of Newala Local
Council, 244, 245; electoral
campaigns of, 267, 271, 308,
315–16, 318; and Mozambique
crisis, 290; nomination of, as
wakili, 168; and organization
of TANU, 258, 259
Slave trade: Arab role in, 15–16,
23, 24, 73, 74, 78; British
role in, 70, 77; French role in,
15, 23; Portuguese role in, 74;
suppression of, 77–78, 129;
Yao role in, 23, 27, 42, 46,
67–68, 70, 72, 73, 77, 128. See
also Kilwa; Mauritius; Mikindani; Slavery; Zanzibar

Slavery: abolition of, 87–88; under British rule, 87–88; under German rule, 87; and Islam, 128; among the Makonde, 67–70. *See also* Pawning; Slave trade
Smythies, Bishop Charles Alan, 27
Socialization, political, 49–52
Songea. *See* Ngoni
Steere, Bishop Edward, 77
Students: aspirations of, in colonial period, 250–52; and conflict with TANU, 277; occupational preferences of, 134–35
Sudi, 23, 48, 69, 75
Swahili, as lingua franca, 76, 292

TAA (Tanganyika African Association), 197, 260. *See also* TANU
Tambwe, Ali M. H., 313
Tanga, 158, 160
TANU (Tanganyika African National Union), 188, 227; banning of, by British, 242; cell system of, 283, 300, 301; and civil service, 281–83; and coercion, 296–97; development policies of, 8–11; electoral machinery of, 321–22; establishment of, in Makonde area, 242–45, 247, 258–60, 307, 308; establishment of, nationally, 240–41, 262–65; influence of, among colonial officers, 253; membership of teachers in, 248–50; National Executive of, 309; and Newala Local Council, 209; and one-party state, 309–12; recruitment campaigns of, 230; as successor to TAA, 260; and trade unions, 277; and traditional chiefs, 276–77; and tribalism, 234, 277; urban strength of, 257. *See also* Elections; TANU Youth League
TANU Youth League, 266, 268, 269, 272, 273, 277–78

Taxes, 17, 81, 82, 113, 158, 212, 268
Teachers: associations of, 242, 248–50; salaries of, 249 n; views of, on development, 247–50
Territorial unit of politics: under Indirect Rule, 101–3; under liwali system, 168–70; in traditional society, 42–45
Thanki, A., 267
Trade unions, conflict with TANU, 277
Tribal groups, in Tanzania, 10. *See also* Chagga; Machinga; Maconde; Makonde; Makua; Maraba; Matambwe; Mwera; Ndendeule; Ngindo; Ngoni; Nyasa; Pogoro; Yao
"Tribal nationalists," 233–34
Tribalism, Nyerere policy on, 291–92
Troup, S. D., 150
Tubbs, S. R., 259–60
Turnbull, A. M., 96, 192, 196
Turnbull, Governor Sir Richard, 266, 267
Twining, Governor Sir Edward, 198, 202, 203, 206, 227, 263

UMCA (Universities Mission to Central Africa), 48, 130, 207–8; and community factionalism, 138, 183; and economic change, 134; educational efforts of, 131–34, 179, 210–11, 247–50; and family structure, 129, 130; and health facilities, 135; and modification of jando, 135, 136; and Ngoni raiders, 29; and status of women, 136–37. *See also* Christianity; Church Province of East Africa
United Nations Trusteeship System, 240, 260–61
"Unity of the Makonde People" (*Umakonde Umoja*), 89, 190–99, 233
*Utani,* 46, 47
UTP (United Tanganyika Party), 264, 266

Uzzy, Abdallah Hassan, 243, 258

Versi, J. A. G., 267
Veterans, 160–62
Village development committees (VDC), 283
*Virambo. See Chirambo*

*Wakulungwa. See Mkulungwa*
Wamakonde Union, 197–98
Water resources, 25–26, 221, 288. *See also* Makonde Water Development Corporation
"White man's madness" (*Wazimu wa Mzungu*), 22, 141–45
Witchcraft, 60, 61–62, 225
Women: attitude of elders toward, 232; and Christianity, 136–37; in community development, 254; education of, 133, 215; in local politics, 319–20; in modern society, 223; on Newala Local Council, 209–11; in territorial politics, 314; in traditional society, 26,
63–64; as wakulungwa, 117, 176
World War I, 33, 84–85, 117
World War II, 160–62

Yao: as German agents, 82–83; as immigrants, 103, 157; language of, 33 n; as Makonde rulers, 29, 46, 48; and marriage with Makonde, 34; and resistance to Germans, 48, 81; and slave trade, 23, 27, 42, 46, 67–68, 70, 72, 73, 77, 128
Young, Governor Sir Mark Aitchison, 173
Youth: attitude of elders toward, 231–32; and delinquency, 222. *See also* Education; Students; TANU Youth League

Zambia, 278, 289
Zanzibar: and control of coast, 74–78, 127; and sale of coast to Germany, 79; and slave trade, 15, 24, 68–70; and union with Tanganyika, 9, 278
*Zikri*, 131 n. *See also* Arabs; Islam; Koranic law

## DATE DUE

| JAN 0 5 2010 | | | |
|---|---|---|---|
| | | | |
| | | | |
| | | | |
| | | | |
| | | | |
| | | | |
| | | | |
| | | | |
| | | | |
| | | | |
| | | | |
| | | | |
| | | | |
| | | | |
| | | | |
| | | | |
| | | | |
| GAYLORD | | | PRINTED IN U.S.A. |